ON BECOMING
A COUNSELOR

On Becoming A Counselor

A Basic Guide for Nonprofessional Counselors

New Expanded Edition

Eugene Kennedy
and
Sara C. Charles, M.D.

Crossroad | New York

1995

The Crossroad Publishing Company
370 Lexington Avenue
New York, NY 10017

Printed in the United States of America

Library of Congress Cataloging-in-Publication Data

Kennedy, Eugene C.
   On becoming a counselor : a basic guide for nonprofessional
counselors / Eugene Kennedy and Sara Charles.—New expanded ed.
      p.   cm.
   "Portions of this book appeared first in Stress I and Stress II"—
—T.p. verso.
   Includes bibliographical references.
   ISBN 0-8264-0505-3 — 0-8245-1333-9 (pbk.)
   1. Counseling.   2. Psychology, Pathological.   I. Charles, Sara C.
II. Title.   III. Series.
BF637.C6K46   1990
158'.3—dc20   89-37258
                                                                    CIP

For a Wise Counselor
William Shlaes, M.D.

Contents

Introduction to the
New Expanded Edition

As life demands growth and transformation, so books seek, almost of themselves, to be revised. The most obvious reason for recasting a book such as this is to include new insights and developments in the field of counseling of which even nonprofessional counselors should be aware. It is just as important to enlarge and bring up to date the references to which those who use the book may turn for more extended and timely information about the subjects of concern to them.

For example, the *Diagnostic and Statistical Manual* of psychiatric disorders, now in a revision of its third edition *(American Psychiatric Press)*, is a landmark effort to develop a common language about the nature and assessment of psychological problems. Although non-professionals may never use it in the same manner as psychiatrists and other specialists, it is a volume of which they should be aware. Some working acquaintance with its carefully delineated behavioral signs may help them understand those people who seek them out for help. In many cases, it will assist them in making a well-timed referral for more intensive treatment. A knowledge of its contents also allows helpers to comprehend and speak the special language of emotional disorder with greater ease and confidence.

If, however, part of the stimulus for revamping this book comes from the professional universe of research and publication, additional motivation arises from continuing contact with that hardy, widely deployed force of nonprofessionals who, on any given day, actually carry out most of the counseling done in the world. Unlike highly trained therapists, they cannot be selective about those they will help. The armies of the dark night of the soul huddle outside their doors, the mendicants of the spirit whose numbers never dwindle, waiting for them even at unlikely hours. The clergy, general physicians, teachers, lawyers, funeral directors, law-enforcement personnel, even you, the tired air traveler who finds the passenger in the next seat suddenly pouring out a troubled life story, lack the professionals' freedom of choice about which persons they feel competent to help.

From the challenges related by such nonprofessionals, we have learned that more helpful distinctions should be made about the limits and possibilities of the help they should offer. This edition has been modified and new chapters have been introduced to clarify the difference between the kinds of responses that should be attempted by professionals and those who lack their advanced training. This by no means places the assistance of nonprofessionals into some second-class category. What such helpers do is often extraordinarily helpful, frequently life saving or at least life renewing. What good they accomplish, however, is a function of their sensible perception of the realistic parameters they should respect in responding to the needy who crowd their lives.

Nonprofessionals should, in the first place, have confidence in their own identity and not apologize for or try to obscure it. Whatever their role, it represents achievement and hard-earned wisdom about a number of theoretical and practical matters. As with the army, which in centuries of dealing with human beings has learned, without any psychological insight or sophistication, a great deal about the pragmatic management of their strengths and weaknesses, so ministers, lawyers, and countless others called on to help people in distress, have acquired, without any deep psychological awareness, estimable stores of practical ways of helping people get through difficult incidents in their lives. Nonprofessionals, somewhat like mothers who have never read Doctor Spock, often have healthy intuitions about how to draw on this information—as well as on the reserves, as with the clergy, of their own traditions—in order to help those who seek them out. Forsaking a well-developed identity casts a vote of limited confidence in those very things that nonprofessionals are already good at. In the wake of a sudden death, for example, bereaved persons depend on the knowledge of the undertaker, the lawyer, the doctor, and the minister, leaning on them for what they know how to do in these painful intervals. Such experience and the wealth of good sense that often accompanies it are hardly to be disowned as extremely valuable strengths in nonprofessionals.

Secondly, what such helpers do as psychological counselors should match their already well-defined roles. The minister who forsakes his spiritual insights to act as a neutral and secular counselor does justice neither to his fundamental identity nor to the counseling in which he engages. For most nonprofessionals, security in their function should be coupled with a disciplined commitment to *supportive* rather than *uncovering* psychological responses. Helpers who stay within the boundaries of sensible supportive assistance will avoid complications that might otherwise seriously entangle or overwhelm them altogether.

The main principles of such healthy supportive assistance suggest that nonprofessional helpers should always focus on the current conscious life situation of the individual seeking help. They should avoid psychological archeological expeditions that lead to levels deep beneath the everyday consciousness of the troubled person. Nonprofessionals should help those who come to them to keep their discussions on the level of what they can, with relative ease, draw out of their consciousness. Such helpers should, therefore, avoid techniques, such as free association, dream analysis, or remaining achingly neutral, that may rupture the defenses that the person has in place against dealing with the unconscious conflicts that lie beneath his or her current difficulties. Nonprofessionals do not want to experiment with approaches, often superficially presented to them in popular literature or in quick workshops, that get them in over their heads psychologically. Here, as the legends once read at the corners of ancient maps, be dragons.

Nonprofessionals can identify and strengthen the healthy defenses, or psychological resources, of those who want their help. Revered ascetic practices, for example, such as "avoiding the occasion of sin," have very practical and useful application in the lives of those troubled by continually falling into the same discouraging life traps over and over again. They assist the person on the conscious level, seal the unconscious conflicts safely away, and, coupled with understanding, are often an enormous and successful source of support for them. Forcing individuals to confront the defenses that are the very structures that are holding them together is a dangerous tactic to employ, for it may cause such persons to regress, to become worse instead of better.

These basic notions are the cornerstones of successful counseling by those without professional training. Maintaining one's own identity, staying out of the unconscious, and strengthening the person's best defenses: Helpers will not err very much by keeping these in mind as they draw upon what is healthy and sensible in themselves in their work with others. It is our hope that this new edition will reinforce the strengths that nonprofessional counselors already possess in such abundance.

Eugene Kennedy, Ph.D.
Professor of Psychology
Loyola University of Chicago

Sara C. Charles, M.D.
Professor of Clinical Psychiatry
University of Illinois Medical School

Introduction

THIS book is written for all those persons who, without extensive psychological training, must deal with troubled people in the course of their work. That includes a wide variety of individuals who cannot be selective about the personal problems that are brought to their door or their office by the confused and suffering, the grieving, or the immature who turn so often to the clergy, teachers, general physicians, nurses, lawyers, or sometimes just old friends for assistance. These are not professional counselors although they are professionals in other fields. But human woe tends to address itself to those nearby who seem capable of some understanding and good sense; the most common cries of pain in the human condition are raised first to people like these. What can they do to prepare themselves better to understand and respond effectively to those who come for assistance?

Such persons may not be able to treat deep and long-standing emotional difficulties. They may not, in fact, be able to spend extended periods of time with many of those who seek their counsel. But they can be more human with these individuals, marshaling their own resources of the spirit and capitalizing on the strength of their best instincts. This book is designed to help the helpers do exactly that without demanding that they become mental health experts or gurus of some gimmicky psychological fad. These chapters are intended to provide them with insights and practical applications of psychological knowledge without challenging or trying to modify their basic professional identity. Teachers can remain teachers and ministers can remain ministers. Changing their identity is not the purpose of this book.

Our first line of response to troubled people cannot be provided by the relatively limited numbers of fully trained psychiatrists, psychologists, psychiatric social workers, or marriage counselors. It must come from the persons who stand on that front line in whatever profession they find themselves. It is all very well to speak about making referrals, but what do lawyers, priests, and other professionals do in the meantime? And what can they do when there is no possibility of a

15

referral or when the problem is one, like the death of a spouse, for which there is no expert treatment?

It is our experience that nonpsychological professionals—nurses, general physicians, and lawyers, as well as those previously mentioned—end up doing most of the counseling that actually goes on in America every day. They have no choice about it because their commitments are not just to aching body parts, conflicted wills, or mortgages, but to the whole living persons who have emotional connections as complicated as a telephone switching center to these and all the other ordinary snags in the human situation. Problems never exist in a pure state; there is always a human being attached to them. As long as those who meet most of the troubled persons in the world are without psychiatric training, they need to know something more than how to say "Stop worrying." These paraprofessional counselors get abundant advice about what they should *not* do; they are reminded regularly of the dangers of involving themselves willy-nilly in the emotional difficulties of their patients or clients. But they are not very often told what they *can* do in constructive ways, nor are they helped to use their very real strengths in assisting those with whom they work with their emotional problems. We have written this book to provide some positive assistance to those paraprofessionals who must, by necessity, do the bulk of psychological counseling in the context of their regular work.

Partly because of a growing distrust of professionals, we are now in an era of the nonprofessional in many fields of endeavor. People are working out their own taxes, mortgages, wills, and even their divorces without the help of lawyers. And we have witnessed the rise of the enlightened nonprofessional in the area of emotional treatment as well. With enormous self-confidence and no training to speak of, many persons have set themselves up as counselors, facilitators, or group leaders. Such presumptions are usually ill-founded in any basic capacity for helping others; they are based more on such persons' need to help or at least to involve themselves in the intimate lives of other persons. This book is not written for such independently established amateurs. Such individuals do not wish to acquire learning in a disciplined or systematic way; they want to fly on what they judge to be their good therapeutic instincts, and on what pianist Oscar Levant called "a smattering of ignorance."

This book is designed to be a source of encouragement and practical help to the paraprofessional counselors who want to learn more about the way they can work effectively with others. It is not a *how-to-do-it* book but one that recognizes both their nonprofessional standing and also their basic strengths of common sense, good judgment, and available humanity. Most persons who are professionals in other fields appreciate the need for some discipline and, far from wanting merely to indulge their own needs, they wish to acquire enough skill to be able to respond to emotional problems with a genuine concern for others and a respect for their own limitations. Such persons need encouragement as well as resources against which to check themselves as they try to improve their counseling abilities. This work is an effort to make the power of disciplined understanding available to them so that they can appreciate and help to translate the complex language of emotional distress.

Therefore, the book offers reflections on the nature of counseling as well as treatments of the typical problems that come to them with living, breathing persons attached to them. Addressing itself to persons who are professionals in some field other than counseling, it does not treat problems and difficulties in the same depth that would be found in a text for psychologists or psychiatrists, but rather it deals with information and attitudes that fit the typical work situations of such persons.

Certain subjects, of course, demand more extensive treatment than they will be give here—for example, counseling or advising persons with sexual problems. These are covered in a companion volume called "Sexual Counselling" devoted only to such subjects. The choice of topics for this book, however, was made on the basis of years of experience in teaching and working with the kinds of professionals to whom the book is addressed.

The clear aim is to reinforce the fundamental identity of those who use it. They need not change their profession in order to work more effectively with people whose problems have emotional complications. If self-confident amateurs stand at one end of the counseling continuum, professionals who have lost confidence in their fundamental identity stand at the other. Instances of the latter may be found, for example, in people in the work of ministry who have become converts to some form of psychological therapy that has gradually replaced the religious content of their work. This is, we believe, an unfortunate development that confuses their primary professional identity and devalues the content of their fundamental occupation. Professionals in other fields need not play down their own role or their competence in order to acquire sufficient counseling skills to operate more confidently with those who come to see them, whether they be termed students, patients, or parishioners. The book is designed to make them more comfortable in their first profession by deepening their human capacity to recognize and respond to the emotional dimensions of the problems, all of which are personal to some extent, and many of which they meet every day.

An increased ability to rely on their own strength enables these professionals to carry out their work with greater integrity and self-possession; they do not feel that they are under siege by totally mysterious forces all the time. Neither do they feel that they must completely solve all the problems of those who come to see them. These paraprofessional counselors can be highly skilled at assisting persons to take greater responsibility for themselves. This is no small gift to bestow on others. The insights into themselves that they develop are also important and enable them to understand their own investment in their work with others. With a little help they can better maintain their own balance and feel free from the cold remoteness supposedly demanded by professional relationships. They can care for others without feeling that they are always on the edge of a punishing emotional involvement.

Nothing is more discouraging to paraprofessionals' willingness to help people than the stinging tangle of emotions, engaged but unidentified, of the trapped absorption with others that destroys their own composure and severely limits their ability to help. They are frequently glad to escape such entanglements, vowing that they will never again get so closely involved with other peoples' personal problems. This book offers a resource for reflection and self-evaluation that helps counselors to remain personal and involved without fearing that they will inevitably be lost in the process.

What can we really do for others? That is a question at the very heart of all the helping professions, and those who counsel in conjunction with other responsibilities ask it of themselves all the time. They want to be constructively helpful, yet they are often puzzled as to how they can best achieve this ideal. It is important to realize that in most emotional problems a little help is a lot of help. A modest enough notion, yet one that many, ambitious that they can deliver more, hesitate to espouse, with the result that they frequently end up delivering considerably less. Paraprofessionals need honest and reasonable expectations about what they can accomplish in their counseling; there is no disgrace in not being able to remake people, for very few fully trained therapists ever come close to this. There is every honor, however, in helping persons to move even a few inches closer to self-responsibility, in assisting them to turn in a new and healthier direction in life. The curse in the soul of "amateur" therapists is their determination to change people at all costs, and they frequently blunder, trampling on the sacred places of others' personalities in the process. Paraprofessionals without such ill-starred notions about their capabilities can both avoid the gross errors of these amateurs and deliver a service that is solid and lasting even though it is modest in scope.

Understanding is at the heart of all good therapy. It is, interestingly enough, a quality that cannot possibly harm others, and it is also something of which all humans are capable. Understanding transmitted through the discipline of counseling skills helps bewildered people to see themselves in better perspective. And all individuals, no matter the primary identity of their profession, can convey it. It is hoped that this book will help counselors use the energy of their own understanding in a measured but powerfully effective manner.

PART
1

1

Emotional Involvement

Stress is a reality—like love or electricity—unmistakable in experience yet difficult to define. However, stress touches everybody sooner or later, and for members of certain occupations it is a daily companion. A person whose chief business is to help others is the most vulnerable to its effects because, unlike other professionals who can at least turn to the stable and uncomplaining world of balance sheets or test tubes once in a while, helpers actually work in the presence of the greatest stress-producers we know—other people. And ordinarily the helping person is alone in this situation, sometimes out of range of supportive colleagues or reference books exactly when they would be most useful. Stress seems to be a dignified burden for the dedicated person, something he or she discounts as part of the personal price of serving others; often it is shrugged off or even denied altogether. After all, does not the goal of assisting others justify emotional sacrifices?

Obviously no helping individual can escape the special stress that goes with concentrating on others' problems. There are no analogs for the sterilized gowns and instruments of the surgical theater available to the counselor, the pastoral worker, or any other kind of therapist. They must learn to handle the stress associated with their work in a constructive manner or it will deal with them in a very harsh way. Too often people do not realize how many Gs of interpersonal stress they have been under until the relationship comes to an end. This is particularly true with the most common problem that helping persons must learn to understand and manage successfully: *their own emotional investment and involvement in the lives of those with whom they work.*

Few people who have ever tried to respond to the needs of others have managed to escape the sting of emotional involvement. It causes an invisible wound that people may not be able to talk about even to themselves because that makes it hurt too much. This situation is to counselors what black lung is to coal miners—an inescapable risk that cannot be separated from their occupation. While working with people in trouble, you come to like them, to feel deeply about their problems and their own efforts to do something about those problems. Caring about them, time, circumstances, or the people themselves, will ultimately pull loose some of the timbers of your own heart.

Sometimes, however, helpers discover that they have cared more than the one they are helping, and they are left with churned-up feelings they do not know how to handle. It is small wonder that once persons manage to make their way out of the seeming wreckage of an overinvolved relationship, they say something equivalent to "Never again!" It hurts too much, they proclaim, to get yourself so involved in such a personal way with other people.

The helper, nursing emotional wounds, may begin to handle stress in a manner that saves something of himself or herself. An individual can become cynical, for example, and turn away from mankind with the familiar protestation that "people are no damned good." Or one may be more urbane and, following a tested and quite acceptable route, adopt an impersonal professionalism that creates a saving emotional distance between oneself and those whom one helps. "You cannot afford to get involved" is the cool advice that is passed out to doctors, nurses, teachers, counselors, and men and women in church work, as routinely as aspirin is given for headaches. According to many observers, this is precisely why we have developed numerous formulations, questionnaires, and other administrative procedures in the helping professions; they allow us to keep that zone of distance between the helper and the helpee as free of emotions as an operating room is free of germs. Emotional involvement, that scourge of the concerned and the vulnerable, is treated as an infection that must be avoided or contained. Of all the interpersonal stresses, it is the most famous killer.

What do we lose when we decide to handle this source of stress by minimizing the chances of its occurrence? We may, in fact, drain our helping potential of its most significant component: the powerful fact that caring about people in trouble—and even actually liking them—is vital to helping them deal more effectively with themselves and with life.

Experience and research have demonstrated that, no matter what school of training or personality theory we choose to follow, two facts of life must be acknowledged by all helpers: First, we must be *in relationship* to the persons we assist; and second, it helps if we like them but *do not try to possess* them just for ourselves. Techniques come and go but these two realities abide. The resultant problem is, of course, one of the chief reasons that helpers often experience so much stress. The very thing that makes counseling or good advice work—that it is done in a personal, caring way—is also the reason it can be hazardous to the emotional health of the helper. "If I could just figure out why I get so hung up on my clients," a typical young psychologist complained recently, "I'd be a better therapist and a calmer person." Fair enough, but how do we do it? How do we walk the tightrope that seems to be anchored in our hearts?

If we are to achieve successful stress-reduction in this area, we must consider ourselves. We begin effectively to deal with "close-quarters stress," not by erecting defenses against an invasion of our emotional lives by those we are helping, but by tearing down defenses so that we can see and hear ourselves better in the midst of our helping activity. If effective interpersonal helping is always tied to the relationship with the other person—a student, a parishioner, a patient—then we must focus on ourselves as we are when we are with that person. Often, we think that it works the other way around and that if we concentrate totally on the other, getting together as much information about him or her as possible, we have done our work well. Nobody will deny the importance of understanding the other well; we must, however, also take ourselves and our own reactions into account at the same time. This is the demanding double focus that is essential for being a good helper both to other people and to ourselves.

Also, we must know what is taking place inside ourselves at the same time that we are trying to grasp what is taking place inside others. After all, these feelings and emotions occur simultaneously and they are often significantly interrelated. We cannot draw close to others without beginning to affect and be affected by them; this is the nature of human relationships. We cannot operate from a protective position. Helping takes place out in the open where we are defenseless. This is precisely why the potential stress of unrecognized and unmanaged emotional involvement is so great; it is dangerous out in the open unless we know who we are and why we react as we do.

Helping is rooted in the human equation in which there should be no unknown term. The unknown term is all too often the person of helpers who, because they are not sufficiently sensitive to themselves, do not know what is happening to them as the course of the helping, no matter how short or long, progresses. Such persons easily get lost, not because the one they help has such complicated problems, but because they have not learned to take their own problems into account.

It is clear that the somewhat cold but presumably prudent injunction not to get involved is simply not good enough in this situation. If we remain uninvolved, nothing much will happen, and the potential stress of emotional engagement will be transformed into a different kind of difficulty commonly known by the reluctant counselor. Such helpers experience the problems of others as burdens or downright impositions; they struggle through relationships like a downed airman crossing a swamp with a parachute dragging behind him. There is nothing sadder than helpers who steel themselves against their tasks, who speak of "having to see all these mixed-up people," and who seem more grimly dutiful than interested in their work. The stress associated with noninvolvement is not very dramatic, of course; the heart does not leap with enthusiasm in these situations. It is like being caught between two great grindstones that crush us slowly into a fine, dry powder. Few things are worse than working with people and not enjoying it.

A Sense of Ourselves

It is better, then, to face directly the challenge of being present to and with other people and to know firsthand the dynamic consequences of being close. This requires a balance between our sense of ourselves and our sense of the other person; it begins, however, with that previously mentioned willingness to listen to what is taking place inside ourselves. Of course, we cannot do this if we are preoccupied with other things or if we so fill the relationship with noise—the sound of our own voice—that we cannot hear the other at all. What is required?

First we must develop a sense of what it means to be in relationship to someone else. This is not the same as just waiting for another person to stop talking so that we can talk. Nor does it mean indulging in our own daydreams while the other tells us what we consider an all-too-familiar story. To be in relationship demands, at the very least, that we give up our own thoughts and interests for a while to be able to give our complete attention to the other person.

There is an invisible sacrifice involved in this, a readiness to empty ourselves of our own concerns in order to make room for those of others. Being in relationship with another calls for a positive effort on our part to inhabit the same life-space as the person speaking with us. This is easy with someone we love; it may take a little practice with those we are just getting to know.

Secondly, we recognize that what stirs in that shared life-space—whatever feelings others express toward us and whatever we experience in feelings toward them—is never just accidental or incidental. What we begin to experience reciprocally constitutes the life signs of relationship; they tell us *that* something is going on, and they also give us major clues as to *what* is going on. If we do not feel anything, then we are probably not close enough to make any difference to the other anyway.

Thirdly, what occurs between ourselves and others—even when this is difficult to listen to—provides us with the key to understand two things: whether we are going to be of any help to the other, and whether we are going to grow ourselves. Unless we can sense the human outlines of the developing relationship we will never be able to understand it or to possess ourselves strongly enough not to be finally absorbed by it. This is true because helping others implicates us in something that is live, not prerecorded or simply intellectual, but in an honest-to-God *you*-and-*me* relationship. We must touch at some level or we will never make any difference to each other at all; we might just as well be on tape or have our lines written beforehand. The strength and vulnerability of what we mean to each other depends to a large extent on our continuing capacity for spontaneity.

These considerations lead us to the questions of *transference* and *countertransference*, notions that are very important yet not very complicated. They describe some of the feelings that take place in helping relationships.

Transference refers to those feelings the person we are helping seems to have toward us in this relationship. They are, however, feelings appropriate to previous, significant persons in their lives, such as parents or those who took their place. These feelings get transferred to the counselor or helper, and they may be either positive or negative in tone. Helpers must be aware that this can happen and not construe them as feelings the person is having toward them as individuals. When a helper naïvely gets involved in responding as though he or she were the direct object of these feelings, complications can ensue.

Example: the priest-counselor working with the adolescent who is in conflict with his own father. The clergyman, already titled "Father," should not be surprised if feelings that are really meant for the boy's true parent get directed at him. These are ordinarily mixed and, if the priest cannot maintain some perspective on what is taking place, he will soon be confused and quite unsure of what is happening. He may, for instance, try to correct the boy's attitude and only reenact an attitude typical of the real father; the quicksand pulls us down very fast in these situations.

Countertransference, on the other hand, refers to feelings (again potentially positive or negative) that we as helpers feel toward the individual we are counseling and that grow from our own past history and needs. These reactions may include feelings of being strongly attracted or unattracted to the other; feelings that are ours and that say something about ourselves that we should try to understand before we proceed further. There is nothing wrong with reacting to other people in this way; a problem arises only when we do not pay attention to the reaction because it disturbs, surprises, or shames us in some way. This feeling is ours at the moment and, rather than turning away from it or denying it, we should gently listen to it and identify it as clearly as possible. Only then can we impose understanding and the freer and unconflicted control that flows from this; otherwise, the feelings will remain alive, dominating and controlling our responses even when we are not aware of it.

Example: the man who finds himself strongly attracted to a young woman client. Defensive about himself, he does not admit these reactions and only expresses them indirectly. He treats the woman harshly, antagonizing her frequently, not because of anything she may have said or done but in response to his own less-than-conscious feelings of attraction to her. He has established distance in a destructive manner in order to handle his own countertransference feelings. Although he does not acknowledge them, they dominate the relationship anyway.

What We Should Not Do

We should not panic; we are not really in danger if we remain calm. The calmer we are, the better we will hear the signals coming from the other person's feelings as well as from our own. The key to being close to others without being destroyed depends on getting these messages straight right from the beginning. This requires self-acceptance, patience, and a willingness to suspend action until we have a fairly good idea of the sources and nature of the emotions involved.

We should not misinterpret, which is the easiest thing to do in such a situation. This only makes the experience more dreadful; it may even be a symptom of our need to master a situation prematurely. We have to let these things come to term; the more carefully we listen, the clearer the meaning will be.

We should not try artificially or dutifully (by force, in other words) *to change either our own reactions or those of the other person.* This will garble meanings immediately and destroy some of the important foundations of our helping work. Instead of covering our emotional tracks, we should learn from them. We may not always react the way we would like or in the manner we would consider ideal, but the way we react defines us, and we look away from it at our own peril. We may not be perfect but we are what we are and we cannot grow unless we can get that into reasonable focus. The beginning of a helping relationship is precisely one of those moments of mutual self-revelation through which we can lay hold of our identity more firmly. This is essential in maintaining ourselves in the kind of balance necessary for avoiding the ravages of unknowing overinvolvement; only when we do not face and label our reactions properly do we have to worry about overinvolvement. We get lost, not only when we do not know the way but, more often, when we do not know ourselves.

As helpers we should wisely remember that we are our own most important counseling instrument and that what we know and possess of ourselves makes a great difference in whether we help others effectively or not. It also makes the difference in whether we can actually be close to these people without losing ourselves in the process. To remain separate as we draw close is fundamental in avoiding the kind of identification with the other that may finally snag and bring us close to ruin. Yet, being separate does not mean being cool or distant; it depends on whether we recognize and respect our own individuality as well as that of the person we are helping. It involves a knowledge of the kinds of reactions—transference and countertransference—that may arise and the sensitive discipline of the self that is required to sort these out appropriately. It demands that we trace down the sources of these feelings without experiencing guilt over having the feelings in the first place. Respecting ourselves begins with respecting our feelings and being able to distinguish between them.

Being a separate individual who can move unafraid into an intimate relationship with persons who want our help is a major factor in our being of assistance to them. When we know who we are and can tolerate and deal with ourselves without impatience or excessive fantasy, we can also see other persons as separate individuals. We can learn to respect and care for them without fearing that every spontaneous concern will draw us closer to the pit of agonized emotional overinvolvement. But this is where we begin: in learning to be separate and in allowing others to be separate from us.

As we pay more attention to the silent stress generated by working closely with people, we may build up a check list that will enable us to keep our relationships in healthy perspective. We need to be able to recognize the signals that inform us about our emotional steps and missteps. For example, we might begin to ask ourselves questions like these:

What is behind my more-than-average interest in this person?

What am I trying to get out of this relationship that I would not like to admit to myself?

Am I always ready to argue with this person . . . or always ready to agree?

Am I beginning to feel more sympathy for this person?

Do I think about him or her between sessions? Do I daydream about this person, and why?

Do I feel bored when I am with him or her? Who makes it so, me or the other?

Do I overreact to statements the other person makes?

Is there a reason why either I or the other person is always late?

Is there a reason that either I or the other wants more time than we had agreed upon?

Why do I say this is the best (or the worst) person I ever worked with?

Do I find myself wanting to end this relationship or to hold on to it even though it should come to an end?

This is only a preliminary check list and we may add items and insights as we proceed. We should move ahead with less belief in old saws like "Don't get involved" and more belief in ourselves and our ability to be close and helpful without being destroyed at the same time.

2

Hard-bought Wisdom

There are things we learn only after we have had some actual experience in counseling other persons. In fact, we are not ready to learn them until we have made some mistakes and, while reassembling our self-confidence, we begin to wonder what has happened to us. Helpers who reflect on the emotional scars they have collected begin to understand things about themselves and their approach to others that they could never learn if they performed like an errorless or unconscious machine. Counselsors have no monopoly on learning from experience, of course, but it is one of their most important methods for improving themselves and dealing constructively with the stress that is intensified in relationships where things do not seem to be going just right.

The following are notions that have been learned the hard way; they summarize things you can find in textbooks but that you only get to know in life itself. While they are framed in terms of laws, they are not intended to be commandments nor are they intended to be a shorthand version of how to be a counselor. They provide a useful framework for our continuing efforts to develop ourselves as helping persons, especially in the area of ministering to others in pastoral work.

Listen to the Patient

Patients, in their own way, are always trying to make better counselors out of us. Indeed, patients are well-named because they are often tolerant of us and our sometimes uncertain efforts to grasp what they attempt to tell us. The fact is that, whether we can hear them or not, the persons who come to us for assistance work very hard telling us—concretely or symbolically—what it is that is bothering them. They cannot do this with complete clarity nor can they explain it, yet in most instances, patients do not hide the truth about themselves from us.

It is a source of wonder that human beings can be so determinedly honest about their lives even when they catch us on a bad day and we cannot seem to grasp their messages fully. They continue on, giving us as many hints as possible in an effort to help us understand them. In ordinary circumstances, the client is not there to outwit or to humiliate us—and even when people can do nothing but this they tell us a good deal about themselves. Most persons, even in quite brief encounters, want to tell us where or how life is hurting them at the moment. Many of our problems as helpers arise simply because we cannot or do not listen to what they so doggedly try to get across to us.

Whether we call them clients, pupils, or parishioners, those persons seated opposite us in our offices actually try to be helpful to us. They tell us, for example, that we may have missed what they are saying. This is done in a variety of ways but none of them is obscure. The person may interrupt quite directly and say something like, "No, that's not what I mean at all," or, making a smaller correction for us, "That's close to what I mean but it isn't quite it."

Sometimes they let us know when we are wrong in our understanding of them by not saying anything at all. This is not necessarily a conscious or deliberate move on their part as much as it is the normal feedback from people who feel that their message has not been received. They stop dead in their tracks because, in the face of misinterpretation of their meaning, they have no place to go with their narrative. They cannot move forward because we have erected a barrier or cut the ground from beneath them. Generally, they move back, regroup their forces, and try again to tell us what we have just misunderstood.

What are some signs that they are doing this? They may switch examples, moving to a different illustration in order to try to clarify their previous point. If we listen carefully to these transitions we begin to realize just how helpful our patients are to us, how, in a very real sense, they are trying to make good counselors out of us. Let us examine the case of Mr. R. for a moment.

Mr. R., a businessman in his forties, tells us that there is something wrong with him, something he would like to correct:

MR. R.:   Well, I don't know what to make of it exactly and I'm not very pleased with it but . . . well, it's like in the morning. I get up and want to have a good day, I want to do my best. Then I get down to breakfast and, before I know what's happening, I'm having a quarrel with my wife. . . .

COUNSELOR: I guess you're upset because you've been having trouble with your wife.

MR. R.: (Pause) No, it's not that. That's not why I'm upset. (Pause) It's more that I can't seem to avoid these squabbles; it's got something to do with me. It's the same way with the car pool I ride in. I want to be pleasant but, well, we don't go a mile before I react to something one of the other guys says. . . .

It is clear that Mr. R. is attempting to communicate his puzzlement and discomfort about his argumentative reactions. He doesn't know why these are occurring and he doesn't know what to do about them. He says this fairly clearly, but the counselor, alerted by the example which Mr. R. uses to try to explain himself, responds in terms of this specific relationship. Mr. R. corrects him immediately in a way that makes it clear that his wife is not the focus of the difficulties. What more, we might ask, could a counselor want? Mr. R. apparently understands this, so he shifts to another illustration, compressing the same difficulty into a new setting. All the counselor needs to do is listen carefully to get all the information needed to recalibrate a response to the client. The helpee, in a very real sense, is trying to make a better helper out of the counselor.

How is it that, despite the clear testimony of the other person, the counselor can miss the point so easily? This can happen to veteran as well as to novice helpers and, because it piles up a sense of dissatisfaction with his or her performance, it not only causes stress but it is discouraging as well. Helpers do not hear well because they are listening to something else, something like their own expectations of what the other person's problem must be. This happens easily, for example, when we feel that we have heard this kind of story before or when something within us self-confidently diagnoses the situation on fragmentary and unconnected evidence.

When, as helpers, we find that we are frequently being corrected by the client or that we are running into roadblocks of frustrating silence, it is a good idea not to berate ourselves but to shift our attitude so that we can discover why we cannot hear what is being stated so lucidly to us. Obviously, not all those we help will be as directly helpful in return as Mr. R., but if we listen more carefully, if we are less preoccupied with our own expectations, we can read the signals—even the symbolic ones—more easily, and we can decrease our stress while we become more helpful ourselves.

One of the chief indications that we are not hearing the client is found in an examination of the whole counseling session, whether it is ten minutes or an hour long. If the person is still trying to say at the conclusion of the period the very thing he was trying to say at the beginning, we must examine our hearing rather than his messages. If we can shake ourselves loose from the course we are set on pursuing, we can listen to the patient and discover just how helpful he is actually trying to be.

Forget About Problems

Closely related to our difficulties in hearing what other people are plainly and patiently saying to us is the difficulty of overfocusing on problems rather than on the people who experience them. Problems do not exist in some raw and unprocessed state, although we frequently speak of them in this way.

For example, a counselor or a member of the clergy might say, "I have another alcohol case this afternoon," or, searching for a psychological cookbook, might ask, "How do you treat alcoholism?" There are, of course, useful things to learn about alcoholism and other human difficulties, but it is also important to remember that the problems do not exist independently of the people who have them. There are only *persons with problems* and our response must always be to them rather than to some disembodied state. Even in the application of behavioral modification techniques, the person remains the vital variable; his or her perceptions and reactions remain central and powerful factors in any course of treatment or approach to helping them.

Helpers who concentrate too much on the *problem* run the risk of missing the *person* who is troubled, or of distorting the situation by underscoring the problem excessively. That can bend the whole helping relationship out of shape. This occurs, for example, if we perceive the problem as separate or even separable from its possessor's reactions to it. In these circumstances we treat it as a package the client brings in and places on our desk for our wise examination and prescription. That is the kind of emphasis we give when we ask too many questions about the problem, or when we feel, for some reason or other, that it must be solved as swiftly as possible.

Actually, we do not have to solve problems; we only have to help other persons accept that responsibility for themselves. To isolate a problem so that we cannot see its organic relationship to the person experiencing it is tantamount to dissecting a living being. All we have to deal with are human beings and their reactions to the particular stresses of their lives; unless we can manage to see the situations they describe, we won't even get a good look at the phenomenon they call a problem. The problem—whether it is alcoholism, school failure, or infidelity—can be understood only in the context of the person who experiences it. If we get the individual into proper focus, we will automatically get the problem into the right perspective. The less counselors feel that it is their responsibility to solve the other person's problem, the more freely they can communicate to the other the strength and support that he needs in order for him to begin finding a solution for himself.

It is a great relief for many counselors when they realize that they do not have to solve every problem or have the answer to every difficulty. This does not lessen the challenge of sensitively understanding people with problems, but it factors out of a counselor's life a considerable amount of unnecessary stress.

Don't Try to Do Good

The suggestion—to avoid trying to do good—is closely related to our awareness that we need not be the world's greatest problem solvers. It also builds on the realization of how much harm has been done all through history by resolute do-gooders—that sturdy tribe whose heavy-handedness with human beings cannot be compensated for by the virtuous gleam in their eyes. Do-gooders are defined as those persons who act on others in response to their own needs. It is clear, therefore, that doing good is not to be avoided as much as setting out purposefully to inflict good on others at all costs.

In any helping situation we hope that the outcome of our efforts will be the good of the other person. This is most often accomplished as a by-product of our sincere interest and effective understanding of him or her. However, trouble arises when we directly—and sometimes unilaterally—decide what must be done and how best to achieve our preplanned outcome.

Thus, for example, we have the college prefect who believes that the junior class member who is seeing him must avoid, at all costs, dropping out of college for a semester. The good end is decided by the prefect and, because he is now personally involved in accomplishing this goal, he may even move outside the counseling session's boundaries to contribute what he can to the goal. He talks to the student's teachers, gets one of them to arrange a special make-up exam, makes inquiries at the dean's office about the student's chances, and begins coaching him in his math course. Massive energies are engaged, in other words, in trying to get the student to do something that has been preordained by the prefect's own judgment—and quite likely by his emotional stake in the project.

This scenario can be rewritten with a dozen different settings and as many leading characters, but the basic dynamics are always similar. The helper suffers from what psychologists call a rescue fantasy—a deep need to rearrange people's lives and to provide them with happy endings designed by the counselor himself. Several questions immediately arise: Whose needs are being met in this situation, those of the helper or those of the person helped? What do we accomplish for others when we decide what they should or should not do and then exert massive pressure on them to conform? How much lasting good is achieved by this common but makeshift arrangement that depends so much on the almost muscular intervention of the helping person?

These are hard but good questions for every counselor to ask, if only to avoid the enormous stress and lopsided emotional consequences of such an arrangement. Not every helping person is inclined to do good in this rather blundering and hardly insightful way, but even old hands at the work may find themselves tempted at times to take over and work out the life problems of another. The reasons can be varied: a need to show a little power; an unconscious response to the attractiveness of the other; a need for self-enhancement. All of these can interfere with responding effectively to the person whose needs presumably come first, the one who comes for help in the first place. The impulse to do good—and to get involved beyond the helping situation in doing it—is one that needs careful periodic examination by every person who works closely with others.

The central difficulty is that the predominance of the do-gooder's needs may make it more difficult for clients to take serious responsibility for their own decisions. It is no favor to anyone to protect him or her from the consequences of their actions or to deny them the opportunity to fail. The overprotected child is the classic example of this; although the child is spared many of the hazards that others must suffer in growing up, he or she is necessarily more vulnerable because of this situation. The capacity of such children to cope with unexpected difficulties or even to be able to stand on their own two feet may be impaired. This was illustrated by the kind of doing good that the college prefect was guilty of. He may feel better that the counselee makes it through to the end of the year, but there is no guarantee that lasting good has been done.

The object of helping others through counseling or other similar work is to assist them in marshaling their own strengths so that they can confront and deal with their lives effectively. This requires understanding and other skills, but it does not need the overkill of doing good through imposing decisions and strategies on others. One element that every good relationship requires—whether in love or counseling—is the kind of self-restraint that acknowledges and respects the potential of the other to begin to put order into the confusion of his or her life. We can give others our time, our understanding, and our honest selves, but what we do beyond that may be quite harmful if it proceeds from our need to do good.

It is an enormous gift to make ourselves present in a responsive and understanding way in the lives of others without trampling all over them. As psychologist Carl Rogers once noted, it takes a lot of discipline to do what we can for others and then, literally, let them *be*. The real good that we accomplish flows from those relationships in which we have come to terms with our own needs to redesign the lives and plans of others. Self-conscious do-gooding may be one of the signs that we should inspect our own emotional lives more carefully and face honestly any need we may have that could interfere with helping others to take care of their own lives. The people we help will be freer and so will we.

Don't Try to Do Well

If *doing good* can interfere with helping other persons and increase the counselor's own experience of stress at the same time, then the urge to *do well* is almost equally destructive. It is common enough, especially in bright people who are afflicted with obsessive-compulsive tendencies. They like to get things straight and carry them out according to the wishes of authority as promptly and effectively as possible. They are easy to recognize in class, for example, because they take their notes and themselves rather seriously. The questions these people ask are endless and all in the service of the need to do well, which is as American as apple pie.

These remarks are not meant to degrade the practical desire to achieve; they are, however, intended to emphasize how much that desire can interfere with what is involved in helping other persons effectively. It is, therefore, something with which we must come to terms before we can become good counselors. What are the elements of this attitude toward life?

Persons who want to do well at all costs are handicapped because this motivation clouds their vision of life and contributes to their perception of human beings as opportunities for achievement rather than as individuals in themselves. Persons for whom doing well is a strong incentive find that it is very difficult to look at life without the feeling that they must produce and earn gold stars or else they will be found unworthy. The reward of approval by parents and teachers seems to be very important to these persons. Worth for them is not something intrinsic; it is always in danger and they must keep earning it. Mix this attitude with an obsessive style and it is easy to understand why, in helping others, these achievers have special difficulties.

Persons who want to do well find it difficult to be part of a relationship with someone who comes for help because they are so aware of themselves, and so concerned about the endorsement of invisible authorities before whom they must prove themselves. Sometimes counselors get to comparing themselves with some expert they know or whom they have heard on a tape or a record; if emulating that expert's technique becomes too important, it can be very hard to be loose and fresh with the client. Yet the major obstacle remains their handicapped vision of other people. As long as they look on others as stepping-stones they will never see them clearly as persons.

Most of this is unconscious on the counselor's part; many have never examined their need to excel or to be approved, and they are terribly frustrated at meeting a challenge in which these familiar approaches do not work any more. They learned this combination for success at some previous time and it is a serious and stressful blow to their adjustment when it no longer opens the way to honor and applause.

Successful helping is an unselfconscious phenomenon and it shrivels when it is forced into the framework of a polished performance. Good counseling demands less and more at the same time; less of the self-regarding attention to the way one counsels, and more of the simple humanity that is considered too ordinary to be impressive. The personality of counselors remains their chief asset, and the more they can liberate it from the grip of the twin needs of doing good and doing well, the more they will be able to respond to others just for their own sake. In the bargain, counselors will feel better about their work and, although they may not think about it so much, they will also be more effective.

3

What Other People Do to Us

Many helpers have occasionally found themselves as lost in the middle of a counseling relationship as they would be in an alien forest. They are not sure of where they are or of how far off the nearest clearing may be, but they keep hacking away as best they can. This is frequently accompanied by rising confusion and frustration, two leading producers of stress. Counselors who want to handle this pressure wisely and constructively must learn to read the signs of the very situation in which they find themselves rather than wait for good luck or deliverance from outside sources. Like the woodsman who takes his bearings in the unfamiliar circle of trees, pausing to study the slant of the sun and to intepret the special language of the vegetative growth, lost counselors can also pause and read the special signals that are present in the relationship in which they are entangled. These make the situation understandable, lead to a way out, and relieve stress all at the same time.

Helpers who do not learn to read accurately the signals of the stalled relationship may only increase their own frustration and bewilderment. They become discouraged and irritated at the client, at themselves, or just at life in general. They may also suffer a loss of self-confidence because of their inability to grasp what is happening to them in this particular situation. Helpers with shaken self-confidence find it increasingly difficult to assist other persons constructively. Such uncertain guides feel helpless and can only be puzzled when the techniques with which they are familiar no longer seem to operate effectively. They cannot impose a rational explanation on a counseling experience that is given shape by conflicting emotional forces that they can sense but cannot identify.

There is also the danger that counselors may blunder badly under the stress of the moment, pushing or pulling the other person in directions that are not helpful. Sometimes helping persons do not even realize that they are contributing to the breakdown of the relationship. They resemble the motorist who makes a dangerous maneuver, then drives off quite unaware of the smashup he has caused among the cars behind him.

It is equally possible that, while counselors may do the right thing in the relationship, they will not understand why they did it nor, for that matter, why it proved to be effective. The trouble with these experiences is that counselors, when they get results, may learn the wrong things even though they do not know what they are doing.

This learning can be very subtle, something we step into without being quite aware of what we are doing, in the same way that a ballplayer or a golfer absorbs an extra and harmful motion into his swing. It is difficult to know how or when it was learned, and it is even more difficult to correct it. The helper can easily confuse causation with association in these circumstances. I once observed a harried man who, having failed to turn the ignition key far enough, could not start his car. He tried twice, shook his head, removed the key and got out of the car. He then climbed back in, slammed the door with special vigor, inserted the key, turned it and, of course, promptly started the car. "Son of a gun!" he said. "Slamming that door does it every time." Learning the wrong responses causes us to misread ourselves and the situation, ultimately adding to rather than relieving our sense of being under stress.

Another Way of Listening

Clearing up our confusion in certain relationships cannot be left to kindly fate or a favorable arrangement of the stars. It requires a willingness to work sensitively at understanding what is taking place and why we are uncertain or troubled in some particular way. There is a library full of literature about learning how to listen to other persons, detailing even the symbolic language of the body. All of this is fine and indispensable for the counselor's professional development. For the moment, however, we want to learn to listen in a new and indirect manner to the person with whom we are working. This is one of the most helpful ways of sorting out the relationships that seem to confuse or dismay us.

When we cannot find our way, we should ask ourselves, "What is this other person doing to me?" We begin to listen, not to what the other says, but to what we can hear of him in our own reactions. Counselors who want to read the signs correctly pause to sense the reverberations the others send through their own personalities. This is a very special but very real language; being able to understand it allows us to get the relationship into perspective and protects us from inaccurate learnings as well as from self-destructive reactions.

There are many ways to know the world and other persons and, although we may have some idea of it, not enough of us have the patience or the disciplined sensitivity to hear the emotional messages that come indirectly but with the accuracy of registered mail into our own persons. It is a valid way of learning, especially in those relationships in which even the client does not fully know what meanings he is conveying. But it is something like staying overnight in another person's room—there are all his things, his photographs, his clothes, the things he likes to read, even his toothpaste. We can feel his presence in this array of inanimate objects; the absent person speaks to us in a special casual language that is completely silent but very powerful in its significance and impact. We have been at close quarters with the private world of another and, even though all the communication is indirect, it is nonetheless clear and unmistakable.

We are at close quarters in counseling as well, and the same kind of messages—often left untranslated by us—are spoken to us throughout the relationship. Something, in other words, of who the other person is comes across in style, in the sometimes quiet but symbolic way in which he presents himself to us. That communication is as important as the words that others speak. We have to listen to the stones that our clients drop into the well of our own personalities. What we hear there frequently helps us to understand why we are uncertain or troubled, and points to the way we can get the relationship moving again.

This style of listening for the messages of the other in our own reactions does not lead us to tortured or brooding introspection as much as it does to a feeling of liberation from forces that we could previously feel but not identify. When we hear these messages we can put names on our experiences; this both relieves our stress and increases our understanding of the one with whom we are working. Some examples will make this clearer:

I Feel Helpless: This can be a rather vague but discomforting experience and, as a first step, we ordinarily attempt to search ourselves for possible explanations. Have we been careless or are we lacking sufficient knowledge or training? These and similar questions are initially appropriate. When, however, they do not seem to fit the situation, we may begin to listen to the other person in the indirect manner that has been described. What is this person doing to me? That is the question.

Are my feelings the result of something that is being communicated to me by the general mood or attitude of the individual I am trying to help? Is he or she, in other words, giving me a firsthand experience of what others regularly feel in relationship to this person? The answer resides in our own reactions and, until we can read it there, we may be puzzled about why things are not going better.

One of the most common transactions of this sort occurs with the person who is passive and dependent and who, despite any verbal protestations to the contrary, acts out a helpless role with everybody, including his or her doctor, clergyman, or counselor. We are particularly vulnerable to this if we are already under pressure from other commitments, or if we have not as yet learned to reflect on our own emotional reactions. This is not to say that the other person deliberately and with full consciousness generates a sense of helplessness and, by a process of psychological osmosis, finally passes it along to us.

Rather, others reveal their whole style of relating with the world, one of clinging expectation in which they turn away from accepting much responsibility for themselves or their actions. The client's helplessness has an infectious quality until we can immunize ourselves successfully through becoming aware of just how this process can and does operate. We feel helpless because someone else has invisibly embraced us with all of his burdens, fully prepared to let us carry him along. Such persons let us know them in the way we find ourselves responding to them.

I Feel Angry: Here again, after searching ourselves honestly but without finding cause for our rising hostility, we may discover that our anger is the end product of the personality structure of the individual we are trying to help. Helpers are notoriously open game for this kind of transfer because they generally involve themselves fairly openly and with a genuine desire to assist. The frustration and irritation that builds inside us can be our best information about the person whose difficulty is passive aggression.

This personality disorder is a lifelong process which, unlike a neurosis, does not make individuals suffering it anxious. They are usually unaware that there is something wrong with them, and they may not understand why they have difficulties in their relationships or at work. The problem can be read in the reactions of others—and, of course, in our own reactions because what we experience from the passive-aggressive person is exactly what everybody else experiences. The style is one of communicating hostility in an indirect and seemingly nonassaultive manner. Passive-aggressives hurt others, not by doing things but by failing to do them; their psychological satisfactions from behaving this way are at personality levels of which they are not aware.

For example, the person who fails to show up at an important meeting commits an aggressive action toward everybody who does; the individual who agrees to support a certain motion and then remains neutral when the votes are taken causes a great deal of mischief. Passive aggression is considered by some to be the most frequently reported contemporary emotional problem—the common cold of the emotions—so that wise counselors will alert themselves to the possibility that the anger they experience may be coming from the passively camouflaged style of the other.

This is complicated by the fact that passive-aggressives do not feel anxiety and so are not strongly motivated to search out reasons to change. Often they are referred for counseling because of the problems that arise in their work or their marriage. Their boss or their spouse sends them. The counselor can learn a great deal from the extremely subtle way in which this type of client reveals the basic difficulty. It shows up in what they cause us to feel—through signs that are sometimes almost too small to measure—like being just a few minutes late or canceling an appointment at the last minute. The passive-aggressive knows how to be uncooperative at just the moment when it will do the most harm. We cannot help being affected by this style of relationship; one of the chief hazards of being a counselor is that one frequently runs into things like this.

Unless helpers can listen and understand that their own anger is a response to the invisible passive aggression of the one they want to help, they may be confounded by it or they may even express their own hostility in ways that are harmful to them and to the relationship. The treatment of the passive-aggressive personality is a separate question that will be discussed later on. For the moment our concern is to turn our attention to the profile of the passive-aggresive that is gradually etched out on the screen of our own emotions. Once we perceive this correctly we can deal with our own mounting anger and see the relationship in a much clearer perspective.

I Feel Frightened: Although this may not occur as often as such reactions as anger, it is just as true an indicator of what is really going on in the helping relationship. When we cannot find the source of our uneasiness in our own experience, it is helpful to pause and listen again to the dynamics of the other person as they sound inside ourselves. Paranoid patients, who are afraid themselves, can transplant their own fear into us, making us restive and uneasy and crippling our capacity to be helpful. Paranoids do not cast a spell on us but their influence is transmitted along wavelengths that defy conscious or rational analysis. Such paranoid persons may be very difficult to detect except by paying attention to what they manage to do to us in the context of our relationship with them.

One clever paranoid person can disrupt a whole school or a whole community, his destructive achievements being written in the reactions of those all around him. Such persons are frequently intelligent and charming and they seem to be deeply concerned about the problem they transmit from levels deep within themselves. The fear they generate in us may lead us to do things we would not otherwise consider; they get us to act inconsistently and, of course, then they have us just where they want us. They are extremely difficult to deal with and, in fact, may require referral for other professional help. This cannot be accomplished, however, if we do not recognize what is happening to us, if we do not read their fearful messages in our own emotional responses.

I Feel Depressed: This is a reaction in ourselves we should read unhurriedly and carefully. When we have ruled out causes from extrinsic sources we should gently inspect the helping relationship in which we are now working. Some clients have an almost eerie sense of how to get at us; getting help becomes the kind of game they play with everyone in their lives. They have to win, to take scalps, to make themselves feel like triumphant chieftains; and, in a very real sense, they cannot help but try to conquer the person to whom they have come for help.

Yet, their objective is not clear to them; in fact, it will only emerge if the counselors can read accurately what the other is trying to do to them. A sensitivity to this brutally effective game is essential not only to relieve the tension that it builds up in the counselor but in order to deal with the core issues of the counseling itself.

Counselors may feel depressed as a reaction to the subtle put-downs and frustrations clients build into the relationship in order to maintain the sense of mastery or superiority. These are at a level that is at first difficult to identify, especially by inexperienced or untrained counselors. Clients goad them, but this transaction takes place at subterranean levels of consciousness. Helpers may not know what is happening to them, except that they feel quite discouraged and depressed. This depression is actually their way of handling the anger that is developing inside them at an unconscious level. Counselors can feel very down but, precisely because the basic emotional transaction between them and the client is outside immediate awareness, it is impossible to say exactly why this should be so.

I recently observed a clear example of this in a role-playing episode in one of my courses. The client, who admitted that he had some real things he wanted to discuss, projected all his unresolved and complex problems onto the person who was taking the role of the counselor. Because the latter was just learning something about the process of helping others, the subtle but powerful attack of the other hit him very hard. He was depressed and very dissatisfied with himself for several days. It was not until he played back the tape of that session and was able to reflect on what was happening to him that he recognized his own deep reactive anger at the situation—the very substance he was experiencing as depression. He quickly dealt with the situation more constructively.

Many of our other reactions are also powerful clues to the difficulty at the heart of the relationship with which we are working. We can, for example, feel bored because the other person is boring us just as they bore everybody else in their life-space. The list of possibilities is almost endless but the important principle remains the same: When we feel lost or perplexed and can find no reason in our own attitudes, we can reasonably turn our attention to what the other person may be causing us to feel.

The Benefits of Listening

First among the benefits of listening is the increased sense of self-confidence that flows from getting a more fully developed picture of what is taking place in the counseling relationship. Helpers have a surer possession of themselves when the reactions they experience are no longer a mystery but a significant clue to what the other person is, however indirectly, communicating. There is an immediate reduction in the pressure that can mount on counselors who are unsure of themselves or who are thrown off their ordinary stride by clients who communicate these subtle and disturbing messages.

It is very reassuring for counselors to understand that their feelings are not all their own fault and that their confusion is not just a product of their own shortcomings in these situations. While it takes practiced sensitivity—and perhaps a helpful consultation with a supervisor—helpers who learn to listen to the other through their own reactions are bound to feel more competent and to perform more effectively.

The capacity to pick up the clues that are scattered inside ourselves

also increases our ability to respond more purposefully and helpfully to the client. As long as we are trapped in our own confusion or
depression we remain crippled in our efforts to be of service, no
matter how well-intentioned we may be. Breaking through to the
truth of our own reactions is a very freeing experience; we can then
use our insights and skills in a far more integrated and successful
manner. In other words, we can begin to deal with the issues that are
really at stake and, even if we come to realize that we cannot take away
all the other person's problems or that somebody else may be able to
assist them more than we can, we will have made real progress. All too
often when these situations arise, counselors slog along, feeling the
burden grow heavier all the time, but never really getting anywhere;
he or she sometimes becomes, in effect, just another part of the
disturbed person's world, an aspect of symptomatic self-expression
rather than any real help to the other. These relationships sometimes
stagger on for months, much to the discouragement of counselors
and not much to the improvement of the clients.

Perhaps the most important learning associated with this way of
listening to others is the insight it provides into the meaning of
human relationships. If we can sense the meaning of another in the
mix of our own reactions, we can also grasp more clearly what goes on
in life between persons all the time. We are forever registering our
messages on each other in many ways and at various levels of consciousness. Helpers begin to understand that the core of their work
consists, not in doing something *to* or *for* another but in experiencing
something *with* the other. Counselors thereby deepen their understanding not only of counseling but of life itself.

When we are in the midst of a relationship, receiving and sending
communications at close range with another person, we are no longer
in the abstract, diagnostic realm. We are part of what is going on; what
we do and what we experience as done to us are not just random or
accidental occurrences. These reactions are profoundly significant in
the living give-and-take context of the helping relationship. This is not
just talking about the other person's problem or analyzing it imper-
sonally from afar. Counselors who work closely with others get a
ringside seat, an inside experiential view of the way the other individual places himself in relationship to the rest of the world.

What the clients do to us is just a sample of what they do all the time
to the people in their everyday environment. Patients not only tell us
about themselves or their problems, they frequently let us experience
these things firsthand. When counselors become sensitive to this reality they can read the signs in themselves far more easily and profitably.

Suddenly their bewilderment, anger, or discouragement take on a new and positive significance.

At this stage counselors begin to be *participant-observers,* as it has been described, in helping others. They will be able to sort out their own counter-transference feelings from the transference feelings of those who come for help. The ability to do this more skillfully frees counselors to understand others better because they understand themselves more completely. Helpers can, therefore, be of much greater assistance because they understand that the static inside themselves is more than meaningless interference with communication. It is *the* communication that, when grasped properly, breaks the dead-locks that can interfere with effective counseling.

4

What We Do to Others

If the ones we help are frequently engaged in sending messages that even they do not fully comprehend, so too do we, the helpers, communicate a variety of instructions and judgements to them in return. This other side of the coin finds us quite actively engaged in doing things to the client, quite often without any idea at all of what we are doing. We may like to assume a neutral or seemingly instant pose in order, as we say, "not to take sides" or "to avoid emotional involvement," but such an antiseptic presentation of the self in a therapeutic role is both unlikely and unrealistic. We need not be consciously aware of any feelings toward the person we are helping in order to have these feelings and, in subtle ways, to get them across to the other. We are never devoid of reactions—the sterile knife of the surgeon is a misleading analog for the helping person—and we cannot help but transmit some of these reactions to the other individual. Of such human exchanges is counseling made; it proves effective, not as an exchange of thoughts that have been cleared of all feeling but as a deeply rooted mixture of human reactions which tells us that people are in contact with each other.

The problem of emotional involvement, as has been previously observed, is not solved by placing an embargo on our feelings but by becoming more aware of them so that we can better understand what is happening to us—and between us and the client—during the hours of counseling. Unless we can hear all the messages, including the ones we ourselves are sending, we find our effectiveness limited and the stress of such work needlessly increased. Even in those presumably less involving helping efforts that come under the heading of "behavior modification," the qualities of the relationship between the helper and the one helped—and their reciprocal messages—are crucial for the outcome. An examination of the complete file of our own attitudes helps us to appreciate what is central to the phenomenon of effective helping.

The Meaning of Relationship

Relationship is something many presume to understand even when they do not. It is also something many persons do understand quite well even though they never think about it at all. Being able to be in relationship to others unselfconsciously is, in fact, a sign of good psychological health. People become friends or fall in love without necessarily describing their experience in psychological terms; it is something that is more on the order of *doing* rather than *theorizing*. Being in relationship for these persons demands a response rather than a philosophical statement.

The problem for certain counselors lies in the fact that they are analyzers by nature and may be accustomed to, as well as adept at, the intellectual description and classification of personal problems. They may, without quite thinking about it, live with an abstract view of helping relationships rather than with an inside experience of them. Because they can talk about them clearly, they may not notice how removed from them they can become. It is not easy to be in intense relationships to many people at the same time, the very thing that pastors, counselors, and educators are called upon to do. The retreat to a more stylized mode of dealing with others can be slow—hardly noticeable at first—but gradually it hardens into a set trend that finds busy counselors on the outside of many of their relationships. This is sometimes the sign of an unconscious effort to reduce the stress that is associated with many hours of close interpersonal counseling. It is also an occupational hazard for the individual who is intelligent and whose education may have emphasized logical thinking and rational analysis.

When, however, helpers retreat from relationships with others, they lose something that may be difficult to recover—the sense of freshness and presence that is the hallmark of living human relationships. Being in relationship is more like being in love than it is like solving a murder mystery or a complicated chess problem. It may take some reflection to discover why or how we have forgotten the way in which this works, but it is a vitally important thing for all of us to do. Perhaps the best metaphor here is marriage, the essence of which consists in man and woman remaining in lively relationship to each other. When couples somehow slip out of this relationship they can no longer see or hear each other very well; the marriage relationship becomes a source of stress rather than of refreshment. So it is with helpers who, for whatever reason, let something die between themselves and those with whom they work. Helping relationships become burdensome when they become extrinsic to our own personalities. Then we have to drag them and ourselves along and, although we may complain a lot, we may never be able to find out what happened to us.

Human relationships are interactions in which neutrality is not really possible; the counselor learns to recognize his own emotional reactions—as, for example, when he or she is deeply moved by the wife's story in marriage counseling and is thereby quickly but subtly enlisted on her side even before the husband speaks—and to take these into account so that prejudice and partisanship do not rule the day. Unless helpers can hear their inner voices, they will not understand why things happen as they do nor why the helping situation can become such a confusing chore.

The helper must see the whole relationship; the focus fails if it cannot be exclusively on the problem of the other person. Counselors respond more freely and effectively when they include themselves in the picture and can understand, accept, and deal with everything that is going on in their personal exchanges with others. It is something like a parent's reaction to a child; this is simply not a one-way street and, until we grasp the transactional essence of the relationship, we can only be on the outside of it. We tend sometimes to overemphasize the parent's effect on the infant, thinking of the latter as almost totally plastic and impressionable. Wise observers, however, know that the very young child also has an effect on parents that may have long-range influence on the mother's and father's responses in return. The laughing child gets the loving response.

It is never too early for this to take place—and it is never too early in a helping relationship for some characteristic of the counselee to shape strongly the nature and degree of our response. The immediately attractive or unattractive client may, in other words, set up responses in us that govern the course of the subsequent counseling. There is nothing wrong with spontaneous reactions to people; they are instructive in themselves. Problems only arise when, unaware of our own responses to these inner promptings, we end up maneuvering the counseling to accommodate ourselves more than to assist others. Seeing all the aspects of the relationship enables us to take everything about ourselves and the other into account so that invisible factors do not determine the direction of the counseling process.

The famed sex researcher, Dr. William Masters, emphasizes a point about the relational nature of healthy human sexuality that can well be applied to the counseling relationship. Dr. Masters notes that human beings have progressed through a variety of sexual attitudes. Some, however, still think that sex is something they do *to* another person, as in the ancient and now fairly well-retired myth of masculine sexual supremacy. The next stage of consciousness-raising about sex gives rise to the viewpoint that it is something one does mainly *for* another person. True maturity of relationship comes about, according to Masters, when men and women understand that sexuality is something they experience *with* each other.

These are fair if approximate categories with which to examine what we ourselves actually do in relationship to those whom we help. It is not unusual for a counselor to consider himself in a class with surgeons or other professions who, in the main, actively *do* something *to* others in carrying out their services. We are not yet sure that this is even the best attitude for a surgeon to assume, especially as we become more sensitive to the psychological factors that are closely associated with operations. But it is clearly not the relationship style of choice for the individual who wants to be an effective helper. This approach makes the counselor the center of gravity and destroys the reciprocal nature of the relationship. It also gives great power to the helper who can use this position of doing something *to* others to make all the important decisions about the goals and content of the counseling process. This is a dangerous and excessive load of responsibility to assume, and it not only makes the relationship hopelessly one-sided but adds considerably to the emotional burden experienced by the counselor.

Why do some counselors unconsciously take this position in their work with others? This is the kind of question that each person must answer for himself or herself because so much of an individual's life history is tied up with the style of relating with others, a style that has developed gradually over the years. It is possible, for example, that helpers who, in effect, take charge of counseling the way a dentist takes charge of teeth, discover protective advantages for their own emotions through this move. We can stay somewhat clear of others when our focus is on doing something *to* them; they do not need to get close to us and our need to reveal ourselves is minimal. In other words, helpers who use this approach defend themselves by the very manner they employ in dealing with others.

The reasons for the counselor's reluctance to disclose something of the self can be many and varied, but the protective effect is nonetheless the same. This may seem to solve the problem of potential emotional involvement and spare the counselor's feelings in other ways as well, but the price for this is high because of the way in which the helper's own personality—one of his or her chief assets—is thereby obscured. This diminishes counselors' capacity to enjoy their work with other people while it seems to save them from being hurt by them.

This situation resembles the bizarre surgery that took place in Vietnam several years ago after one of the Vietnamese soldiers, in a freak outcome of battle, came to the hospital with a live shell embedded in his back. The operating theater was sandbagged, a wall of shatterproof glass was erected, and the surgeon in heavy protective garb, used specially constructed elongated tools to perform the delicate surgery. Understandable in these circumstances, one might say, because the patient was literally a threat to the doctor and everyone else around. Unfortunately, some counselors don psychological armor and operate from a protective distance in their helping relationships because they are afraid these will also explode. Doing something *to* others is often accompanied by such defensive maneuvers.

Counseling as a service *for* others also deserves careful examination because it may be built on inner motives that have a powerful effect on the nature of the counseling process. Individuals determined to do something *for* their clients may actually be doing something through them for themselves. In other words, counselors with this approach are not in relationship with others as much as they are with themselves. They may counsel to meet needs of their own or to fulfill some set of expectations they have set up for themselves.

Helpers who must do something *for* others may not feel worthy or productive—or lovable for that matter—unless they assist others in this manner. The difficulty is that such helpers most frequently respond to their own inner needs; they do not perceive others as separate persons and, although the thought would horrify them, they are, in effect, using others to satisfy themselves. This style of counseling is both wearing and ultimately lessened in effectiveness precisely because the helper has not yet learned to deal with his or her own feelings. Such counselors are trapped by their emotions and consequently they find it very difficult to understand much less actually enter into the free flow of relationship that is essential to good counseling.

As with friendship, love, or good sexual relationships, the essence of helping lies in experiencing something *with* another person. This is a different realm as well as a different range of experience from those that concentrate on doing things to or for others. It is far freer and is, therefore, less stressful in the long run than any other approach. This is not to say that it is easy or without its problematic moments; that could never be said about the best of love and friendship either. However, helpers who begin to understand their work as sharing rather than performing both decrease the pressure they experience and increase self-confidence and a sense of more significant participation in life itself.

Counselors who can let go of themselves more freely in counseling find that the list of appointments on the desk calendar no longer looms like the labors of Hercules at the edge of the day. Helpers who experience things *with* others lessen the demands on themselves because they no longer need to know exactly what the next step will be nor what lurks around the next bend in the counseling process. One of the greatest sources of a sense of decreased stress is the realization that counselors really do not have to know more than the client, nor do they have to prove anything. They are liberated to employ the instrumentality of their own personality, to let the truth of themselves show through more honestly and with less need to explain or defend themselves.

Such counselors enjoy the work of the day because it is no longer an occasion for defensiveness or for self-justification. Being aware of greater inner freedom, these helpers can go more deeply into the relationship itself; this provides a deeper experience of life because the exchange between client and counselor becomes one of reciprocal and creative discovery. These fancy words have a down-to-earth significance for counselors. The "Blue Collar Blues" may exist on assembly lines because of the boredom generated by doing the same thing over and over again, but this is not the problem for the liberated counselor. This helper possesses the closest thing we will ever get to a boredom-proof job by the fact that he or she is constantly in relatively deep contact with the most interesting of all phenomena, the human person. Each one of them is different, and when helpers can see them that way they see individuals in all their wonder.

Counselors who see everybody as the same as everybody else need to examine the reasons for this unfortunate view. They miss one of the aspects of their work that is truly refreshing and genuinely re-creative of their own energies; it is a part of counseling where helpers can freely receive as well as give. Until they can free themselves enough to experience at least some of the spontaneous rewards of counseling-as-experience-with-others, they will only find a desperate increase in the pressures that spring from doing things *to* or *for* others.

It is no secret that the strain that accumulates in the lives of some helpers comes from their conviction that they have the responsibility for the success of the counseling as well as for improvement in the client's behavior and an increased maturity in his or her goal-setting and decision-making. Enormous energy is expended by some in trying to solve the problem that the needy person causes by coming to see them in the first place. These and other considerations—sometimes it is just the volume of people that a counselor must see—make it difficult to ask the simple question we all must answer honestly for ourselves: *What can I really do for others?*

The stress in many helpers' lives is made worse by unrealistic answers to this question, or perhaps from their failure ever to ask it seriously of themselves. We cannot change people's parents or their experiences; neither can we cry or grieve for them, much as we sometimes might like to do this. We cannot even keep them from making mistakes or bad decisions. And we cannot provide guaranteed happy endings for them the way the movies used to do.

A more modest and realistic approach to the possibilities of helping others not only keeps the responsibility for their lives with them, where it belongs, but it also frees the counselor from being the superperson or savior to everyone who enters his or her life. That, in fact, is the role to which counselors cannot aspire without making life more complicated and difficult for themselves.

The capacity to be there with another person without letting our own needs intrude or determine the course of the counseling; the willingness to experience with others their own patient and sometimes painful exploration of their lives; the improvement of our ability to move with them in their inner lives without trampling all over them: these are not small gifts and they are extremely important ones in counseling. In order to give them freely and generously we must get to know our own selves very well so that we can avoid spoiling the best things we have to share with others. Sometimes when we think that we can or must do more for others, we end up frustrated because we have set goals for ourselves that are unrealistically high, and, failing to achieve these goals, we may abandon our efforts to offer them the far simpler but substantial wealth of our presence and understanding.

One of the most difficult lessons for most of us to learn is when to let go, that is, when to give clients enough freedom and trust—even when they seem to have made a miserable botch of their lives. We tend to think that we still know best and that we must keep such persons and their choices fairly well under our control. Giving up control, however, does not mean giving up interest or turning away; it does mean that we permit others to be the center of the stage in their own life. Can we or should we really try to prevent or control that? Can we, in fact, ever successfully or for very long maintain a guiding control over the destiny of other persons? When we find out why we are at times reluctant to give people this operational freedom, we discover the secrets about our own needs that free us from their domination.

5

Our Approach to Others

We have been exploring the living nature of our relationships in counseling, underscoring the importance of seeing them as dynamic experiences rather than as rigid exercises in applied science. As we look at and listen to our relationships, we learn far more than we expect to, finding in them what we can never discover in textbooks—ourselves in action with other people.

The more we perceive ourselves as living although imperfect persons—and the more we can accept ourselves that way—the more we can let go of falseness and self-consciousness, the elements that bind us so hard to the role-expectations of being a helper. The latter situation deprives counselors of the freedom and spontaneity through which they best express their strengths. Only as free counselors do we experience our work with others as personally re-creative rather than as a stressful chore.

Some persons examine themselves rather harshly out of motives that are a mixture of fearfulness and a need not to be found wanting. It is not difficult to raise guilt feelings in people, as most preachers and fund-raisers know, and it is not hard to make helpers feel bad about the shortcomings that can be found in their counseling work. Progress, however, does not come out of feeling guilty any more than it comes out of an unrealistic striving to be the supercounselor who always does the right thing. Raising unnecessary guilt gives self-examination a bad name and may be the reason that many people shun it or postpone it and, therefore, never realize its values.

There is another way to look at ourselves; it is more the way a professional does it—whether a doctor or an athlete—accepting the need for a particular discipline in view of freeing the self for a steadily improving performance. It is part, in other words, of what healthy professionals do, not to punish but to improve themselves.

When professionals get uptight it is difficult for them to perform at all; relaxation allows professionals to see the self in action, to note the false moves or the extra steps they have unconsciously incorporated into their behavior, and to deal constructively with these discoveries. There are no exceptions to the need to explore the self in view of

55

improving performance; this means bringing forth the best blend of natural ability and acquired skill. It helps if we can approach this good-naturedly, realizing that escaping this self-examination only sentences us to an increased experience of stress.

The need to keep refining ourselves, even as counselors, is expressed well in the old saying, "If you have always done it that way, it is probably wrong." The following questions are offered to stimulate the examination of our approaches to other persons with a view toward improving our professional capacity to be of help to them:

Do we want clients to like us? It is not unusual for us to look for a positive response from the individuals who come to see us. Although this may be hard to admit, there are not many people who are indifferent to the way in which other people regard them. This need for a response is only a problem if we make it a chief determinant of the helping relationship and its style. It is, for example, over-emphasized in those textbooks and other urgings that put so much importance on "creating rapport."

Ordinarily, this notion of "rapport" means that the client and the counselor should, right from the start, work at becoming comfortable in each other's presence. On the face of it, this is not a bad idea; the problem arises when our efforts to create rapport become artificial; then we do more harm than good. The best rapport arises, not out of some direct effort to get along well with the client but out of a simple and sincere effort to listen and hear accurately what he or she has to say.

Rapport automatically exists when we are concerned enough about others not to worry about whether they like us or not. Efforts to find out where the other went to school, or if you know somebody in common, or whether they are interested in sports or art, merely interfere with a process that is immediately initiated by placing ourselves, insofar as we can, directly and sincerely in relationship to the client.

Do we judge others? Psychologist Elias Porter has suggested that our tendency to evelute others is so much a part of ourselves that we hardly realize that it is present. It is understandable that we pass judgment on the world and people around us, but this tendency often interferes with our effectiveness as counselors and, as a consequence, increases the pressures we experience in our helping relationships.

In reflecting on our inclinations to evaluate, I am not necessarily disputing the need for accurate diagnosis, nor am I condemning our capacity to put rational order and meaning into life as we observe it.

The penchant to evaluate refers to a deeper and less conscious need to compare ourselves to others, to give a grade to our performance or to their behavior and, in general, to preoccupy ourselves with judgments that may keep us on the outside of relationships when we really belong on the inside.

To stand in judgment on others means to evaluate—to place a value on—persons or events based on our own special point of view. For most of us it resembles a reflex by which, when we leave a movie or a lecture, the first question that comes to our lips may be, "Well what did you think of that?" The question is not, "What was the director or lecturer trying to communicate?" Rather, it places us in the role of the critic, the individual who looks out on life and confidently judges it in terms of his own perhaps limited experience, education, and tradition. This judgment is also affected by our prejudices and unconscious motivations. The effects of excessive evaluation from our own narrow viewpoint are many. It may create a subtle distance that keeps us from ever really getting into relationship with a person who seeks help because we are so busy applying our own homemade labels to them.

Excessive evaluation makes the experience and communication of genuine understanding difficult because it keeps us on the outside looking in. If we are to be effective, we must suspend our own judgments for a while in order to get the other person into accurate focus. Too much evaluation also closes us off from learning about other persons and about life. When we feel that we have it all down perfectly and that we can fit everything into the categories of our own knowledge and experience, then we have closed ourselves in a windowless room where our effectiveness is quietly stifled. The signs of excessive evaluation can be heard in the remarks that we make ourselves. It takes a great deal of self-assurance even to say things like, "It's too bad that you did that," or "It's good that you can tell me these things." How we can be sure, from our viewpoint and limited information, about the correct courses of action for others is a mystery. If we find that we are inclined to be moralistic or that we lead clients by reinforcing certain of their statements, then it is time to examine our approach in this regard.

Do we enjoy interpreting? A better title might be: *How to be wrong even when you are right.* Some counselors, especially amateurs, feel that the art of helping others consists in weaving some interpretation of their behavior out of a smattering of Freudian principles and overconfidence in their own powers of analysis. It is sometimes interesting to note that the person who is given to interpreting too much always gives the same or a very similar interpretation to the behavior of others. Such a counselor-savant may, for example, always tell people that they have not resolved the oedipal situation; this says more about what is going on inside the counselor than what is necessarily the experience of the other.

Interpretation is a valid aspect of skilled counseling, but the therapist who understands its place knows that it is not something that can be used carelessly, out of some desire for mastery or as a demonstration of cleverness. The brash interpreter, however, is out to teach others about their behavior and to add meanings that the others may not be ready yet to recognize. Persons skilled in interpretation know that they must time their interpretive statement to that moment when the other individual is prepared to see, accept, and profit from this kind of response. Good interpretations are characterized by understanding rather than mystery.

Counselors who define their work as searching for the right psychological analysis to apply to the other person's conflicts may badly misunderstand the nature of interpretation and retard their own development as competent counselors. The risk involved in premature interpretation is that, even though we may be right, we may be wrong because of our poor timing. Most of us resent having our behavior interpreted. We are defensive on this matter and interpretations only work when we are quite close to accepting and making them for ourselves. Otherwise they can be threatening and thus only increase the defensiveness, if not the total withdrawal, of the person we are trying to help. Interpretations may display our cleverness or they may help us to feel powerful because we seem to know more about others than they seem to know about themselves. This approach to dealing with them is filled with dangers and if we find that we are indulging in it, or excessively insisting upon our judgment of things, then it is time for a careful self-examination on this matter and, on occasion, consultation with a skilled psychotherapist.

Do we like to ask questions? This might be subtitled: *What to do when we don't know what else to do.* Approaching others through asking them for information, through saying to them, in other words, "Tell me more about this or that," is very common, especially among inexperienced counselors. If we look into our own experience, we know that nothing is more frustrating for us when we are trying to tell somebody about ourselves than to be interrupted by a number of questions that interfere with rather than facilitate this process. It is like being required to fill out a long medical inquiry at a desk in an emergency room when we have a sick child for whom we want some immediate attention. Questionnaires and forms of inquiry have become staples in American culture, however, and some people think that nothing can be done validly unless documents in triplicate are filled out in advance. This can happen in many different spheres of helping other persons; it occurs whenever counselors are bent on getting information they feel is more important than what the client is trying to say. Misplaced or excessive questions may, in fact, be part of the style through which we keep control over our work with others.

Obviously, counseling cannot proceed without any questions. They are sometimes very important in order to clarify certain points the client makes, or to check to see that the counselor has really heard correctly what the other has communicated. Although sensible questioning clearly has a place, the approach that depends too much on soliciting information may be motivated more by curiosity or by the simple fact that the counselor does not know what else to do.

When people come to us in order to talk, they usually do not need to be questioned very much. All we have to do is to make it possible for them to tell us their story and to clarify their own perceptions of it as they do. When we cannot follow what they are trying to say, or when we have not honed our skills at listening to their statements, we may find ourselves at sea, using questions as we would life rafts to keep ourselves afloat. This does not really help the other person very much. It also involves us in more convoluted uncertainties that ultimately multiply our own experience of stress.

Sometimes questions are asked because we are uncomfortable when the client is silent for a while. This is a common problem in counseling, one that is a source of stress for many helpers. Silence can have many meanings; it can be the embarrassed fruit of noncommunication, but it can also be the sign that something meaningful is going on in the relationship. Good friends need not talk to each other all the time, and lovers share many silences that are signs of the depths of their relationship. When clients pause and seem to be thoughtful, they may be absorbing what they have been able to discover about themselves. The good counselor understands this and allows these silences to happen without panicking. We need to learn to live with the significant silence that follows on genuine self-exploration. To break that with unnecessary questions is to destroy the mood and meaning of counseling itself.

Do we like to reassure people? To be supportive is an important function of good counseling. We must, however, ask ourselves where support comes from in the counseling process. It arises in those situations in which the helper is in contact with the person seeking help and accurately communicates an understanding of the other's view of the world. Great strength flows from a relationship in which the client is taken seriously as a person; support arises in the context in which the client feels accepted and heard by the counselor.

Sometimes counselors approach the question of support in a very different way. They stress reassurance rather than the solid exchange that has just been described. To be reassuring is not necessarily to be supportive, although it may sound this way to bystanders. Nonsupportive reassurance consists in telling people that they need not feel the way they are feeling. It denies their experience. This is, of course, the very opposite of acceptance and understanding and, in the long run, can only be destructive.

Falsely supportive reassurance is found in the way that clergymen and counselors sometimes sound in the movies or on television. It is a sad thing to see these professionals portrayed as having nothing really to say to persons who are in trouble. The phrases, "It isn't as bad as you think," or "You'll feel better tomorrow," or "You shouldn't feel so upset about this" are run-of-the mill reassurances that discourage rather than help others. I remember a real-life incident in which I heard a well-meaning person gently tell a weeping widow not to cry. I felt that he was really saying, "Don't cry. It makes me feel bad because I don't know what to say to you." Recent studies of grief and mourning show that "jollying" people along during periods in which they must experience deep feelings of sadness is not at all helpful.

Real support arises from entering into the experience of other persons, being able to stand there with them as they explore themselves, and not in backing away when the experience threatens to become hard on us. To reassure another falsely is to find an escape hatch for ourselves that may isolate us from our counseling work and leave us empty and lonely. In an effort to avoid stress, counselors who only reassure others end up increasing the pressure on themselves. Such counselors may not realize that this stress may reflect their whole approach to other persons; it keeps them on the outside of their experience and therefore prevents them from feeling or being effective in their lives.

Do we try to be understanding? Understanding is essential in approaching all human relationships and is indispensable in any work that comes under the heading of counseling. It is contained in all schools of psychotherapy and in all techniques or applications of counseling principles. When understanding is lacking, nothing very effective can take place. It is the single most important aspect of our approach to others and, even when we fail to be completely understanding, the very effort to approach others in this fashion is helpful both to them and to us.

The effort to understand puts aside a tendency to evaluate or to pass judgments from some distant authoritarian vantage point. Understanding attempts neither to agree nor to disagree with clients as they express their feelings or experiences. Genuine understanding does not condemn the person seeking help but neither does it condone or enlist itself needlessly on their side of an issue.

Accurate understanding begins with an effort to get out of ourselves and to let drop away from us our own narrow viewpoint and traditions. It grows with an effort to see from the viewpoint of the other. It demands that we suspend our tendency to impose our own meanings or judgments on them. Through understanding we are able to get on the inside of the world of another and to stand there without trampling on or confusing their meaning.

This approach to others, which requires great sensitivity and plain hard work on the part of the helper, is powerful, and it is essential if we want to improve our counseling and control our own experience of stress. The willingness to understand and to work consistently from this point of view strengthens our capacity to be helpful, frees us of a need to prove ourselves or demonstrate our mastery, and increases our sense of lively participation in the deep and meaningful work of counseling.

6

What Is It Like to Be Real?

A special stress associated with counseling arises when a helper feels uncomfortable in attempting to fill the role requirements of the counselor. Being a counselor, in other words, is frequently perceived as being different from oneself, requiring individuals to assume attitudes and behaviors that would ordinarily be unnatural to them. A conflict arises between acquiring disciplined skills and being oneself, between trying to do something correctly and doing the right thing spontaneously.

It is as if counselors had to play a part that makes them sacrifice their own reactions in favor of those prescribed by their teachers or supervisors. As a young counselor once said to me: "It seems that everything I do on my own is wrong and that everything I'm supposed to do as a counselor makes me feel artificial."

Our growth as helpers may be measured by our handling of this common challenge. It involves our developing a sense of unity about ourselves that incorporates what we learn with what we are. The continuing task is to integrate our professional counseling skills with our own personal identity. There is no necessary conflict between what a good counselor does and what a good person does.

The discipline of counseling does not engage us in activities that are antagonistic to the truths we understand about ourselves. The discipline requires us to concentrate on and refine more fully our genuine human strengths; it offers a systematic way of tapping the healthy resources of understanding and concern that are hardly foreign to the best side of ourselves. Maturing counselors appreciate the fact that what they do in counseling does not ask them to change themselves as much as it invites them to come closer to their best but frequently unrealized selves.

What Goes into Being Real?

Being ourselves does not mean saying or doing anything we feel like at any moment in the counseling process. This erroneous interpretation of what it means to be natural—that is, responding to one's impulses without reflection—echoes a general misunderstanding about achieving our individuality. "Being my own man" not only rings of male chauvinism but it is a prime cliché that sums up one of our lesser national illusions: It is far easier to proclaim we are our own person than it is to be our own person. Being our own person involves us, not in employing contemporary aphorisms that supposedly confer identity on us, but in developing ourselves as fully as we can. It takes a serious appreciation of one's talents and some mature concern for the meaning and possibilities of existence itself.

However, these are precisely the opportunities that are available in counseling work. Far from being vague and dreamy notions, concern for meaning and existence is precisely what we encounter whenever we listen carefully to the life experience of another. When we are in a relationship of serious purpose we do experience a kind of meaning that others can only talk about. The essential predisposition is that we be ourselves.

Being oneself does not mean being carelessly different. It suggests, rather, that we take our personalities and our gifts in a serious manner and that we try to involve ourselves in the purposes of life in some depth. Being serious, of course, is much different from being solemn. We only achieve this seriousness by refining our abilities—using ourselves wisely. This means ridding ourselves of the defenses or habits that interfere with our coming more completely alive and expressing ourselves more fully in our work.

Counseling does not ask us to be startlingly different but to be more genuinely ourselves in our work. This is the side of counseling to which only counselors can attend. It is important for them to realize that counseling offers them the opportunity to bring their best disciplined performance—the best of themselves, in other words—into relationship with other persons in emotional need.

As we reflect on and become more comfortable with this, artificiality drops away and the atmosphere and the exchange become less studied and more genuine. Stress decreases and the experience becomes more intensely real for both ourselves and those with whom we work. We discover that our best responses match our best potential as human beings; the developing sense of oneness about ourselves and our attitude in counseling resolves this frequently painful conflict. It creates an environment in which much greater therapeutic progress is possible in a much easier and more spontaneous atmosphere.

As things become more real we experience not only greater personal ease but also a deeper sense of contentment about our work. It is no longer a burden or a test of our laboriously acquired techniques. Counseling becomes a truly recreative experience because we are more fully and freely involved in it. This builds a sense of security that makes the counselor's person more available. A decrease in stress is an inevitable by-product of this.

Some Reality Principles

It may be worthwhile to recall some things that any person who engages in counseling activity will recognize as true. Reflecting on them enables us to consolidate at the same time our sense of ourselves both as human beings and counselors. We feel less as if we are changing costumes and more as if we are entering at a deeper level into an important human relationship. Among the reality principles that help reduce the stress of counseling are these:

People are always trying to tell the truth about themselves. It is helpful to understand this because so many people who find themselves involved in counseling perceive the work in quite a different fashion. They think that human beings more naturally try to hide the truth about themselves. Counseling then becomes an arena in which a battle, sometimes muted and sometimes intense, takes place. Counselors who feel that they are engaged in a battle of wits, a power struggle, or a demonstration of their own cleverness, clearly increase their chances of experiencing stress during their therapeutic work.

Our cultural awareness of the "Freudian slip" offers us an example of this attitude. One of Freud's powerful insights, in *The Psychopathology of Everyday Life* (New York: Norton, 1971), tells us that apparent mistakes in what we say are actually signals about our real intentions. Thus, the man who says, "I now close this meeting," instead of "I now open it," tells us what he really feels about the gathering. This understanding of the meaning of slips of the tongue is closely associated with the reality principle we are discussing.

However, for some persons Freudian slips have become clues in a detective story in which they try to discover a culprit rather than be an aid to a subtler and more penetrating understanding of another human being. Catching a person in a Freudian slip, in other words, has become a triumph, a way of exercising higher wisdom, reassuring oneself, and possibly even putting other persons down. There is a gamelike quality in interpreting Freudian slips this way that diminishes rather than enlarges human relationships. Counseling is not a situation in which we are trying to get the goods on others or demonstrate that we know more about them than they know about themselves.

When we say that people are trying to tell the truth about themselves we refer to the totality of their communication. Most persons do want to get the truth out even though they are sometimes confused or deceived about it themselves. They do this through many styles of communication, some of which are direct but many of which are symbolic and proceed from unconscious levels of their personalities. Even when people are saying one thing in their words, frequently they are communicating just the opposite by their tone, their gestures, or by other behavior. It is the counselor's task to read with an ever-increasing sensitivity the many languages in which we speak to each other so that the message being delivered can be correctly received. The problem is not that the message is not sent; it is that we miss it.

Sensitivity of this sort demands a high level of skill as well as an accepting attitude that tries to understand people rather than to catch them in their inconsistencies. Inconsistencies, after all, are part of the language people use in expressing themselves. When we use our sensitivity to Freudian slips against the client we may obscure rather than get closer to the truth. We may also separate ourselves from the client, accenting the relationship as one of competition rather than cooperation.

Some examples may be helpful in assisting us to unravel what other persons are actually saying to us. Clients who verbally attack us, saying that as therapists we are not helpful or do not seem to be very experienced or that they would like to end the counseling, may well make us uneasy. As we become more sensitive we begin to understand their meaning more clearly. We know that the client is actually saying something like, "I'm getting involved in this counseling relationship and it makes me uncomfortable. The only way I can respond to my discomfort is by trying to put some distance between us through these attacking statements."

Individuals who use defenses extensively in counseling, intellectualizing about the process or about psychological difficulties, reveal something of the truth about their inability to deal with their own inner problems. They are saying, in effect: "This is the best I can do, the only language I know in which I can feel safe telling you about my anxieties and about the sense of threat I experience when I try to talk about what is bothering me."

Clients who attempt to manipulate us by getting us to do extra things, such as granting additional time, make us uncomfortable, but they also reveal a good deal about their own style. They are saying:

"This is the way I handle people. I'm showing my style to you, trying it out on you, displaying to you exactly the manner in which I relate to people in the rest of my life." Counselors who understand that people are really trying to get the truth of themselves across feel less combative toward this type of client and are able to read their behavior with much greater accuracy. They catch the meaning of the whole person and this both increases their effectiveness and decreases the experience of stress in their counseling work.

The things about people that drive us crazy are the things that are keeping them sane. This is merely a commonsense way of understanding the functional nature of the symptoms and complaints people bring to us. It also heightens our awareness of the fact that the rough edges of the sample of behavior people offer us during a counseling session provide a profile of their painful and difficult adjustment. The things they do wrong, the defeats they inflict on themselves, the trouble they get into—the things that bother both them and us—reflect their inadequate attempts to solve their life problems.

There is a pattern to the behavior and, if we sense its outlines, we develop a feeling for the fuller dimensions of the client's psychological motivations; we get a look deep down behind the surface activity. This enables us to see persons in better perspective and to appreciate the functional nature of the defenses they employ. Looking at the situation this way enables us to factor out the annoyance we sometimes experience at the kinds of problems some of our clients repeatedly manage to get themselves into. Remembering this enables us to possess ourselves more easily and to be more understanding of our clients as total persons. It also gives us a fresh way of dealing with the stress of transference and countertransference.

We shouldn't try to open people up. There are strong cultural and personal reasons that sometimes make the objectives of friendship or counseling converge in the phenomenon of "getting the other person to open up." Counselors or overhelpful friends occasionally perceive themselves as psychological safecrackers, spinning the emotional dials sensitively and urgently in order to have the doors swing open on the presumed treasures within.

It is almost an accepted principle that the objective of a good talk or a good counseling session is for opening up the person in distress. Perceiving this as an objective leads certain helpers to invest great energies in bringing this outcome about. They decide beforehand, in other words, that the revelation of the inner life of the person seeking help is the sign that all is going well. They are frustrated when this does not easily come about and they shift from strategy to strategy in an effort to find the precise one that will get clients to talk about what is really bothering them.

Working intensely from their own outside point of view leads some counselors to miss the important things that are going on inside the person who has come for help. These counselors are so anxious to get the person to open up—and consequently so disappointed if the person does not do this according to their expectations—that they easily miss a great deal of what is significant. Also, they try too hard for the wrong goal.

Persons do not come to a counselor to be opened up. They come to open themselves up, a process that is only successfully accomplished if the energies for it come from within. The objective of the counseling relationship, or even of a friendly talk, is not to get others to open up. This is something they will do if they experience the qualities that seem to be indispensable for good counseling; they need to be accepted and understood in a relationship where they are respected and prized as persons capable of taking more responsibility for their own lives. Counselors must periodically reflect on whether they have been caught up in the cultural tide that makes opening up such an unquestioned ideal in counseling work.

But counseling does not have this oversimplified ideal. We go a long way toward relieving our own stress when we can wait for things to happen instead of deciding when and how they should. There is an ancient Chinese proverb that says we can chase butterflies all day long, but only when we finally sit still will one come and light on our shoulder. Waiting is more important in counseling than pushing hard.

Counselors who have not learned to wait compound the experience of stress for themselves and never know quite why. Clearly some gentle listening to themselves will help them track down the sources of their own impatience. It will also give them some clues about why it is so difficult for them to see things from any perspective but their own.

Respond to the person instead of trying to make a good response. This may be the most basic reality principle of all counseling, the common thread that runs through friendship, love, and any kind of relationship in which individuals reach out to enlarge each other's lives. The more we actually see each other as persons—the more, in other words, we perceive each other as distinct individuals rather than as extensions of ourselves—the more freely we can respond to each other. We see each other less as cases, as psychological burdens, or annoying time occupiers. However, when we do not see our clients as persons they quickly get pigeonholed in one of the above categories.

Counseling becomes harder work when people are seen this way; the stress we experience multiplies in exact relationship to our failure to appreciate the individuality of those with whom we work.

We can tell we have this difficulty when we find that much of our counseling effort is going into making a good response rather than in responding to the person. It seems like an oversimplification to remind ourselves of this, and yet, in their efforts to do well, many counselors find it difficult to disengage themselves from the process of making artful-sounding responses. They get self-conscious because they want to sound like accomplished therapists.

The only way to avoid this syndrome is to concentrate on others and not completely on ourselves. When we respond directly to others, we lose the studied and contrived quality that can creep into so many of the things we say in counseling. When we put the other person first, always asking what their experience is in sharing this difficulty with us, then our responses take care of themselves. They may be ragged and incomplete at times but, if they catch the core of the person speaking to us, all that is unfinished about them is compensated for.

All the effort that goes into sounding good only makes counselors more conscious of themselves, and this cannot help but make them less aware of their clients. Persons do come first, but it is a lifelong task to learn to respect them practically and genuinely in our counseling work. The more we do, however, the more effective and freer we are in counseling because it will be less something outside ourselves and more a reflection of our best attention and concern.

7

What Can We Do for Others?

The issues connected with answering the question of what we can do for others may cause counselors their greatest professional and personal discomfort. Varied feelings arise because of the inevitable intersection of counselors' desires to be helpful with the realistic possibilities of actually being helpful. What they long to do collides with what they can do. That people cannot do everyting they want to do for others seems to be a well-established fact of life; it is nonetheless a very difficult reality for many counselors to accept and make operational in their own activities.

Answering this question—or at least asking it honestly—is an important factor in managing the problems that accompany the intimate work of dealing with the personal difficulties of others. Counselors need to develop, for their own good, simple and reliable estimates of what they can accomplish in trying to help their clients.

The question of exactly what we are able to do for others is also related to many burgeoning issues in the broader community's own attitudes toward emotional problems and the variety of issues—legal, ethical, and psychological—that arise in connection with determining the community's own response to its emotionally needy members.

The need to do good has been discussed sufficiently in a previous chapter. It is clearly operative in trying to shape any answer to the question we have asked about the counselor's capacity to help clients. There is no reason to deny the impulse to do good, which is shared by so many people who do counseling on a full- or part-time basis. It is a strong motive that has been associated with some of the great religious and humanitarian achievements of history. That it can be over-balanced in favor of meeting the counselor's need to help, rather than the need of others for help, does not mean that it should be banished from our considerations. It is a factor that influences persons in every profession that defines itself in terms of service to the community. It is central in motivation for ministry.

We grow with an adult grasp of our own need to do good and an awareness of this motive's strength in shaping our choices in helping others. We need not deny the need to help, but we must understand it if we are to integrate it successfully into our personalities and relate it sensibly to the external reality in which we work. This takes a continuing refinement of our own self-understanding; we constructively blend our impulse to do good with the facts about our own abilities and opportunities and the genuine capacity of others to receive and make use of our "rescue fantasies."

Optimism is an important strength in counselors; they can never do much if they are plagued with a negative and unhopeful approach to people in need. Adult optimism, however, is not the same as the dangerously naïve expectation that we can remake successfully all the persons who come to us for help. This latter attitude carries many counselors into deep waters where they soon find themselves floundering in bewilderment and guilt at the confused state of things. It is possible that some counselors unconsciously design their own defeats. Most, however, want to succeed in reasonably human fashion. The first step toward this goal is to come to terms with the facts about their therapeutic power to help others.

Practical Points

The following notions help illumine the self-investigation that counselors carry out as they attempt to give their own answers about their ability to intervene constructively in the lives of others.

Every therapist is limited, no matter how many degrees or how professionally advanced he or she may be. No one therapist can do everything, can work effectively with every kind of patient, or can guarantee cures for every problem. There is an obvious quality to this statement that is often forgotten, especially by counselors who are always comparing themselves to a therapist beyond them whose skills they admire and may even try to imitate. The perfect therapist is like the perfect wave. The quest in search of this kind of perfection would carry us throughout the world and we would never be completely satisfied. Some therapists are clearly more experienced and far more skillful than others; part of the reason for this may lie in the fact that they do understand their limitations, that they have, in other words, answered for themselves in a practical way the question of how much good they can do for others.

No one is expected to succeed all the time. Success may be a peculiar American preoccupation. It is generally defined in concepts of "more" rather than "better." In counseling, the only way that success can mean anything is in terms of a continuous improvement of our performance. It is unrelated to seeing more people, making more money, or having more people impressed by us. Therapy, like growth and life in general, is a series of approximations. It is never magic, and it is difficult to observe when it is going on. Counseling works because it is like life; it matches the imperfect way in which we come to terms with the truth about ourselves and brings this more into practice. Therapy is built on the basic stuff of human experience that underlines the personal growth that, by its very nature, is limited and never takes place overnight.

The counselor who cannot accept limitations and at least occasional defeats is probably in the wrong work. This is especially true in pastoral work. To have expectations of always being able to provide the right answer at the right time is self-enhancing in theory but it never works out that way in practice. Counselors suffering from a "savior complex" only multiply their own experiences of stress by insisting on total therapeutic victories that they cannot possibly achieve.

Counselors who acknowledge their limitations no longer need to prove anything about themselves. They do not have to win the power game with their patients, get their clients to like them, or even impress their colleagues. Counselors liberate themselves through making a pact of truth with life. They are thereby freer to be effective because their defenses are automatically minimized. They do what they can with integrity and do not feel guilty about it. They are less neurotic and, therefore, interfere less with the factors that contribute to genuine success in therapy. They can understand and manage the challenges of countertransference honestly and cleanly because they have learned, in a real sense, to be counselors to themselves. This relieves them of unnecessary stress and permits them to achieve a deeper involvement in their relationships with their clients.

Becoming a counselor to oneself is indeed a necessary aspect of our growth as helpers. Often, the counselor's self is left behind as though it could safely be overlooked or disregarded in view of fulfilling an ideal of service to others. A failure to listen to what is going on inside ourselves, under the banner of heroic self-forgetfulness, may increase our experience of stress and place a heavy mortgage on our effectiveness. It may also make us vulnerable to being slowly consumed by our own unrecognized needs. The reverse of the golden rule applies here: Counselors should do unto themselves what they try to do unto others. This means that they should listen carefully to their own feelings in an accepting and nonjudgmental manner.

We should try to understand and forgive ourselves for our share of human fallibility. Unfortunately, many counselors are hard on themselves and uncomfortable with their own humanity. The understanding they can share with others they curiously deny to themselves. Until we can open ourselves to our own experience we will be caught up in the tension between our ideals and our ideas about counseling.

Revisions of counselors' self-ideals follow automatically from a more realistic perception of themselves. The key to answering the question about how much we can help other persons is found in the realism with which we look upon ourselves, our talents, and our expectations about life. Our self-concept can be revised, of course, but only if we can lay aside our habitual defenses against the truth about ourselves. As defenses harden to preserve a distorted self-understanding, it becomes increasingly difficult for us to process the truth about ourselves. We become rigid, dogmatic, and unyielding because we must insist on the view that we have of our own personalities.

Once we can modify all this—call anger or longing by their right names, and not feel undone because we have a surprisingly rich capacity for emotional reactions—we can more easily be ourselves. This step toward assessing and accepting our own personalities allows us to define our ideals more realistically. There is a correlation, in other words, between a truthful sense of oneself and an appropriate and attainable set of professional and personal ideals. Our personal ideals of helping everyone are tempered sensibly by a good grasp of the facts about ourselves.

In other words, the less we know ourselves in depth, the less appropriate will be the expectations we place on our performance. People feel guilty when they perceive themselves habitually falling short of their ideal. This leads to stressful recriminations and regrets, the twin killers of many persons who engage in counseling. An honest appraisal of ourselves necessarily leads to a modified and more attainable counseling ideal.

The central question that enables us continually to review our own potential in a realistic manner comes to this: What do I think I can actually do for people? Can I undo the compounded experience of years? Can I change their childhoods or eliminate their realistic griefs? Can I compensate them for their bad breaks, their lack of love from others, or their own genetic disadvantages? Can anybody remove the obstacles that are found in everyone's life?

There is a philosophical tone to these questions that takes us slightly beyond what we might term the mechanics of counseling. We cannot forge an answer about our own capacity to help others unless we are philosophical about the many things we cannot change. Hard as it is to admit, there are some people we simply cannot help, some people for whom we will not be well fitted as counselors, some clients with whom we can never establish a helping relationship. Being honest in this context is the beginning of wisdom for counselors. This implies some common sense about human nature as well as some humility about ourselves.

Some Contemporary Issues

Counselors need informed realism about themselves for their own professional work with others. However, they are also shapers of public opinion, mediators who are asked to translate the issues connected with mental health for the understanding of the general community. Even if counseling is not a full-time activity, professional persons have an obligation to be well-informed about the major psychological questions that are relevant to the community. This cannot be done without reading and reflecting on these important issues.

The community has genuine concerns about the claims of counseling to be able to help people on the one hand and the capacity of many persons to be helped on the other. These concerns cover a broad range of issues, including the legal rights of patients, the nature of psychiatric hospitalization, and even the nature of prison reform. Some of the issues about which counselors must continue to educate themselves in order to be agents of understanding for the community include the following:

What do we do with patients we cannot help? It may be well for us as counselors to come to terms with the fact that we cannot assist everybody and that we cannot solve every problem perfectly. It is often appropriate to take the next step and use available referral resources. Beyond this, however, the community is concerned—sometimes because it has not been properly informed—about the implications of our professional failure to be successful in treating everybody. There are practical questions related to this about the nature and length of hospitalization, and the reasonableness of returning certain psychiatric patients to life in the community itself.

Strong feelings can accompany these discussions when persons can cite news accounts of recently released patients who commit crimes, especially if these are crimes of violence. It remains true that most crimes are committed by nonhospitalized persons. This does not lessen the horror that spreads across a community in the face of some shocking murder committed by someone who has received psychological treatment or who has been dismissed from a hospital. All persons who engage in counseling have a responsibility to clarify and to help people face and deal with the strong emotions that can block a mature discussion of the various issues involved here. These are perennial sore spots in every community. The fact that we cannot treat everyone successfully is a problem that the community shares. And the community can only deal with the problem if it is helped to understand the facts about psychiatric treatment, hospitalization, and the need to rehabilitate many psychiatric patients in the environment of the community rather than in an institution.

Associated issues center on the heavy attacks that have been launched against the very idea of psychiatric hospitalization. These have been spearheaded by lawyers who make the case that the patient's civil rights are frequently violated in these circumstances. The increasing number of legal challenges to psychiatric hospitalization cause medical authorities to be understandably defensive about the possibilities of civil suits or lengthy courtroom wrangles over the clinical judgments associated with hospitalization.

The issues are important, of course, but this discussion sometimes obscures the fact that hospitalization is oftentimes absolutely necessary. The perfect solution for preserving patients' rights while providing them with the environment necessary for treatment and control has not been found as yet. It is a major public question to which there is no fully satisfactory answer. The answer must be worked out every day in each concerned community. Pastoral counselors can assist in this, not only through their input of up-to-date information but also through their sensitivity to the emotional issues that surround such questions. They can be effective in clarifying and mediating the discussion of these problems.

The counselor's sense of realism about what can be achieved in a reasonable balance of the medical, legal, and ethical issues connected with community psychiatry has no cut-and-dried formula. Counselors contribute to the continuing resolution of our understanding of these issues if they avoid committing themselves to related causes. Idealogues are impassioned in their demands for hospital and prison reform and for a general renewal of community psychiatric practice. Heightened personal emotions do not help the community arrive at reasonable answers about improving its response to emotional problems.

Counselor to the Community

Counselors can respond better to their communities when they have struggled with some of these questions in their own professional work. In this way they provide the seasoned view that enables steady and mature progress in the community's quest for improved mental health. The notion of the counselor to the community is hardly a new one. It is as old as the idea of priesthood and ministry. The need for professionals with emotional sensitivity to take on this function is one that may be appreciated fully only by the very professionals involved.

Oftentimes members of the community look toward those who do counseling as possessors of solutions; they turn to them for answers in times of crisis. This is frequently very unrealistic; it is the product of a set of commonly held expectations about professional counselors— that they know everything and should be able to handle anything. The inversion of the counselor's unrealistic view of himself or herself is found in the community that makes magicians out of mental health workers.

Magic is, of course, hard to resist because it confers a special kind of power on those who are presumed to have it. One of the best ways to lessen our own stress and to help our communities is by refusing to don the wizard's robes even when others urge us to accept them.

This is particularly so in relationship to the growing problem of the homeless, especially those who are mentally ill. The counselor will sometimes be contacted to aid in evaluating or in helping to find solutions to the problem. Such individuals, by virtue of their home-lessness, may no longer receive their social security checks or be able to comply with prescribed medications for their medical and/or psy-chological illnesses. In these instances, familiarity with community resources is especially helpful.

Everyone with counseling responsibilities shares in the obligation to help the community understand and utilize counselors in a realistic and timely way. This is one practical way in which counselors can lessen the stressful demands made on them by communities or col-leagues who do not appreciate what they can do—and what they cannot do.

8

Questions for Counselors

Sooner or later every person involved in helping others must face and deal with the complex issues implied by the following questions:

Can I be a friend to my counselees?

Can I be a counselor to my friends?

Those inquiries require self-examination, the kind of survey of one's own inner life that is of continuing importance in understanding exactly who and where we are as helpers to other persons. Such questions take on added importance for counselors who have heavy workloads or who have occupations into which counseling fits as an added and sometimes major feature of their responsibilities. Counselors can be so busy that they do not take the time to reflect on the stance that they have assumed in their relationships with others. They come to understand that it is only through periodic investigation that they are able to note whether shifts have occurred in relation to their counseling work and what kind they are.

The questions stated above draw the personality of the counselor into sharp focus. In answering these, counselors must examine basic personal and professional attitudes that have implications for their lives both in and out of counseling.

For many years the model for therapy—and one still found in the professional work of many psychiatrists and others—defined the helping relationship in a highly specific way. It is described in a nationwide study of psychotherapists in this fashion:

> The unique nature of a therapeutic relationship undoubtedly contributed to the therapist's ability to distinguish between intimate personal and intimate professional relationships. Unlike close personal relations, a therapeutic relationship is affect-laden but asymmetrical. That is, only the patient is supposed to reveal the intimate details of his life. The psychotherapist is not only free to determine what he will reveal and conceal about himself, but also to choose how to react to what the patient is saying, if indeed he decides to respond at all. The relationship

is also asymmetrical in that only the therapist is supposed to interpret and impute meaning to what the patient is saying and only the therapist can evaluate the degree to which therapeutic objectives are being achieved in the relationship. In sum, the therapeutic relationship is a highly circumscribed, personal relationship conducted in accordance with the ground rules laid down by the therapist. These rules result in relationships in which the therapist comes to know all about the patient as a person while the patient never comes to know the therapist as anything but a therapist. Thus, from the therapist's standpoint, the therapeutic transaction provides intimacy in close personal familiarity without, at the same time, involving the risks entailed in revealing one's inner thoughts and feelings to another. (*Public and Private Lives of Psychotherapists*, W. E. Henry, J. H. Sims, and S. L. Spray. San Francisco: Jossey-Bass Publishers, 1973, pp. 218, 219.)

This traditional view has, as most counselors realize, been questioned sharply in recent years. Inspired by the personalistic emphasis of people like Carl Rogers and Everett Shostrom, counseling has come to be described more in terms of friendship and in terms of equal relationship between helper and client. Indeed, the face of therapy has changed so that, to some extent, therapy has been defined operationally by some as that which a therapist judges to be therapy. This has led Hans Strupp to remark that "in many respects the field must be characterized as chaotic." (*Psychotherapy and Behavior Change 1973*. Chicago: Aldine Publishing Co., 1974, p. VII.)

We have reflected previously on the impact, not only of the expanded notion of therapy but of the American cultural ideals on the shift of our understanding in the dimensions of the therapeutic relationship. American optimism and traditions have democratized therapy, making it, in many forms, something in which all participants, including the therapist, are equals. This has been reinforced by the widespread rejection of professionalism and an outright denial of the therapeutic value of professional training and skills. We have reached the age of the naïve but confident psychotherapist. In extreme forms, these attitudes might be summed up by saying that it is OK to be a therapist as long as you are sincere.

Common Ground

The theoretical agreement that therapy and friendship contain many qualities in common has also led, even in more disciplined therapies, to a greater emphasis on the characteristics of genuineness, openness, and equality in the relationship. The qualities of ordinary friendship became the basis for describing the elements that are important in any counseling relationship.

Powerfully influential over the last thirty years in shaping this thinking were Carl Roger's famous reflections on "The Necessary and Sufficient Conditions for Therapeutic Personality Change," first published in 1957 and later incorporated in his book *On Becoming a Person* (Boston: Houghton Mifflin Co., 1961). Rogers hypothesized explicitly the similarity between good therapeutic relationships and good personal relationships in general, noting that the formal qualities of therapy permitted a more intense and consistent experience of these. The publication of William Schofield's *Psychotherapy: The Purchase of Friendship* (New York: Prentice-Hall, 1964) symbolized this understanding of therapy as a specialized form of friendship.

A subsequent massive review of the research inspired by Rogers and others led to the isolation of certain common qualities as characteristic of a wide variety of therapeutic relationships. These included genuineness, a capacity for empathy, and the expression of "unconditional positive regard." (C. B. Truax and R. B. Carkhuff. *Toward Effective Counseling and Psychotherapy: Training and Practice*. Chicago: Aldine Press, 1967).

Hans Strupp, a long-time student of the nature of the psychotherapeutic relationship, has sharply questioned the friendship model. He stresses the helping relationship as resembling that of a good parent to a child rather than that of a friend to a friend. Good therapy, he suggests, is analogous to good child-rearing practices. He writes:

> The problem of how our external controls are transformed into internal controls is one of the most basic issues of psychotherapy as well as child rearing, and the two are indeed analogous in very important respects. . . . Psychotherapy . . . resembles child rearing . . . and makes use of the psychological mechanisms although in more refined and self-conscious forms. (Hans H. Strupp, "On the Basic Ingredient of Psychotherapy," *The Journal of Consulting and Clinical Psychology*, 1973, Volume 41, No. I, pp. 1–8.)

One can conclude that the debate about which model is appropriate for understanding effective counseling is far from over. The fact of these developments suggests that it is important for counselors to explore their own way of conceptualizing their counseling work. This is especially true for counselors who do their work in relationship to other professional responsibilities or who work in smaller settings where they cannot help but know socially many of the people they also see in counseling.

This advice does not mean that counselors should take back anything they sincerely understand about the utilization of their own personalities in therapy. This is still important. As Richard Felder has written: "It is appropriate to use the Self in psychotherapy because it is the Self which is doing the psychotherapy anyway, and it works out best to recognize this." (*Counseling and Psychotherapy, Overview,* Dugald S. Arbuckle, Ed., New York: McGraw-Hill Book Co., 1967, p. 109.) The question is one of balance—knowing where one stands as a counselor and a friend, and understanding the many issues that are implied in any such discussion. It does not mean a retreat into coldness, aloofness, or benign paternalism.

Friend or Counselor?

Counselors alone can tell just what their emotional investment is in their relationships with their clients. Indeed, some helpers experience stress because everything does run together in their work and social world. They are in the middle of pressures that come from professional expectations as well as from their own personal need and the needs of their clients. Sorting this out is not just an intellectual exercise but a vital and indispensable form of self-supervision.

Helpers may ask: Is my emotional life led in counseling? Do I get enough response there so that I limit or otherwise contain, consciously or not, my emotional reactions in the other relationships in my life? Some of the research on psychotherapists mentioned earlier suggests that some counselors lead most of their emotional lives in their offices and that there is little left over when they return to their families. They are midway, in other words, between two intimate worlds, never entering either one of them fully, and caught somewhere outside both camps. If this happens, does it have the effect of estranging the counselor from those who may have a legitimate claim on a more intimate personal response from him? It is possible for the emotional commitment of therapy to drain away the kind of emotional commitment that should be present in marriage or in other relationships. Therapy, in other words, becomes not just like friendship; it is the operational friendship in the counselor's life.

It is not a small issue to find out whether the counselor is leading a balanced emotional life. The pressure of work is often invoked as an excuse for letting one's emotional life become distorted. The need to respond to those in distress has legitimated or rationalized many semineurotic adjustments on the part of helpers. If the therapists are not working at maintaining a balanced life, they may find that their own needs predominate whether they want them to or not. Such emotional confusion constitutes a major source of stress for practicing therapists. It is not something that takes care of itself.

Several years ago George Lawton provided a series of reflections that can assist helpers who are interested in examining the style of their therapeutic relationships. Dr. Lawton offers a review of some of the unconscious possibilities that may strongly affect the way counselors place themselves into relationship with others. These include the following:

Counselors may need to dominate their clients and often very subtly assume stances that enable them to do this. They may need the affective response of the client to such an extent that they find themselves in competition with other figures in the client's life. Such counselors want the clients to listen to them and seem to fear the fact that others may also be important and influential in other aspects of their lives. Counselors may shower too much love and attention, too much concerned treatment, on clients in an effort to make the bonds of friendship more secure. This is a common danger in many professions which involve people in helping others.

It is also possible for some counselors to suffer from the "Pygmalion complex," in which they wish to remake clients, especially those for whom they may have some deep but unverbalized feeling. It is instructive for counselors to recognize that they are very resentful of certain seeming demands made by their clients. Another signal indicating a need for self-examination is the counselor's fear of possible client hostility, which often leads counselors to try to appease clients at every stage of their work together.

Contrasting sweet and aggressive therapists, Dr. Lawton speaks of seduction as a two-way street, reminding counselors that seduction on the part of the client is generally more a form of resistance to therapy than a means of cure. This is true despite the impoverished sense of ethics and diminished personal integrity of those therapists who suggest sexual relations as an important part of the treatment process.

This issue has become more prominantly debated in recent years with a publication that reported that six percent of surveyed psychiatrists acknowledged having sexual or inappropriately intimate relationships with their patients (Gartrell, 1986). The American Psychiatric Association not only prohibits such activities with patients but also recently endorsed a statement that warns that sexual involvement with a *former* patient is also almost always unethical (*American Psychiatric Association,* 1989).

These questions merely suggest certain areas where self-examination can be extremely profitable for counselors who take themselves and their work with others seriously. The greatest stress occurs when there are strong potential sources of conflict operative about which the counselor is uninformed. These are generally unconscious aspects of the transference-countertransference phenomenon and the questions help us to examine the complexities of such issues. Counselors who neglect this self-supervision almost certainly sentence themselves to problems that will generate great stress in their lives.

In a recent article, John M. Reismann and Tom Yamakoski explore the kind of communication that goes on between friends. It does not, in fact, very closely resemble the communication that takes place in therapeutic relationships. While this is only the beginning of much needed careful research in this area, the article does suggest some very practical ways in which counselors may explore the manner in which they handle themselves in their personal and professional relationships. ("Psychotherapy and Friendship: An Analysis of the Communication of Friends," *The Journal of Counseling Psychology,* 1974, Volume 21, No. 4, pp. 269–273.)

Perhaps one of the chief dangers, especially to people who are just starting on their counseling work, is not that they will be friends with their clients but that they will act like therapists with their friends. This is a major clue to the fact that counselors can submerge their true selves in a role that not only destroys their spontaneity but generally distresses their friends as well. It is not uncommon, however, for certain therapists to transfer their counseling attitudes to their social activity. They look solemn, pause, use reflections or interpretations in place of ordinary conversation, and quickly give the impression that they are not being themselves with others. This kind of reaction may be the result of fascination with the therapeutic process or may come out of a sincere desire to be helpful. It leads to a falsification of the counselor's personality, and thus to a destruction of the mature use of the self that is so essential to effective therapy. Persons who find that they are changing into therapists in all their relationships need a careful look at why this is happening. They will feel relieved—as will their friends—when they free themselves from assuming the therapeutic stance in social activities.

Common sense dictates the need for careful and consistent self-

examination about these issues. It also validates something professionals have understood for a long time. Neither doctors, lawyers, nor
clergy should take family members or close friends for clients. The
unconscious factors, the overlapping areas of relationship, all create a
stress that cannot be handled easily even by mature therapists. Clear
thinking and self-discipline remain essential even in this era of free-
wheeling therapeutic styles.

Recommended Reading:

Allred, G. B. (1988). Sensitizing Nursing Home Staff to Residents' Needs: A
  Workshop. *Journal of Counseling and Development*, 66:248–49.
Aponte, H. J. and Winter, J. E. (1987). The Person and Practice of the
  Therapist: Treatment and Training. *Journal of Psychotherapy and The Family*,
  3:85–111.
Barnett, M. A., et al. (1987). Reasons for Not Helping. *Journal of Genetic
  Psychology*, 148:489–98.
Barrow, A. C., English, T., and Pinkerton, R. S. (1987). Physical Fitness
  Training: Beneficial for Professional Psychologists? *Professional Psychology:
  Research and Practice*, 18:66–70.
Beitman, B. D. (1983). Categories of countertransference. *Journal of Opera-
  tional Psychology*, 14:82–90.
Beresford, T. P., Low, D., and Hall, R. C. (1983). Ego Defense Mechanisms
  among Medical House Officers. *Psychiatric Medicine*, 1:151–63.
Blochen, D. H. (1987). *The Professional Counselor*. New York: MacMillan.
Bowman, J. T. and Reeves, T. G. (1987). Moral Development and Empathy in
  Counseling. *Counselor Education and Supervision*, 26:293–98.
Brammer, L. M. (1985). *The Helping Relationship: Process and Skills*. Third
  edition. Englewood Cliffs, NJ: Prentice-Hall.
Brown, N. (1986). Empathy and Accuracy of Interpersonal Perceptions of
  Affect. *Journal of Social Behavior and Personality*, 1:639–43.
Buckley, M. (1986). The Concept of Confiding Ties: Implications for Social
  Work Research and Practice. *Journal of Social Work Practice*, 2:60–76.
Cassata, D. M. (1983). Physician Interviewing and Counselor Training. *Inter-
  national Journal for the Advancement of Counselling*, 6:297–305.
Cole, K. D. and McConnaha, D. H. (1986). Understanding and Interacting
  with Older Patients. *Journal of the American Optometric Association*, 57:920–
  25.
Collins, G. R. (1987). Lay Counseling: Some Lingering Questions for Profes-
  sionals. *Journal of Psychology and Christianity*, 6:7–9.
Combs, A., Avila, D., and Purkey, W. (1971). *Helping Relationships: Basic
  Concepts for the Helping Professions*. Boston: Allyn and Baron.
Corey, G. (1982). *Theory and Practice of Counseling and Psychotherapy*. Second
  edition. Monterey, CA: Brooks/Cole.

Cormier, L. S. and Hackney, H. (1987). *The Professional Counselor: A Process Guide to Helping*. Englewood Cliffs, NJ: Prentice-Hall.

Derrickson, P. and Ebersole, M. (1986). Lasting Effects of CPE: A Five-Year Review. *Journal of Pastoral Care*, 40:5–15.

Deutsch, C. J. (1984). Self-Reported Sources of Stress among Psychotherapists. *Professional Psychology: Research and Practice*, 15:833–45.

DeWald, P. (1971). *Psychotherapy: A Dynamic Approach*. New York: Basic Books.

Diagnostic and Statistic Manual III—Revised. Washington, DC: American Psychiatric Press, 1987.

DiMatteo, M. R., Hays, R. D., and Prince, L. M. (1986). Relationship of Physicians' Nonverbal Communication Skill to Patient Satisfaction, Appointment Noncompliance, and Physician Workload. *Health Psychology*, 5:581–94.

Dinkmeyer, D. C. and Dinkmeyer, D.C., Jr. (1982). *Developing Understanding of Self and Others, DUSO-1 Revised, DUSO-2 Revised*. Circle Pines, MN: American Guidance Service.

Eber, M. and Kunz, L. B. (1984). The Desire to Help Others. *Bulletin of the Menninger Clinic*, 48:125–40.

Eckler-Hart, A. H. (1987). True and False Self in the Development of the Psychotherapist. *Psychotherapy*, 24:683–92.

Egan, G. (1986). *The Skilled Helper: A Systematic Approach to Effective Helping*. Third edition. Pacific Grove, CA: Brooks/Cole.

Elliott, R. (1985). Helpful and Nonhelpful Events in Brief Counseling Interviews. An Empirical Texonomy. *Journal of Counseling Psychology*, 32:307–22.

Franklin, D. L. (1986). Does Client Social Class Affect Clinical Judgment? *Social Casework*, 67:424–32.

Fremont, S. and Anderson, W. (1986). What Client Behaviors Make Counselors Angry? An Exploratory Study. *Journal of Counseling and Development*, 65:67–70.

Freud, S. (1971). *The Psychopathology of Everyday Life*. New York: Norton.

Fuller, F. and Hill, C. E. (1985). Counselor and Helpee Perceptions of Counselor Intentions in Relation to Outcome in a Single Counseling Session. *Journal of Counseling Psychology*, 32:329–38.

Fultz, J., et al. (1988). Empathy, Sadness, and Distress: Three Related but Distinct Vicarious Affective Responses to Another's Suffering. *Personality and Social Psychology Bulletin*, 14:312–25.

Glick, P., et. al. (1988). Keeping Your Distance: Group Membership, Personal Space, and Requests for Small Favors. *Journal of Applied Social Psychology*, 18:315–30.

Goldberg, C. (1986). Understanding the Impaired Practitioner. *Psychotherapy in Private Practice*, 4:25–34.

Guy, K. C. (1987). Touch: An Exploration of Its Role in the Counseling Process. *Journal of Mental Health Counseling*, 9:142–49.

Hansen, J. C., Stevic, R. R., and Warner, R. W., Jr. (1982). *Counseling Theory and Process*. Third edition. Boston: Allyn and Bacon.

Hellman, I. D., Morrison, T. L., and Abramowitz, S. I. (1987). Therapist

Experience and the Stresses of Psychotherapeutic Work. *Psychotherapy*, 24:171–77.

Hellman, I. D., Morrison, T. L., and Abramowitz, S. I. (1987). Therapist Flexibility/Rigidity and Work Stress. *Professional Psychology: Research and Practice*, 18:21–27.

Hendricks, G. (1977). What Do I Do after They Tell Me How They Feel? *Personal and Guidance Journal*, 55:249–52.

Henry, W. E., Sims, J. H., and Spray, S. L. (1973). *Public and Private lives of Psychotherapists*. San Francisco: Jossey-Bass.

Hopkins, P.E. (1986). On Being a Compassionate Oppressor. *Pastoral Psychology*, 34:204–13.

Hornblow, A. R., Kidson, M., and Ironside, W. (1988). Empathic Process: Perception by Medical Students of Patients' Anxiety and Depression. *Medical Education*, 22:15–18.

Irwin, E. C. (1986). On Being and Becoming a Therapist. *Arts in Psychotherapy*, 13:191–95.

Ivey, A. E. (1988). *Intentional Interviewing and Counseling: Facilitating Client Development*. Second edition. Pacific Grove, CA: Brooks/Cole.

Ivey: A. E., Ivey, M. B., and Smiek-Downing, L. (1987). *Counseling and Psychotherapy: Integrating Skills, Theory and Practice*. Second edition. Englewood Cliffs, NJ: Prentice-Hall.

Kafner, F. H. and Goldstein, A. P., Eds. (1975). *Helping People Change*. Elmsford, NY: Pergamon Press.

Knight, J. (1986). Transference and Countertransference in Social Work. *Journal of Social Work Practice*, 2:4–14.

Larson, D. G. (1987). Helper Secrets: Internal Stressors in Nursing. *Journal of Psychosocial Nursing and Mental Health Services*, 25:20–26.

Latting, J. E. and Zundel, C. (1986). Worldview Differences between Clients and Counselors. *Social Casework*, 67:533–41.

Levy, S. B. (1982). Toward a Consideration of Intimacy in the Female/Female Therapy Relationship. *Women and Therapy*, 1:35–44.

Lichtenberg, J. W. (1984). On Potential. *Journal of Counseling and Development*, 63:101–102.

Lutwak, N. and Fine, E. (1983). Countertherapeutic Styles When Counseling the Learning-Disabled College Student. *Journal of College Student Personnel*, 24:320–24.

Marks, J. J. (1985). Professional Narcissism in Psychotherapy. *Current Issues in Psychoanalytic Practice*, 2:95–109.

Miller, M. A., Smith T. S., Wilkinson, L., and Tobacy, K. J. (1987). Narcissism and Social Interest among Counselors-in-Training. *Psychological Reports*, 60:765–66.

Morris, M. (1986). Communicating with Adolescents. *Adoption and Fostering*, 10:54–55.

Murphey, T. J. (1984). Encouraging Client Responsibility. *Individual Psychology: Journal of Adlerian Theory, Research, and Practice*, 40:122–32.

Nievard, A. C. (1987). Communication Climate and Patient Care: Causes and

Effects of Nurses' Attitudes to Patients. *Social Science and Medicine,* 24:777–84.

Norcross, J. C. and Wogan, M. (1987). Values in Psychotherapy: A Survey of Practitioners' Beliefs. *Professional Psychology: Research and Practice,* 18:5–7.

Patterson, S. L., et al. (1988). Effectivenss of Rural Natural Helpers. *Social Casework,* 69:272–79.

Peca-Baker, T. A. and Friedlander, M. L. (1987). Effects of Role Expectations on Clients' Perceptions of Disclosing and Nondisclosing Counselors. *Journal of Counseling and Development,* 66:78–81.

Ponzo, A. (1985). The Counselor and Physical Attractiveness. *Journal of Counseling and Development,* 63:482–85.

Ratliff, N. (1988). Stress and Burnout in the Helping Professions. *Social Casework,* 69:147–54.

Reyes-Netto, B. (1985). Hidden Agenda in Cross-Cultural Pastoral Counseling. *Journal of Pastoral Care,* 39:342–48.

Rogers, C. (1961). *On Becoming a Person.* Boston: Houghton Mifflin.

Rolfe, D. J. (1985). The Destructive Potential of Psychological Counseling for Pastor and Parish. *Pastoral Psychology,* 34:61–68.

Schoenfeld, W. (1964). *Psychotherapy: The Purchase of Friendship.* New York: Prentice-Hall.

Schroeder, D. A., et al. (1988). Empathic Concern and Helping Behavior: Egoism or Altrusim? *Journal of Experimental Social Psychology,* 24:333–53.

Smith, R. C. (1986). Unrecognized Responses and Feelings of Residents and Fellows During Interviews of Patients. *Journal of Medical Education,* 61:982–84.

Strupp, H. (1973). *Psychotherapy and Behavior Change.* Chicago: Aldine Publishing Co.

Talbott, J. A., Hales, R. E., and Yudofsky, S. C. (1988). *Textbook of Psychiatry.* Washington, DC: American Psychiatric Press.

Toro, P. A. (1986). A Comparison of Natural and Professional Help. *American Journal of Community Psychology,* 14:147–59.

Tracey, T. J., et al. (1988). Changes in Counselor Response as a Function of Experience. *Journal of Counseling Psychology,* 35:119–26.

Tracey, T. J. and Dundon, M. (1988). Role Anticipations and Preferences over the Course of Counseling. *Journal of Counseling Psychology,* 35:3–14.

Wachowiak, D. and Diaz, S. (1987). Influence of Client Characteristics on Initial Counselor Perceptions. *Journal of Counseling Psychology,* 34:90–92.

Watkins, C. E. (1983). Transference Phenomena in the Counseling Situation. *Personnel and Guidance Journal,* 62:206–10.

Williams, R. L. and Lond, J. D. (1983). *Toward a Self-Managed Life Style.* Third edition. Boston: Houghton Mifflin.

Wright, P. G. (1984). The Counseling Activities and Referral Practices of Canadian Clergy in British Columbia. *Journal of Psychology and Theology,* 12:294–304.

Zautra, A. J., Eblen, C., and Reynolds, K. D. (1986). Job Stress and Task Interest: Two Factors in Work Life Quality. *American Journal of Community Psychology,* 14:377–93.

PART
2

9

How Do We Interview?

As we apply our theoretical convictions about relationships and the art of counseling, we confront the practical considerations that surround its normal setting, the helping interview. Many questions that may seem incidental to the process of interviewing open up areas in which we can see outselves and our work more clearly. Sometimes the stress that helpers experience is related directly to—possibly even compounded by—attitudes and behavior that seem peripheral to the main substance of the counseling interview.

A great deal of communication, in other words, takes place on the edges of the interview; some of the attitudes or personal styles that are expressed at the beginnings and ends of interviews, for example, may powerfully affect what goes on in the heart of the counseling session. Unless counselors learn to read the messages they send and receive in connection with these issues—which may appear to be of only secondary importance—they may fail to comprehend what is going on with the other person, and will also increase their own subjective experience of stress.

Appointments

Although one would not expect any great difficulty connected with something as uncomplicated as making an appointment, important questions do arise about the way appointments are arranged and kept. Most professional counselors or therapists, for example, try to make as clear as possible to clients the conditions under which they will be seen. It only takes a few minutes to do this and it usually involves nothing more than stating the time, place, and duration of the appointment. It may also involve other simple matters, such as explaining how to get to the office or some other routine procedure, to eliminate unnecessary mystery and confusion. These are straight-forward matters.

The time of making an appointment is also a good occasion for a brief structuring of the helping relationship. This does not take much time either; if it is not done, however, it may consume a great deal of time when we need to straighten it out later on in the counseling. For example, counselors—whether they are members of the clergy or more clearly identified as psychotherapists—may well take this moment to state their understanding of why the appointment is being made.

"I'll see you in my office, then, at 7:00 o'clock. We'll be meeting for an hour to discuss this problem you've been having at home." In a few sentences both the time, duration, and nature of the discussion are helpfully recapitulated. The time of setting this appointment is, in other words, an occasion for clarifying some of the contractual issues connected with the counseling relationship. In the interest of clearing up ambiguity, the counselor may even wish to add something about what the counseling experience itself will be like. This makes clear to the client the counselor's perception of the service that is being offered and permits the client to question it so that he will not misinterpret or expect something else.

The helper can, for example, say something like this: "When people come to see me about questions like this I usually just try to listen while they explore their feelings. They usually find that helpful. I don't give a lot of advice or tell them what to do. I try to help them deal more constructively with their problems." There are many possible variations of this, each one appropriate to the counselor's style or purpose. Such statements reveal something of the counselor's approach and describe briefly the clients' accountability for examining and taking responsibility for their own personal problems. Such a brief structuring statement is an honest commitment on the part of the helper and not an effort to manipulate or control the client. Obviously, it would not be helpful to offer some structuring unless it reflected the true nature of the experience the client is about to undergo.

It is sometimes surprising to find that people who do extensive counseling operate on an approximate or somewhat vague basis. Instead of making a precise appointment they feel that it is adequate to say that the person should "drop around after supper on Tuesday." This may seem to preserve a kind of informality, but it also leaves the boundaries of the interview shadowy. This may lead to expectations on the part of the client that will not be realized and that will therefore only complicate the relationship itself. If counselors feel hesitant to make a definite statement about the counseling session and its length, they might well examine themselves to uncover the source of their hesitancy. A number of rationalizations may be employed to support this strategy: "Making appointments is too official sounding," for example. Such approximations may, however, reflect a general uncertainty on the part of the counselor concerning his objectives and his capacity to describe and achieve them.

A prime source of stress for many counselors who find reasons for not making definite appointments springs from the way in which their counseling sessions can drag out. Such helpers say that they would rather spend the time and get something settled in one evening than see the person for several weeks. Prolonged sessions of counseling do not necessarily mean more effective counseling, however, and may only exhaust both the client and the counselor.

Some helpers need to exhaust themselves in pursuit of what they think is helpful to the other; but such stances can be very self-serving and, in the ordinary course of events, a reasonable amount of structure does not interfere with more effective counseling but actually contributes to it. Counselors who feel that they cannot set an end point for their helping may reveal something about their own psychological needs, such as their inability to say no, or some similar inner dynamic. Such counselors frequently experience severe stress and often complain about the long hours for which, in fact, they themselves are responsible.

The Physical Arrangements

Most professionals take great care in seeing that their offices provide the environment that will minimize unnecessary stress both for the client and for themselves. The surroundings and general arrangements for counseling immediately say something about a helper's sensitivity to these issues. The counselor who is not aware of how much surroundings communicate attitudes toward clients—at least on an unconscious level—should examine some of these issues.

For example: Is the office soundproof so that one neither hears noises from the outside nor is concerned about other persons hearing the conversation going on inside? Is some precaution taken against unnecessary interruptions, such as the interruption of phone calls, or someone coming to the door with a message, or other people unexpectedly showing up for help? These can be very disruptive of counseling; they also reveal carelessness on the part of helpers about the nature of their work and the seriousness of their commitment to the client. Helpers who are willing to be interrupted convey very clearly to the client that during the time they are together there may be many other things more important than the person of the client. This unrestricted potential for interruptions may also reflect a distracted and ill-organized person whose counseling clearly reflects this. A counselor who cannot anticipate and make arrangements to minimize or eliminate altogether these interruptions introduces jarring and stressful conditions that only frustrate and complicate the helping work.

The place of counseling need not be luxurious but it should be reasonably comfortable and devoid of any harsh or distracting stimuli. The counseling room, in other words, is not the place where you display the model airplanes you make as a hobby or where you exhibit photographs of your family, travels, or the famous people you know. It is not a place for unnecessary "conversation pieces" placed strategically to give client and counselor something to talk about when they cannot seem to get going.

Most counselors know that the seating arrangement in their offices can also sharply define the relationship right from the start. They recognize, for example, that helpers who feel that they must sit behind an imposing desk may have needs to protect themselves from other persons or to impress them in some way or other. The excessively causal counselor—the barefoot guru or the one who looks like he just left an interesting football game on television—also communicates something, and it is not always mere informality. Underscoring the unconventional may reveal the counselor's reluctance to be disciplined or his need to display his own sense of inner freedom. These are not necessarily helpful to the client, and they may well reflect unresolved stresses in the life of the counselor.

The way that the chairs are arranged can also be instructive. Counselors may, for example, choose the chair that puts them always in an elevated position; there is nothing very subtle about such a choice. The amazing thing is that counselors may at times do this without realizing how much they are revealing about themselves. Obviously the chairs used should be reasonably comfortable and not positioned so as to give the helper any psychological advantage over the client. The important thing here is for counselors to examine such features of their work; they may learn a lot about themselves in the process.

In connection with this, helpers may be able to learn a good deal about the client from observing the way in which the latter chooses a place to sit and the manner in which he or she does it. This is not to "get" something on the client but to learn from all aspects of the interview behavior in order to understand as completely as possible the person who needs help. The client who sits as far away as possible may, in fact, be distancing the self from the counselor just as he or she does from everyone else in life. Clients who cannot decide where to sit and who allow the counselor to make the choice may reflect a habit of dependence and indecision that is also found in their relationships with other persons. One cannot jump unnecessarily to a hard and fast conclusion on the basis of such behavior; this should be judged in relationship to other verbal clues or symbolic gestures through which the client portrays himself and his concerns. The important point is that there is something to learn from every dimension of counseling.

If there are to be any charges connected with the counseling, it is crucial to deal with this matter early in the relationship. Sometimes it is the first concern expressed by the person, who may need the opportunity to explore why he or she is so uneasy about it. At times this has no direct bearing on their capacity to pay, but it does tell something about their general style or the level of their character development. It is not an issue to be left in a vague or ambiguous state, not something to be put off until later on. It does not take long to clear this up or to arrange for payment of whatever cost is involved.

While there are many counseling situations—such as those with the clergy—where this is not a direct issue, it may be important nonetheless. For example, a person may tell a member of the clergy, "I was going to see a psychiatrist about this but I thought it would be better to see you because it wouldn't cost any money. . . ." There are many implications in such a statement, and the counselor should be ready to respond to them even if no actual financial charges are going to be involved. Such a statement may reflect the way the counselee perceives the value, the professional competence, or the manipulable qualities of the counselor.

Great Expectations

Expectations of one sort or another are shared by both the counselor and the client. These are factors that operate even before the first interview to shape it, factors that can sharply affect the way the counselor and client perceive each other and the goals that they try to achieve together.

Clients, for example, may come to a counselor with the uneasiness that arises from misunderstanding the nature of counseling itself. They may expect that they will be diagnosed by a person of superior intellect and professional competence who will know more about themselves than they possibly could. This is a part of the cultural mystique connected with various types of counseling assistance.

For example, a person whose opening statement is: "I guess you're the kind of doctor who can tell if I'm crazy or not," may be making a joke in order to handle uneasiness; it does, however, say something about the client's expectations. This is obviously an issue that the individual brings into counseling, and it should be dealt with as soon as possible. Counselors should not get involved in long explanations of their work; rather, they should respond to the client's uneasiness and try to make it possible for him to work it through on his own. Straightforwardness also dispels the unfortunate overlay of mystique that makes counseling seem magical.

In the same way, persons who go to religious figures for counseling may have expectations that are based on a confusion of psychological counseling and religious ministration. This is a difficult area, one to which a counselor who is also a religious figure must be particularly sensitive. Otherwise he or she may find that clients expect absolution or a guarantee of salvation rather than an opportunity to explore themselves and their own behavior. The counselor who allows himself to be perceived in a confused way in this regard not only hampers the work of counseling but also adds to his or her own experience of stress.

Counselors must also be aware of the possibility that they may be perceived as authority figures. The expectations that the client, quite silently and often unconsciously, brings to the relationship provide the counselor with a good firsthand experience of the challenge of transference. Clients, in other words, react toward the counselor as they have toward previous authority figures in their lives. It is clearly important to sort out these expectations and not to confuse the experience of transference with any direct feelings of the client toward the counselor.

Such challenges are commonplace in the work of counseling. The sooner counselors learn to understand and appropriately incorporate them into their awareness, the more fully and easily they possess themselves and the more effectively they carry out their work. While opening themselves to the range of expectations that may be brought by the client, counselors need to check off their own expectations and the role they may play in giving form to the counseling activity.

It is possible for counselors, even against their best intentions or firm acts of their will, to look on people who darken their doors as problems they must solve so that they can get back to other work. To perceive a client as an interruption in one's otherwise busy schedule is an attitude that can drastically affect the course of counseling. Counselors who find themselves looking at a person as "just another case" have abundant material for exploring their own attitudes. Such counselors may be overtaxed by a larger number of clients or patients than they can effectively handle; to admit this can be difficult but therapeutic.

Some counselors, laboring under the urge to save everybody, diminish their capacity to assist anybody when they are worn down or worn out by excessive burdens. They may investigate the expectations they make on themselves in the work of counseling. Until these expectations are understood, the helpers will be affected by them without understanding why. A failure to admit one's own expectations is a prime source of stress for those engaged in psychological helping activities. A prudent modification of schedule—even though it seems to admit some partial defeat—is a far more sensible thing than to carry on counseling that has become a genuine burden.

Helpers need to examine their own expectations if, for example, they are surprised or thrown off balance by the counselee. If they find that the client is not at all what they expected, counselors should wonder why. This may lead them to a healthy survey of the role of their own expectations and the manner in which these affect their attitudes and anticipations in the counseling process. By such reflection, helpers can free themselves from much of the unnecessary stress that builds up when the peripheral factors connected with interviewing are not attended to.

10

More Aspects of Interviewing

In reflecting on interview style, the counselor must avoid applying even the most practical reflections in a cookbook fashion. This causes the helper to fall into the trap of trying "to do well" in an exaggerated fashion. Too much emphasis even on the most sensible suggestions can rob the counselor of his best strength, his own free and available personality.

The themes in these chapters that are connected with interviewing are not prescriptions to help the obsessive counselor become perfect in a stiff and therefore destructive manner. They are meant to be thought about in the perspective of the overall helping relationship, especially insofar as they help the counselor understand and deal positively with the many levels of communication that are always present in an interview. The helper who wants to be more at ease with himself in the work of counseling gradually absorbs fresh insights about interviewing and makes them a part of his approach. Insights that are applied in too studied a fashion increase rather than decrease the possible awkwardness of interviewing work.

The Telephone

The telephone has become an important factor—and sometimes a source of considerable stress—in the lives of many counselors. It is their first point of contact with a large number of the persons who want help. Because many potential clients are initially a voice and only later a full presence, the exchange by telephone is a highly specialized but increasingly common beginning for many counseling relationships.

Counselors who understand the positive possibilities of helping others over the phone immediately decrease their own sense of stress. They can perceive the phone as presenting an opportunity rather than just a hazard or a burden; they may, in fact, employ it in a sensitive and therapeutic way that builds a solid foundation for a continuing relationship with the caller.

The realization that the helping relationship begins with the initial phone call makes it an interview of special possibilities. Even though the call may come at a difficult time or find us unprepared, it can still be developed as a brief but substantial encounter. The helper need not extend the conversation unduly in order to make it into a real meeting with another person. Counselors can begin to build a relationship with unseen callers by taking them seriously rather than by putting them off, and by structuring important elements of their possible future relationship in the time that is available.

When we receive a call from someone who wants help from us we should, in ordinary circumstances, use the call as a bridge to a face-to-face meeting. Although this is sometimes impossible in the lives of certain people who do a great deal of counseling—members of the clergy, for example—it is still the preferred goal. Anyone who gets many calls for help is vulnerable to the "let's settle this on the phone" attitude. This approach demonstrates one extreme of the emotional spectrum associated with telephone calls. The other approach is demonstrated in the person who sits waiting for calls to come, like the emotionally needy professor who once told me that he would not go out at night for fear of missing a call from a student with a problem.

But effective uses of the phone are actually much simpler and more constructive; they center on gathering essential information about the caller and the reason he or she seeks our help. Our imagination can run wild when we only hear someone else's voice; instead of talking to a phantasm of our own, it may be helpful to get some facts about the age, marital status, and occupation of the caller. Secondly, we should hesitate to get into a long and involved discussion of a specific problem with someone we have never met. Counselors may gently provide a framework for a personal meeting by displaying interest while indicating that a detailed discussion should wait for an appointment. As helpers we should also explain to the caller something of the way in which we operate. It is helpful to make ourselves less mysterious and to simply explain something of our approach or what the face-to-face meeting will be like. It is often helpful to describe a meeting in terms of a mutual decision to be made as to whether the counselor and the prospective client can work effectively together. Grandiose promises obviously can get us in very deep water before we really have our bearings or a good sense of direction about the relationship.

The telephone is frequently the instrument of emergency calls, and counselors must learn to react sensibly and without panic to these. It is still helpful to get a name, an address, and a phone number in case the emergency is of such a nature that someone else must be notified. The helper may, for example, need to notify some emergency squad if the caller announces that he or she has just taken "a lot of pills." This may be a relatively rare occurrence but it is one for which we should be prepared with practical courses of action. It is also clear that many calls are not quite the emergencies the caller may make them seem; a measured response through which we do not immediately alter our own schedule in a major way is better than trying to extinguish all the emotional blazes that are actually false alarms. Counselors must restrain their potential for melodrama in order to lessen their own stress and be of real service to others. This can be done, even within the limitations of a phone call, quite simply and effectively.

What Do I Call A Client?

How to address a client seems a simple enough problem, one that a professional should be able to solve on the basis of the right instincts about a situation. The titles employed, however, do display something about our relationships with other persons and therefore deserve to be examined closely. Some counselors do not make much of the question of titles, allowing themselves to be called by their proper designation, and referring to the other in a formal way. It is far more usual to call adolescents and children by their first names than it is to address other clients whom we have not previously met in this informal way. As a relationship develops, it may seem appropriate to call the client by his or her first name; the best judgment on this can only flow from the counselor's mature sense of what is fitting as the relationship grows.

The helper, on the other hand, may want to display a certain informality or easiness of relationship by addressing clients by their first name right from the start. Here again, counselors may profitably serve their own motives in doing such a thing. If it is an easy and spontaneous approach, something that reflects the helper's own personality, it is probably the right thing to do. If, on the other hand, such informality is forced, it may be perceived incorrectly and misinterpreted by the other person. This is particularly true of certain patients who consciously or unconsciously attempt to manipulate the counselor in the first place.

The corollary of this concerns the manner in which the client refers to the helper. If there is a premature effort to reduce professionalism in the name of friendliness, the counselor may wish to explore what the client is attempting to do through this mode of address. The helper need not make a big deal of it and may, in fact, merely restructure the situation by saying something like, "Most people call me Dr. Smith or Mrs. Jones or Father Brown. . . ." The point is that there is some significance to the way the client and the counselor address each other even at the early stages of their interviews. It is not to be ignored nor is it to be seized upon with excessive zeal. It is a signal to be noted and gradually understood correctly in the context of a developing relationship.

Hostile Clients

Counselors should prepare in advance for the possibility that persons coming for help will test out their reactions right from the start. The first initiatives can be very revealing in this regard and the helper should not dismiss these statements or symbolic actions as though they were of no account. For example, a hostile client may act aggressively from the moment the interview begins. The way the counselor handles what constitutes an attack may have a marked influence on the effectiveness of the subsequent counseling.

Clients who enter the room and seat themselves in the chair that is obviously meant for the counselor give a clear message that cannot be ignored. What would the helper do in such a situation? This definite challenge may be issuing from levels of consciousness of which the client is not aware. It is conceivable that the counselor could become defensive, as people do when they have been attacked symbolically. When the client tries to pick a fight—and there are many ways of doing this besides sitting in the counselor's chair—the helper must try to see this in a larger frame of reference. This meaningful gesture telegraphs the client's style of dealing with others. The counselor should deepen his or her sensitivity to the potential meaning of the assault and maintain self-composure to avoid overreaction.

The counselor is always, first and foremost, one who learns from all his or her experiences in the interview. To take the bait by becoming angry in such a situation would be equivalent to allowing oneself to be manipulated quite effectively by the client. Few things increase counselors' stress more rapidly than allowing themselves to be drawn into a power contest with the client at the beginning of their relationship.

A variant of the aggressive testing of the helper may be found in the client who inquires, in a tone that indicates some skepticism, about whether the counselor has the training or the experience really to be of help. This direct challenge can unbalance helpers if they are not prepared to deal with it, especially if it taps into some sense of their own insecurity they have not previously resolved. "Where did you go to school?" or "What special training have you got to help me with this problem?" can irritate counselors and increase stress for them. "How long have you been doing this kind of work?" or "You haven't had much experience, have you?" are very similar inquiries. These questions can upset even experienced counselors; helpers must be at peace with whatever training or experience they have.

Counselors may find that they are suddenly caught in a lengthy explanation of their training or why they feel that they are competent to work with the person. This is almost always a mistake because it represents an acceptance of a defensive and explanatory role. The important issue is to understand the significance of these questions and to respond to what motivates the inquiries rather than to their factual content. The meaning of these questions must be read at a level beneath their outward appearance. Either they should be accepted and not responded to directly or the counselor should attempt to key his answer to the feelings behind the question. This can be done simply and even gently with a statement that reflects a capacity to accept and understand the attack without responding in kind. A counselor may, for example, say "You really want to get some information about me, don't you?" or "It seems important for you to examine my credentials."

The first moments of an interview, even when they are not marked by a subtle attack from a hostile client, still constitute a time of reciprocal stress. It is hard for persons to come and talk about their problems; it is also difficult for busy counselors constantly to readjust their emotional reactions in order to be open, accepting, and understanding toward the long line of people who come for help. It is not unusual to detect some awkwardness in a situation that is not only novel for a client but also stressful for the counselor.

Instead of small talk, as has been noted before, it is always sensible to start with something that is real, with feelings that flow out of the context in which the counselor and the client have met each other, even if they do not know each other very well. The counselor must read the beginning of each interview with understanding and as much naturalness as possible.

If, for example, the client has been referred by another teacher in the school, the counselor may begin with some sentence that sets the stage for the interview very easily. "Your teacher tells me you have had some problems lately," is a sentence that is rooted in the reality of how the client got to the counselor's office. It is not imaginary, nor is it based on some effort to please or persuade the client to talk. It recognizes his or her situation and recapitulates very briefly the manner in which the individual has been referred.

At times counselors have very little information about the client. They may have only the name of a stranger who finds it difficult to open up. Such a person may often ask, "How do I begin?" This can have many meanings and the counselor finds the correct one in the tones in which it is spoken rather than in its literal content. It can be a statement of dependence or a declaration of genuine bewilderment about what to do in this new and unusual situation.

The counselor should respond to the emotional coloring of the statement, realizing that not all clients are trying to test the counselor's skills, and directly acknowledging the difficulty the client expresses. It is simple enough, for example, to accept the uneasiness of the client with some statement like, "Sometimes it is hard to talk about yourself, isn't it?" This puts both the client and the counselor more at ease, especially if the beginning problem is not related to some deeper obstacle. Counselors can learn to tell the difference, especially if they develop a sensitivity to the feelings expressed in the statements as well as in the face and gestures of the other person. Later on, more will be said about the difficulties of client resistance. For the present, we are merely concerned with the common problem of how hard it is for people to talk about their own emotions.

In connection with this, counselors may be tempted by two extremes. The first convinces them that they must never say anything, that they must never break the silence or communicate a sympathetic or understanding response until the client takes the responsibility for the first remark. This "stone-face syndrome" is too rigid a posture for effective counseling, one that does not shape itself to the practical, real-life situation and that often does more mischief than good. No counselor should hesitate, if the emotional climate seems appropriate, to ask something as simple as this: "Can you tell me something about why you came?"

At the other extreme, a helper may be overanxious to be of assistance to the faltering client and may supply a bewildering number of possible leads or topics they may discuss. This ends up confusing both the client and the counselor. Both of these extremes increase the stress of beginning a counseling relationship—and it is a stress the counselor himself may be able to lessen.

As counselors develop experience, they trust their own reactions more, sensing that they can communicate interest and understanding in a human manner without needing to prove anything or to win any contest with the client at the beginning of counseling. Self-confident counselors avoid stereotypes or theoretical imperatives and let their own spontaneous reactions lead the way.

Endings

Since the counselor has arranged to see the client for a certain time, there need be no unnecessary concern about reminding the latter of this arrangement. This should be adhered to carefully and the counselor should avoid unnecessarily shortening or lengthening the initial interview. The beginning interview sets the pace for those that follow, and very few clients express much difficulty if the subject of the length of the appointments is handled in a straightforward manner.

Counselors may profitably remind the client near the end of the interview that a certain number of minutes remain in their meeting together. This can be done very gently and to good effect: "We have about five minutes left." This enables a person to bring things together and avoids the abruptness of suddenly stopping a client in the middle of an important statement. It is not unusual for persons to produce important material near the end of the interview precisely because they know that the end is in sight; some of the most significant self-explorations may be reserved for these closing moments. This possibility should not necessarily cause counselors to prolong the interview, but they should be prepared to deal in summary fashion with important closing statements and indicate that they can be talked about more at the next meeting.

The counselor, in other words, should try to bring together any loose ends; this can be done briefly, effectively, and with due respect for the feelings of the person seeking help. To bring an interview to an end is merely to place a relationship in the context of a broader reality. This is a healthy thing for both the client and the counselor. If it becomes a source of stress or struggle, then here again the helper has an occasion for studying his or her own reactions. This may indicate an emotional involvement with the client to which the counselor should attend in order to keep the relationship in balance. It may also suggest conflicts that have not yet surfaced. These possibilities point to the helpfulness of reviewing each counseling interview at its conclusion and of making some notes about its significant dynamic movement.

It may also be appropriate to write down questions about one's reactions. Self-reflection can frequently clear up most of these difficulties, but it may at times be necessary to talk these things over with a colleague or with someone who can serve as a psychological supervisor. As counselors learn to take advantage of the difficulties they encounter in their work, they free themselves from these problems and work more effectively with others.

In conclusion, the counselor should make clear arrangements for the next meeting and not leave it up to some chance arrangement by saying, "Call me about this," or "I'll be in touch with you about this." Few experienced counselors ever use these strategies, but in the life of a busy educator or other professional for whom counseling is not the whole of the day's activities, these somewhat vague arrangements are not uncommon. They can be a prime source of stress because they indicate that something is always left up in the air. The counselor who links one concluded interview with the time and place for the next one indicates a good sense of managing and minimizing his own experience of stress.

11

The Resistant Client

Stress multiplies, especially for persons who must blend counseling with other professional work, when people who ask for help do not seem to want it. These counselees either quickly drop out of the counseling process or never let themselves get deeply involved in it. Such behavior can be confusing and frustrating because it strikes at the heart of counseling and at the counselor's heart at the same time. There is a double importance in understanding the issues connected with this phenomenon because it has implications for the meaning and extent of the help that may be given; it also affects the counselor's own self-confidence and self-esteem. When people reject the counseling they came for, some counselors automatically assume total responsibility for this state of affairs. This is often an unnecessary and destructive burden of guilt for them to bear.

It is important for all persons who engage in counseling, on either a full-time or a part-time basis, to understand the nature and source of these derailments of the helping process. We will begin by distinguishing between two very different situations with which every counselor sooner or later must deal. These are *resistance* and *reluctance,* separate realities that have the common result of blocking the progress of therapy. These phenomena—and strategies to handle them—will then be discussed in turn.

Resistance describes an attitude on the part of the counselee that seems to fight the treatment. It is the motive for the famous line ascribed to fictional doctors, "You're fighting me." People resist treatment in order to stay the same; that is, to maintain their repressive defenses so that they need not look at the truth about themselves and so that they can keep anxiety at bay.

Reluctance is another situation altogether. This describes the reaction of clients who are present in the office of the counselor, lawyer, doctor, or member of the clergy, and who do not want to be there in the first place. Their presence is the idea of somebody else; they are neither motivated nor interested in getting help for themselves. This is almost as common as resistance but distinct from it. It will be discussed in the next chapter.

The Faces Of Resistance

Resistance, as psychiatrist Fritz Redl once described it, occurs because "that part of the personality that has an interest in the survival of pathology actively protests each time therapy comes close to inducing a successful change." This is usually carried out without any conscious planning on the part of the client and is expressed in symbolic ways that the alert counselor should be able to recognize. Resistant clients are not necessarily directly resisting the counselor; they are not even necessarily consciously resisting the idea of getting well. Resistant individuals do not want any changes to occur; they do not want any rearrangement of the dynamics within themselves. They attempt to preserve and hold on to ways of acting that, even if obviously full of shortcomings, nevertheless manage to satisfy them and help them to adjust to life even if in a psychologically crippling way. The symptoms exhibited by these people do not constitute an ideal solution to their problems but they at least enable them to hold themselves together and ward off anxiety. Resistance occurs, in other words, when people are willing to settle for an adjustment that is defective but functional.

Freud discussed several types of resistance besides this main one in which the central feature is the effort to maintain repressive defenses. He mentioned, for example, the *transference resistance*, through which the client or patient identifies with the physician instead of resolving his or her inner conflicts. Such a patient may be looking for the counselor's affection or, in certain situations, may even be trying to compete in some subtle way with the therapist. There is also the resistance that comes when people are unwilling to give up what psychiatry describes as the *secondary gains* of being sick. These include attention, freedom from ordinary occupations, and other benefits that sometimes accompany affliction. There are also those who resist positive treatment because, at an unconscious level, *they wish to continue to punish themselves.* They do this by refusing to give up their painful symptoms.

Resistance ordinarily manifests itself in the communication style of the counselee. One of the most common ways in which this occurs is through silence. A person who comes for help and who does not or will not talk can raise the stress level of a counseling interview considerably. Many experienced counselors find this almost intolerably uncomfortable, especially if they are unfamiliar with the deeper meanings of resistance.

What does the counselor do in this situation? Does he make the relationship into a tug-of-war by waiting out the person grimly? Or does the counselor try to coax or manipulate the person into speaking, thereby getting himself into an impossible position in the relationship? It is easy enough for a counselor to do either of these things. The most effective response, however, and one that is consistent with the best professional counseling attitudes, is to make an effort to hear the person in the silence itself. Many tones are communicated even when there are no sounds from the voice of the other person. There are, nonetheless, many things to be heard and to be seen that contain important aspects of the counselee's resistant communication. The feelings are there and, as some people say, one can almost touch them or cut them with a knife in certain situations. It is better to try to sense what these may be rather than to go after the other person's jugular vein because they have made us angry.

Listening carefully, the counselor may pick up the tones of hostility in the very presence and nonverbal gestures of the client. The counselor may also hear other things, such as confusion and uncertainty. The response should be to this predominant tone. For example, if the tone is one of confusion, the counselor may ask, "It seems very hard for you to get your bearings in here." If the individual seems hostile, the helper may appropriately say something like this, "You seem to be mad at the very idea of being here." The advantage of such statements is that they are directed at the feelings rather than at the person. They make it possible for the other to take a look at these feelings with the counselor. That can provide the beginning of more positive counseling.

Recognizing and responding to resistance requires sensitivity and skill. Inexperienced counselors, quite like rookie ballplayers flustered into errors by the tough old professionals around them, sometimes make mistakes that only add to their own subjective experience of stress. This happens, for example, when counselors make a direct attack on the resistance, especially if they seem to take it too personally or if they think that the other person is deliberately and consciously trying to circumvent them. To ask something directly like, "What's the matter with you that you can't say anything to me now that you're here?" illustrates the kind of response that may deepen rather than dissolve the silence. It is probably good for counselors not to try to break the silence at all, even though this is what they are sorely tempted to do. The task of attempting to understand and to respond to the other individual is far more important and remains the most significant aspect of the counseling. Counselors should consistently try to do this. They should see the silence itself within the context of the client's overall personality.

Sometimes overeager counselors who want the other person to be able to participate at least minimally in the counseling begin to ask questions that demand only a *yes* or *no* answer. This is another dangerous strategy because it means that the counselor is taking responsibility for the success of the counseling on his or her own shoulders. Whenever we take unto ourselves major responsibility for progress we encourage passivity in the client. If we do the work, the client does not have to. This complicates the problem because it rewards the person for being resistant.

It is also a mistake to trample all over the communication in some effort to improve it. This happens when counselors, for whatever motivation, begin to talk about themselves or to interrupt the silence prematurely. When there is a direct attack on the silence rather than an effort to understand it, this is almost certain to create more silence and, therefore, more discomfort and distress for both participants in the counseling.

Other styles of resistance that a counselor may meet in the course of a day's work include:

The Laughing Client: This person treats everything lightly, staying on the surface of even the counseling relationship in order to stay away from the material that would multiply anxiety if it were ever discussed more clearly. The laughing boy never lights down for very long on any subject and the smiles and jokes are not substantial or rooted in genuine experience.

The Talking Client: This individual talks constantly, the verbal barrage achieving the same purpose as the laughter in the individual just described. Both keep at a safe distance, protecting their emotions from involvement, and escaping any serious commitment to the counseling process. What is the counselor to do when resistance such as this emerges?

The principle to be applied remains the same: Counselors should attempt to understand the persons beneath the laughter or the excessive talking. How can we reach them so that they may be able to lower these defenses just a little bit? In order to do this we must make some genuine commitment of ourselves to them, one that recognizes their difficulty and that does not threaten them by judging them as consciously uncooperative. The counselor may say, for example, "I wonder why you are making it so hard for us to really meet each other, or to talk seriously to each other"—or some other statement that directs the other's attention *to the process* and at the same time does not indict the other too severely *as a person*. It is an effort at a mutual recognition of a difficulty.

The same approach may be used with persons who, in small and sometimes undetectable ways, hesitate, stop, interrupt themselves, or shift the emphasis of their remarks whenever they get close to emotional pay dirt. The counselor's task is not to trap them, pointing out what they are doing and thereby making them more defensive. It is more appropriate for counselors to sense the struggle that is going on and to respond to this by saying something like, "You seem all tied up," or "You don't seem to feel free to talk about yourself very easily."

The Intellectualizer: The defense of intellectualization is a natural for a therapeutic process that is built on verbal communication. It is almost an occupational hazard. Intellectualization refers to the manner in which some persons talk about their problems with apparent clarity and in great detail but without much emotion. They drain away their emotions by abstracting their problems. They do not sound like resisters because they are speaking about serious personal subjects. They are doing it from a distance, however, and the most important clue is the fact that their feelings do not seem to be present.

New counselors have difficulty in recognizing intellectualization and responding to it effectively. It must be dealt with without destroying the other person, who is, after all, not indulging in it as a matter of conscious choice. The counselor can communicate understanding by saying something like, "We seem to talk and talk but not really get anywhere." Good counselors also remember not to encourage intellectualization by indulging in it themselves; it is very easy to use jargon or to retreat into psychological abstractions for reasons of our own. We should not be surprised if the client picks these up and uses them against us.

The Generalizer: This very effective form of resistance is displayed by the individual who avoids tying his or her feelings down to any specific subject or person. As long as these individuals can continue in general terms, they can approach their emotions without making them concrete or associating them too closely with their real lives. This is not the time—it probably never is—to use that familiar line, "You're fighting me." Anything like that is always taken as an attack. It is much better to try to move in with an appreciation for the other's difficulty by saying something like this: "You seem to talk in general about your job—or your wife, or your children. . . ." If the counselor can point to the area in which clients are generalizing, he or she will show an understanding of the difficulty the patients experience and make it possible for them to break through themselves. The counselor who speaks only in generalizations can expect to get this back from other persons. It is also helpful not to get caught in the trap that the resistant client can spring when he finishes a sentence by saying, "You know what I mean." It is much better to say that we do not know what the client means than to give the false impression that we do. We can never get that ground back once we have surrendered it.

The Scene Maker: There is no more clever or effective way to interfere with the progress of counseling than through making an emotional scene. Like a lawyer with more bravado than facts, clients can sometimes weep, pound their fists, or get wrathfully indignant in order to keep away from the kind of material that might make them change. Making a scene is a way of getting attention, but it is also a way of avoiding something else, something that would be more painful by far. The person who gets angry in counseling may, for example, be covering shattered internal feelings that they strongly resist examining. Counselors cannot afford to become angry when their clients do this in order to create a diversionary action. Here the skill of the counselor is tested, for he or she must understand the other at a deeper level than that of the dramatic scene that the client engineers. The response must not be to the anger or indignation but to the inner reason that makes the client choose the noisy demonstration as a defense.

The Happy Talker: Sometimes people who come for counseling sound like news announcers on those impossible TV teams whose members are always smiling and kidding each other. This very subtle form of resistance can be found in statements of claimed happiness that do not ring true but that effectively prevent discussing anything that may have a painful aspect. The counselor must never misread false heartiness for genuine contentment. This takes sensitivity, patience, and a willingness to attempt to explore with the other the reasons that such a reassuring defense should be chosen. People only say that everything is fine when they are afraid that things will get worse if they get down to business about their problems.

The Counselor's Involvement

Many other subtle behaviors exist that involve the relationship—and some aspect of transference—between the client and the counselor.

These may quietly slow down the progress of therapy while the counselors are unaware of how these signs of resistance are connected with them.

The individual who switches appointment times frequently may have a good reason for it. On the other hand, it profits counselors to examine this behavior, which is always explained in terms of external factors. Counselors may be more involved than they think. This includes all behavior related to appointments and coming late. If we try to feel our way into what is going on we ask, without any quick readiness to retaliate in kind, whether such clients are trying to avoid moving ahead or whether they are trying to seize control of the therapeutic situation itself. In both cases the counselor is involved because the client is doing something to him or to her in order to modify the pace of the counseling. This obviously needs careful reflection and exploration or the counselor will easily become the victim of it.

At times the patient unconsciously attempts to compete with the therapist. Counselors who find clients trying to "one-up" them or "put them down" will suspect that subtle behavior is present. The counselor needs to take a hard but sensitive look at this in order to sense the reasons behind it, or the unconscious level of the client's personality.

Seductive behavior on the part of a client can be disturbing, especially to inexperienced counselors, and therefore can easily achieve its desired effect of slowing down counseling progress. Seductive behavior is intended to be disturbing and it can have many meanings. It suggests that the client, quite unconsciously, may be trying to flatter the counselor in order to get his or her attention or care. It may also be another way of seizing power in the situation by changing the relationship and taking the upper in it. In either case, of course, the resistance strategy can be very effective. It is also very stressful, especially for counselors who are unfamiliar with it and who may dangerously misread it. They should recognize it as a form of resistance and not take it too personally. That is to say, they should not conceive of themselves as suddenly sexually attractive, nor imagine that the greatest crisis of their counseling career has suddenly arrived. It is a familiar resistance device.

As with the other strategies this must be seen in terms of the total personality of the other. The person is saying, in a dramatic way, "I do not want to go ahead with the business that I should be attending to in therapy." The person is definitely not saying, "I find you irresistible," or "I want to spend the rest of my life with you." It is deflating in a healthy way for counselors to face the reality of such situations.

Sometimes clients attempt to mitigate the influence of the counselor by talking to other people about their problems. If they talk to others, they need not talk deeply or directly about their difficulties to the counselor. That is one of the reasons that bartenders sometimes get in the way of other person's troubles. It is also the reason that people sometimes go to their parish priest or their internist and talk about difficulties they should be discussing with their psychiatrist. All parties to this kind of resistance should be aware of it as a possibility in their own experience. It is quite easy for some of these patients to enlist the support of an outsider by saying that the psychiatrist or other counselor is unsympathetic and that they need a new kind of help. The proper thing is to refer them back to discuss their problems with their original therapist and not to be manipulated into this diverting game. The original therapist must also recognize what is going on and not become so irritated that he or she cannot respond with the kind of sensitive understanding that such a maneuver deserves.

It is also true that some people are not good candidates for counseling or therapy. This is so because of their personality structure. People who were once called *psychopaths* and are now termed *antisocial personalities,* seem to have great difficulty in establishing any kind of relationship with other persons. Such persons are obviously resistant when, for whatever reason, they meet with a therapist for counseling. Counselors who are unaware of this kind of personality difficulty may feel that they have failed personally when they cannot reach persons who are psychologically inoculated against relationships.

To sum up these reflections, it is clear that the therapist must work with the client in order to explore the nature of resistance. This may be the first step to a deeper, more effective, and longer lasting therapeutic change. If the resistance is misunderstood or mishandled, then counseling may be sidetracked and its purpose completely defeated. It is important, then, to listen to the whole person and not to attack merely because the resistant behavior irritates us. Counselors need to recognize resistance as a form of defense that cannot immediately be torn down or taken away. Such defenses have important purposes in the lives of troubled people; they employ them in order to avoid a deeper and more truthful look at themselves. Counselors who see whole persons and respect their defenses will manage quite effectively the stress of the inevitable resistant behavior.

12

The Reluctant Client

Who is the reluctant client? It is the unwilling person who finds his way against his own inclinations to the counselor's office, and who rejects the role of helpee that was chosen for him by other persons. Reluctant clients literally do not want to be there, and they generally make this clear in a variety of ways. Two important elements must be remembered in any discussion of this problem:

Reluctance is as common a problem for a counselor as low back pain is for a general physician. Far from being an unusual phenomenon, it may, in certain situations, seem to be the rule rather than the exception. Dr. William Glasser, author of *Reality Therapy* (Harper & Row, 1965), has described the universal experience in telling of his work as a school counselor. "They put you in a small room, about six by eight, and then they throw a kid at you and close the door." The counselor is expected to take things from there and to return the student in improved shape to the school environment.

Reluctance on the part of clients need not be a sign of something wrong. It is not necessarily the same kind of signal as resistance to therapy, which indicates a need to maintain repression. Not wanting to be in the presence of a counselor can be a natural and understandable response to a situation of which the individual is not the author. As two students of the problem, John Vriend and Wayne Dyer have written, "It may be the most reasonable and realistic approach for a client to take. . . ." When clients do not want help, it should not surprise us when they express this clearly and directly in their behavior.

This combination of features makes the reluctant client one of the most formidable sources of stress for counselors of every stripe and theoretical persuasion. Reluctant clients are found in many settings, from schools to jails, but the emotional context of their appearance in the helper's office is frequently the same. Counselors, whether formally in that role or not, are expected by others to "cure," "adjust," or otherwise "solve" a problem person referred from the outside. This weight of expectation from the sources of referral can be very great; it seems almost a test of the counselor's skills and resources. It is as if other people were implicitly saying, "You're supposed to be able to help others; now, here's a chance for you to prove it."

Added to these external expectations are those the counselor may make on his or her own performance. Many counselors feel that they should be able to reach and change most of the persons who come to them. This is because they have high ideals, personalistic value systems, and optimistic outlooks from their training and reading that make them feel that they can constructively transform most of the persons who come to them. These are the assumptions that lead to trouble for counselors just as surely as the unrealistic assumptions of diplomats lead to war. Reluctance resides primarily in the client, but counselors would do well to inspect their hierarchy of expectations about their work. Until they can come to terms with a semimessianic conviction that they can help everyone, they may increase their own stress in a way that is not fair to themselves. Counselors may also have to retranslate the notion of help into a more modest and sensible concept. A little real help is a great deal of help. When counselors can accept that, they lessen their experience of stress and increase their chances of assisting other people in a positive way.

Who Are The Reluctant?

Reluctant clients may be described in terms of the settings in which they are found. For example, counselors whose work involves them in any way with a school find many young people coming to their offices at the suggestion or command of someone else. This may be in connection with situations as different as academic counseling about appropriate courses or transfers, and it may include disciplinary cases whose behavior has caused their teacher or supervisor to "send" them to the counselor.

These referrals frequently solve the problem of those who recommend counseling by relieving them of dealing further with such problems and by substituting presumed therapeutic counseling for some kind of punishment. Counselors in school also see students who puzzle administrative officials because of their poor attendance record, their failure in certain subjects, or because they are suspected of things like drug use. A student who is in danger of dropping out is often referred to the counselor's office along with those who are not living up to their potential in class performance. It has been suggested that a very high percentage of clients in schools are nonvoluntary. They knock on the counselor's door because somebody else thinks this is a good idea. Some counselors spend most of their time with these reluctant referrals.

There are many other settings in which enforced counseling is common. Those in ministry often find persons in their parlors who have been sent there by frustrated parents or relatives who hope that the religious counselor may be able to straighten out the behavior or attitudes of the one sent. The clergy are particularly exposed in this regard because they cannot, like members of other professions, pick and choose the clients with whom they feel they can be effective. Their ideals commit them to see everybody and to try to be of some help to them, which places enormous pressure on them. Many other counselors, because of institutional or societal regulations, find themselves in a similar position.

Counselors who work in community agencies, for example, find that they must see persons referred by the courts, no matter what the motivation or attitude of these referred people may be. Judges, feeling themselves enlightened in the matter, dictate that prisoners, as a part of their sentence, must seek psychological assistance for their personal problems. Sometimes the possibility of parole is contingent upon the prisoner's complying with this regulation. It is obvious that such referrals may run a high risk of being pro forma arrangements. The clients must show up because of external motivation, but they are minimally committed to changing themselves. Certain states and other localities demand that married couples contemplating a separation or divorce must see a marriage counselor for a prescribed number of visits before taking any further steps. Some church jurisdictions require people below the age of twenty-one to accept marriage counseling before the church will approve of their marriage plans.

All these people, who may be very different in background, interests, and personality features, share the reluctant client syndrome in common. They are not asking for counseling; they are required to get it.

Counselors who deal with unwilling clients come to recognize a wide variety of behaviors that tell the same story and offer the same challenges. The non-voluntary counselee may, for example, express himself or herself in silence. This silence can be very loud and can seem to be very long for the counselor who is unprepared for it. Such periods of silence are not without expressive gestures, shrugs of the shoulder, or other examples of body language. Sometimes the client can do something as simple as fiddling with a loose button on a jacket to indicate his or her genuine removal from the counseling situation.

Hostility may be expressed by silence but it can also come out more directly. "This wasn't my idea," the client says, and the room fills with a feeling of forces engaged on a field of battle. The hostility can be raw and unprocessed, but it can also be subtle, as when the client knows how to tease the counselor or how to go through the motions of counseling without getting any help. Some clients who have been referred frequently for help have learned a lot through their experience, and they begin to look on each succeeding counselor the way a matador looks at a bull. They learn to lead the counselor by telling colorful stories that are more fiction than fact. They play the role of a productive and cooperative client on the surface but withhold themselves or turn off completely when they feel like it, much to the exasperation and frustration of the counselor. One is reminded of the famous cartoon, drawn when America was becoming conscious of psychoanalytic concepts, of the young prisoner being led from an interrogation room. He turns to speak to another young prisoner just being led into it. "Tell them your mother beat you," he says with a knowing smile.

Other clients who do not want to be there may indulge in distracting behavior that gets silly at times in a self-conscious way but that, nevertheless, achieves the goal typical of reluctant clients: It delays or interrupts the helping process itself.

Beneath Reluctance

Nonvoluntary counselees may have many motives for not wishing to engage in therapy. They may share these in common with all persons who are not motivated to deal with their problems or to change themselves. The only difference, of course, is that they find themselves in the helping situation. It is not surprising that they balk at this; it may even be a reasonable reaction on their part. It is helpful, however, to explore some of the possible reasons that explain why people do not wish to engage in counseling. These include the following:

Reluctant clients resist the idea of facing things that they do not wish to examine or admit about themselves. These may not be causing them enough subjective anxiety to move them to seek help; in fact, their behavior may be getting them some secondary gains that tend to reinforce it and therefore they are reluctant to deal with it.

Talking to a counselor frequently involves a loss of self-esteem— which may already be a basic part of the individual's problem—

because it seems tantamount to admitting failure. In certain institutional settings, seeing the counselor is what you do when there is something wrong with your head. Going to see the doctor becomes another way of admitting painful failure.

Some individuals are referred for counseling as a logical consequence of their being against the establishment in general. As they act out against it—or against any symbols of authority—they become annoying to the institution and they are referred with the admonition that "You'd better get your thinking straightened out on this." The counselor's office may merely provide an extended stage on which the individual can act out even further; now, however, he uses reluctance as a new weapon against the expectations of the uncongenial establishment.

This is an area in which it is easy to fail. This is especially true for new counselors who bring to their work high expectations on their performance. They are vulnerable, therefore, to the reluctant client who will not cooperate and who may, by his or her behavior, slowly pick apart the substance of the counselor's self-confidence. New counselors frequently try too hard to do good or to do well, and so they overinvest in succeeding rather than in understanding what is going on in the counseling relationship. They sometimes live with the fear of meeting a noncooperative client and, once repulsed by one, they are not eager to try again.

According to Vriend and Dyer, counselors, both old and new, sometimes fail because they project the client's reluctance onto themselves personally and thereby feel rejected. They blame themselves for the counseling failure and, not sorting out the elements of the emotional exchange that are relevant to the situation, they feel trapped or engulfed unnecessarily because they have taken on too much responsibility for the success of the relationship.

The most important learning for the counselor dealing with such clients is the ability to accept the person as reluctant or as uninterested in counseling. The key to any successful therapeutic relationship is related to our capacity to let people be what they are in our presence. If we try to make them into cooperative clients when they are, in fact, just the opposite, then we impose a demand that interferes with the institution and development of helping counseling. We treat feelings of reluctance, in other words, in the same way we would treat any other emotions expressed by those who come for help. There is no need to get into a psychological wrestling match with nonvoluntary clients or to present ourselves as extensions of the environment or other societal forces that brought them to us in the first place. It may be easy to fail, but it is not difficult to succeed if we keep clearly in mind the notion of accepting the *person* of the other. We may need to explore the reasons we find it difficult to accept reluctant clients as they are; whatever the situation, authentic acceptance is the appropriate response.

The pressure involved in dealing with reluctant clients is often associated with the context in which counselors work with them. Counselors who are part of a larger institution, like a school or a prison, may find that their function is presumed to serve institutional ends as much as individual needs. No one thinks this out clearly or writes regulations about it; it is part of the logic that comes alive in almost any institutional setting. All helpers who have institutional affiliations must be aware of this in order to survive and work effectively. Institutions, in other words, process all experience to fit their own contours; they need to accomplish their ends and this becomes, through no one's fault, an impersonal exercise. Institutions, whether they are universities or churches, expect other people to adjust to them, and this includes counselors. This fact creates an immediate stress for the helper whose philosophy of counseling commits him to serving the individual rather than to carrying out institutional purposes in regard to other persons.

This individual versus institution dilemma creates an abiding tension in the life and work of a variety of helpers. It cannot be totally eliminated any more than institutions can be persuaded to transform themselves so that the individual good is always the goal of their functioning. Counselors must view this difficulty seriously and try to get it in perspective in terms of the work in which they are engaged. This may be an occasion to follow the advice of psychiatrist William Glasser, who was quoted previously. He suggests that, just or unjust, right or wrong, there are situations and relationships in which we cannot effectively change other things or other people. The only thing we can do is change something about ourselves; if that is all we can do constructively, then that is what we should do.

It is a much better alternative than getting angry at uncooperative clients or ruling out those who do not seem interested in seeing us. It is certainly better than backing away from the people who challenge us through their hostility and thereby put us on the defensive. Some counselors attempt to deal with reluctant clients by trying to win them over. This only adds to the problem. So too does any attempt to transform negative feelings rather than to explore them with the client. These approaches intensify an already stressful phenomenon.

It is also true that many counselors have simply not had sufficient training to deal easily or skillfully with reluctant clients. They may want to seek additional training or supervision, or at least to read and reflect on this problem in order to be able to avoid some of the pitfalls that are so common in these nonvoluntary relationships.

Courses Of Action

Counselors should begin by examining themselves, as has been suggested in earlier chapters. The counselor must ask, "What is he doing to me?" and, "What am I doing in return or in retaliation?" In other words, counselors need a *feel* for the flow of the relationship so that they may judge whether they are allowing themselves to be trapped or if they are further provoking reluctant behavior because of their responses. Counselors may well focus on the source of reluctance to see if they are rewarding it in some way and therefore strengthening and extending it.

The primary task is to deal with the reluctant feelings of the client instead of merely getting angry or attempting to coax or cajole the client out of having them in the first place. Fundamental to this is the acceptance of the individual as unwilling or uninterested in seeing us. When we can convey an understanding of the way clients perceive the situation in which they find themselves we may relieve a good deal of the distress we experience with them. This also reveals something of the counselor's own wholeness and of his or her capacity to convey understanding while remaining a separate individual. Then, too, it permits clients to experience themselves as persons who are dealing with another concerned person rather than with a blind bureaucracy. It may be the first such experience the client has in which he is recognized as an individual with feelings and rights that are completely his own. This de-fuses the situation, takes the reward out of any behavior that may be designed to bait or to defeat the counselor, and may open up the possibility of the client's exploring his own feelings of reluctance. If the counselor is not defensive, the client may learn that he need not be defensive either. As these unnecessary defenses collapse, the client can take a step closer to the reluctance he feels inside himself.

The emphasis is on dealing with the reluctance as a mutual exploration of a serious business. The counselor takes clients seriously and does not engage in trying to win them over or in other such unproductive behavior. If nothing more is accomplished than that the client and counselor perceive each other in a more personal and less official way, small but substantial progress has been made. This attitude toward the reluctant client must be present in order to carry out effectively any one of the many practical strategies that may be used to assist the client in exploring himself further.

Counselors should explain the process of counseling so that it is not strange or mysterious. Reluctant clients may never have allowed themselves to learn anything about the way counseling ordinarily works. As this is explained to them—especially when they feel they are being taken seriously—they may feel a lessening of their own reluctance to participate.

The counselor may also set up a brief contractual arrangement with reluctant clients offering them a series of appointments at a certain time in order to explore whether they wish to go on or not. Many counselors may find it helpful to explain to the reluctant client some of the various aids to self-knowledge that the counselor is capable of providing. For example, clients may become interested in taking certain psychological tests that may provide helpful information about themselves and may assist them in dealing with the roots of behavior that brought them to the counselor's office in the first place.

Reluctant clients must be recognized for what they are: people who do not want to be in the counselor's office and who need to be accepted and understood as such before any real progress can be made.

13

The Problem of Diagnosis

At times counselors think of diagnosis as an activity appropriate to medicine or to some other specialty such as clinical psychology or psychiatric social work. It is true that members of these professions have special training and tools for developing judgments about the problems experienced by those with whom they work. There are many sides to diagnosis, however, and every helper may profit from regular reflection on the pertinent issues. Most helpers diagnose informally whether they acknowledge it or not; this is particularly true of the many individuals whose counseling work is only part of a larger responsibility in teaching, ministry, or similar professions.

It is fair to ask whether helpers who experience the stress of seeing many new persons with a wide range of problems each week have the time or even the need to diagnose exactly the psychological state of their counselees. This is a controversial area; certain theorists clash strongly with practitioners who are beleaguered by the difficulties of overcrowded days. Some classical texts on counseling insist on thorough diagnosis as the indisputable prerequisite for any successful work with others. Part of the stress that busy helpers experience flows from the fact that they realize they are falling short of the therapeutic ideals they have read or heard about. They justify their light touch with diagnosis through citing the pressures to deliver service to numbers of people who would otherwise go without help. Such counselors do what they can, looking on extensive diagnosis as a luxury rather than a necessity.

The overworked counselor may not have the time for careful evaluation or diagnosis according to the classical model of the textbooks. Occasionally they also lack the skills or the experience to deliver a complete or sophisticated description of the problem. These facts do not, however, excuse anyone from making the judgments that are necessary for the welfare of the persons who seek their assistance.

This is a complicated area for many reasons, among which is the widespread contemporary conviction that judgments of any kind in regard to a client are inappropriate. While counselors wisely hesitate to evaluate the moral quality or desirability of the behavior or motivations of those with whom they work, this does not mean that they can never indulge in intelligent and informed reflection about how counselees can best be helped in view of their difficulties. To make sensitive judgments about the individuals without condemnation of them as persons is a serious obligation for the mature counselor. The helper has much to decide: Questions about his or her capacity to help the other, as well as about the client's capacity to manage himself or herself through life. These judgments eventually resolve themselves—in the shipwreck of overambitious counseling, for example—if the helper fails to take timely responsibility for them.

The combination of democratic ideals, scientific objectivity, and the current fashionable stance that it is society rather than individuals that is sick also militates against even tentative diagnosis. These forces have strongly shaped a generation of attitudes toward the work of counseling, one in which brief, symptom-oriented treatment has come to replace more complicated and time-consuming approaches. We are not trying to settle, much less mediate, these clashing theoretical positions; we are merely pointing out how they affect the atmosphere in which we all live and work. According to some current therapists, for example, it is absurd and insulting to people to attempt to diagnose their problems, because mental illness is a myth and going "mad," as it is called, is a way of staying sane in a schizophrenic world. The work of writers like Thomas Szasz and R. D. Laing is stimulating but does not reduce our responsibility for treating others as effectively as possible.

In addition, many behaviorally oriented schools of therapy do not consider diagnosis vital to helping persons learn to deal more constructively with life problems. The whole idea of diagnosis, some say, is an inheritance from the medical model of treating people and it is not so significant in patterns of counseling that are built on the principles of learning and personal reeducation.

No system, no matter how advantageous, can be applied without any regard for the psychological structure of the persons involved. The same may be said of a wide variety of other psychological techniques, from sensitivity training to bioenergetic feedback. Only the amateur who literally does not appreciate the subtleties of human behavior or the potential for harm applies techniques with more self-confidence than understanding. This is not to criticize any specific approach but to observe the ever-present need for at least some informal diagnostic capability.

These are the current features of a discussion that is not likely to be soon settled. While the learned papers are being read and pondered, however, counselors still face and must respond to many persons each week. What are the practical questions connected with intelligently and responsibly helping these people? If the helper is to avoid getting caught in a web of theoretical uncertainty, he or she must face and deal honestly with the question of diagnosis.

When Diagnosis May Not Help

Diagnosis does not help if it ends up placing distance between the helper and the one seeking help. This can occur when diagnosis becomes a species of intellectual exercise played largely within the confines of the counselor's own personality. It happens in the amateur's approach in which a detective-story excitement of "figuring somebody else out" dominates the intention to help. This is not, of course, genuine diagnosis in any therapeutic sense, but rather is a response to the counselor's own need to keep people from getting too close. The intellectual assaying of another's strengths and weaknesses is a strategy that spuriously builds the confidence of the counselor through promoting the illusion that he or she is in better control of others.

Diagnosis does not help if it becomes a formalized and self-conscious activity that robs the counselor of the very qualities that are most important in assisting others: warmth, true acceptance, and a healthy spontaneity. Categorizing others cannot be done "cookbook style" without doing more harm than good both to client and counselor. When diagnosis interferes with establishing a good relationship with another person, it is obviously not helpful no matter what the textbooks say. This leaves helpers on the outside of the relationship, increases their experiences of stress, and ultimately lessens their self-confidence. They will sense that they are not getting through to others even though, as a counselor, they believe they know what is wrong with them. When diagnosis is awkwardly attempted, it has the classic bad effects that go with anything that is done poorly despite good intentions. We are all made uncomfortable when we realize that someone else is trying to categorize us rather than understand us.

And When It May

Although there are times when attempting a diagnosis seems undesirable, it is clear that no counselor can fly blind; indeed, no conscientious helper wishes to do so. There are theoreticians who claim that even the most elaborate diagnosis does not change the client or the counselor very much, and that, in the long run, the course of the relationship will be determined by the capacity of both to experience it in a reasonably deep way together. There is something almost admirably open in this stance; it would surely be naïve, however, to insist that a sensible diagnosis of the client's condition is of absolutely no value whatsoever. Just as those who insist that no counseling can occur until diagnosis is complete exaggerate their claims in the face of life's practical demands, so those who make a principle of avoiding diagnostic inferences exaggerate in another direction. Responsible helpers need to have some sense of what is going on inside other persons in order to place themselves in an appropriate and helpful relationship.

This is important because of the manner in which certain disturbed or extremely anxious persons may distort or misinterpret our interest in them or our responses to them. One of the more important reasons for a diagnostic sense about the other is our need to calibrate his or her response in accord with this information; this can be done without sacrificing any genuineness and without becoming involved in manipulation. For example, counselors who sense that the individual with whom they are working has a paranoid flavor in his or her reactions may wisely temper their own friendliness because this is so often misperceived by persons with this difficulty. Paranoids may become suspicious and uneasy with persons who appear to be assaulting their own inner castles by what healthy people would describe as openness. The counselor who does not try to balance such factors by applying the lessons that sensible diagnosis provides only invites problems into what is already a highly stressful work. More detailed examples of how we may need to modify our behavior in the presence of certain kinds of emotional problems will be discussed in later chapters.

How Deep Is The Diagnosis?

In popular language, the counselor needs a feeling for the processes or dynamics that govern the behavior of others. This is not solely an intellectual problem; indeed, in a certain sense, acquiring such a feeling is an art in itself. It is dependent on intellectual understandings of psychological processes, but it also requires that we develop our sensitivity to emotional messages even when they come in whispers or half gestures. One need not be a poet to possess this capacity to sense the stirrings inside others; it can be cultivated and strengthened as a reliable source of clinical judgment. Many things go into that hazy phenomenon we term clinical judgment; it is hazy, however, precisely because it is human and consists of a blend of reactions, intellectual information, and the kind of responses that are refined by experience and that cannot be exactly specified.

This sounding board for the inner experience of others receives radarlike echoes that enable us to appreciate the quality and intensity of the process taking place in them. As counselors our challenge is not just to categorize the dynamics of others but to understand them with as much sensitivity as we can. The depth of their emotions must be gauged if we are to make a proper evaluation that will be helpful in our counseling work. It is possible to listen to the emotions of another person and to tune them, as one might a radio, too softly or too loudly. An accurate feeling for the depth of the person's experience is a most useful tool in operational diagnosis. The individual resonates at a certain pitch; hearing that, and neither increasing nor diminishing it, permits us to understand with the kind of accuracy that informs our judgment prudently.

Our best guide in this exploration of the internal life of the other person is the feedback we constantly get as we place outselves in steady relationship to them. In other words, as we react to the person as understood by us, we send out forces that induce a response from the other. In the waves that return to us we get our best sense of how the other not only functions currently but how he structures his private world. As we sit closely with others we are permitted a view of their world that we cannot ignore if we seriously propose to be of help to them. This is fundamentally nonrational communication, which we learn to translate into terms that enable us to understand and interact in the manner that will be appropriate and helpful. This is a practical form of diagnosis that must become second nature to the counselor.

Obviously, we cannot assist others unless we are in contact with their real personalities, that is, with the factors that are governing their behavior. These are not necessarily the same as the reasons they themselves offer to explain their attitudes or actions. Neither are they the same as some notions we may have formed from previous experience or because we once worked with another person with remarkably similar difficulties. Diagnosis need not be understood as an elaborate and distancing method of assigning persons to psychological categories; it is simply getting as. true and clear a picture of them as we can manage. It does not necessarily turn them into objects; sensitive and sensible diagnosis permits us to see them much more clearly as individuals.

This type of diagnosis is important for our own effective work with persons, and it is also significant if we have the responsibility of deciding whether they should be referred to some other helping resource. An accurate diagnosis enables us to balance our feeling for others with our own abilities to help them. A crucial judgment with long-range implications is in order here, and it cannot be made if we do not possess an appreciation for the quality of the psychological difficulty the person is experiencing.

Neither can an intelligent referral be made unless we have some basic sense of the contours of the underlying problem. The correct and well-timed referral is one of the most important decisions a counselor can make. It is a profound recognition of reality as perceived by a helper whose commitment is to the decision that will best serve the counselee and best reflect the counselor's own well-developed diagnostic sensitivity.

We can best help people—and ourselves—by getting them to the right sources of help as soon as we make a judgment about their needs and our own ability to respond to them. Sometimes counselors regard a referral as an indictment of themselves; more often than not it is an example of good judgment exercised at an appropriate moment, a responsible professional decision.

Who Is Diagnosable?

Many helpers never meet anyone whom they would classify as seriously disturbed or in need of a different and more specialized kind of treatment. This is partly because so many problems are subtle and difficult to detect with a high degree of confidence; it is also partly due to the fact that many individuals who have need of counseling simply cannot be put very neatly into any diagnostic category. They experience difficulty in adjustment or in coping with life—they may drink too much or fight with their spouses—but their basic problem seems no greater or no less than that of the average person. These, in a profound sense, are residents of the human condition: the people who from time to time require some understanding assistance to regain their composure and to take charge of their lives once more.

Persons in this category—and perhaps there should be a special classification for the ordinary syndrome of facing life—do not fit into textbook pigeonholes. They do not have hallucinations, nor do they suppose themselves to be great historical figures. They have the garden variety of human problems and they need to be understood accordingly. These are the people who come to talk to old friends, their clergy, former teachers—sometimes even bartenders—in their quest for a better grasp of themselves. The fact that they are not classically diagnosable does not mean that they do not need a sensitive effort at understanding from us.

To realize the way an individual feels when he or she is caught in the web of the human situation is a great and appropriate diagnostic gift to offer. This is built on the same foundations of intellectual understanding and emotional sensitivity as are more elaborate diagnostic formulations. They feel—and we as counselors may deservedly feel as well—more like persons because of our effort to understand thoroughly and well.

Every specialist tends to view a patient through his or her own profession's interpretations. So the dentist may interpret your moods in terms of your teeth, the internist in the vocabulary of your metabolism, and the preacher in terms of your prayer life or lack thereof. There may be no area in which a sense of diagnosis is more appropriate than in winnowing out emotional problems from those that could be termed spiritual. Confusion in this area has existed for a long time and, despite our resolves, it will not easily be cleared up. The need to confront this distinction, however, is very real. It illustrates a seldom cited but important justification for the process of diagnosis.

Spiritual problems do exist; one needs only to consult the daily papers or magazines for documentation of a widespread spiritual malaise that is complicated rather than abated by affluence. Such problems, however, do not exist independent of human personality; they do not grow without roots in the person. One of the difficulties with sexual problems and their discussion in our day comes from the fact that they are often talked about as if they existed in a world of their own independent of human personality. This is commonly referred to as "sex out of context"—sex, as it were, disintegrated from the person who is sexual. Few people would imagine that spiritual problems could suffer from the same difficulty. And yet in a manner that parallels sexual problems, they are regularly separated from and talked about as if they possessed a life of their own and were not anchored and entangled in the same human soil from which all our difficulties grow. Spiritual illnesses cannot be spoken about out of context any more than sexual problems. Diagnosis aims at understanding all the longings—whether for meaning or as a result of unresolved conflict—in the human situation that are the common ground for our difficulties.

The mature counselor, then, will not be too quick to apply purely spiritual solutions—like prayer and fasting—to problems that usually have deeper and more complicated origins. Diagnosis aims at understanding the person—including his spiritual and sexual dimensions—and it makes sense only when these dimensions are in true and full perspective. The counselor cannot ignore a person's spiritual nature any more than the clergyman can ignore a person's sexual nature. It is the person who suffers in these various areas and the person who needs to be understood in all his or her complexity. There is no great help in encouraging sexual behavior as a solution to spiritual pain, and there is certainly no lasting assistance in recommending spiritual remedies for sexual conflicts. A balanced and fully developed diagnostic sense permits us to see the interrelated aspects of personality and to respond with the sensitivity which acknowledges and illumines the person's search of the self. A healthy attitude toward diagnosis can turn people not into numbers but into unique individuals.

Practical Issues

Making room for some diagnosis does not demand that we probe deeply into the psychological wounds of other persons immediately. Asking a great many questions from our own viewpoint may, in fact, interfere with our hearing the message that tells us best what we should know about the other person. Most anxious people want to talk when they first see us; they want to get their feelings out into the light and the air as best they can. To block the flow of these initial communications by inappropriate or ill-timed questions may interfere with counseling and with our best chance of diagnosing wisely.

Let the other person start where he or she wishes; this will lead us in the right direction if we pay attention to what is being said. The word *diagnosis* comes from Greek roots that mean "to perceive apart" or "to distinguish between things." It might be approximately translated as "discernment" or "seeing sensitively." The process involves all our capacities in developing a special kind of pervasive human understanding. This is very different from harshly judging clients or yoking them with a psychiatric label from which they will never be free. Diagnosis is a living, interactional process the strength of which comes from our awareness of the ways in which others struggle to deal with their conflicts and problems in life. It is not branding someone with a rigid unchangeable clinical opinion.

The first thing to listen for is the reason the other gives us for coming. The story of how other people get to our offices generally includes important information about their previous experience and the way others have reacted to them. An appropriate question to ask in an initial interview is: "Where do we hear the pain?" Closely related are the feelings the other person has toward this principal pain. How, in other words, do they experience their problem? Only this reveals their presenting the problem in the context of their own personality and their ongoing life. Here we get a sense of the general sweep of the others' psychological experience; this allows us to understand them in depth rather than just cross-sectionally. Permit the clients to speak, and even in their silences and hesitations they will say much that will help us to understand them and their current functioning.

The counselor who wants to understand others is well-advised to count to ten before asking any questions at all. This is to restrain overeagerness, curiosity, or the use of a question to cover up for not knowing what else to do. Questioning can back already anxious persons against the wall, making them raise their defenses against us so that it becomes more difficult to understand them. The manner of asking questions, and the sensitivity with which they are shaped and directed to important issues, not only carries a message of respect for the other but brings forth information vital to an understanding discernment of their current functioning. Our inquiries, phrased in gentle tones, should be directed toward those parts of the other's story where the flares of hurt are burning. There is obviously a message in our manner of approaching sore points, and our skill in doing this gently but clearly assists the other in clarifying his problem both for himself and for us. The best diagnosis comes from those moments in which both the counselor and the client learn together.

Counselors are neither prosecuting attorneys nor members of a senate committee; they are not trying to expose guilt but to understand the texture of the other's experience. In framing our questions there is hardly ever any need to ask *why*. This is asking for an explanation that most persons seeking help are unable to give in a rational or completely logical manner. They come for help in order to be able to answer this question for themselves. It is better to frame our inquiries in an open-ended fashion that decreases threat and allows others enough room to develop their answers in their own way. Our questions should be more like invitations to self-search rather than commands for the production of evidence.

Counselors also need the opportunity to reflect on what they have heard and on their own manner of reacting to it. To reduce their own experience of stress they should try to build some time into their schedule in order to integrate the experiences they have with individual clients. This is a necessary step if diagnosis is to be mature and helpful. Counselors, in other words, need some perspective on their work in order to perceive their counselees distinctly and not have them fuse into some overall impression of emotional struggle.

To maintain the balance needed for healthy diagnosis, counselors often find a check list of their own reactions helpful. Is this an emergency? That is a fair question if the evidence of the interview has revealed behavior on the part of the counselee that is increasingly agitated and destructive. In the light of this, for example, must some judgment be made about the place and number of future appointments or even the possibility of an early referral to other facilities? One of the most important elements in a good referral is its timing. If a counselor senses that clients need more help than he or she can provide, then the manner and moment of arranging for the client to see somebody else becomes an important operational consequence of diagnosis. The referral should be made when the counselor has reasonable certainty about the seriousness of the psychological difficulty. The manner of referral should be gentle and constructive rather than a response that seems to be made out of the counselor's own anxiety about the other person's behavior.

It is possible for some counselors to refer in an excited and premature fashion out of a sense of romantic emergency. This may well bewilder persons who come for help and make them feel worse about themselves; it may also be a kind of disowning response through which we make them feel that they are too sick for us to have anything to do with them.

An Extension Of Understanding

The strong egalitarian emphasis of humanistic psychology makes suspect any diagnosis that involves a presumed "expert" passing judgment on the behavior of another person.

To presume to diagnose seems to smack of excessive scientism and a generally depersonalized attitude toward others. As has been mentioned, however, this need not be the case at all, and appropriate effort to grasp the significance of another's symptoms can and should be an exercise in enlightened personalism.

Helpers sincerely committed to the good of those with whom they work are not trying to "get something" on their clients or to dominate them through categorization. Their attitude is best described as an effort to broaden and extend their understanding of others. This is very different from the impersonal pigeonholing that creates distance between clients and counselors. When diagnosis is seen as an aspect of understanding another person, it demands an appreciative closeness that is concerned and positive. The more deeply counselors understand the private world of others the less they need to distance themselves from their clients out of fear of them—and the more easily will the relationship develop. Diagnosis and the recommendations that may follow from it are never threatening when the recommendations are in the context of concerned personal understanding. Diagnosis, in other words, need not be employed as a defense; it is truly up to the counselor.

The steady effort to extend our understanding of others so that we have a feeling for them and their needs requires hard work and the self-awareness that keeps us free of emotional ensnarlment because we are committed to increasing the freedom of others. This takes concentration, self-knowledge, and professionalism. In the long run, however, this intense approach is far less stressful for counselors than the uninformed groping in the dark that can easily characterize imprecise relationships. Sensitive diagnosis makes us work harder at developing the practical understanding that is at the heart of effective counseling.

It is axiomatic that the counselor must be alert to the attitudes and behavior exhibited by clients during the interview. These contain powerful signals about their condition. Even small gestures or statements—things we might not ordinarily pay much attention to—can contain important indications about the individual's way of looking at himself or herself. There is a need to balance one's sensitivity prudently so that judgments are made only when sufficient, consistent clues are combined.

Some counselors may miss other manifestations of disturbance, or they may misread the ones they do observe, because of a lack of experience or a failure to integrate for themselves the impressions they gather in their relationships with their clients. Among the items the counselor should note are these: Is the patient so deeply depressed that it is difficult to make contact with him or her, and difficult for him or her to speak about problems? This depression needs to be examined more closely. How deep is it and what overt behavior has it given rise to in the client? Is the other person able to report the situation in a coherent way, with reasonable continuity and with some satisfactory sense of time or place? Where there is some interference with these aspects of their communication, counselors should take the possibility of major disturbance more seriously.

This is also true if there are obvious abnormalities in the way people talk about their lives or experiences. For example, persons who derail their narrative with a flight of ideas, one association leading in wild distraction to another, exhibit symptoms that demand careful evaluation. The same is true if clients perseverate, that is, if they cling to one concrete and inappropriate part of their narrative and cannot seem to get away from it.

A counselor must also ask if the emotions displayed by the other are appropriate to the events he is describing. A gap here prompts the counselor to listen more carefully to what the other is attempting to describe. No counselor should read things into the statements or the behavior of others that are really not there; helpers cannot, however, ignore indications of major difficulties. Questions of diagnostic judgment and prognosis are tricky. We do not reduce another's stress or make progress in handling major symptoms by ignoring them; neither can we do it by ignoring our own reactions. Our diagnosis may need to be provisional, something to be confirmed by the judgment of somebody else. The tentative nature of a diagnosis does not lessen its significance, nor should it make a counselor hesitant to develop a psychological hypothesis that may have important practical implications for helping others.

Once the counselor has developed a general feeling for other persons, he or she must ask: Am I the best qualified person to assist in this situation? Or am I unnecessarily taking over what might be done better by some other professional person? Am I well acquainted with the referral resources in my community? Do I want to get rid of this person because I am afraid? The answers to these serious questions only come from the counselor's willingness to pursue the possibilities of sensible diagnosis.

While we need not distract persons who are anxious to talk by asking them unnecessary or ill-timed questions about their life histories, there are basic items of information we should try to secure during or close to our first interview. Many of these may naturally emerge in the context of the story the person tells. So much the better if this is the case. If these do not come in this fashion, however, the counselor should try to elicit the information in as warm and genuine a manner as possible. This information is not hard to get, especially if we match our questions to similar material in the patient's story. These include the patient's age, marital status, and something about his family life and his children. It is helpful to know something about his parents, his job history, his current living circumstances, and whether he has had previous or concurrent treatment. These provide the framework for a rich appreciation of the other's life.

Counselors should develop some communication with the professional resources of their community. Too often this is done only under the pressure of making a referral and on the word of someone else. Some preliminary relationship with other resources would increase self-confidence, lessen stress, and make the process of referral much easier on both client and counselor.

Counselors should learn to speak the professional language of diagnosis; the best road to this is through studying the descriptions in the *Diagnostic and Statistical Manual of Mental Disorders,* American Psychiatric Association, Washington, D.C., 1987 3rd edition, revised *(DSM-III-R).* Counselors can also expand their appreciation for diagnosis by making use of supervision when this is possible or through continuing appropriate reading.

14

Diagnosis: Goals and Resources

The democratization of therapy in American culture has led, among other things, to a sense that the professional and the patient stand on a level plane with each other, neither with an advantage in knowledge or experience. In such a framework diagnosis is sometimes considered an unfair and improper "labeling" of another person, as if, as we have noted, this process somehow diminished the humanity of those being assessed. Diagnosis remains indispensable, however, as a deepening and refining of our efforts to understand other persons. It is, in fact, a way of taking them and their complaints seriously, of valuing and respecting them enough to be sure that we choose a course of treatment that matches their needs. A professional dehumanizes others by not making the effort to appreciate them individually, by eliminating diagnosis and responding to everyone in some benign generalized fashion. Nonprofessionals can also profit from developing their gifts for diagnosis. There are many reasons why this is of practical importance for them.

Why Diagnose?

Diagnosis serves three general purposes:

1. It provides a common language for all mental health professionals so that if one professional assesses a client as suffering from a given disorder, those with whom he communicates about this client can accurately conceptualize the nature of this particular client's problems.
2. It enables us to cluster the distinguishing characteristics of a given disorder together and to study its natural history. In so doing, a diagnosis often points the way to the most effective treatment.
3. The ultimate purpose of classification is to develop an understanding of the causes of the disorder and, with this knowledge, making a sensible treatment plan for the person experiencing it. For

most mental problems, the etiology, or cause, is unknown. Currently, there are numerous theories about the origins of specific disorders. They usually depend on the observer's theoretical orientation. In this book, we will conceptualize a number of these disorders from the psychodynamic or psychoanalytic viewpoint—the theory that views psychological reality as a living, influential, interactive universe— because this theory not only plumbs the meaning of observed behavior but shows the relationship between symptoms and their psychological roots.

How Do We Define A Mental Disorder?

In the *Diagnostic and Statistical Manual III-R*, (*DSM III-R*, for short) we read that "each of the mental disorders is conceptualized as a clinically significant behavioral or psychological syndrome or pattern that occurs in a person and that is associated with present distress (a painful symptom) or disability (impairment in one or more important areas of functioning), or a significantly increased risk of suffering death, pain, disability, or an important loss of freedom. In addition, this syndrome or pattern must not be merely an expectable response to a particular event, for example, the death of a loved one. Whatever its original cause, it must currently be considered a manifestation of a behavioral, psychological, or biological dysfunction in the person. Neither deviant behavior—for example, political, religious, or sexual—nor conflicts that are primarily between the individual and society are mental disorders unless the deviance or conflict is a symptom of a dysfunction in the person." (*DSM-III-R*, p. xxii)

In deepening our appreciation of diagnosis and in facilitating at least our occasional use of this basic work, we understand that the categories of illness are not distinct, that there is considerable overlap of symptoms between categories, and that individuals with the same disorder may vary considerably in the way that they manifest their illness. We will now examine some of the basic principles and methods of this standard reference work for the classification of mental illness.

Current Classification—*DSM-III-R*

Because we do not know the origin of the majority of mental disorders and since there are numerous ways of understanding these problems depending on one's theoretical tradition, this system is based on descriptions of the disorder rather than on efforts to trace its etiology. Most clinicians and researchers can agree on the descriptive terms for specific signs and symptoms. This behavioral emphasis is therefore atheoretical and defines disorders in terms of what we observe in our experience with troubled individuals. Using these agreed-upon descriptions enables clinicians to apply their own theoretical tradition in developing an appropriate and consistent treatment plan.

An innovative dimension of the current system of classification is its multiaxial approach. The basic concept of this system is that several different domains of information that are assumed to be of high clinical value are examined for each person. Considered together they offer a more comprehensive view of the person than an evaluation limited only to the symptoms of mental disorder. This is organized around five axes:

Axis 1—*The clinical syndrome.*

Axis 2—*The developmental disorders and personality disorders.* This permits thinking about disorders in the context of the person's basic personality. We are thus able to understand why some patients are compliant and perhaps do well while other patients, because of their fundamental personality characteristics, experience more complicated courses of illness.

Axis 3—The listing of all *current physical disorders.* The importance of this arises from the fact that a person's physical condition can affect the manifestations of the disorder as well as its treatment.

Axis 4—*Severity of psychosocial stressors.* This provides a six-point scale for assessing the overall severity of the psychosocial stressors, such as job loss or death of spouse, that have occurred in the year preceding the evaluation.

Axis 5—*The Global Assessment of Functioning Scale.* This scale summarizes the psychological, social, and occupational functioning on a continuum of mental health and illness.

Nonprofessionals should have some knowledge of the major classifications found in *DSM-III-R.* They are as follows:

1. Organic Mental Syndromes and Disorders

This group includes disorders such as dementia, delirium, and a number of disturbances, such as intoxications and withdrawal conditions, associated with the use of substances such as alcohol and cocaine. The underlying feature of these syndromes is a psychological or behavioral abnormality related to transient or permanent dysfunction of the brain. Such dysfunctions can cause myriad clinical manifestations and are often difficult to diagnose even for the experienced clinician. This is particularly true in the early stages of some of these disorders.

Counselors may have contact with individuals suffering from such problems in their early stages but are more likely to be consulted by friends or family members of those so afflicted. It is useful, therefore, to have some familiarity with the nature of these disorders in order to provide needed and informed support and to be of practical and sensible assistance in obtaining resources for the suffering person. .

If a counselor, on the basis of comparing behavior to the list of signs and symptoms, feels that a client—or a person described by a friend or relative—may be suffering from such a disorder, an appropriate and prompt referral is indicated. Such serious entities need effective medical evaluation and management and cannot be dealt with wisely through any time-buying improvisation or through the use of unproven remedies. The use of the latter visits an even greater cruelty on afflicted individuals and on those around them.

2. Psychoactive Substance Use Disorders

This group of disorders classifies, for a wide range of substances, indications of dependence on and abuse of those substances. The criteria for determining drug dependence are defined, and the clinically significant behaviors, cognitions, and other symptoms that indicate loss of control over substance use are described for each drug.

Because of the pervasive use of recreational drugs at all levels in our society, nonprofessionals will surely encounter persons with problems associated with this social reality. Their ability to respond is enriched by a grasp of the signs and symptoms of the most common types of drugs. These will also be discussed in more detailed fashion in a later chapter.

3. Schizophrenia

Here the nonprofessional will find the basic criteria for the inclusion and exclusion of the diagnosis of schizophrenia as well as a description of the subtypes of this major disorder.

Most counselors, even nonprofessionals, have some familiarity with the explicit symptoms of psychosis, such as delusions, hallucinations, and other signals of gross disturbances in thinking. Such seriously troubled individuals should always be referred as quickly as possible for professional treatment.

4. Mood Disorders

This group includes the behavior associated with both manic and depressive syndromes. The manic and hypomanic disorders are distinguished by the marked impairment in the person's social and occupational functioning and often require hospitalization. Depressive disorders include a wide range of mood disturbances.

Counselors will often be the first to interview individuals who manifest depressive symptoms. Knowledge of the various kinds of depression is, therefore, extremely helpful as they try to make judgments about the persons with whom they are working. These will also be reviewed in a later chapter.

5. Anxiety Disorders

In this group of disorders, the troubled persons experience anxiety directly or act in ways that help them ward off anxiety through other behaviors that may seem strange but actually constitute a language of distress that nonprofessionals must learn to interpret accurately. It is good for counselors to recall that what drives them crazy about other people is often what is keeping them sane. This vocabulary of symptomatology can only be read correctly in the context of the client's total life situation. This group of disorders will also be discussed in a later chapter.

6. Somatoform Disorders

This group of problems involve physical symptoms suggesting a physical disorder but for which there are no findings that indicate any organic basis. Nor is there any known pathophysiologic mechanism that could account for the disturbance. There also exists a strong presumption, or even positive evidence, of a link between the somatic symptoms and underlying psychological factors or conflicts.

7. Adjustment Disorders

This disorder may be read as a maladaptive reaction to an identifiable psychosocial stressor. It must also occur within three months after the onset of the stressor. A relationship may be observed with symptoms of depression, anxiety, physical complaints, withdrawal and/or occupational disturbances. These are, in fact, the problems with which counselors may be most familiar and with which they may be able to intervene most effectively.

8. Personality Disorders

Such disorders represent pervasive patterns of disturbance in personality functioning that make themselves present in a variety of settings in the person's life. The behaviors, of lifelong duration, often cause problems for those who suffer from them in their social and work life. These latter problems cause these persons to experience subjective distress. The problem is so much a part of their nature that they cannot observe it in themselves and suffer from the reactions they trip off in others, such as employers or acquaintances. Counselors will be very familiar with this group of disorders and need to understand some of the more familiar patterns of behavior that constitute these disturbances.

Conclusion

It is important for counselors to understand that our knowledge of mental disorders and our classification thereof is in a state of constant development and refinement. During the past thirty years, for example, we have learned that many disorders that we considered due primarily to psychological factors have far more complex origins. Considerable research data suggest that disorders such as schizophrenia, mania, depression, panic attacks, post-traumatic stress, and impulse disorders are often associated with genetic, neurochemical, and neurophysiological abnormalities. As a result, approaches to the treatment of these disorders have been rethought and developed in fresh ways. To attempt to treat a serious depression without careful assessment and the consideration of medication may deprive clients of the currently accepted and available treatment. Counselors, especially those who have not had extensive training, can ony improve their chances of being truly helpful by acquainting themselves as thoroughly as they can with the ever developing insights of contemporary diagnosis.

15

Listening to the Story

Counseling is a process of many languages; people use their eyes, their hands, and their shifting feet to punctuate and underscore what they attempt to understand and communicate about themselves. Much of what clients relate to counselors is in anecdotal form, a storytelling mode as old as mankind. We talk to each other all the time by telling stories; even our tall tales tell something true about us. Telling stories to communicate our experience is as human and natural as breathing. Stories and illustrations are found in abundance in the garden variety of common, personal problems with which counselors deal all the time. What do they mean?

When we tell a story about ourselves we bypass logic in order to reach the unconscious level of another person in a way that completely defies rational analysis. That is why stories have always been a part of the civilized person's resources. Myth and symbol remain potent means of communication and the art of the novelist consists in telling the truth about us while telling a story at the same time. Counselors may understand this but fail to appreciate or develop an adequate sensitivity to the dynamics of the storytelling that they hear so much of from their clients. There are dangers and opportunities here with which effective counselors will wish to acquaint themselves.

Novelist Graham Greene tells us something of the unconscious sources of a novelist's work in his autobiography, *A Sort of Life* (New York: Pocket Books, 1973, p. 160). He recalls that what he has forgotten returns regularly in his novels. "If one day [these forgotten details] find their way into a book, it should be without our connivance and so disguised that we don't recognize them when we see them again. All that we can easily recognize as our experience in a novel is mere reporting. . . . Perhaps a novelist has a greater ability to forget than other men—he has to forget or become sterile. What he forgets is the compost of the imagination."

Clients are not trying to entertain counselors through their stories; they are trying to explain themselves. They sift through their own experience, describing their relationships and the things that have

139

gone wrong and the things that have gone right, always searching for the root of their complaint. They attempt to trace down the source of their anxiety by describing the circumstances or events in which they face it in their lives. These narratives, then, are an invaluable source of raw material from which counselors can draw an understanding of the persons who tell them.

This is particularly true with children who almost always describe their life events in terms of simple stories. As psychiatrist Richard A. Gardner has suggested, adults sometimes fail to communicate with children because they respond to these stories with rational arguments or explanations. To reach the unconscious level from which the child's story proceeds, it may be important for adults to respond in terms of stories themselves. Stories bridge the gap between persons' unconscious levels more swiftly and surely than logic (*Therapeutic Communication with Children: The Mutual Storytelling Technique,* Richard A. Gardner, M.D., New York: Science House, Inc., 1971). We are not suggesting that adult counselors should tell stories in response to their clients' stories; we are pointing, rather, to the richness and subtlety of the material to which counselors should attune themselves if they wish to hear the inner resonations of the persons coming to them for assistance. These constitute a rich lode to be mined carefully by counselors who can gently attempt to "hear their way into" the meanings beneath the narratives of the clients.

Problems arise when counselors lose themselves in the details of the story and miss both the person and the message in the process. Many life stories are interesting and intriguing; they can easily capture the counselor's attention. Helpers often get hooked on the story, wanting to know how it comes out rather than the reasons for its being told. Some even wish to alter its ending.

This is a common problem for novice counselors; they discover they are so intrigued by the details of the illustrations the individual uses that they mistake a clear understanding of the story for effective counseling. To be stranded in illustrative material is both bewildering and a source of stress for counselors; it is like finding oneself in quicksand—any slight movement to escape seems only to worsen the situation. Counselors easily lose their perspective when they become absorbed by the stories or so identified with them, that they miss the client's motivation for using the illustration.

Counselors may also get so caught up in trying to untangle or straighten out the details of a story that they lose their own spontaneous reactions to the clients with whom they work. They get trapped, as if they were in an elaborate erector set, out of which they are required to manufacture responses that fit the stories of the client the way scaffolding fits outside of a building.

Getting stalled at the level of the illustration means the counselor is preoccupied with the technique rather than the human essence of response. This may be the honest counselor's most serious distraction. Through this stressful detour counselors get out of the flow of experience with the other. They are caught up in doing good and in doing well, the twin burdens of counselors who have become too self-conscious about what they are trying to achieve.

Getting trapped in constructing responses to illustrative material makes it very hard for such counselors to respond simply and directly to the persons. The stories reveal the other person, painting his or her concerns. Our responses must be to the persons as they reach toward us with their interesting narrative, not just to the story itself.

Counselors who hear themselves respond by tracing over every detail of the client's story are almost surely trapped by their own obsessiveness. It is one of the classic ways by which helpers miss seeing the forest for the trees. They can profitably style their responses in accord with the old cliché about "making a long story short." Responding to the point of the illustration is the core of effective counseling.

The many stories clients use are attempts to convey to us the story of their lives. In effective therapy the response that is most helpful cuts through the story material to its origins in the personality of the other.

Each anecdote is filled with echoes from less than conscious levels of personality. When we pick these up we begin to hear the real story which others are trying to tell us, and which they themselves are trying to hear. The counselor's response resembles the way a friend answers a friend who is in trouble, the manner in which a husband or wife respond to each other when one of them is in distress. They are not distracted by the details because they sense the pulsating core of the distressed person. That is what is important, and it is to this level, from which all the illustrations flow, that they respond. They understand that the illustration is just a way of getting this deeper message across. Counselors must listen to clients in the same way.

This is not to say that the stories are completely unimportant in themselves. It is important, however, to put them into proper focus in relationship to the person who is telling them. Clients, after all, offer us the context of their self-perceptions when they tell us the stories of their difficulties. They describe the significant figures in their lives, peopling the stage for us so that we can see their particular way of looking at themselves and their relationships with others. Stories are full of significant stage directions, entrances and exits, conflicts and expectations. The clients stand at the center of this, and it is how they emerge rather than how the story ends that is important. The question that is most helpful for counselors in getting this into perspective remains: To what am I responding, the person or the story?

Other pertinent reflections center on why we find ourselves so distracted by a story that we may run the risk of missing the person who is telling it. In other words, as we listen to others talk we not only hear something about them but, through our own reactions, something about ourselves. We may find that we pay attention only to those things that stir us or remind us of something in our own lives. We may avoid things to which we are sensitive, episodes that cause us embarrassment or about which we would rather not think or speak.

A profile of ourselves stands out clearly in the way we hear and respond to the illustrative communication of others. Counselors who are aware of their own curiosity realize that if they satisfy only this, it will lead them away from the individual and toward a projection of their own concerns onto the client. Such counselors may end up responding to themselves more than they do to other persons. Counselors can unravel this and lessen the stress that is associated with it if they take the time to listen to their own reactions to others' stories. They will find there is a great deal about their own life story.

As we become more sensitized to the value of illustrative material in revealing the essence of a person's difficulty, we become less concerned with the narrative details and more alert to other aspects of what the clients have to say. These include:

The feeling tone: This is always a key element in counseling and it is quite possible that, no matter what the content of the story may be, the feeling tone will still be the most significant source of understanding for us. The person may be describing what sounds like a trivial or neutral incident—such as a minor disagreement between a married couple or an argument at work—and reveal much more in the tone than in the detail. Is the individual telling this in a depressed way? Is there anger bubbling up beneath these words? Is there some prizing of power involved in what seems such a simple tale? The counselor's response in these circumstances would be to the underlying tone which gives this story its color and its meaning.

The perspective: Is the individual telling the story solely in terms of things that have happened in the past? Or is it integrated with life's continuity so that it opens the person to the future? Is something over and done with in this person's view? Or are there still possibilities for some growth and development? Are they mourning something? Or are they preparing to deal with a problem that is just emerging?

Prospects: This subject is closely related to the previous reflections. It indicates the attitudes the persons have toward the challenge or difficulty before them. Are they hopeful or despairing? Do they feel betrayed, deserted; or is there some self-confidence on which they seem to draw in order to confront this difficulty?

Central identification: How, in these stories, do the persons describe themselves? Are they active or passive? Do they assume responsibility or portray themselves as victims of circumstances? Do they accept some blame for what is wrong, or do they consistently locate the blame in sources outside themselves? The roles in which persons place themselves reveal a great deal about their self-concept.

The theme: This is central in any narrative and is especially important as the thread of meaning that links several illustrations together. The theme is a potent clue about the individual's experience of himself, significant others, and life in general. Frequently clients are not aware of how clearly they describe themselves and their lives in the stories they tell. This is because the material may be coming from subconscious levels; that's why they may employ recurring themes, such as stories of conflict. In these scenarios the central questions become: What is the nature of the conflict? With whom is it experienced? What are the prospects for resolving it? The explanation of conflict through stories gives counselors clear signals about what the client sees as his or her most important struggle. These are scenarios of the self, not just interesting stories.

Practical hints: Counselors should avail themselves of the great assistance that clients give them by patiently telling their stories many times and in many different versions. Clients are always helpful in this regard. All we have to do is listen to them and hear them. An important question becomes: Have I heard this story before? It may not be the same story in setting or details, but it is identical in theme and central conflict. Clients repeat such stories over and over again for a simple reason—because counselors don't catch on or respond adequately in the first place. When clients repeat a story they are clearly saying, "This is important and I want some sign that you have heard it."

The beginning of wisdom for distressed counselors arrives when they can ask themselves, "What is the source of my block? Why am I not able to get the meaning of the story the client has told me in so many different ways?" In this regard, it is sometimes very practical for counselors to propose a challenge to themselves. They should try to finish the following sentence: The client would move forward if only I could understand _____. When counselors can finish that sentence and use it as the basis for a response to the individual, they have taken a big step toward resolving the block in their understanding of the other. They will also be getting closer to the unconscious material, even though they may not completely understand it as yet. Understanding moves slowly, not with the swift finality of a detective story.

Understanding responses should be made as soon as counselors get a real feel for the essential communication of the client. This requires a professional sensitivity and a sense of timing that builds on what seems to be natural and appropriate. It is ordinarily not very helpful for counselors to interrupt clients unexpectedly or before they have finished telling the story in the terms they want to use. Nor can counselors wait too long to respond or they will project themselves as dull and passive in the relationship. There is a rhythm to storytelling that makes it possible to integrate the counselor's response at some natural break or point of conclusion. Clients almost always provide these pauses for us.

As counselors become more sensitive to the undertones of the stories their clients tell them, they make rapid progress in getting at their real communication. While they do this they must be aware of their own potential for interfering with the communication of the client, either because of curiosity or defensiveness on their own part. When they can understand and control these reactions, they are much more capable of receiving loud and clear signals from their clients.

Counseling is not a task to be accomplished but a relationship to be experienced; we are not solving a puzzle but trying to respond to persons rather than illustrations. As we become accustomed to hearing *into* the narrative, we respond more freely and with more of our genuine selves. Counseling becomes less a stressful test and more a satisfying real-life relationship for clients and counselors alike.

16

The Problem of Referral

Referring clients to other professionals for continued assistance is an issue faced regularly by counselors, especially those whose helping work is part of other occupational responsibilities. Although not much has been written about referral, there are varied and complex feelings concerning it. Some of these arise because neither the counselor nor the one getting help have more than a vague idea of what referral means. Other complexities develop because of the uncomfortable personal implications of referral both for the counselor who refers and the client who is referred. Referral remains, however, an inevitable issue, and each helper needs a clear understanding of the process as well as of his or her feelings about it.

The process of referral is like a blank screen on which we project many of our own inner experiences; we do, in fact, find out a good deal about ourselves when we face and deal with the question of recommending that a person go to someone else for continued assistance. What we feel about ourselves and our own professional helping work comes under our own close scrutiny at such moments. Among other things, referral may represent:

An abandonment of the person: Some counselors feel guilty about turning their clients over to somebody else, especially if they have previously had ambiguous feelings about the individual. The moment of truth in referral may stir these up, especially in counselors who are very hard on themselves, the type who allow no margin for error and not much room for the kind of common mistake that even seasoned professionals make from time to time with their clients. A good referral is not an abandonment of the individual but a recommendation in his or her best interest.

Getting rid of the person: Some helpers regularly put most of their energy into solving the problems that people cause by knocking on the office door in the first place. Referral can easily represent more of a solution for the counselor than for the client. This is not true, however, in the great majority of cases in which successful referrals are made.

About all these attitudes we may, as counselors, feel either good or bad. Whatever we feel at the time of referral—relief or anxiety—we will necessarily communicate to the client even if only in nonverbal language. We cannot hide our genuine inner attitudes, and this underscores our need to become more sensitive to our own reactions to the process of referral.

Referral often surfaces countertransference feelings, the complex of emotions the counselor experiences toward the client. It is difficult to proceed in counseling without an awareness of the many levels of emotional reactions we can have toward our clients. One of the best preparations for the process of referral is to review our feelings in each individual situation, to try to face them and accept them as honestly as possible so that we can modify our own self-image as well as the expectations we make on ourselves as counselors. Such feelings, if they are denied or distorted, only imprison the counselors who have them. The more clearly counselors can symbolize these feelings to themselves the freer they become in all of their counseling work. Unrecognized countertransference feelings contribute a principle source of stress for many counselors. The moment of referral reminds us of our need to listen carefully to ourselves so that we can control rather than be controlled by our inner experience.

Unless we deal with our inner experiences before we proceed with the process of referral we may easily give the impression of rejecting the individual with whom we are working. This can be fairly complicated, especially if the person coming for help has had a lifetime of being rejected by others. We hesitate to add another rejection to this, but, in the commonplace entanglements of counseling, the client may be testing us out to see if, in fact, we are going to be as rejecting of them as others have been. Obviously the counselor must be aware of several levels of interchange with clients if he or she is to move forward without being trapped or needlessly manipulated.

The possibility that a client may be testing us, or even edging us toward rejecting them, may make some counselors hesitate even when a referral is appropriate. A referral should not be put off merely because such possibilities of manipulation exist. They need to be recognized and, in some cases at least, even talked about with the client. There are sensible ways to handle even this situation without trapping ourselves or needlessly hurting the client. It takes listening, however, and an awareness of how many strands of the counseling relationship are drawn together at the time when referral becomes a possibility.

We should not be uncertain or hesitant about the referral itself; this will only make the client feel the same way. This may rob the process of some of its potential value and leave the relationship of the referring counselor to the client unsettled and ambiguous as well. Referral calls for clean edges to our relationships. We can only profit by attending to and making clear to ourselves all of our inner experience at the time of discussing a referral.

The feelings of the client can also be very complicated. Just as the counselor's countertransference feelings play a role at the time of referral, so the transference feelings of the person coming for help are also activated at this time. The client may openly like or dislike the counselor; this may be the fruit of transference feelings rather than of any direct emotional response to the counselor. We should not be afraid of letting others express positive or negative feelings toward us, but counselors should not attempt in-depth exploration of them. The referral is being made in order to allow a decision about that to be made by an expert in a better position to do so. Handle these feelings and don't take them too personally; see them as essential parts of the human process of helping.

Counselors who are not aware of their countertransference feelings, or who do not know themselves well, may find that they cannot easily face the strong feelings others may express about them when referral comes up for discussion. They become victims of excessive softheartedness and back away from this important point of decision, allowing themselves to be manipulated in the process and missing the chance to help the other person more significantly. Certain professions—especially those entered by persons with a warm interest in and a need for close contact with others—are particularly vulnerable to this kind of difficulty. These people cannot bear to face hard truths because they feel this will cause them not to be liked, which is not an attractive idea at all. This experience is a paramount source of stress in such counselors' work and, while they recognize its results, they may not realize that they can deal with it more forthrightly by acquiring a better understanding of themselves as well as of the process of therapy. They are far freer, for example, when they realize that not all of the emotional reactions of their clients are directed at their person, but that they have become the object of transferred feelings from other important individuals in their clients' lives. Such counselors can prepare themselves by self-examination and by a deeper awareness of the transference feelings of the clients.

It is not uncommon, for example, for a client to tell certain counselors, such at those working in schools or in church settings, that they cannot afford to get any help except what the present counselor is giving to them. This can be a major source of conflict for warm-hearted counselors who do not understand the symbolic issue that may be involved and who may find this a very persuasive argument against affecting a needed referral. Any time feelings about money come up, they should be explored like any other attitudes that are verbalized during the counseling process. Counselors operate far more effectively when they do not take everything personally and when they can appreciate the symbolic significance of many aspects of their relationship with their clients.

The process of referral should be integrated into the counseling relationship as closely as possible. It should not, in other words, represent a distinct break but rather the outcome of the kind of growth the counselor and the client have shared together. Referral represents a moment of decision at which, for the greater good of the client, he or she is transferred for help to another professional person. This should not come as a total surprise to the client; counselors can easily and honestly make this a possibility right from the start. Referral fits the context of the counseling in which the helper is open and honest with the client.

This includes telling the truth about the reasons for referral. Manufactured reasons never hold up, and a simple short statement of why the counselor believes that referral is necessary takes very little time and effects a great deal of good. The counselor may feel that the client's needs are beyond his or her competence at the moment. That is an admirable reason to get another therapist. It may be that the counselor feels the client needs help on a more regular and long-term basis, something that, because of circumstances, the counselor cannot provide.

Referral may be appropriate when the relationship does not seem to be working out very effectively and, despite good will and efforts on the part of both, it does not seem possible to disentangle it. Some counselors and clients are not well-matched because of personality factors that may be unconscious. It is not always possible to refer people in these circumstances, but it is an important factor to acknowledge and to deal with even if it does not lead to referral to someone else. Referrals are appropriate if either the client or the counselor is moving away; reality necessitates such a change in many helping relationships. This may be seen on a minor scale if either party is going to be away on an extended trip, a vacation, or an assignment. It is important to anticipate this well in advance and to arrange for an adequate referral to cover the period of absence. This is not something that should be brought up at the last moment. It is hard enough for some clients to survive a counselor's being away on vacation for a few weeks. They should never be surprised about an absence if it is at all possible to anticipate it and discuss it beforehand.

The general context is always the greater good of the individual. This is the final determination of any referral: What is the best thing for this client at this time? As the counselor balances all the factors that may be involved in such a decision, this becomes the overriding final consideration. The counselor should also be willing to answer questions about the referral and to explore a client's feelings about it so that their relationship can be full and clear even though it may shortly be terminated.

Counselors should have the names, addresses, and numbers of referral sources ready well in advance. This takes some reflection— and at times consultation with other professionals—to make a referral to the helper who, because of professional training and personal characteristics, seems best qualified to take responsibility for the counseling. It is helpful for any counselor to have relationships with a number of professionals in the community to whom referrals may be made. It is a common practice to make a brief note or a phone call announcing your intention to refer a patient and to receive an acknowledgment when a contact is made. Clients, however, should ordinarily make the contact for themselves. Counselors should send only the information that is asked for by the referral source and agreed to explicitly, generally in writing, by the client.

The process of referral is completed by the counselor's stepping out of the picture, making it clear that the client is now the responsibility of another professional. The completed referral marks the end of their participation in the therapeutic process. This requires self-knowledge and self-discipline. Counselors' feelings can betray them in these moments, especially if they find it hard to let go of a certain client or if their own curiosity prompts them continually to find out how the person is getting along. Mature counselors recognize these possibilities in themselves and are neither surprised nor scandalized by them. They can deal with them without panicking or experiencing any lessening of their own professional competence or self-esteem.

Sooner or later every counselor faces the following situation: The client referred to another person calls up to complain about the new therapist in terms something like these, "I just can't talk to him the way I did to you," "She's not as understanding as you are," or "I just don't like him and I don't think I'm getting anywhere." The words vary but the theme is generally the same, counselors may experience great stress when they feel that a referral has not worked out. Sometimes they are tempted to intervene, to take back the responsibility of the client, or even, in some circumstances, to try to find yet another professional person for the client.

All of these are moves in the wrong direction. As soon as a counselor makes any one of them, the former client has him in his power. It is very difficult to escape once we have allowed ourselves to be manipulated back into managing or trying to rearrange a referral we have already made. Sometimes we do it because we are flattered by the former client, and sometimes we do it because of the kind of softheartedness previously described. The general principle involved demands that once a referral is made we stay out of the picture and that we resist any impulse to assist or otherwise interfere with the newly developed relationship.

It is appropriate to acknowledge the feelings of the person who calls; this can be done with understanding and without brusqueness. But it should also be done to avoid getting any deeper into the new problems of the person. In a gentle and understanding way, a counselor can suggest that the client should discuss these problems in the only place in which it is appropriate to do so, the office of the person whom he or she is now seeing.

It is not the end of the world for clients when they find difficulty in relating to their therapists. It is often a sign that something significant is happening. Counselors might verbalize this in a general way as they direct the person concerned back to the referral source for an in-depth exploration of his current feelings toward this new relationship. The counselee is now somebody else's client, and we may do damage to the person we say we want to help if we allow ourselves to become unnecessarily involved after the referral has been made.

Most helpers, whether counseling is full or part-time work for them, can easily contact the local medical and psychological societies to get lists of psychiatrists and psychologists for referral purposes. Other specialities, such as that of social work, can also be extremely helpful, especially in certain problems involving the families of those with whom we are working. Counselors should be aware of the hospitals with psychiatric facilities or clinics through which referrals may also be made. Every community has certain agencies, some run by the state and some privately, whose directors know well the local communities' referral capacities. A number of organizations—Alcoholics Anonymous, certain drug units, suicide prevention centers, and even Travelers' Aid—can be extremely useful in dealing with the varied problems that come up in the work of the counselor. A contact at one of these places can relieve a great deal of stress and make it possible for a counselor to be far more helpful to a client. The counselor who knows whom to call at the right moment is well equipped for referrals.

Self-help Groups

Since the mid-1970s, there has been an expansion within most communities of resources that emphasize self-help. These groups focus on peer support and education and are available at low or no cost to vast segments of the population whose members are coping with developmental disabilities, chronic emotional and physical conditions, as well as specific life events such as divorce or the death of a child. These groups do not provide treatment per se. The treating professionals, in fact, often suggest that their patient participate in such groups in order to cope more effectively with the problem. These resources ordinarily consist of people who share a common experience and who serve as helpers to assist others and participate in providing and disseminating information about the common issue, often engaging in constructive actions related to the commonly shared experience.

Counselors should be familiar with some of the more than thirty self-help/mutual aid centers that have been established throughout the country. States such as Illinois and California have established detailed directories of self-help resources within those states as well as "800" numbers to expedite the process of referral.

Although many persons who do counseling say that they have neither the time nor the finances for it, some regular supervision or at least consultation about their work is indispensable to keep them fresh and alert in their helping activities. Counselors need continued clinical education, not just intellectual stimulation, and the regular exploration with another professional of the various factors that may enter into one or the other of their helping relationships. Nothing is a more significant source of support and development to a counselor than the opportunity for regular supervision or consultation.

It is a common practice in many areas for a group of persons who do counseling to gather together to discuss their work with some other professional person on a regular basis. When each member of the group contributes a small amount it makes it possible for a sensitive professional consultation to be obtained without the cost becoming overwhelming. This offers a valuable forum in which to make decisions about referrals as well as to acquaint oneself with the resources of one's community. It is also a fundamental way of dealing with the accumulated stress of working on a day-to-day basis with persons with emotional difficulties. It is, in other words, a source of professional development and personal integration at the same time. This is the kind of professional assistance to which hard-working counselors can gladly refer themselves.

17

When Can I Say What I Feel?

The question of when to say what one feels arises frequently with counselors but it is not a simple one to answer. Why is it asked?

Many therapists feel some need to involve themselves more actively and personally in their helping work. Sometimes this is a reflection of their usual style of relating with other persons outside of counseling. Some individuals seem to need to be personal with others; they are disappointed with relationships in which other persons do not seem to "like" them. They are anxious until they can get some sign that the people they help have warm feelings toward them. The anxiety that results when they do not feel "liked" causes some inexperienced therapists to insert themselves and their own feelings into the therapy early in the relationship.

The expression of the counselor's feelings or the revelation of the counselor's problem may also reflect a current generalized notion about the democratic conditions of psychotherapy. This is part of the antiexpert point of view, which demands that everybody stand on roughly the same ground at the beginning of therapy with nobody wiser than anybody else. The counselor who operates according to this democratic imperative may feel that an expression of his personal problems helps to put him on the same plane with his clients.

Some counselors become anxious to express their own feelings in counseling because they are frustrated—unconsciously at least—in their obsessive efforts to follow what they presume to be the "professional" rules of carrying out therapy. They generally perceive these as a collection of "Don'ts." They are not, for example, to be personal; they are not to express their own feelings; they are not to interpret, nor even to answer any of the client's questions. A need to break through this hedge of commands may make self-expression more attractive to many counselors who have been overinstructed about their work.

Some of the above experiences and other phenomena associated with the expression of the counselor's feelings may be the evidence of the countertransference feelings of the helping person. That, in other words, is what operational countertransference can look like. There are many countertransference possibilities that go unrecognized, especially for persons who do their counseling in connection with other professional responsibilities. Countertransference is, however, a common problem for all therapists, something with which they must deal systematically if they are to be effective in helping others. Countertransference, as has been discussed earlier, refers to the feelings—negative or positive—that arise in the therapist toward the client. As with transference, the emotions that are really appropriate to other persons in the therapist's life history become projected onto the clients. Counselors who have not dealt with their own emotional problems and conflicts are particularly vulnerable to these difficulties. They tend to act out their own problems during the counseling process and use the expression of their own feelings as a way of handling these.

The presence of countertransference feelings may be unsettling and stressful for counselors who do not have much experience or who lack opportunities for adequate reflection on their own experience or for proper supervisory consultation. These last experiences are the counselor's best help in dealing with the many and varied emotional reactions that can arise in the course of therapy. It is hard for counselors who have not had extensive experience to separate themselves enough from their own feelings in order to examine their source and deal with them in a mature way. Unresolved countertransference feelings, however, can be a prime reason for the premature expression of the therapist's own feelings in the counseling relationship.

Countertransference feelings can inspire a number of subtle efforts to involve oneself more personally with the client. It is clear that some counselors live their own emotional lives with their patients because they need the affection they feel in the responses from those they help. Counselors who make themselves dependent on their clients for emotional reinforcement may permit their own needs to dominate the counseling. This is a traditional hazard for inexperienced counselors. It can also plague overworked helpers who may have forsaken emotional satisfactions in other areas of their personal lives in order to meet their large case loads.

Dependence on the client can develop easily, for example, in a counselor who has always dealt with human problems in an intellectual fashion and who lacks much in-depth experience with others. It can also develop for the counselor who has had little experience with members of the opposite sex. The sudden rewards of dealing for the first time on a fairly intimate level with a member of the opposite sex can be extraordinarily satisfying, especially if the therapist lacks self-awareness.

There are readable signs of this kind of countertransference phenomenon, however, and they should motivate more careful self-exploration on the part of counselors who discover them in their own lives. Anything that smacks of "going well out of one's way" for a client may indicate that this problem is present. Counselors who observe themselves needlessly rearranging and extending appointments, or offering help for situations quite separate from the counseling, have firsthand evidence of emotional involvement.

Counselors should pay attention to their urges to overimpress their clients; to brag to them, for example, about other cases they have handled, about how hard they work, or about how little they are appreciated at home or by their colleagues. This expression of the counselor's own feelings is aimed at getting an appreciative response from a client. The same thing is reflected in the behavior of counselors who insist too much on controlling or supervising the lives and decisions of those with whom they work. Some counselors seem afraid to let people take responsibility for themselves because they fear that they may lose some influence over their clients and therefore lose their affection as well.

Counselors who wish to avoid or deal intelligently with the complicating stress of these problems may profit from deepening their understanding of the transference phenomenon itself. Reading is helpful in this regard, but in the long run some opportunity to discuss one's cases with another person or to explore systematically one's reactions is the most beneficial antidote to stress. Even the busiest counselor can take time to read and reflect on his or her own experience.

Counselors who take time for reflection can notice the clues to countertransference problems and begin to trace them down to their source. The chief clue, as MacKinnon and Michels note, is signaled "when the therapist is unable to recognize or refuses to acknowledge the real significance of his own attitudes and behavior" (*The Psychiatric Interview in Clinical Practice.* Philadelphia: W. B. Saunders, Co., 1971, p. 30). This points to the disparity between what the counselor *does* and what the counselor *thinks* he or she is doing. The evidence for countertransference involvement may be clear, but the refusal to recognize or to interpret it accurately becomes further proof of the existence of the problem.

Examples include counselors who overidentify with the person being helped. The patient's struggle becomes their struggle, and the involvement deepens into making decisions and plans that affect wide areas of the person's life. A classic example of overidentification is the encouragement of behavior in the counselee of which the counselor himself strongly approves. Standing up to one's parents, for example, may represent a victory of the therapist over the authority figures in his own life rather than really constructive progress for the client.

Another stressful area that may draw out the therapist's own feelings springs from the fact that patients may learn more about their counselors than what can be perceived during the hours of their relationship. Counselors who discover that their patients have picked up information about their families, their interests, or their own problems may find themselves actively on the defensive, or they may discover that it is difficult to get the focus back to the client's life. Should counselors allow themselves to be manipulated into discussing their own problems, they seriously compromise the therapeutic goals appropriate to counseling. The same kind of thing can occur if counselor and client get involved in some kind of business deal together. Counselors who, for example, buy things or make other financial arrangements or investments through their clients add elements to the relationship that can only complicate and increase their own experience of stress. They make it virtually impossible to avoid inappropriate expressions of their own feelings.

The reciprocal transference-countertransference area must be surveyed with sensitivity and care. It is obvious that counselors who prematurely involve their own feelings without understanding what is happening may do more harm than good both to themselves and their clients. The occurrence of transference-countertransference feelings also offers constructive occasions for the direct and fitting expression of the counselor's feelings.

All counselors must reflect on the democratic-antiprofessional notions that motivate many therapists to disclaim any special skills or training in helping other persons. An exploration of why counselors feel they must prove that they are human by washing their own dirty linen in a therapy session is therefore relevant. It may be that such counselors have not resolved their own feelings toward authority or professionalism, or that they do not realize the extent to which being accepted and liked by their clients is important to them.

Counselors who impose their own problems on the therapy situation out of due time may place themselves so much at the center of the relationship from the very beginning that they interfere with serious progress. In this regard it is important for counselors to reflect on the image they are trying to project. Sometimes they dress, speak, and even grow beards or affect other mannerisms that show their clear identification with some other therapist or teacher. There is some problem when a professional person borrows or excessively leans on somebody else's identity. Such counselors find it difficult to get themselves into the relationship in an honest and clean fashion because they are so preoccupied with acting like a master therapist. One is reminded of a popular lecturer in the 1970s who confessed that, as he gazed at his shaving mirror in the morning, he reminded himself that he was not Freud. That is an extraordinary but classic reaction of those who are uncertain of their identity.

Most of the "Don'ts"—those special rules that many therapists obsessively try always to keep in mind—do not exist in any absolute form. As therapists begin to trust their own instincts they do not feel bound by any of these commandments never to express their own feelings or their own opinions, or to answer questions that are proposed by clients. They find a certain freedom to let themselves show through in counseling, which is constructive and in the long run quite helpful to the counseling itself. It is perfectly safe, in other words, for therapists, when they are aware of themselves and able to listen to themselves while in relationship to others, to express their feelings in a number of situations. These include such occasions as:

When we do not understand what the client is trying to tell us or, for some reason that we cannot define, we feel that we are not in contact with them on a particular theme or point. When this occurs it is almost always more stressful to fake understanding than it is to admit that we are confused or that we have missed something. An honest expression of how we are experiencing the relationship at this point is perfectly appropriate. This can be done in a self-possessed and direct manner that expresses both our genuineness and our concern. Such a statement of our true feelings fits into the therapy; it is part of its truth and can only advance its purpose.

When we are distracted or cannot otherwise deal with some feeling that interferes with our capacity to respond to the other person. Such feelings operate on us whether we admit them or not. We begin, of course, by admitting them to ourselves. If this does not make them more manageable, it may be appropriate to mention these feelings in the course of the therapy. They are already present in the relationship because of their reality inside us. "I'm sorry but I cannot seem to hear you because I keep thinking about . . ." is a valid way of introducing this kind of annoyance. When expressing such feelings one must exercise care that the client will not misinterpret what we are trying to say. For example, counselors who prematurely tell their clients of their attraction to them may find that this kind of expression—made to clear the air—is interpreted by the client in a way different from that intended. Counselors must use good judgment and not express feelings that are ambiguous, that may easily be misinterpreted, or that serve only to relieve them but do not help the relationship itself.

When a genuine expression of interest or caring fits the flow of the relationship. We know that counseling seems to improve if we like our clients. Counselors have been notoriously hesitant to express spontaneous concern for clients out of fear that this would violate one of these famous "Don'ts." This may be to deny to the therapy an ingredient that is indispensable for its success. It is also very helpful for counselors to realize that it is not only acceptable but appropriate for them to express their own affection or concern for clients at times. It is a liberating experience for clients to realize that the counselor may like them but still does not try to take them over or possess them. This nonpossessive liking is a powerful component of successful therapy, just as it is in real life. It is the kind of response that mature persons are able to give because they no longer feel that they will necessarily become emotionally overentangled or will be lost if they let these true feelings surface. The counselor who discovers the freedom to express genuine feelings of caring also achieves a new freedom of spontaneity that removes much of the stress of counseling work.

Reasonably self-aware counselors come to trust their own experience because it has been refined through their own sensitivity and reflection. Mature persons can always trust their own feelings because these feelings are integrated into their personalities. The best advice for mature counselors is to allow them to feel their own way as far as expressing their own feelings is concerned. They possess a reliable sense of when to do this because they can hear what is going on inside themselves as well as within their various helping relationships. They know when to listen and when to speak; they do not let artificial rules outside themselves predetermine their behavior.

18

Supportive Psychotherapy

The Approach of Choice

The type of therapy practiced by most counselors should be predominantly supportive. This is not second-rate assistance but the sensible, possible approach for helpers who do not have the time or the luxury of selecting the people who seek out their assistance. Supportive help does not rule out the achievement of what is best termed limited but true insight. This insight is described as limited because it is restricted to explorations of the conscious and pre-conscious aspects of troubled persons' experience. That is to say, nonprofessionals will focus on those materials that can be recalled easily or with modest effort. They will avoid any attempts to tap into unconscious aspects of experience—that is, that area, entered only with highly skilled guides and with a real expenditure of effort. That is the proper province of long-term, insight-oriented, or uncovering therapy, in short, the task of thoroughly trained professionals in psychiatry and psychology.

Important Distinctions

Counselors with some training sometimes feel that the recommended choice of supportive therapy is a somewhat unnecessary fettering of their helpers' wings. In truth, however, most of the treatment being carried out by professionals is, because of circumstances such as time, counselee's aptitude, or mutual choice, that of the supportive variety. Some leading authorities, for example, the psychoanalyst Paul Dewald, have described long-term, insight-oriented treatment as on a par with elective surgery. Nonprofessionals will treat themselves and those who seek their assistance in a healthier way if they proceed with some appreciation of the differences between these approaches.

Insight-oriented treatment has as its goal the resolution of conflicts,

159

that is, the deep exploration of the unconscious psychological roots of the problems whose twisted outer growth emerges in patients' conscious lives in disguised and discomfiting ways. Therapists aim at unearthing these roots so that the individuals can, in a sense, break them open, examine, and render their psychological power neutral through understanding them. The objective of such treatment is the development of fresh ways of adaptation and reintegration of the personality. This goal is very demanding because it calls for the maturation, from within, of the patient, with all that this implies in the development of talents, better personal relationships with others, and greater freedom of choice about how the person will function.

Such treatment, which may take several years, also requires a major personal commitment of energy and time on the part of the person entering treatment. Not everyone can make such sacrifices because of their life and work circumstances. And, even if the latter are favorable, those seeking help may lack the psychological stamina to persevere in treatment. The decision to go ahead is made very carefully between therapist and patient and only after long and careful assessment of all significant internal and external factors.

It should also be observed that, if such serious treatment is undertaken without properly considering all the impinging elements, the process may fail, or result in stalemate, with the last state of the patients worse than the first. Their symptoms—the surface manifestations of their inner conflicts—may intensify and they may regress so that they become increasingly emotionally disabled.

In summary, the therapist undertaking this mode of treatment intends to enter the unconscious and must possess the finely honed skills to do this in a constructive and controlled way. The overall aim of reorganizing the personality is lofty, difficult, and extremely demanding. Nonprofessionals should not deliberately initiate such a treatment plan. Nor should they naïvely employ techniques—especially those offered in short courses or workshops, such as dream analysis—that may accidentally dislodge unconscious material.

Supportive Treatment

Supportive treatment, informed by a dynamic understanding of personality, views the conscious, current life situation of the other as the proper field for constructive intervention. Those who employ it avoid any strategies that might, even indirectly or accidentally, pierce the membrane of repression that keeps the contents of the unconscious out of the person's active awareness.

The purpose of such treatment is to relieve the symptoms experienced by the person seeking help. This is done without any attempt to alter or rebuild the person's basic character structure. Counselors aim at bringing about external behavioral changes within the present, psychologically flawed adaptation of the client.

Nonprofessionals, therefore, choose to strengthen the healthiest defenses of others, assisting them in a consciously insightful way to improve their functioning without descending to the depths of the unconscious or disturbing the latter in any way. We are not, as incidental if indispensable helpers, interested in rebuilding other persons but in assisting them to examine their conscious behavior and of altering it constructively. To this end, counselors may and should use any sensible and healthy device available to troubled persons to accomplish this goal. The latter will, in the course of this help, achieve insights but they will be into preconscious aspects of their motivation rather than into the remote unconscious sources of their behavior.

It is clear, in the course of daily life, that many people, through supportive treatment, learn to live much happier lives without changing their basic personalities. They may, as in physical illness, be forced to learn to live with chronic problems; that is, one of the outcomes of counseling may be that they accept and live more comfortably with themselves despite their psychological liabilities. Nonprofessionals must recognize that such persons, although functioning better within their limitations, may continue to have—and need to have—various neurotic symptoms. Helpers must always be careful about demanding that people give up their symptoms or, even worse, about promising them that they can help free them from their grip. The objective of supportive treatment for nonprofessionals is frequently that of helping others to weather a crisis successfully. And supportive techniques are the strategies of choice in dealing with people in crisis situations. (See the companion volume, *Crisis Counseling*.)

Some nonprofessionals, thinking that they would do better by attempting more in-depth therapy, not only make a mistake in that regard but also fail to utilize the many resources they already have at their disposal. Lawyers, for example, may provide enormously stabilizing responses by drawing on their technical expertise to help people understand and exercise their legal rights, or to straighten out their legal affairs, or put their wills in order. Pastoral counselors possess a rich armamentarium of responses from the spiritual tradition of those they work with that can strengthen their defenses enormously. Prayer, ascetic self-denial, the avoidance of the occasion of sin, reassurances about God's love and forgiveness: These, among countless others, can be strong and positive reinforcers for changing people's troubled and troubling behavior.

How They Differ

These basic approaches are employed differently by the counselor doing supportive work and the therapist engaged in insight-oriented treatment. The basic difference lies in the way the helpers use the instrumentality of themselves in the process. In insight-oriented treatment, for example, the therapist strives to maintain a neutral stance, keeping himself or herself a vaguer presence in the relationship for the express purpose of exerting a pull on unconscious material. The more neutral and the less sharply defined the therapist is in the relationship, the more the patient will project transference reactions onto them, thus forwarding the essential work of getting at unconscious conflicts.

In supportive approaches, however, counselors should avoid engaging in behavior that will, in effect, act as a poultice to draw out this buried dynamic material. They can feel freer to speak their own opinions, give measured advice, and, in other ways, remain concrete, well-defined personalities, thereby minimizing or dulling any magnetism for the iron filings of the unconscious. The less neutral we are, the less we challenge the main defenses, and the more we keep the focus where it belongs—on the current conscious stage of the person's life and activities. This strengthens positive rapport and helps to avoid the complications of regressive transference distortions that can be so dismaying to nonprofessionals. The latter can, in a real sense, function as their best disciplined selves; they can *be themselves* as long as they respect the overall dynamic realities of the relationship. In general, supportive counselors want to use the relationship to promote identification and to strengthen specific defenses.

By the latter, we mean that counselors should recognize the defensive system employed by the other and adapt to it in the process of giving help. If, for example, persons use intellectualization as a main defense, we may realize that they are thereby avoiding emotional content, but that this is, in what is certainly not the best of all possible worlds, the best they can do to manage their way through life. We may choose actively to strengthen that defense, perhaps by recommending books for them to read, rather than challenging and weakening a defense they need in order to keep their psychological balance. The same may be said of allowing persons to depend on us—literally, to lean on us—during a crisis period. While we might ordinarily view dependence on the counselor as less than ideal, we also recognize that this is indeed the most sensible way of managing this critical interval. Such techniques would not, of course, be employed in this way in insight-oriented treatment.

A Rule of Thumb, Repeated

It may be helpful to restate here the rule of thumb for nonprofessionals in understanding their commitment to the supportive approach. If we can define the person coming to see us as still in the role of our parishoner, our general medical patient, our bereaved mourner, or our pupil, we are on safe and solid ground. If the person becomes our therapy patient, we have shifted to a form of relationship that is beyond what we should attempt or engage in. When we sense that the needs of this person go far beyond what we can provide in a supportive relationship, we initiate referral to an appropriate professional resource.

Recommended Reading:

Adams, J. E. (1980). *Helps for Counselors: A Mini-Manual for Christian Counseling.* Grand Rapids, MI: Baker Book House.

Argelander, H. (1976). *The Initial Interview in Psychotherapy.* New York: Human Sciences Press.

Benjamin, A. (1981). *The Helping Interview.* Boston: Houghton Mifflin.

Biggs, D. A. (1987). *Foundations of Ethical Counseling.* New York: Springer-Verlag.

Blocher, D. H. (1987). *The Professional Counselor.* New York: MacMillan.

Book, H. E. (1988). Empathy: Misconceptions and Misuses in Psychotherapy. *American Journal of Psychiatry,* 145: 420–24.

Bragan, K. (1987). I and Thou: An Examination of Empathy. *Australian and New Zealand Journal of Psychiatry,* 21: 575–79.

Chused, J. F. (1987). Idealization of the Analyst by the Young Adult. *Journal of the American Psychoanalytic Association,* 35: 839–59.

Collins, G. R. (1986). *Innovative Approaches to Counseling.* Waco, TX: Word Books.

Combs, A. W. (1985). *Helping Relationships: Basic Concepts for the Helping Professions.* Boston: Allyn and Bacon.

Corey, G. (1984). *Issues and Ethics in the Helping Professions.* Monterey, CA: Brooks/Cole.

Derlega, V. J. and Berg, J. H. (eds.) (1987). *Self-Disclosure: Theory, Research, and Therapy*. New York: Plenum Press.

Diagnostic and Statistical Manual of Mental Disorders: DSM-III-R (1987). Washington, DC: American Psychiatric Association.

Donaghy, W. C. (1984). *The Interview: Skills and Applications*. Glenview, IL: Scott, Foresman.

Dorn, F. J., (ed.) (1986). *The Social Influence Process on Counseling and Psychotherapy*. Springfield, IL: Thomas.

Dryden, W. (1985). *Therapists' Dilemmas*. Cambridge: Hemisphere Publishing Corporation.

Evans, D. R. (1979). *Essential Interviewing: A Programmed Approach to Effective Communication*. Monterey, CA: Brooks/Cole.

Everstine, D. S. and Everstine, L. (1983). Communication Principles for High Stress or Dangerous Situations. In D. S. Everstine and L. Everstine, *People in Crisis: Strategic Therapeutic Interventions*. Brunner/Mazel.

Faustman, W. O. and Miller, D. J. (1987). Considerations in Prewarning Clients of the Limits of Confidentiality. *Psychological Reports*, 60: 195–98.

Felder, R. (1967). In *Counseling and Psychotherapy: Overview*. Arbuckle, D. S., (ed.). New York: McGraw-Hill.

Fonagy, P. (1984). *Personality, Theory, and Clinical Practice*. New York: Methuen.

Fortune, A. E. (1987). Grief Only? Client and Social Worker Reactions to Termination. *Clinical Social Work Journal*, 15: 159–71.

Friedman, M. S. (1985). *The Healing Dialogue in Psychotherapy*. New York: Jason Aronson.

Gartrell, N., Herman, J., Olarte, S., et al. (1986). Psychiatrist-Patient Sexual Contact: Results of a National Survey: I. Prevalence. *American Journal of Psychiatry*, 143: 1126–31.

Garrett, A. M. (1982). *Interviewing, Its Principles and Methods*. New York: Family Service Association of America.

George, R. (1986). *Counseling: Theory and Practice*. Englewood Cliffs, NJ: Prentice-Hall.

Gladstein, G. A. (1987). *Empathy and Counseling: Explorations in Theory and Research*. New York: Springer-Verlag.

Goldberg, C. (1980). *In Defense of Narcissism: The Creative Self in Search of Meaning*. New York: Gardner Press.

Gorden, R. L. (1980). *Interviewing: Strategy, Techniques, and Tactics*. Homewood, IL: Dorsey Press.

Greenspan, M. (1986). Should Therapists Be Personal? Self-Disclosure and Therapeutic Distance in Feminist Therapy. *Woman and Therapy*, 5: 5–17.

Hartman, C. and Reynolds, D. (1987). Resistant clients: Confrontation, Interpretation, and Alliance. *Social Casework*, 68: 205–13.

Hatcher, C. (1977). *Innovations in Counseling Psychology*. San Francisco: Jossey-Bass.

Havens, L. L. (1986). *Making Contact: Uses of Language in Psychotherapy*. Cambridge, MA: Harvard University Press.

Hedges, L. E. (1983). *Listening Perspectives in Psychotherapy*. New York: Jason Aronson.

Hummel, D. L. (1985). *Law and Ethics in Counseling*. New York: Van Nostrand Reinhold.

Hunt, G. T. (1987). *Interviewing: A Communication Approach*. New York: Holt, Rinehart, and Winston.

Ivey, A. E. (1978). *Microcounseling: Innovations in Interviewing, Counseling, Psychotherapy, and Psychoeducation*. Springfield, IL: Thomas.

Ivey, A. E. (1987). *Counseling and Psychotherapy: Integrating Skills, Theory, and Practice*. Englewood Cliffs, NJ: Prentice-Hall.

Jacobs, M. (1985). *Swift to Hear: Facilitating Skills in Listening and Responding*. London: SPCK.

Janis, I. L. (ed.) (1982). *Counseling on Personal Decisions: Theory and Research on Short-Term Helping Relationships*. New Haven: Yale University Press.

Josephs, L. (1988). A Comparison of Archeological and Empathic Modes of Listening. *Contemporary Psychoanalysis*, 24: 282–300.

Kemper, J. (1988). Deadlocking and Stalemating: Primitive Defense Mechanisms against Progression in Psychoanalysis. *American Journal of Psychoanalysis*, 48: 138–55.

Kernberg, O. F. (1984). *Severe Personality Disorders: Therapeutic Strategies*. New Haven: Yale University Press.

Kirsch, P. (1986). How They Cling Like Shadows: Object Relations and the Difficult Patient. *Psychotherapy Patient*, 3: 43–54.

Kir-Stimon, W. (1986). Boundaries: A Metaphoric View. *Psychotherapy Patient*, 2: 21–28.

Korchin, S. I. (1976). The Interview. In *Modern Clinical Psychology*. New York: Basic Books.

Kottler, J. A. (1986). *On Being a Therapist*. San Francisco: Jossey-Bass.

Kuhlman, T. L. (1984). *Humor and Psychotherapy*. Homewood, IL: Dow Jones Irwin.

Lawton, G. (1979). Neurotic Interaction between Counselor and Counselee. In *Helping Relationships: Basic Concepts for the Helping Professions*. Boston: Allyn and Bacon.

Lehmer, M. (1986). Court-Ordered Therapy: Making it Work. *American Journal of Forensic Psychology*, 4: 16–24.

Lowman, R. L. (1987). Occupational Choice as a Moderator of Psychotherapeutic Approach. *Psychotherapy*, 24: 801–08.

Mays, D. T. and Franks, C. M. (eds.) (1985). *Negative Outcomes in Psychotherapy and What to Do about It*. New York: Springer-Verlag.

MacKinnon, R. A. (1986). *The Psychiatric Evaluation in Clinical Practice*. Philadelphia: Lippincott.

Millen, L. and Roll, S. (1986). Common Impediments to Good Psychotherapy: Or Hell Is Other People. *Journal of Contemporary Psychotherapy*, 16: 115–20.

Moursund, J. (1985). *The Process of Counseling and Therapy*. Englewood Cliffs, NJ: Prentice-Hall.

Okun, B. F. (1987). *Effective Helping: Interviewing and Counseling Techniques*. Monterey, CA: Brooks/Cole.

Palombo, J. (1987). Spontaneous Self-Disclosures in Psychotherapy. *Clinical Social Work Journal,* 15: 107–20.

Pascal, G. R. (1983). *The Practical Art of Diagnostic Interviewing.* Homewood, IL: Dow Jones-Irwin.

Pasternak, S. A. (1988). The Clinical Management of Fees during Psychotherapy and Psychoanalysis. *Psychoanalytic Annals,* 18: 112–17.

Peterson, J. V. (1987). *Orientation to Counseling.* Newton, MA: Allyn and Bacon.

Redlich, F. C. (1986). The Use and Abuse of Power in Psychotherapy. *Psychiatric Annals,* 16: 637–39.

Schulman, E. D. (1978). *Intervention in Human Services.* St. Louis: Mosby.

Seligman, L. (1986). *Diagnosis and Treatment Planning in Counseling.* New York: Human Sciences Press.

Sharma, S. L. (1986). *The Therapeutic Dialogue: A Theoretical and Practical Guide to Psychotherapy.* Albuquerque: University of New Mexico Press.

Shea, S. C. (1988). *Psychiatric Interviewing: The Art of Understanding.* Philadelphia: Saunders.

Shectman, F. and Smith, W. H. (eds.) (1984). *Diagnostic Understanding and Treatment Planning: The Elusive Connection.* New York: John Wiley.

Skopec, E. W. (1986). *Situational Interviewing.* New York: Harper and Row.

Smith, J. T. (1988). Therapist-Patient Sex: Exploitation of the Therapeutic Process. *Psychiatric Annals,* 18: 59–63.

Stahler, G. J. and Eisenman, R. (1987). Psychotherapy Dropouts: Do They Have Poor Psychological Adjustment? *Bulletin of the Psychonomic Society,* 25: 198–200.

Strean, H. S. (1986). Why Therapists Lose Clients. *Journal of Independent Social Work,* 1: 7–17.

Strupp, H. H. (1973). On the Basic Ingredient of Psychotherapy. *Journal of Consulting and Clinical Psychology,* 41: 1–8.

Strupp, H. H. (1977). *Psychotherapy for Better or for Worse: The Problem of Negative Effects.* New York: Jason Aronson.

Talbott, J. A., ed. (1978). *The Chronic Mental Patient: Problems, Solutions, and Recommendations for a Public Policy.* Washington, DC: American Psychiatric Association.

Thomas, E. J. (1984). *Designing Interventions for the Helping Professions.* Beverly Hills, CA: Sage Publications.

Tolchin, J. (1987). Telephone Psychotherapy with Adolescents. *Adolescent Psychiatry,* 14: 332–41.

Tolor, A., (ed.) (1985). *Effective Interviewing.* Springfield, IL: C. C. Thomas.

Truax, C. B. and Carkhuff, R. B. (1967). *Toward Effective Counseling and Psychotherapy: Training and Practice.* Chicago: Aldine Press.

Vriend, J. (1985). *Counseling Powers and Passions: More Counseling Techniques That Work.* Alexandria, VA: American Association for Counseling and Development.

Yokin, C. and Berman, J. S. (1987). Third-Party Payment and the Outcome of Psychotherapy. *Journal of Consulting and Clinical Psychology,* 55: 571–76.

PART
3

19

Problems of Healthy People

Stress is a somewhat mysterious if pervasive concept. Everybody has some ideas about it, most of us can recognize it when we experience it, but no one can give a completely satisfactory definition. We can judge stress in its effects, and research has helped us to understand something about its causes. It is, however, a concept used to describe both our inner and outer experience concerning reactions that are both physical and psychological. The notion of stress fits the human person, catching the varying qualities of tension that necessarily surround any kind of active living. Stress, like a headwind in sailing, can also be a positive and necessary life experience.

Counselors must deal with their own stresses while they deal with the stresses of other persons. In the work of some counselors, the stress is strong and almost without letup. Chaplains, doctors, and persons working in correctional institutions or in environments where there is extreme pressure for diagnosis or administration may find that stress is a large part of their daily diet. It is, in other words, an occupational hazard for many counselors. Either the persons with whom they work are under severe stress or they find that they themselves experience it because of the urgency of the demands for decision and response that are made on them.

One of the mechanisms most often employed in getting through the situations of life is denial, a common denominator of all psychological defenses. This does not necessarily make denial a bad thing. Were we not able to deny certain aspects of our experience, it would be almost impossible to carry on in any kind of serious emergency situation. We can, however, employ denial to protect ourselves against examining the stress that we need to look at in order to be well adjusted in our life and work. We can end up wearing psychological blinders so dark and stiff that we miss other things quite important for us if we are to be effective in working with others. Stress deserves examination for the clues it gives us about ourselves and our work with others.

Only a basically healthy person can live an average life well. All too often, we associate strength of personality with the heroic dimensions of adventure and challenge. Some persons, however, court great challenges for neurotic reasons. It is quite another thing to lead an undramatic, quiet, and, one might say, common sort of life. Living in this fashion does not attract publicity, headlines, or perhaps any great financial reward, but it does demand a sound sense of oneself and a capacity to withstand stress in its constant, everyday forms.

There is plenty of stress associated with being a teacher, a husband or a wife, a mother or a father; this stress arises from what we usually regard as the healthiest conditions of life. When persons are in a close relationship with each other—such as the relationship of husband and wife—they necessarily experience the stresses that go along with what most persons prize as one of life's greatest blessings. People who are close to each other can easily hurt each other; they also miss each other more when they are apart; they feel life more intensely than they could had they remained at a distance from persons. It is the same for persons with great integrity who are dedicated to their work. The kind of performance given, the sincerity of the commitments under which the individual works—all these become more important and, therefore, more capable of producing stress than they do in the lives of persons who approach work more casually or with less responsibility. This is why it takes a healthy person to live an average life well.

Adjustment Disorders

This is the description given by psychiatry to the kinds of problems that are found in the lives of fundamentally normal people. These are to the emotions what the common cold is to the physical body of the ordinary individual. They arise in the situations that, sooner or later, everyone must face and adjust to at the various stages of life. The adult stage is characterized by events that have the following elements in common: (1) a difficult situation; (2) a fundamentally normal person; (3) the failure of the psychological mechanisms with which the individual ordinarily handles difficulties.

In practice, this means the kind of problem or situation that would upset most people. That rough, thumbnail description includes a great deal of human activity. In other words, these are the problems experienced on a wide scale by most people. It is important for counselors to be able to distinguish between these problems and problems of a more serious and disabling nature. The counselor also profits from understanding this type of difficulty in his or her own life.

Quite often the counselor only sees the symptoms of these transient episodes. Often such distress signals get the response of reassurance—the "buck up and carry on" advice—that denies them a chance to explore just why this situation should be so difficult for them. Persons experiencing these disturbances cannot quite tell what is wrong with them. They know that they are different and they recognize the presence of reactions or behaviors that are not ordinarily characteristic of them. Mere reassurance often undercuts the person while overdiagnosis may lead to a graver interpretation of the person's condition than is necessary; both approaches are anything but constructive in the situation.

It is more helpful if the counselor listens for the kinds of events that are usually associated with adjustment disorders, occurrences that can easily be identified in the life history of the individual seeking help. This underscores one of the reasons that it is helpful to have an understanding of the context of the client's life. Often the background information contains clues that are extraordinarily helpful in making a mature and prudent judgment about the difficulties the client is experiencing. One of the features that the helper should be alert to is:

Loss: The loss, to have a notable effect on the individual at the time he or she is seeking the counselor, may not even be in the immediate past. Losses are of various kinds, ranging from the death of a loved one to the loss of a position, a familiar living place, or one's reputation. We have already seen that until the person can recognize and admit the loss, it is difficult to carry out the work of mourning through which the individual reintegrates himself into the continuing process of life. Depressive reactions to stress are to be expected in the lives of persons who sustain serious losses. Sometimes an interval of several months, or in some cases even of years, may occur between the actual loss and this response. In other words, at times the fundamental loss is denied or disguised so that the person never does deal with it on a psychological level. An event then takes place that lays bare the initial wound or symbolizes it in some fashion, and denial no longer works. Here we have a case of a postponed failure of adjustive mechanisms and a consequent uncovering of the formerly masked stress.

Typical of these situations are the depressions persons experience on anniversaries or during holidays when their isolation and loneliness is heightened. There is a retrospective aspect to such symptoms and the counselor should not be surprised to find that the loss is more remote than he or she would have supposed. As one allows the person to talk, one can pay close attention to the amount of emotion that is connected with the losses described.

Threats to Self-Image

We all make our way through life in terms of the picture of our own personalities we develop over the years. We identify ourselves according to the strengths and weaknesses we allow ourselves to recognize in our personalities. We hold on to that picture, and we may be subjected to severe stress if our regard for our own persons is shaken by some life event. Any threat to self-confidence or self-esteem can lead to a depressive reaction in an adult. If we can no longer preserve intact the image we have of ourselves, we become vulnerable to the kinds of situational disturbances previously discussed. Challenge or take away a person's self-esteem and the depression that follows will be a clear sign of the sudden onslaught of stress.

Self-confidence and self-esteem may be attacked in many ways, of course, and counselors can only allow their clients to tell the story of their own lives as simply and truthfully as possible. When individuals speak of their self-esteem they speak of a very particular and significant view of themselves. We cannot make unwarranted suppositions about the self-concepts of others from the outside; we can only let others tell us about themselves. Listening is the key; restraint of our own impulses to support or reassure is equally important if we are to give enough room to normal people to solve their own problems.

Helpers can make it easier to explore the recent past by general questions about the events that have taken place lately that seem to be related to the client's coming for assistance. General and understanding statements inviting recollection of recent occurrences lead quickly to some experience of loss. That loss is the core of the problem with which the individual is attempting to deal.

The fact that people carry on under enormous burdens is one of the continuing mysteries of psychology. Some individuals can sustain very severe blows and yet seem to right themselves and handle life with continuing self-confidence. Others find that the struggle is always a difficult one and that any single stress may throw them off balance so that it is hard to continue their ordinary activities. Counselors need to reflect on the soundings they take about the losses in another person's life. Clients are very helpful in this regard because they are anxious to talk to someone who will be understanding about the experience that has cost them so much. Their capacity to react one way or the other depends on many factors; only as counselors listen carefully can they develop a satisfactory sense of the client's strengths.

The first focus is on the particular situation that precipitated the problem. Was it abrupt, unprepared for, unsoftened by support or understanding that was expected? All these elements can alter the impact of loss in a notable way. Closely associated with this is the personality structure of the individual. The normal range of personality is very wide; so too is the range of the ability to respond to the losses that affect everyone in life. Past experience is also an important consideration. Individuals who have been through a number of difficulties, who have literally learned the hard way about life's power to alter or take away the things we prize most, are generally better prepared to deal with a new experience. The ordinary stresses of life are also complicated if there are no available solutions; most of us cope better with problems when there are alternatives from which we can choose. It is only as choices are removed completely that the stress may have its greatest effect on us.

How many other stresses is the person experiencing at the same time? An accumulation of stressful experiences will naturally be far more injurious to the individual than a single stress in an otherwise well-balanced life. Helpers need a feeling for the total picture in order to gauge the kind and amount of assistance that may be most significant for the counselee. It is always dangerous to shrug off persons as self-pitying, or to fail to appreciate their difficulties because we think we know how people should react. As we allow them to tell the full truth about themselves, we develop the special appreciation that is needed to help them regain their balance in dealing with their problems.

The Symptoms

Anxiety is one of the chief psychological reactions in adjustment disorders. This is manifested in many ways from tension to an obsessive preoccupation with a detail or obligation of life. At times persons experience restlessness and irritability or find that it is difficult to concentrate on their ordinary work. Anxiety has a hundred homely faces.

It is also not unusual for persons to complain about depressive symptoms such as not being able to sleep or of not being able to eat regularly. Somatic complaints are frequently rather vague, including generalized fatigue, abdominal pains, or the other physiological symptoms. People talk to themselves and to us through these complaints.

Occasionally persons are surprised by new and unexpected behaviors in their lives. They find that they are trying to deal with situations by activities that compound their problems. These efforts are usually described by psychologists as *maladaptive*. Persons under stress are attempting to solve their problems but the choice of strategies often makes them worse. In their effort to reduce their anxiety they may do things that cause them other difficulties. They may seek other satisfactions to make up for the loss they have experienced. For example, the individual who begins to get into fights in order to settle difficulties at work is exhibiting maladaptive behavior. The person who finds that he is taking time off from work to spend in some vain and expensive pursuit of relaxation has chosen a poor solution to his basic difficulty. So too an individual may psychologically make up for what he has been deprived of by drinking or promiscuous sexual behavior. These behaviors sometimes suddenly appear in the lives of persons who have suffered a recent loss. A widower who starts drinking is a good example.

Maladaptive behaviors affect the work and relationships of persons under stress; they give clear signs to others that some difficulty is present. There are stresses that are related to an event that is limited by time itself, such as the length of a trial. Other stresses are not of this order, however, and as they continue the counselor may observe an increase in the symptomatic signs of an adjustment reaction. These need to be read carefully and always in terms of the context of the person's life.

Research

A number of research projects have explored the kinds of life experiences that seem to produce or multiply the experience of stress. A study of over five hundred middle-aged men in Finland who had either survived a heart attack or died from one showed that about two-thirds had experienced stressful life changes within a year before their attacks. In a report published in *The American Journal of Psychiatry* (November, 1973), the researchers suggested that "if many of these subjects had not been exposed to this significant increase in demands on their lives, they might not have developed an infarct [heart attack] or have died at the time they did." The authors also suggested that those involved in the helping professions should assess the recent life changes in middle-aged persons if they want to improve their accuracy in predicting or preventing heart attacks. The same researchers had previously found that individuals were more likely to become ill or to have an accident within a two-year period following major life changes.

This appreciation of the major role of change in precipitating adjustment reactions of a severe nature parallels the work of Holmes and Rahe who developed what is called *the social readjustment rating scale*. This gives a list of forty-three life events associated with varying amounts of disruption in the average person's life. The scale lists these stresses and gives them a numerical value so that, theoretically at least, one could add up the number of stresses present in any client's life. In this list the following categories are found:

Occurrences	Numerical Impact
Death of Spouse	100
Divorce	73
Marital Separation	65
Jail Term	63
Death of Close Family Member	63
Personal Injury or Illness	53
Marriage	50
Fired at Work	47
Marital Reconciliation	45
Retirement	45
Change in Health of Family Member	44
Pregnancy	40
Sex Difficulties	39
Gain of New Family Member	39
Business Readjustment	39

There is a remarkable overlap here with the list published in the Finnish study. These lists have been widely reprinted and, while it is obviously a scientific effort in its very preliminary stages, it does dramatically chart for us the impact of stress in the life of the average person.

Not all experts agree on the way such information should be used. Dr. Holmes suggests, for example, that an accumulation of two hundred or more life change units in a single year would constitute more stress than the average individual could withstand. Anybody working closely with such persons would wisely suggest that they avoid adding units of change to their life and perhaps work out some of the emotional complications of these situations with the help of the counselor.

Others believe that it is not the absolute number of stresses that is important but the manner in which the individual is able to handle them. Dr. Lawrence Hinkle of the Cornell University Medical School in New York suggests that some people who have many illnesses are particularly susceptible to the effects of life events, and others seem almost immune to the effects of stress. This latter group, he described in an interview in this way: "They seem to have a shallow attachment to people, goals or groups, and they readily shifted to other relationships when established relationships were disrupted. Others endured prolonged deprivations, boredom or sustained hard work without obvious adverse effects." The key for some of these people, according to Dr. Hinkle, is the fact that they realized their own limits and avoided situations that would tax them beyond their ability to respond.

It is clear that an inspection of the life events of those who come to us for help will broaden our capacity to respond to them. The counselor must be ready to see the individual in the context of the occurrences, especially the major changes, that have taken place in their lives. These changes can produce stress whether they are positive or negative. It might be wise for the counselor to note that his own toleration of stress in working with others can be severely complicated if he is sustaining other life changes that are making great demands.

The counselor should avoid reassurance or supportive therapy that ignores the person's highly individual perception of the meaning of these events. The effect on the individual's self-esteem is also important in these considerations. Persons need assistance in identifying a loss and its meaning in their lives, as well as the continued understanding that enables them to put these experiences into proper perspective. This is the best gift that a counselor can give to a person experiencing the difficulty of adjusting to a major change in life.

20

Translating the Languages of Inner Trouble

If a generalized anxiety disorder represents the undifferentiated, unshaped, and somewhat unpredictable experience of relatively pure anxiety, the other symptom disorders channel it into distinctive shapes and patterns through the development of specific symptoms. No one is completely happy with the categories of diagnosis by which these neuroses are sorted out and roughly described, and yet these classifications, despite their shortcomings, do provide some means by which we may better understand and respond to persons who speak to us about their conflicts in the varied language of neurosis. In many ways, the counselor's task resembles that of a person learning another language. It is possible, for example, to become an expert on the fine points of grammar and to amass an extensive and obscure vocabulary. One can be a technician of a language, a master of information about language, and despite this accomplishment, not speak it very well.

It is helpful for counselors to have as much scientific information as possible about these disorders, but it is essential that they be able to understand their language as the vehicle of painful human communication. Counselors need to feel for the expressive side of such symptoms; their task remains that of understanding them rather than controlling them by excessive intellectualizing. As counseling is understood, not as a technical tool or a competitive game between helper and client, and as it is better appreciated as a special human exchange filled with symbols and shifting currents, counselors feel more comfortable, deal with their own stress more constructively, and are able to respond with a far greater effectiveness to those persons with whom they work.

Most of the disorders that we will discuss are familiar to experienced counselors. Those who are just beginning counseling work or who do it incidentally in connection with another occupation will recognize the symptoms and may begin to put them together in such a way that their meaning emerges more clearly. They may begin, in other words, to understand this special language that distressed people are speaking to us all the time. As we penetrate it with understanding we become more confident and less hurried in our manner of dealing with these people. We take a larger view and are able to see and respond to the person experiencing the symptoms rather than just to the symptoms or to the problem side of things.

Somatoform Illness/Conversion Disorder

Colloquially, the word *hysterical* is used to describe someone who is running around shouting or weeping uncontrollably. This is not, of course, the meaning that it has in conditions known as a somatoform illness, termed a conversion disorder. The latter offers us a clear example of the way the general dynamics of neurotic symptom behaviors work. In this case the unconscious mechanism allows the inner unresolved psychological conflict—the source of anxiety—to be represented by a physical symptom. The anxiety, in other words, is no longer of the undifferentiated variety. It is no longer the free-floating phenomenon we have discussed before. It is shaped, instead, into a specific symptom that bears the weight of the conflicts—indeed, tells the world about it—while relieving the patient's anxiety at the same time. It is easier to have a well-defined somatic complaint one can complain about specifically than an uneasiness of the spirit to which one cannot readily point.

The symptom is a symbol of the conflict, an image for our contemplation. It may be, for example, a paralysis of a hand or a foot. This can occur, thereby demonstrating the close affinity between symbol and reality, in a person whose conflict centers on aggression. The hand that would strike or the foot that would kick becomes the vehicle for the neurotic symptom. What makes sense of this conversion of an inner conflict into an outer problem? The genius of neurosis is the way it handles anxiety beneath the surface. In a double stroke it makes it difficult for the person to carry out the threatening impulse and it provides a kind of compromise about the internal conflicts. If, for example, a person suddenly loses the capacity to speak, he or she can no longer become involved in certain types of conflict. If such persons can no longer hear, they are removed to an even safer psychological distance from the kind of psychological warfare that may surround them.

These conversion symptoms are often in the form of anesthesias—losses of sensation in some limb or through a form of blindness or deafness. Unless the neurotic individual is an anatomist, the loss of sensation will not follow the nerve distribution in the body. There is a clear message about the nature of the problem in that. Paralysis of muscles, or groups of muscles, as well as various ticks, convulsions, or strange, unusual movements or postures, may also serve as the symbolic symptoms in this conversion difficulty.

The vocabulary of conversion is very rich, and as we learn to understand it we realize how ill-advised we are to focus too directly on the symptom and how disastrous it could be if we tried directly or with excessive determination to stop or change this special behavior. Patience and understanding—a willingness to listen to this language of neurosis—permit us to place these activities in the life context of the experiencing person. We may then respond to the persons who author the symptom rather than just to the signals they are producing for us.

Correlates of the Conflict

Students of the problem of conversion symptoms have observed that there are certain other behaviors or attitudes that may go along with this problem. It is helpful for counselors to be aware of these because they fill in details that make the picture more understandable. For example, people with conversion reactions often have sexual problems as well. It is true that some of these sexual problems, such as frigidity or impotence, may be conversion symptoms themselves. It is not surprising, however, to find clients who have difficulties in their sexual adjustment speaking this special neurotic language of conversion. It is enough to make the mature counselor pause about focusing too directly on solving the sexual problem, a common attitude in our culture where a little learning about sex is indeed a dangerous thing.

Secondly, persons suffering from this particular difficulty may exhibit a somewhat bland attitude toward the problem and the disability that it causes them. They do not seem to be very much concerned about what the average person would find extremely inconvenient. This has been labeled "la belle indifference." Such persons sometimes employ dissociative styles in their relationships, and they may also do this with the counselor. They may, for example, behave seductively without seeming to realize the impact of their behavior on those around them. In the same way, they seem to crave attention and also are considered by many to be highly suggestible.

The *secondary gain* that arises from this difficulty is one of the great signals by which we may understand and interpret this problem with accuracy and sensitivity. There is a secondary gain connected with any kind of illness, but in these situations one feels that it is of particular importance and advantage to those involved. Secondary gain includes sympathy, concern, and all the other aspects of being the one on whom everybody else has to wait or worry about. The person on the bed becomes the central dominating figure, not only in the household but in the lives of people all around. Being sick with a conversion symptom frees somebody from certain tasks that would otherwise have to be performed. It may also even allow some compensation for the entailed loss of work.

The secondary gain is the core of the adjustment around which we can see many other behaviors cluster. Unless we try to put the situation into greater perspective, we may miss this information and may misinterpret the events because we have distorted the meaning of the illness. Some people are forced to build their own lives around the secondary gain that this kind of person manages to achieve. You can see this in the people who are made to delay their own plans, such as marriage, to care for a person whose illness is, in fact, a way of maintaining control over the individual who might otherwise depart. There is a web of psychological effects that one can make out and trace back patiently to the person who is literally in the eye of this psychological storm.

Current Understandings

The language counselors encounter with these disorders is puzzling and yet eminently human. Somatoform disorders may be understood because they are expressed in their native tongue, that of physical symptoms that seem to indicate an underlying bodily problem. Medical consultation will support that there are, however, no demonstrable organic findings to support this, nor any identifiable physiological structures with which it can be associated. The prudent clinician, examining all the evidence, judges that the symptoms are the special vocabulary expressing unspoken psychological factors or conflicts.

It is possible that, as noted in Talbott (p. 534), "difficulties in acquiring the capacity to verbalize may leave the individual developmentally fixated at a predominantly somatic level of experiencing, conceptualizing, and communicating psychological conflict." For such persons, this language may be the only one in which they can speak of their inner pain.

It is also possible that individuals learn to express themselves this way in their family of origin because "physical symptoms may gradually become a route to obtain nurturance, attention, love, and support that might not otherwise be forthcoming" (Talbott, loc. cit.). When counselors suspect that they are overhearing this kind of language, they should, as in other serious and complex matters, refer the person for psychiatric evaluation and treatment.

Things to Think About

Counselors may begin by reflecting on the compromise nature of most of the neurotic symptomatology with which they will deal. There is a message in it about the second-best nature of the solution represented by such problems. Through neurotic symptoms people are striving to solve their life problem—something bothering them on the unconscious level—but their solution is far from ideal. In a real sense, they are caught between the world in which they live and the anxiety that is generated by their own inner conflict. What emerges tells the story of this dilemma in symbolic form.

Neurotic language is fairly clear in the sense that the symptoms are sharp, distinct entities from which most neurotics want to separate themselves. They do not, in other words, recognize how they are speaking to themselves through this symptom formation. What they see is a problem that does not seem like themselves, a difficulty that they cannot consciously explain or rationally interpret. It is something they want to be rid of and that is why they come for help.

This is why an effort to interpret the client's behavior reasonably is not usually effective. It may make sense intellectually, but if the person could make the emotional connections, he or she would be able to handle the problem without assistance. The art of helping effectively lies in being able to translate the neurotic version of the psychological conflict that people speak to us about through their symptom life. It is true that some people never do get very much insight into their neurotic difficulties. They settle for having them because the neurosis accomplishes the original purpose of saving them from experiencing greater anxiety, and because they just may not be able to come to terms with what will always seem to them a mysterious and difficult aspect of their personality.

Wise counselors understand that a complete cure of a person's neurosis may not be possible or desirable. Since neuroses are not totally disabling, we should not be surprised if, in a sense, people seem to get used to them and are reluctant to probe very deeply into themselves in order to uncover basic conflicts. Neuroses pursue an erratic course, sometimes seeming to disappear and at other times seeming more intense than usual. It takes a long and understanding look into a person's life in order to appreciate the role that any set of symptoms is playing. They are not to be forcibly changed nor quickly transformed unless the individual is ready and able to follow through in the course of treatment.

There is, in other words, a question of judgment involved that is quite significant in working with patients who exhibit neurotic symptoms. One can never be absolutely sure of such decisions and yet, weighing the complex of factors involved, the counselor must make some determination about what courses of treatment the individual is ready to follow.

Seeing the whole person is a vital aspect of working effectively with such individuals. This is why the ability to listen, the sensitivity to the entire case history, and the readiness to read even the seemingly obscure messages of the language of neurosis increase a counselor's effectiveness manyfold. Insisting on curing everybody, focusing excessively on symptoms, and taking too much responsibility for the outcome of counseling may only increase the stress experienced both by counselor and client.

21

Other Dialects of Symptomatic Language

We get an even better feel for the way in which the symptomatic individual adjusts to conflict when we look at the symptoms that puzzle and frustrate so many observers—those of the phobias. Everyone experiences irrational fears, but most relatively mature people are able to manage their lives without having these interfere with them in any marked way. It is interesting to note that the psychological mechanism beneath the minor irrational fears of healthy people is the same as that found in more troubled persons who seek help because of the way a phobia interferes with their life or work. We all, in other words, speak this dynamic language at one time or another. We may not be aware of its meaning but there is a similar kind of psychological significance in our experience of it as that which we discover in those who come to us for help.

Pathological Fear

A person suffering from a phobia experiences what is called pathological fear. This is originally and unconsciously associated with some situation that gave rise to an inner psychological conflict. The phobic mechanism works by displacing this anxiety onto some other situation or object. The person can then fear this latter situation as a substitute for facing what would be so anxiety producing in the original difficulty. Thus people can fear riding in certain conveyances, being in certain kinds of rooms, or having certain kinds of pets. These specific phobias represent the distillation of another very strong fear that is associated with an unresolved and unattended inner conflict.

Whatever the object of the phobia may be, it does symbolize the original source or anxiety. Here again we have the striking of a compromise, that common feature of neurotic adjustment. People suffering from phobias actually substitute the experience of fear for the experience of anxiety. They would rather be afraid of a specific, identifiable object or situation than be hounded by a nameless and vague kind of anxiety. They are uncomfortable but in a different and more acceptable way. They know, at least on the intellectual level, that what they now fear cannot really hurt them because they can do something to avoid it. They make their anxiety manageable by displacing it onto some place or object that they can avoid. They are thereby able to control the situation and, through this, their own experience of anxiety.

Counselors suffer from the widespread temptation to interpret the conflict in terms of the kind of phobia the individual experiences. Most people are familiar with the long list of phobias to which Greek prefixes were once added—such things as claustrophobia (fear of closed places) or agoraphobia (fear of open places)—because the symbolic connection is often quite striking. This is the same kind of temptation to which minor novelists, with a smattering of Freudian understanding, sometimes succumb in motivating their characters. Thus one can understand a phobia about subway riding for a young girl, not only because of the cultural worry associated with the safety of this mode of transportation, but because sexual analogies can easily be drawn with the train, the darkened tunnel, and the excitement and stimulation of the trip.

It is very tricky to try to interpret the symbolic meaning of the phobia, and the temptation to do so should be repudiated. It is much safer to listen patiently and compassionately than it is to demonstrate how clever one can be. The problem is that the same phobia may, in different persons, represent very different kinds of conflicts. Counselors who relish the role of master interpreter of the language of neurosis may make more mistakes than they expect. It is very easy to be wrong because so much depends on the individual life history of the person coming for help.

Treatment Approaches

In the area of phobias, behavior modification has been used with great claims of success. This has resulted in freeing people from the kinds of fears that have kept them from being able to enjoy or participate in life more fully. Counselors may also be attracted to using this form of therapy because the results can be so dramatic and so relieving to persons who have suffered for an extended period of time. Behavior modification, however, only *sounds* easy, and the careful planning and carrying out of such treatment requires expert knowledge and technique. Counselors must know what they are doing in order to make this their choice of treatment. They should also remember the qualities of personal concern, associated with all forms of therapy, that are extremely important in considering whether to use any of the methodology of behavior modification.

It is also important to recognize that the vocal critics of behavior modification suggest that, in phobias, the language of the problem is never really understood and that one symptomatic symbol may merely be exchanged for another. One should not automatically rule out the usefulness of behavior modification, however, merely on such philosophical or theoretical bias. That something is not the perfect cure means that it is like every other cure, medical and psychological, with which we are familiar; it does not mean that it is not helpful. There may well be situations, especially in extremely crippling phobias, when its use will be dictated. Sensible consultation is clearly desirable, just as it would be in taking responsibility for any other specific form of treatment.

At times, when obsessive rituals and anxiety reach an intolerable stage, it may be important to see that the person is hospitalized until the severity of the symptomatic complaint has lessened to an acceptable level. Counselors should also make referrals to family therapy for those close to the afflicted person. This has proved very helpful in reducing the marital discord that can result from the disorder and offers general support to loved ones who can be severely tried by the presence of this problem in the close quarters of family life.

The language of phobias is a bewildering and a complex one. Phobias give a shape to anxiety by changing it into fear but, unlike many other psychological phenomena, they can spread and, at times, can even seem to be catching. In the latter case, the companion or person who cares for an individual suffering from a phobia can become quite anxious about the person's success in accomplishing tasks that are filled with fear. For example, companions who bring clients for counseling may find that many of their reactions center around the very thing about which the phobic person is afraid. It is not contagious, of course, in the same way a disease is, but there is little doubt that phobic persons can touch off anxiety, not only in those around them but also in the counselors who work with them. Therefore, counselors ought to recognize it as a possibility because it can complicate and interfere with the therapy.

Phobias can also spread from one situation to another. Gradually, a person may blot out all external stimulation or travel as the number of objects or situations that give rise to fear multiply. Such persons may end up prisoners in their own home or in their own room. Some indication of the intensity of the anxiety with which they are dealing is derived from the multiple experience of avoidance they create for themselves.

Counselors who have some appreciation of the dynamics of the phobic neurosis will not be surprised by the presence of the characteristic defenses in the therapeutic situation itself. The classic mechanisms employed by phobic persons are those of *displacement* and *symbolization*. These are at the very heart of the phenomenon; without these psychological means the neurosis could not be established as a defense at all. Displacement and symbolization make the phobic neurosis work. Counselors should not be surprised to find these mechanisms operative in the course of counseling. It could hardly be otherwise.

Beyond that, counselors should expect these clients to use projection somewhat extensively. The whole idea is to get their fears outside of them. As MacKinnon and Michels (p. 153) note: "Like the paranoid, the phobic patient uses relatively primitive defenses, with denial playing a prominent role. He thinks concretely, focusing on the external environment rather than his inner feelings, and keeps secrets from the interviewer. However, in contrast to the paranoid patient, the phobic maintains reality testing." A counselor will feel the effects of this defense; it may, in fact, be used directly against the helper but the sensitive counselor will be able to keep this in the perspective of the overall behavior of the person. Persons suffering from phobias may repress their hostile feelings and present themselves at times as almost naïve innocents who invest a great deal of trust in what they presume will be the magical powers of the counselor or other helper to assist them in overcoming their difficulty. This is one of the faces of their adjustment. It is a way of relating to the counselor that displays their unconscious tactics and that can easily incorporate the unwary helper into their whole defensive symptom.

Avoidance

At the very core of all phobic neurotic behavior is a massive effort to avoid anxiety and to sidestep the conflict that gives rise to it. The phobic patient tries to get anxiety into a corner that can then be carefully avoided. Counselors should expect to encounter this strong avoidance behavior in many different ways during the course of therapy. It is another way in which the language of neurosis is directly spoken.

These clients, with an almost paranoidlike reactivity, seem to sense danger and to move very cautiously in their relationship with the helper. There are many manifestations of this, many signals, in other words, that make the difficulty quite clear to the counselor who understands the language. These include the following kinds of behaviors:

The avoidance will be expressed in the kind of resistance to moving forward that these clients can express in counseling interviews. The counselor may feel this resistance and recognize it as part of the pattern of avoidance that so characterizes the phobic patient's way of dealing with anxiety-provoking material.

Resistance will be expressed in a variety of ways. These clients may seem to forget certain things and so manage not to tell the counselor significant details that are important for a total understanding of this psychological problem. It is important, for example, to understand when and how this experience of a phobia first began. The context for the onset of the difficulty frequently provides a dynamic picture of great significance. It may be related to some events, a series of life-style changes, big decisions, or the possible change in relationships around the client. Whatever it is, the onset will be closely related to the governing dynamics. When the client leaves out these details, or cannot seem to remember them, avoidance in the form of resistance is clearly present.

These clients may also steer the conversation away from important topics, displaying the deft footwork that enables them to stay so far away from anxiety-producing stimuli. They may do this very subtly, however, and counselors may realize that they have been led up a blind alley only after they have arrived there. They have not recognized that this is exactly where the client wants to be.

The client may refuse to speak. This is a classic form of resistance that has obvious dynamic significance. Such clients are behaving in front of the counselor exactly the way they behave in the grip of this neurosis. The counselor can experience and almost feel the outlines of it in the course of the relationship.

Counselors should be aware of the phobic client's typical maneuver, which can seem so inoffensive, of requesting permission not to talk about such subjects. Counselors may find themselves agreeing to these arrangements because they feel sorry for such clients and do not wish to disturb them further. This, of course, is another way in which these persons are able to avoid confronting their conflict and so keep their anxiety at bay. Counselors create their own failures when they become accomplices in this defense.

It is not surprising to find such clients telling of self-treatments. They buy books, read articles, and sometimes seem ready to try almost anything in order to cure themselves. Some observers have noted that these clients are collectors of treatments; they can tell the counselor, at great length, about the different ways they have experimented in trying to deal with their problems. Again, such behaviors must be seen in the context of the overall difficulty and recognized as the symbols of avoidance behavior they truly are.

It is also characteristic of persons suffering from this difficulty to strike bargains with themselves. For example, if they are afraid of going above a certain floor in a building, they will make a deal with themselves to go halfway. This is a way of doing something but not really getting close to the tight circle of fear that symbolizes their conflict for them. Such a compromise can sound like a brave effort, or even progress, to counselors unless they understand how characteristic these "deals" are in this neurotic problem.

Helpers understand this disorder more deeply if they can identify the secondary gains associated with the avoidance behavior. This gives a sense of the pattern of the person's life and may point to the area of sensitivity, whether it is family relationships, business conflicts, or concern about their own behavior. Counselors who take a longer and larger view are much more able to assemble an accurate picture of these persons than those who focus only on the symptoms.

A Role for Reassurance

Counselors may be called upon to offer a good deal of reassurance at certain times to these clients. This can come through recognizing with them the fact that other people have had these experiences, that it is not unusual for them to have such concerns; in other words, that the counselor does comprehend and is able to express, without censure or disdain, an appreciation of what their life means to them. Frequently these people seem rather desperate and ask either explicitly for equivalently something like, "Can you help me?" or "Am I going crazy?" These are questions that do not have literal answers. They are symbolic of the enormous concern the clients feel about their lives. The counselor's response is made not to the content of the question but to the level of concern. This is always appropriate and will, in itself, offer the kind of reassurance that the person may need in order to be able to move forward.

It is quite important for counselors themselves to remain calm. They will often feel their own anxiety being spurred by the phobic concerns of these patients, who can even penetrate the defenses of the counselor. When this happens, and the counselor himself becomes anxious, the counseling is upset. This represents a triumph for the avoidance techniques of the person, is self-defeating, and greatly increases the stress on the counselor. Only when counselors control their own reactions are they able to function effectively in assisting persons very slowly and carefully to come closer to the significance of the phobias that plague their lives.

Counselors may wisely ask: How much anxiety can this person stand at this time? The answer will help them decide on the level of response and the effort to develop insight that they will employ in the course of counseling. When dealing with people who have already substituted fear for anxiety, counselors are walking on an emotional minefield where their tread must be carefully measured. They must move forward but at a pace that interacts sensibly with the experience of the client.

It is not unusual for phobic patients to experience bouts of depression in the course of their treatment. This should neither surprise nor dismay counselors. The fact that these people experience depression is generally a sign that something is going on, that they are coming to terms with their difficulty at some level. Counselors may have to ride along with this depressive experience, recognizing it as a sign of progress and not trying to overcome it and thereby throw the rhythm of the counseling off.

Counselors are tempted in two directions with phobic patients. It is very easy to treat them like children, to accept their desire to invest us with magical qualities, and to dominate them as though the counselor is an all-wise and powerful parent and the clients merely infants. The magnitude of this mistake hardly needs to be pointed out. The other possibility is that counselors can become so frustrated, especially by the nimble avoidance devices these clients can use, that they get extremely angry at them. Counselors who wish to read the language of this problem sensitively must read their own reactions carefully, take them into account, and see that they do not destroy the progress of counseling. The counselor's self-possession remains a key variable in working with these persons.

22

Fear and Trembling: Context for Anxiety

The poet W. H. Auden christened ours as the age of anxiety, inspiring Leonard Bernstein to write his Symphony No. 2 as an expression of our cultural uneasiness. Indeed, the theme of this anxious age has been almost overdone; it is a cliché that hardly stirs us anymore. As the poet's voice diminishes, those of television commercials, convincing us that we are tense, rundown, and irritable, grow louder. There is much to learn about fear and anxiety, about worry and uneasiness; helpers, in particular, must have an appreciation of these notions—and their various manifestations in human beings—if they are going to be effective in their work.

We realize that there are other remedies to which people turn these days in order to cope with anxiety. The use of soul-placating drugs prescribed by some physicians is well known. The growing interest in meditation, homegrown or Far Eastern, attests to a widespread intuition that there are ways to transcend the pressures of the moment and to find a haven of peace inside the soul. But cures or distractions are not enough if we lack an understanding of the basic psychological character of both fear and anxiety.

It was Sigmund Freud who made a clear distinction between normal and neurotic anxiety. It is one that most people now appreciate quite clearly. Fear, he noted, was caused by "real danger . . . which threatens from some external object" (*Inhibitions, Symptoms and Anxieties*. Standard Edition, Volume 20. London: The Hogarth Press). Neurotic anxiety, on the other hand, is present if we can judge a person's reaction to be "disproportionately . . . greater than in our judgment it ought to be. It is by this excess that the neurotic element stands revealed" (p. 148). While this latter anxiety, especially in its free and undifferentiated form, is our chief concern in this set of reflections, there are facts about fear with which counselors should be familiar.

190

The Management of Fear

The classic definition of fear associates it with some definite object—a person, a thing, or an event—in the environment. A logical connection can be made between this phenomenon and the subjective experience of fear. The latter feeling is an appropriate and helpful response in many situations in life. It is suitable in many of our interactions with persons and events around us. A healthy fear protects us, for example, from danger. We would be totally vulnerable to our surroundings were it not for the information that fear gives us.

Frequently, counselors work with persons who have quite legitimate and understandable fears. These may be connected, for example, with some event that is forthcoming, such as a major examination or a surgical operation. Psychological research leads us to believe that these fears should not be ignored; rather, we should assist people to understand the meaning of the experience that prompts the feeling. Often, when people are not helped to understand the source of this reaction, they use faulty mechanisms to preserve their psychological integrity. They may look away from the fear, for example, and place themselves in greater peril. There are, in other words, sensible things we can do to help people manage their realistic fear constructively.

The first attitude to avoid is that which tells people they really don't have anything about which to be afraid. Since their fear is telling them exactly the opposite, a sensible and measured effort to understand the true dimensions of the circumstances in which they find themselves is of basic importance.

Research by psychologist Irving Janis (*Psychological Stress.* New York: Wiley, 1958) illustrates this situation for us. Recognizing that major surgery involves pain as well as a serious threat to bodily integrity and a variety of other frustrations, Janis investigated the experience of fear in the surgical wards of a general hospital. He found three patterns of emotional response. There were those patients who worried excessively in advance of their surgery. They openly admitted their extreme feelings of vulnerability, attempted to postpone the operation, were unable to sleep without sedation, and constantly sought reassurances from the hospital staff. After the operation these subjects were much more likely than the others to be anxiety ridden.

Another group of patients experienced a moderate kind of fear in anticipation of their surgery. They were, as Janis noted, sometimes worried and tense about certain aspects of the operation such as the nature and mode of the anesthetic. They did, however, ask for and receive realistic information about what was going to happen to them. Although they felt somewhat vulnerable, their concerns were focused on realistic rather than imaginary threats. These people were much less likely than the others to display any emotional disturbance after the operation. They evinced high morale, cooperated well with the hospital staff, and were not so disturbed with the many nursing procedures that they had to undergo.

A third group of patients had very little fear in anticipation of their surgery. They were always cheerful and optimistic about what would happen. They denied any experience of feeling worried and they slept well and seemed to operate in a fairly normal way. Janis suggests that they "appeared to have unrealistic expectations of almost complete invulnerability." After the operation their vulnerability dawned on them and they were much more likely than the other patients to display anger and resentment toward the staff. They complained and were uncooperative.

Janis concludes that a moderate amount of fear in anticipation of the realistic dimensions of some forthcoming event is helpful because it prepares people to deal with actual dangers and the experience of deprivation they will undergo. The first two groups were able to rehearse in advance some of the unpleasant things they were going to go through. They could listen to and take account of the realistic information that was given to them. As a result they were not caught by surprise and they felt fairly secure as the events unfolded around them.

The key variable here seems to have been *the amount of information that was provided in advance*. The third group of patients, who displayed practically no fear beforehand, had no idea what was really going to happen to them. Those who experienced a moderate amount of fear were much better informed. What can helpers conclude from this kind of research? It makes sense not to cajole people out of a valid experience of fear. It is not constructive to hide from them information that, if delivered in a mature and not overwhelming way, they can use to prepare themselves for a difficult event. There is a constructive side to fear in that it allows people to prepare themselves sensibly for the realities that lie before them. The old idea of helping people to keep a stiff upper lip, with the coda that what you don't know won't hurt you, simply does not work. Counselors can frequently serve as significant mediators for the kind of information—whether it has to do with going to a hospital, a courtroom, or a strange distant place—that can help people manage their fear constructively. They can also wisely apply it in their own lives.

Anxiety As A Signal

One of the great insights given to us by Freud concerns the informational nature of anxiety. He said that anxiety is a signal the ego sends out to warn of some internal conflict the person is experiencing. This is usually between some unacceptable impulses and the psychological forces trying to suppress them. This anxiety also serves to mobilize defense mechanisms to protect the ego itself. There is, in other words, a clear meaning to the experience of anxiety even when this cannot be associated consciously with any distinct event or object. It is not uncommon for counselors to work with people who are experiencing raw and undifferentiated anxiety. This is not just a case of "nerves" but a symbolic manifestation of an internal psychological reality.

Just feeling on edge does not indicate that a person is experiencing a state of pathological anxiety. Everybody goes through periods of uneasiness, especially when they are exposed to stress. But most normal people can manage these anxieties. We speak here of anxiety as a constant visitor to the psyche, a steady disturber of the individual's peace, which is difficult to describe even though its effects are deeply felt. Typically, persons who are experiencing a genuine anxiety neurosis feel some kind of uncontrollable dread and apprehension. Their physical reactions—rapid pulse, elevated blood pressure, difficulties in breathing—are the signals of the emergency measures the body is taking to prepare itself for the nameless threat. Psychologically, these people feel that something bad is going to happen but they are not sure when, where, or why this will be. They live under a dark cloud and they cannot overcome their tensions and restlessness by an act of the will or through the reassurance of their friends. This condition can interfere markedly with the pursuit of their individual lives. This is when they come for help or when someone suggests that they should see a counselor and try to get to the bottom of their worries.

Victims of acute anxiety cannot explain much about their difficulty in a conscious or orderly way. When the experience of the anxiety is episodic—that is, when the experience is not steady but comes in intense and unpredictable bursts—they cannot tell why it has happened or when it will end. They frequently feel that they are about to die. It is a haunting and disturbing experience. These people are not faking nor are they merely trying to get sympathy from those around them. It is very wearing on them and occasionally it is equally taxing on counselors or others who are supposed to help them.

It is possible for this anxiety to disappear by itself. It is difficult to explain why this should take place, just as it is difficult to explain periods of remission in physical illness. However, it is also possible for the anxiety to worsen. It may, in fact, begin to take the shape of another and more distinctive symptom disorder. This happens when the person begins to use defenses characteristic of other difficulties. They may become phobic, for example, and fear contact with anything that might have germs on it. At the bottom, however, an anxiety state is undifferentiated; it has not yet taken on the form of some disorder symptom through the person's adaptation of specific kinds of defenses. It is just a bubbling, disturbing, queasiness of the spirit.

Sensitivity is needed in the diagnosis of this difficulty, especially because of the complications occasioned by physical complaints. It is helpful for counselors to remember that many organic states cause the same symptoms that are found in anxiety states. These include hyperthyroidism, organic heart disorders, disturbances of the cerebellum and the semicircular canals, some toxic conditions and disorders, as well as many other organic diseases. These symptoms should be attended to carefully because they constitute the special language of the suffering human person, a language that, above all others, counselors must be able to understand. Counselors should not be surprised at the indirect and disguised way in which conflicts make themselves known to us.

At a time when our country is unsettled, or is trying to come to terms with economic and other persistent difficulties, many persons are subject to anxiety. They fear the loss of their position or their pension, or they worry about the stable future of the country. When social status and financial well-being are threatened, people are more subject than usual to this free-floating experience of anxiety. The reason is that the air is filled with so many potential threats. There may be layoffs, strikes, recurrence of war, the increase of inflation, or something like an alienating change in life-style, which leaves the person feeling out of step with or lost in contemporary society. These triggering events are not the direct causes but are rather the occasions for exposing conflicts within individuals. Counselors cannot control the economic status of the world nor much else about the environment. They are aided considerably, however, when they can appreciate the stress these factors introduce into the lives of those with whom they work. It is against this setting that they can appreciate the nature of the various manifestations of anxiety.

What Can Counselors Do?

It is stressful to work with anxious individuals because it is difficult for them to explain what their problem is. The very nature of it, wrapped in vagueness, complicates the effort to understand them right from the start. It is the classic situation in which knowing what to avoid is almost as important as knowing how to proceed sensibly.

Sometimes well-meaning friends only complicate the difficulties of people suffering from extreme anxiety by blindly urging them on in some effort to overcome it with a General Patton-like determination. When persons are already experiencing something close to panic, this can be extremely destructive to their adjustment. They can only try to escape and, in fact, it is under just such pressure that some people leave counseling altogether. Counselors who respect the fact that they are clearly dealing with unconscious variables will never push people too hard on the conscious behaviors or decisions of their lives. These persons need a great deal of acceptance and understanding. This is complicated for them by the fact that they have grown very cautious of committing themselves to other persons precisely because of the nature of their anxious difficulties. These persons can only take one small step at a time; hurrying them along merely makes them stumble and become more uncertain of their direction. This is, of course, very trying on the patience of the counselor who may find the symptoms bewildering and, in an effort to establish some core understanding of the problem, may push people too hard toward a definite conclusion. This is a way of alienating and making things worse for clients.

Another temptation in the age of anxiety and stress is to intellectualize about the tensions and difficulties under which we all live. Philosophical and theological ruminations about the star-crossed conditions of modern life may sound soothing but they do not touch the heart of this difficulty. It is a mistake to associate the cultural awareness of existential anxiety with the individual's experience of anxiety that is the result of an inner and unverbalized conflict.

Sometimes counselors or other people become suspicious of the complaints of those experiencing severe anxiety because anxieties are so hard to describe and because they have so many signs that resemble the indications of psycho-physiological illnesses. Conveying some attitude of suspicion or uneasiness about the authenticity of their symptoms can only complicate their own experience of themselves and cause a further recession. This would be just as unhelpful as telling them to buck up, put a good face on things, and confront the difficulties of life with some determined optimism. Counselors must be prepared, not to demand more than these people can deliver, but to allow them time to approach the underlying conflict a little more closely. A counselor's commitment to understanding the special language of emotional difficulties is under genuine trial at these times. Dealing with people who experience anxiety can be very stressful, but with a feeling for the difficulties these people experience counselors can work much more effectively with them.

As in many other situations, counselors must be alert to their own experience of anxiety, not only for what it tells them about themselves but for the clues that it gives concerning the conflict the other is experiencing. Sensitive helpers can hear many things in their own resonations. They may, for example, realize that they too are vulnerable to the same kind of difficulties, that whatever the person is dealing with is coming close to something that may affect the counselor as well. Counselors who are aware of this will be able to avoid unnecessary defensiveness. They will avoid, in other words, making themselves part of the problem because they will be able to factor out their own reactions from those of the anxious client.

It is also true that the specific kind of anxiety that others give rise to in us can tell us a good deal about them. A person with free-floating anxiety may make us generally uneasy and restive, while a person who is more paranoid will upset us in a very different way, making us feel that we are the object of their attacks in an effort to diminish our authority. Counselors sometimes undervalue the information they can receive in consulting themselves as they work at close range with others. Far from being merely a source of stress, their own reactions can be a part of a constructive help in their counseling activities. They can read clients accurately in their own reactions to them.

23

The Everyman Illness: Depression

From the ordinary blues to the depths of a severe psychotic depression there runs a broad band of bad feeling. We have all crossed its borders at one time or another during our lives. Feeling down is personally familiar to everyone who does any counseling, indeed to any human being. Famous men like Churchill and Lincoln are known to have experienced severe depressions during their lives.

English author Evelyn Waugh wrote a novel based on his own depressive experience, *The Ordeal of Gilbert Pinfold*. Everybody knows depression at least in its milder forms. Nobody goes through life smiling all the way.

Depression can mean something in general as well as something quite specific. In general, it refers to a symptom that can be present in many different psychological difficulties. Specifically, it can refer to a distinctive problem of which it is a dominant or important feature, as in a diagnosable mood disorder. As mentioned previously, the person experiencing depression is shot through with sadness, feeling helpless and at the same time valuing the self less. A threat to security exists because something treasured—usually a loved one—is lost or is in danger of being lost. Individuals riding toward the far end of the continuum of depression cannot cope with life, yet they often resist help. Almost intentionally, they dig a deep hole for themselves. They will not come out of it and they may not let you in even when you want to be of assistance to them. Having known some depression ourselves does not mean that we understand all its forms. Indeed, counselors can save themselves from serious errors by not generalizing from their own experience to the experience of those with whom they work.

As one moves from the milder to the more serious experiences of depression, one notices that individuals who suffer from them react in certain systematic and predictable ways. At the outset, depressed persons try to make contact with other people. They want to get help and so they make some effort to establish relationships with others. They are seeking, at some level of consciousness, some way to restore what has been taken from them in life. Sometimes this is through an

197

unrealistic wish for a magical restoration of things as they once were. We may not notice this kind of thinking unless we can closely inspect the life of the depressed person.

As the problem becomes more intense, however, depressed individuals begin to give up. They appear more helpless and it is difficult for them either to seek or to allow themselves help. Difficult as it may seem, even this is evidence of a psychological attempt to find a solution to unconscious problems. Persons who are deep in the quicksand of depression not only feel bad but end up being bad for themselves. Depressives can be their own worst enemies, and it is common to observe self-destructive tendencies, either subtle or pronounced, in the depressed individual. Suicide, which has been discussed earlier, is the ultimate self-destructive act. It does not come suddenly, however, and counselors should always take soundings in their relationships with depressives to pick up the signals of an increasing will to self-destruction.

It is also possible to encounter depressed persons who do not look at all like depressed persons. They are able to deny their bad feelings and keep up a good front, which earns them the title "masked depressions." These people can be identified by the depressed mood that is evident when their defenses are pierced even briefly in the course of helping them.

Experts also speak of "depressive equivalents," through which the person wards off the conscious experience of depression by having some other kind of problem. The classic example of this, of course, is the person who has some bodily ill to complain about while at the same time denying any emotional upset at all. This is the kind of person who comes to a general practitioner or talks about problems to clergymen or other professional associates, perhaps elaborating on the physical concerns and, in the process, garnering a good deal of medical advice, vitamins, and other suggestions about nutrition and exercise. It takes sensitivity to realize that such physical complaints are a substitute for the real problem about which such persons are unable to speak.

Depressed persons can wear many disguises, and counselors must be able to read these in order to create effective relationships with them. Sometimes the signals only come to counselors in their own reactions to clients who come with these problems. They feel that there is something more beneath the surface, something dark and sad hidden beneath the exterior. In well-balanced helpers, these signals should be taken seriously because they will lead to a deeper level of understanding the person. Counselors can, in other words, discern on the radar screen of their own feelings the shapes of the depressions that others cannot consciously describe.

The experience of depression is generally marked by some mood change. Individuals become sad or gloomy or tend to feel hopeless about life and its possibilities. They pull back from existence, seeming to lose zest for life, finding that interests they once had no longer stimulate them. They slow down in many ways, both in their behavior and in their thought processes. When people are suffering only a mild difficulty, they may be able to go through the motions of their regular activities but they do not enjoy them. They will, however, perform them, especially at the urgings of others who think this activity will be "good for them." As the depression gets worse, however, they give up going along with others. They become indifferent to their surroundings and they withdraw into a quiet and somber outlook toward the people and events around them.

It is possible to observe the presence of anxiety especially in these or atypical depressives who cannot settle down and who pace the floor, shifting from one place to another in a dramatic display of the fine edge of their concern over their situation. These signals may also disappear and depressed persons who have been obviously anxious can seem to quiet down. Those around the depressed individual may interpret this as evidence of improvement. It is more often movement toward apathy. Doing nothing is rewarding to the depressed person because, if they do not move or engage themselves in life, it does not hurt so much. They do not feel the pain but they do pay a very high price in the kind of withdrawal from normal activity that enables them to achieve this. Sometimes one may observe a miserable style of adjustment in depressed persons. To them, however, such a situation is not as miserable as it could be, and they remain in an emotional holding pattern to avoid making things worse for themselves.

A Constant Factor

Sensitive counselors understand that no matter how quiet and subdued the depressive may be, anger is almost always churning not far beneath the surface. This anger may be expressed directly, as when depressed persons complain that they are unloved or that they are being treated poorly by their friends and relatives. This is a constant theme and it is one that, to a certain extent, works against the depressives; people get tired of those who complain all the time and seem to think they are the only ones who have ever suffered in life.

At other times the anger is expressed far less directly but it nonetheless gets through to others. The sufferings of the individual in this case radiate out to make the lives of everybody around them miserable. This can be accomplished very subtly. One must look and listen very carefully in order to sense how often this type of transaction does happen. Depressed persons are preoccupied with themselves and with the specific problems that dominate their thoughts, and they cannot seem to get away from their own situation. Focused on these things, they talk about little else and so a certain dull monotony comes to characterize their conversation. They are not fun to be with and this has the effect of driving away the very people whom they feel they need most for support and affection.

Those who are severely depressed may brood over long-past incidents, still feeling guilty about them, or discovering special messages or significance in their present experiences. They also tend to generate their feelings outward through the use of the psychological mechanisms of projection and displacement, catching other people up in the net of their depression and blaming them for their difficulties. Sometimes the only language that the severely depressed person can speak is one of concrete symbols. They are preoccupied with disease, with bodily illness that stands for their own very painful feelings.

It is always useful to remember that depressed people have a way of distorting their recollections of the past. It can seem as if nothing good ever happened to them. Their life stories are so appalling that it seems that they have had neither a good break nor a blessing of any kind. They do not remember happiness, the way normal people do not remember pain. This reveals something about their present vision of life. This distorted perception is an important element for counselors to understand. In fact, its presence can complicate helping the client. As MacKinnon and Michels note (p. 177): "It is not unusual for the patient to portray his mood as long-standing and gradual in onset, whereas others describe the symptoms as relatively recent and abrupt. In a sense the patient is right; he has simply been concealing his depression from others, and perhaps from himself. As he improves, this process may reverse itself; in the early phases of recovery the depressed patient sometimes sounds much better than he really feels. This may lead to premature optimism on the part of the therapist, and is one of the factors that contributes to the increased risk of suicide as the patient starts to improve."

In addition to perceiving themselves and their difficulties differently, depressed persons also have a narrower range of thoughts than normal persons. They seem to move intellectually at a slower pace, and they display little drive or innovation of their own. This slowness and restriction also shows up in the outer behavior of depressed persons. They move more slowly and without the evidence of purposefulness that characterizes the behavior of better adjusted people. Depressed people do not get into things on their own or they move out of them quickly once they get into them. They tend to do things that do not demand much in the way of active participation or social involvement. They may, for example, sit and stare at TV, hardly noticing what is taking place before their eyes.

Typical Complaints

Depressed persons frequently talk about the signals of the depression rather than about the depression itself. They may, as has been noted, express concern about their physical rather than their emotional health. They may, in fact, give evidence of certain changes in their physical functioning. All this is matter for determination by competent physicians. It is not unusual, however, to note this kind of complaint along with such typical complaints as difficulty in falling asleep, waking up early, general fatigue, loss of appetite, or other dysfunctions. An amazing amount of medicine is sold in response to these specific complaints every year, as most counselors recognize, but the medicine never touches the underlying depression for which the complaint is a familiar signal. However, one must not dismiss these symptoms as those of some self-pitying crackpot. This is the only voice through which depressed persons may be able to express their difficulties.

The temptation to shake them loose with some common-sense confrontation is very great for certain counselors. Such an approach is not ordinarily effective and may, in fact, do some damage. Far better is the effort to sense the tone and the symbolic meaning of the complaint. Whatever symptoms the persons display contain a message for those working close to them. Translating this language of symptoms in the context of the person's life is an essential activity of sensitive counselors. Sometimes the complaints of depressed persons have very specific meanings. Persons who develop foot trouble, for example, may be accomplishing many ends by having this difficulty. They will need service from others and must be excused from many duties and functions. It is also true that they may be punishing themselves through such symbolic difficulties. Bad feet, after all, mean that a person loses mobility and must be more isolated and withdrawn than would otherwise be the case. Standing back in order to get some perspective on the person's whole life enables counselors to test this kind of meaning; a sensitive perspective saves them from trying to respond with an individual remedy to every complaint the depressed person may have.

Persons suffering from depression genuinely do want the attention and affection of other persons but, in the grip of their difficulty, they find that they are not able to respond in kind. Relationships then tend to break down because they cannot give of themselves the way they would like others to give unto them. This is why depressed persons seem to grow more isolated. It is not uncommon to observe a process through which they try to reach others only to turn them off because all they have to offer is their own self-preoccupation and their need to cling to others for help. This psychological infection tends to worsen because, since they are afraid of rejection, depressed persons may redouble their efforts to get other people to like them. This just puts these other people off because they sense that the persons are project-ing their own needs rather than warmth or concern for them. What takes place under these maneuvers for friendship is an effort on the part of the depressed persons to cover over their own anger and aggression. But the outlines of the conflict cannot be hidden com-pletely and others receive a confused message from them.

It is characteristic of depressed individuals, as was noted earlier, to seek out social relationships in the beginning phases of their difficulty. Because they run the risk of alienating others, however, they experi-ence a kind of rejection they have unconsciously inflicted on them-selves. It is not surprising that they should withdraw and stop trying to be socially successful. This situation is all the more desperate because they tend to suffer in silence, mad at themsevles and at others for the fix in which they find themselves. The hostility that marks this adjust-ment may be apparent to those around depressed persons, but they are themselves unaware of it. All they know is that others tried to reject them and this confirms their feeling of being unliked; it just makes them feel worse.

Counselors must determine whether the evidence of depression in the persons with whom they work is a sign of a very serious episode, a chronic life difficulty, or merely an aspect of a normal grief reaction. It is sometimes very difficult to sort this out. For this reason the helper must always try to maintain enough distance to be able to view a total picture of the person's life. This is very helpful, as is the information that can be gathered from members of the family or friends of the depressed individual. Experienced counselors will be able to sense differences in those who are deeply disturbed from those who are suffering from milder difficulties. One of the most informative feelings is that which helpers experience in their own emotional reactions. For example, counselors dealing with psychotically depressed persons will feel at a greater distance from them, sensing that they are harder to reach and identify with; it is more difficult to experience empathy for their situation. Counselors will, in general, feel more alienated from a seriously disturbed person.

They will feel closer and will be able to identify better with those suffering from milder forms of depression. The ordinary guidelines for sensing the difference between a major psychosis and a milder dysfunction are also relevant here. The milder depressive and dysthymic, after all, are able to function in society. There is a logic to their life; their depression may make sense in the context of their lives. They experience a certain impairment in their social and working activities that can be traced back to inner conflicts.

There is also the kind of depression that is an element in normal grief and mourning. In these situations bereaved persons gradually work their way back into life. Grieving people do not suffer the other emotional evidence that can be found in seriously depressed persons. They do not usually suffer, for example, a major loss of self-esteem. Nor do they have an excessive and illogical feeling of guilt about their lives. They may feel terrible but they know, at some other level of their being, that they will come out of it, that they have a serious challenge to work through but that there will be an end to it. Grief has a terminating point when the individual reemerges into the normal activities of life. This sequence can be expected in persons suffering the normal blows of the human situation. Individuals who do not come out of their experience of grief within a reasonable time may be providing some evidence that they are experiencing depression of a more serious sort.

24

Further Aspects of Depression

Our current understanding of the genesis of mood disorders tells us that afflicted persons possess a biological vulnerability to depression. The degree of this susceptibility is reflected in the intensity of the person's problem. Almost all the cases with which counselors deal will be reactive depressions in persons experiencing deep sadness and a loss of self-confidence because of a serious break or traumatic experience in their lives. The depression can almost always be associated, in other words, with an external event. There is an external trigger in life somewhere; to identify this may be one of the first constructive steps that can be taken in a counseling situation. Much of what depressed persons say in speaking about the event that turned their lives sour helps the counselor to understand their general approach and reactions to life. It is a key element around which is clustered a mass of relevant psychological reactions.

The ordinary precipitating stress is that of loss, a death, or a separation from a loved one. It is sufficient here to recall that threats to self-confidence and self-esteem are common and that when these are present counselors can be fairly certain that they are dealing with depressed persons. It is not only a defeat that can get some persons down. Success can also trigger depression in some individuals. They do not feel up to it, or they feel unworthy, and the big promotion that seems like a reward when viewed from the outside is actually the beginning of a depression for them. The success is too much for their self-confidence or self-regard to handle.

Characteristic Defenses

Working with depressed persons is indeed stressful. It is helpful for counselors to appreciate some of the psychological patterns ordinarily encountered. It is not uncommon, for example, to see persons who have experienced some loss employ the psychological mechanism of identification as a means of getting the person or object back. They absorb the lost person in some way into their own personality, introjecting them to a degree that they possess the lost friend or relative in a new way. It is sometimes obvious that depressed persons have taken on the characteristics, interests, or even hobbies of the person who has been lost. They may carry on the work or cause of the lost person as an effective way of symbolically recapturing and holding on to what has been denied them.

Depressed persons almost invariably experience some anger. They may be angry with the person—a spouse, for example, who died—for abandoning them, but it is very difficult for them to express this directly or outwardly. Much of the anger gets thrown on those who are around trying to be of some help. This creates certain difficulties of which the counselor must be careful to note. The reason is simple: When persons suffer a loss and they come to a counselor for help, they really want more than help. They ordinarily want more than just being told that the counselor will help them to help themselves. In truth, they want the counselor to become a substitute in terms of offering affection and support in place of the person who has been lost. They want the guide to solve their problems, and they may be very disappointed when counselors resist this. Depressed persons want more than healing. They want everything back, and this need, mostly unconscious, can become an important dynamic in any counseling process. Counselors who do not realize this can easily be lost in the ensuing confusion.

Stress builds up very dramatically when the person has strong expectations for help that the counselor really cannot provide. This intimidates certain counselors, especially those for whom counseling is not a main occupation, and they may feel very guilty and uneasy in not being able to give more assistance to these genuinely suffering people. The counselor's own guilt can then become interwoven in the counseling dynamic. This can happen quite easily and quickly, and counselors must be very attentive to their own reactions as well as very self-disciplined in the face of what can be heartrending situations. If they are not, they may find themselves trapped in a position they cannot really fill and that will destroy their capacity for helping.

Depressed people often feel bad because they experience such hostile feelings toward those around them. They are angry with people enjoying life and carrying on as usual. These feelings make them anxious, so they find themselves in a psychological bind. They cannot really survive emotionally unless they have these persons around them, and yet they can still feel great anger toward them. They cannot express this, however, or they place their friendships in jeopardy. They therefore turn their anger in toward themselves, accusing themselves of various things and condemning themselves without much compassion. Self-condemnation is a common feature in persons who seek out counseling for their depressions. This anger at themselves, because there is no other permissible direction it can take, underlies and explains their depressed feelings. For this reason some observers call depression "inverted anger."

The High Riders

Most people are familiar with the phrase *manic-depressive* or, in more recent years, *bipolar illness.* The notion of mania suggests agitated and enthusiastic activity that seems to be quite the opposite from what is observed in the midst of depression. Manic people are always on the go, they seem difficult to contain or to keep on one subject, and after some exposure to them, one suspects that the roots of their enthusiasm are not as simple as they at first seem.

Such individuals do not seek counseling because they do not find their agitation and increased activity uncomfortable. If manic depressive patients experience, or their families observe, symptoms necessitating professional attention, they should be referred to a psychiatrist for evaluation and appropriate treatment, such as with the drug lithium carbonate.

The Paranoid Flavor

The edge of paranoia can be felt, not only in the world at large, as some novelists tell us these days, but in the adjustment style of depressed persons. They sometimes alternate between a paranoid and a depressed outlook. The use of projection enables depressed people to shift the blame for their difficulties onto others. Paranoids find this a very functional defense; it serves their purpose well. Paranoid styles do not come cheaply, however, and the amount of distortion that this adjustment introduces into their lives is quite marked. The ability of paranoid persons to make accurate discriminations about the world around them is genuinely impaired. So too are their social relationships. People can only take so much of the paranoid style. The high-riding paranoid will then slump back into depression. It is not unusual to observe these emotional shifts even within the same interview with a person suffering from this difficulty.

A Common Feature

One of the chief but not well-understood traits found in depressed persons is their capacity for hurting themselves. Some people just seem accident prone, and others to suffer a long string of bad luck; nothing seems to work right and misfortune dogs their steps. These may be difficulties into which these persons unconsciously get themselves or that they attract toward themselves. Counselors must be alert to a pattern in the problems of such persons. There are many interpretations of the meaning of such masochism. Some observers feel that individuals can only justify the experience of pleasure by first inflicting some kind of denial on themselves. Others feel that self-punishment is a way of maintaining control over events. If you take the blow before someone can inflict it on you, you have to maintain control of your environment. That, they say, explains why some people always volunteer for the most dangerous jobs.

Self-punishing behavior can be easily misinterpreted by others and can, in fact, be the source of what is called "secondary gain." Benefits in sympathy or concern are paid when people have misfortune or sickness. It is important to reflect on this because counselors may sense this dynamic occurring in therapy sessions with depressed persons. Recalling the principle that clients always re-create for us what is typical in their behavior with others, detecting masochistic behavior can be highly significant in counseling with depressed patients. For example, clients who take each new awareness or insight and use it, not to go deeper in a constructive way toward understanding themselves better but rather as further evidence of their own badness or general wretchedness, may be exhibiting a strong streak of masochism in the relationship with the counselor. They are using what is discovered in counseling to prove the case against themselves. It is clear that such persons are not ready to use insight constructively. Therefore, counselors should proceed very slowly and not push too hard lest their efforts to help the client understand amplify what is part of the dynamic difficulty in the first place.

Current thinking about these trends suggests that although these patients seem depressed and their mood disturbance may be their primary reason for seeking help, their underlying problem is actually a disturbance in personality. In the 1988 edition *DSM-III-R*, such patients are assigned the diagnosis of *self-defeating personality disorder* but they may also have associated depressive features. This entity is described by T. A. Widiger and A. J. Francis as "a behavoir pattern characterized by chronic pessimism, a submissive and acquiescent attitude, a resignation to failure, suffering, defeat and exploitation, boredom with or disinterest in success and supportive relationships, a belief that their misfortunes are justified, expected, and fated, and the tendency to continually place themselves within situations that are harmful, painful, disappointing, or abusive" (J. A. Talbott, R. A. Hales, and S. C. Yusofsky, *Textbook of Psychiatry*. Washington, D.C.: American Psychiatric Press, 1988).

During the Interview

Working with depressed patients is very demanding. Not only do counselors need special sensitivity to the signs of the dynamics that are taking place beneath the surface, but they may also have to take a counseling stance that differs markedly from the one with which they are ordinarily familiar. Counselors may have to be more active, for example, than they usually are with other clients. In the initial phases of counseling the counselor may have to reach out and introduce more structure into the relationship than ordinarily.

Such departures are necessary because the person is incapable of saying much or doing much about or for the self at the beginning of therapy. To wait for them is to impose on them a psychological burden that they are really not capable of carrying at this stage. Depressed persons may want far more than the counselor can ultimately give them. They will, in one way or another, try to get this right from the start of therapy. These persons approach counseling with pessimism and passivity and with little willingness to commit themselves with much determination to dealing with their problems. Understanding this, counselors will need more than the usual patience and may have to take on some additional responsibility for initiating the counseling itself. This is not a betrayal of principle but a practical extension of what it means to understand someone in trouble.

When very seriously disturbed people come for help, somebody else often comes with them. Sometimes depressed persons are so withdrawn or so passive that they can hardly speak for themselves. They have others with them to describe their problems. It is a good idea to get as much information as possible from their companion. Although counselors must always avoid the impression of talking behind the client's back, they can, without subterfuge, question the companion thoroughly.

In an attempt to respond directly to depressed persons, counselors may deal first with their difficulty in speaking, or even in seeming interested in speaking, about themselves. This is clearly a symbolic message to the counselor and may indeed be the first one to which an effective response may be made. Such depressed persons are telling you why they present themselves in this special kind of silence. This is a clear communication: It hurts too much to talk. It can be responded to directly.

Counselors who understand that depressed persons will relate to them the way they relate to other persons will not hurry them. Nor will they become impatient with the slow pace, hesitations, and repetitions that may characterize the depressed person's presentation of himself or herself. These are all ways in which depressed persons reveal what it is like to experience their dark difficulties. They are constricted, emotionally and logically, and pushing them too hard is distinctly counterproductive. Those counselors who enjoy confronting their clients may feel an urge to do this with depressed patients who present such a halting vision of themselves and their difficulties. This is not a good time or place to challenge them, however, because that would only be flexing the counselor's own muscles. Depressed people, perhaps as much as any other group of patients, need receptivity, patience, and a great willingness on our part to discern and understand their tortured patterns of life.

Reassurance is not helpful if it is the only response. When people are rather mildly depressed they will be critical of themselves. They need to express these negative feelings, and counselors should not abridge their right to do this. They should allow clients to get the poison out and deal with it at their own pace.

Concerning depressed persons who are very withdrawn, counselors may be required to deal very gently with the fundamental emotional barriers to communication before they can expect these patients to deal with more serious or profound material. In other words, counselors may have to do more than they are accustomed to in the initial counseling sessions with these people. Therapists who are too passive, who play the waiting game too exclusively, may make already depressed people feel greater frustration and incompetence about themselves. They will be more depressed as a result. The first thing counselors must accept is a modified mode of helping these people. The conseling will be slowed down and, unless we can move at this reduced rate of speed, we will only increase our own experience of stress and not help the client much.

Physical Complaints

While the diagnosis of genuine physical symptoms should be referred to other competent professionals, it is not wise for counselors merely to check these symptoms off as though they were of no significance. Counselors should refer these complaints, if possible, to the larger context of the client's experience. In hearing depressed persons speak about their physical complaints, counselors may get a clear glimpse of the way these individuals deal with many of their problems. Their style emerges—their general approach to themselves and others—as they describe, for example, their manner of dealing with the fact that they cannot get to sleep or that they wake up early. These are windows into the person's world, and even though the counselor may not be medically qualified, the client's attitude toward these difficulties is always an act of self-revelation.

It is sometimes very helpful to reassure such persons in general about physical complaints with some statement like, "It's not unusual for people who are depressed to have these physical difficulties," or something similar. This simple acknowledgment relieves anxiety, does not make little of their symptoms, and leaves room for referring them for other medical diagnosis.

Summary: What Counselors Should Know about Depressive Symptoms

1. Mood disorders span a wide spectrum of conditions, ranging from reactions to loss and other negative life experiences to severe, recurrent, debilitating illnesses. Counselors will generally work with the former, those persons who exhibit relatively normal states with some evidence of mood and cognitive disturbance.

2. Moderate to severe depressive illness pervades the person's life so that despairing and hopeless feelings and thoughts, including suicidal ideas, are common. Their sleep and appetite are disturbed, they cannot concentrate or think rapidly, they take little interest in life, and often complain of fatigue, headache, and various physical disturbances. Such patients should be referred for psychiatric evaluation in order to understand the true nature of their problem and to rule out a diagnosis of a major depressive episode.

3. It is not uncommon for patients who may seek counseling for mild depressive complaints to develop the signs and symptoms of major depressive illness. If such a change is noted, the patient should be referred for psychiatric evaluation.

4. It has been estimated that in patients who suffer symptoms of major depressive illness, approximately fifteen percent are at risk for suicide. Any communication about an interest in or threat of suicide should therefore be taken seriously by counselors and referrals should be made promptly.

5. Despite counseling efforts, some persons fail over time to show significant improvement. They may be suffering from what is defined as *dysthymia*. Such persons, many of whom would previously have been described as neurotic, have mild complaints and symptoms similar to those of major depressive disorder. Here again, a timely referral for a thorough psychiatric evaluation can be of great benefit to such clients.

6. If a counselee should suddenly evince an elevated, expansive, or irritable mood, increased activity, pressure of speech, decreased need for sleep, and marked grandiosity, helpers should suspect the development of bipolar illness (formerly called manic-depressive illness) and refer the person for psychiatric evaluation and treatment.

7. A number of individuals who seek counseling assistance may, in late fall or early winter, begin to complain of an increased need for sleep, a lack of energy, and a craving for carbohydrates. Such persons may be suffering from seasonal affective illness and should, as with the above patients, be referred promptly.

8. Because biological as well as psychological and social factors appear to play an etiological role in the development of mood disorders, counselors will find it helpful to question clients about whether other family members have experienced similar symptoms. If so, the person may be more vulnerable to the development of serious mood disturbance.

25

The Core of Depression

Counselors need to listen actively in working with depressed patients. These clients hide certain parts of themselves, especially the anger and hostility they feel. They are willing to talk about almost anything else, which just confirms the significance of anger in their whole psychological adjustment. Depressed people may not exhibit the kind of curiosity that is found in other patients, the kind of interest in discovering more about themselves that is a helpful motive in therapy. Depressed persons are too taken up with their particular feelings of uneasiness or shame. Counselors will have to "hear around" these things in order to get a full picture of what such persons are trying to convey. Again, counselors must take a more active stance than usual, making connections very gently and not pushing too hard in any circumstances. Meanings are drawn together slowly; at all times counselors must show great respect for the person.

Suicide will be discussed in later chapters; it is sufficient to note here that counselors should not hesitate to discuss suicide out of fear that they may thereby promote this possibility. As a matter of fact, if people can talk about the feelings that may impel them to suicide, this can reduce their need to act out these impulses. Talking about suicide lessens rather than intensifies its danger. Allowing people to talk offers a situation in which they are able to control the feelings that could otherwise lead them to the brink of self-destruction. Suicidal individuals are always telling others about these plans. Their major problem lies in finding others who can really hear them.

This was illustrated some years ago when the host of a television talk show in Florida shot herself on the air, having written a script in advance describing what this event would be like for the audience. She had previously told her co-workers that she was contemplating suicide. As the Associated Press story read: "No one took her seriously. Co-worker Rob Smith said she told him, 'Wouldn't it be neat if I were to take the gun, pull it out on the air, live and in living color, and blow myself away?' 'I thought at the time it was just a bad joke and changed the subject.'" Her mother, in describing her, gave a vivid picture of the depressed person's life. She said that her daughter had been "terribly, terribly depressed. She constantly said that she had no close friends. She was already twenty-nine-years old and it bothered her. She was very sensitive. She tried. She'd say, 'Hi, how are you, won't you have some coffee?' They'd say, 'No.'"

This story dramatically exemplifies the counselor's need to sound out the suicidal possibilities in the depressed patient and not hold off from this for any of the many bad reasons that people offer to excuse themselves from this difficult task.

Counseling depressed persons involves helpers in a dual role. They must understand that they are called upon, first of all, to be supportive and, secondly, to help work out the psychological explanation of the individual's difficulties; they must help to get the meaning clear. Support for depressed persons is important for lessening the suffering and guilt they experience, for giving birth to hope in their lives, and for protecting them from harming themselves. It is only as and if this is done that such persons may be able to explore the meaning of their depression. Counselors, of course, should be prepared to refer such suicidal persons as promptly as possible. They will feel more confident and be of greater assistance if they develop a practical understanding of the multidimensional possibilities of depression. They will better understand the treatments, the one medical, the other psychological, for depressions of a biological or psychological origin.

It is true that there is a wide range of pharmacological aids that may be used for depressed persons. Many persons are already taking drugs that are prescribed specifically for alleviating their feelings of sadness. This is a medical matter, but counselors should be aware of whether or not the people they are seeing are taking drugs. They should not give advice about the dosage. They should confer with the person's physician or refer him or her to a psychiatrist if there is some question about the dosage or the kind of drug being taken.

At the heart of the matter, counselors must be aware of the fact that transference works all around them, because they are taking the place of whatever has been lost in the depressed person's life. Without some awareness of this, counselors will not be able to understand the maneuvers and unconscious strategies that depressed patients may evince in the course of counseling.

Understanding this transference is tricky but essential. Hope is given to persons through a real committed interest in them. They do not need sermons about this. It arises from an open and concerned presence and a willingness to move at the person's own pace in dealing with difficulties. As the counselor reflects on saving these persons from harming themselves, more than the possibility of suicide must be kept in mind. People can harm themselves in many small ways, by quitting school, for example, or needlessly giving up on a chance for promotion. Many major decisions about life, marriage, and work can be and are often made in the grip of depressed moods. The counselor's sensitivity may help depressed people to consider these things more carefully. A very simple response to a person who is about to make a major decision impulsively can be something as simple as, "I wonder if you're really ready to do that." This conveys concern, understanding, and a willingness to wait while the person examines the issue further.

It is helpful if counselors remember that depressed patients ordinarily get uncomfortable if the counselors themselves are too warm and friendly. This is the natural bent of some counselors, especially in the face of somebody who seems to be very sad and may be crying about life's difficulties. Counselors must remember, however, that these people do not feel good about themselves and they really cannot give back the affectionate warmth they so desperately seem to want. When depressed persons do not respond to friendliness, of course, many counselors just try harder, attempting to be even more jolly and warm, and they are dismayed when the depressed person seems to move further away from them. The nicer they try to be, the more anxious these counselors make them. Depressed people simply are not ready to deal with over friendliness, and false heartiness can be downright harmful.

Moving Forward

As the counseling progresses it will be necessary to deal with the dependency that characterizes depressive clients. It will also be necessary for the person to assume a more active role in the counseling. This is a great difficulty for depressed patients who use denial in order to get rid of their symptoms because this psychological mechanism affords so much relief. The problem with denial is that, although it is functional, it works directly against gaining insight. Denial and insight cannot coexist. Nor should counselors press too soon or too quickly to resolve the conflict that contributes to depressive problems. They can, with great patience grounded in an understanding of what is taking place, allow clients to approach this discovery on their own.

Counselors are not wise to push anger too directly either. Individuals may become frightened if confronted with the presence of so much anger in themselves, and they may feel that their own controls are slipping. This feeling sometimes drives depressed persons out of treatment. Unfortunately, some counselors, reading something about depression and its relationship to anger, use this as a linchpin in their efforts to interpret the person's difficulties in a persuasive but sometimes hurried fashion. This illustrates the danger of having some insight into a clinical difficulty. Some insight is not enough in dealing with depressed people. Here again, the use of such knowledge helps the counselor to understand the client, but it should not be employed as a club or as some demonstration of the counselor's wisdom.

On the other hand, depressed patients may on some occasions seem to confront the therapist. They may use articles, talk-show quotes, or current books about the origins of depression to prove to counselors that the pursuit of insight is vain and unavailing. This challenge to the counselor should really be seen as an effort on the client's part to continue to deny elements of his or her own depression. It is not a situation that is helped if counselors are made defensive and end up trying to explain in great detail their theory or their methods. Such defensiveness merely goes against further therapeutic advances and increases the experience of stress for the counselors themselves.

In the same way, a patient in a hypomanic phase can throw a counselor off very easily. They have an aggressive way of being sarcastic and of playing on the weaknesses of others (in order to avoid looking at their own) that can unbalance the helpful counselor. They may parody counselors, use derogatory nicknames to describe them, or in some other way put them at a personal or professional disadvantage. Here, as in many other situations, the counselor asks, "What is this person doing to me, and why?" Instead of becoming defensive, the capacity to respond to this individual with understanding and acceptance is far more helpful than getting the last word or triumphantly putting him down.

Transference

The main difficulty centers on the transference problem in which the client truly wants to make a wonder-worker out of the therapist. Appearing victimized and helpless, with an added mix of dependency and hostility, such clients can move very subtly to get the counselor to take over responsibility for their lives. While we have suggested that counselors may have to be more active than usual in the beginning phases of counseling these people, this does not mean that they take complete control over the therapy. It is not the counselor's ultimate responsibility to solve the problems of depressed persons, to change their lives, or to make decisions for them. This is a very tricky area and unless counselors are aware of the interplay between the dependency and the anger of the client they may be caught up in a situation from which escape will be very difficult.

Frustration can quickly arise in the client when it is clear that counselors cannot be magicians or good fathers or mothers making all things whole again. Depressed patients will be disappointed and may express this with real anger. This tends to cause countertransference feelings of irritation and anger in the therapist. Here, however, we are at the heart of the transference-countertransference phenomenon, and a response with understanding of the whole complex relationship is far more important than one that is generated by frustration.

As Edith Jacobson notes, writing specifically of analysts but speaking to all counselors: "There must be a continuous, subtle, empathic tie between the analyst and his depressive patients; we must be very careful not to let empty silences grow or not to talk too long, too rapidly, and too emphatically; that is, never to give too much or too little. In any event, what those patients need is not so much more frequent and longer sessions as a sufficient amount of spontaneity and flexible adjustment to their mood level, warm understanding, and especially unwavering respect—attitudes which must not be confused with overkindness, sympathy, reassurance. . . . With these patients, we are always between the devil and the deep blue sea; this cannot be avoided" (*Depression*. New York: International Universities Press, Inc., 1971, pp. 299–300).

Counselors must be very attentive while working with these patients and they must avoid panicking even when suicidal patients tell them about the pills or the gun they have and that they will use if they have to. These are frequently dramatic-sounding statements that draw counselors into the life of the depressed person far more deeply than they expected to go. Counselors, for example, thinking they are using common sense, make the person promise to bring them the gun or the pills. Some counselors may even go and get them. This, however, takes away the power that the individual is trying to exercise over the counselor and makes him feel helpless. The issue centers on this symbolic use of power. Stripping them of whatever they unconsciously feel as power may be more harmful to them than some exploration of the dynamic significance of making this kind of threat. This is a classic example of doing good that frequently does harm instead.

One of the greatest tests for the counselors working with these patients will be the fact that they have a good sense of how to irritate the counselor, or of how to make him feel guilty or uneasy. They can do this, for example, by commenting about what a pleasant life counselors must have even when their clients cannot enjoy things quite so much. Frequently such a crisis occurs when it is time for the counselor to take a vacation. If counselors allow their guilt feelings to be played upon successfully, they will end up trapped by these persons. Here again these statements only take on meaning in a much broader context; they reveal the style and unconscious purposes and problems of the depressed persons.

Many counselors are tempted to respond strongly, to get angry at these people, or sometimes even to get depressed about their lives in some sympathetic fashion. Counselors who are aware of this danger have already taken a step to avoid such difficulties. However, counselors must also resist taking on the omnipotent role in which these people are sometimes willing to cast them. So too, counselors must avoid paternalism, being overprotective, or assuming other roles that seem to take over the helpless person's life.

What Am I Telling Myself?

Counselors must examine their feelings during the course of therapy. They will find that they are different with depressed patients than they are with other clients. They may, for example, experience boredom and uneasiness because these clients can seem drab and dull and uninteresting. Our boredom may tell us that we are not getting beneath the surface. It is sometimes helpful for counselors to explore the way they treat their clients. For example, take a look at the list of people you see to discover which one you would feel free to cancel out or switch if some emergency came up. It may often be the depressed persons, because they are not very inviting and we can unconsciously respond to their subtle anger with some powerful subtle anger of our own. Such indirect signs reveal much about our countertransference feelings.

Depressed patients are indeed a severe test of counseling skills. Counselors cannot afford to doze, make check marks, or not listen very carefully to the clients or to their own very informative reactions. There is always something going on even if it is of a slower rhythm and a duller external appearance than usual. Keeping in tune with this reduces stress, enlarges the experience of counseling itself, and enables counselors to work far more freely and effectively with depressed patients.

26

Introductory Notes on Personality Disorders

It is not unusual to discover—although it is difficult to admit—that despite our best efforts there are persons we cannot seem to help. We fail to reach them or they do not seem able to respond. For whatever reason, we fall short of what the textbooks urge us to achieve: a healthy and helping relationship. This is a particular source of stress for many counselors, especially those who do their counseling work in connection with other professional responsibilities. The reasons are clear:

Most counselors like people and for this reason they get into this special work of helping other persons. When they meet people who do not like them or with whom they cannot establish a successful relationship, they are frustrated and disappointed. Such clients represent a challenge to many counselors' basic stance toward people and life in general. Failures can intimidate and upset them.

These clients also frustrate other typical ideals of counselors; namely the optimistic American and democratic notions that, with a little effort, we can stand on common ground with almost anybody; that things can be worked out; and that no matter what the difficulty, some kind of a solution is always possible. It is extremely stressful when non-cooperative clients challenge such basic personal and professional beliefs.

It is always typical of many conscientious counselors to blame themselves too much in these circumstances. They feel guilty that things are not working out when, in fact, the problem may not be entirely their fault. It may be helpful to recognize certain clinically defined groups with whom counseling is characteristically difficult. Without a sensitive appreciation of their personality structure, it may be bewildering to attempt to understand or work with them.

Moreover, it is difficult to manage the feelings these clients can generate in us. These two dimensions are closely linked with the immediate and long-range possibilities of helping them even in a

219

modest way. Some feeling for their life-style and their way of relating to others makes us more positively helpful and assists us in dealing with our own countertransference feelings. When we see these persons in perspective, we can keep these issues clear and also make more sensible and appropriate referrals to other sources when this seems the right thing to do.

Some of those with whom it is difficult to work in counseling can be best understood under the descriptive category of *personality disorders,* a classification taken from the *Diagnostic and Statistical Manual of Mental Disorders-III-R.* Some object to any kind of labeling of the behavior of clients, but the descriptions of this manual—with which all counselors should be familiar, as has been suggested before—can have practical positive benefits for both counselors and their clients.

Persons suffering from personality disorders are neither neurotic nor psychotic. Personality disorders "refer to behaviors or traits that are characteristic of the person's recent (past year) and long-term functioning (generally since adolescense or early adulthood). The constellation of behaviors or traits causes either significant impairment in social or occupational functioning or subjective distress" (*DSM–III-R,* p. 335).

These persons do not manifest symptoms; rather, they display a distorted way of living and of managing their affairs and their relationships with other persons. Personality disorders, like many other things difficult to define, may suffer from the use of analogies; they do, however, resemble the proverbial tree that grows the way the twig is bent. Individuals with personality disorders do not come for help in an anxious state unless their underlying problem has precipitated some other difficulty in their lives, such as the loss of a job or the breakup of a marriage. Ordinarily, they arrive in counselors' offices because of collisions on the behavioral level. Such persons do not have subjective complaints about the state of their souls as much as they have problems in living and working in reasonable harmony with others. Because they do not have much subjective anxiety, they do not ordinarily seek counseling help on their own.

Lawyers, members of the clergy, personnel managers, and other such persons meet a great number of people suffering personality disorders without ever recognizing the nature of the disturbance. These truly affected persons may recognize that things are going wrong in their occupations or in their domestic lives but still be unable to know why. They know that things are just not working out, but they have little insight into their own involvement in the situation. Frequently they are referred by other persons, such as supervisors or family members, who know that they are in trouble but feel incapable of being much positive assistance to them. Very often this is because the disordered person has had a long record of losing jobs or of marital difficulties and is finally pushed to seek assistance by those around him.

They do not see themselves as the major contributing cause to their own difficulties. It is much easier to blame others for the problems that arise with the boss, or to make their spouse the responsible party in any difficulties at home. They cannot perceive the flaws in their own approach to life, and they are therefore not discomforted by the way they do things. They may be puzzled by the consequences, but these can be projected out as the responsibility of others. The twist in their personality seems so much a part of their self-enclosed system that they may not realize it is there.

In a strange but true way these persons are frequently never told the real reasons when they get into conflict at school or in their work. Supervisors and educators choose to rationalize rather than to tell the truth when they fire an employee or dismiss a student—a common problem for many people in authority. Individuals suffering from personality disorders are not helped to understand that the patterns of their behavior get them into trouble; they are usually told that the reason lies in poor academic or occupational performance, or that extraneous considerations have dictated the move. These efforts to avoid the hard truth leave such persons in the dark, which they already find difficult to pierce or comprehend. Because they are seldom confronted about their behavior and its inadequacies, they are denied even an elementary option about doing something about themselves. The work histories of such individuals often contain a record of similar incidents of dismissal after conflict with co-workers or with authority. Despite this, these people fail to observe their pattern and their own responsibility for it. There is a kind of psychological naïveté about them that permits them to seem innocent or oppressed when they explain themselves to counselors.

Psychiatry does not know enough about human personality to make final judgments on the development of personality disorders. Although they can be recognized, it is difficult to sort out their antecedent causes. Some theorists believe that there is a constitutional predisposition for this difficulty; others emphasize early life experiences. What is important for the counselor who must face and respond to such persons is some appreciation of the kinds of situations that seem correlated with these difficulties. When counselors hear clients describe similar life experiences, they can be alerted to the possibility of a personality disorder.

The person who grows up in a family in which the other members have suffered from personality disorders—such as being fearful and suspicious of all strangers and remaining in isolation from them— may identify strongly with these defective adjustments because no other model has been provided. The experience of a childhood in which few discriminations between good and bad are made by elders, or in which there is great inconsistency in the application of discipline, may give rise to confusion or misunderstanding about what is appropriate human behavior. Children who develop personality disorders may have learned early and in a confused way the patterns of reaction in which they persevere throughout their lives largely because of the inadequacy of their early uncorrected experiences. The child who is reinforced in deviant behavior, or who is allowed to get away with misbehavior without ever being corrected, may emerge into adult life with the very problem we have been discussing.

As counselors listen carefully, they may get a feel for the lifelong quality of the personality disorder pattern. Such a judgment is made, not to trap the person in this category of diagnosis but to define the terms of the relationship and to allow counselors to develop their own role in an intelligent and informed manner. Counselors can thereby avoid errors both in responses and in the expectations that they place on the client's behavior and their own capacity to be of help. Some understanding of the diagnosis of a personality disorder frees counselors from experiencing unnecessary frustration and inappropriate guilt when they find such persons are difficult to work with or to help very much.

The Passive-Aggressive Personality

The passive-aggressive personality is a specific instance of a personality disorder. Some experts claim that it is the most common psychiatric disability in the United States today. A few have speculated on the cultural reasons contributing to this; these include overcrowding and the other sources of frustration that are generated in a modern-day technological society. The passive-aggressive designation is self-descriptive and is ordinarily characterized by conflicts over dependency needs and relationships with authority. Persons in authority are often puzzled by these individuals who seem too difficult to understand. They may make every effort to reach the passive-aggressive only to find that little success follows. This is very frustrating for persons in authority who do not understand the subtlety of the situation or the effectiveness with which persons with this personality disorder transmit aggression in indirect ways.

The essence of the behavioral style of these persons lies precisely in this—their hostility comes out indirectly and in disguised forms. They are able to irritate or hurt others as clearly as if they employed direct aggression. Because their passive style is elusive there is an unsatisfying fuzziness to their relationships which is very difficult to handle.

One must observe carefully in order to see how, by withdrawing from life or through half-hearted compliance with its demands, these individuals act out their problems. At work, for example, the passive-aggressive persons are only partially engaged. He or she is there but, in another sense, not there at all. They are able to devise ways of having things left hanging or unfinished or grudgingly done that delay and cause discomfort or pain to a great many people around them.

They can do this in many ways. They can inflict passive-aggressiveness by failing to show up at a long-planned meeting, by not answering their phone or mail, or by playing the role of dropouts in important discussions. It is hard to pin anything on passive-aggressive persons but it is easy to recognize the results of their style of relationship. We feel the effects of the invisible aggression on ourselves; they know how to hurt us without seeming to. That is precisely why their behavior leads them into conflicts and why they have such repeated difficulties at home and at work.

The chief characteristic is the self-defeat that is written into the scenario of their life-style. This personality difficulty explains many of the failures or disappointments we observe around us that are otherwise difficult to understand or appreciate. Such things are not planned consciously. Passive-aggressive persons do not understand what they are doing nor do they experience anxiety over what they do. The anxiety comes only when their spouse leaves them or when the boss threatens to fire them. Otherwise they can only be spotted through their passive, hurting style. This is sometimes exemplified through overcooperation; applying the letter of the law, for example, to such an extent that they finally defeat its purpose. They are not very happy or successful people; their relationships do not seem very deep or lasting and, because of their personal characteristics, other people find it very difficult to like them. And counselors can feel that way about them too. This is why they are a source of stress.

What Can Counselors Do?

Counselors are almost certain to meet and work with passive-aggressive persons weekly if not daily; their preparation for this lies in deepening their understanding of the personality disorder itself. It is also helpful to realize that persons experiencing this disorder will bring their style of relationship with them when they come for help. In other words, counselors can expect to experience from passive-aggressives what others who have been close to them have already experienced, the painfulness of aggression expressed in a subtly passive way. Counselors who are sensitive to the mode of cooperation or noncooperation of those with whom they work will be able to recognize and identify this particular personality problem early in the relationship.

One of the first sources of information will be in the counselor's own feelings. As has been stated in this book, this is the first place we look when we want to understand what is taking place in our relationships with others. The problem arises precisely because passive-aggressive persons can be so irritating that they cause us to react harshly to them in some sort of self-defensive retaliation. Realizing the high probability of this kind of reaction in ourselves enables us to catch it as it develops, and to control it so that it does not obstruct or destroy our counseling work.

Counselors may be caught between two feelings, especially if they do not have much experience working with these persons. On the one hand there will be the inclination to strike back, to hurt those who have hurt us; on the other hand there may be some inclination to win them over, to please them, to convince them that we, as counselors, are really nice and lovable people. Counseling is no place to apply this kind of "how to win friends and influence people" approach; it will not work. It will merely ensnare us in the embarrassing and ultimately self-defeating game of trying to get people to like us.

The counselor's primary task is to accept passive-aggressive persons as they are. This is difficult because they do not engender much sympathy and they do not seem to be attractive persons. They seem rather to be troublemakers and it is difficult to keep them in focus as persons who have a very taxing and unfortunate life. Even basic acceptance can be a great help as we try to work toward helping them to see the pattern of their family adjustments. Counselors should not reward passive-aggressive maneuvers, thus cutting off the gratifications unconsciously sought by the client. This may enable the person to see the self-defeating behavior for what it is, even if he or she lacks insight into its causes.

This attitude, coupled with the acceptance of the fact that we cannot completely save or perfectly cure everybody, makes us more available—even on a limited basis—to be of assistance to the passive-aggressive. The relaxation of our own expectations and the control of our own irritation make it much more likely that we will be some help instead of just being frustrated in dealing with personality disorders. Related problems with personality disorders will be discussed in a later chapter.

27

The Gift of Tongues: The Obsessive Style

Obsessive difficulties are common and tough; they are the source of great stress for counselors who work with people suffering from some variety of the obsessive-compulsive syndrome. The obsessive person needs assistance but makes it difficult to get; obsessives are not very happy and don't quite know how to make themselves that way. Reaching them with any kind of effective therapeutic help is a challenge to the most skilled therapist. Because these difficulties occur so frequently (psychiatrist Leon Salzman says the obsessive-compulsive personality type "is today's most prevalent neurotic character structure"—they are thought to constitute about twelve percent of all neurotic disturbances), counselors need an understanding of them and of their own potential reaction to their frustrating style. Perhaps professional persons who are not full-time counselors will never "cure" many truly obsessive persons, but they can learn to avoid many mistakes both in working with them and in managing their own reaction to them.

Defining Terms

Not everything described with the words obsessive or compulsive necessarily reflects the same kind of difficulty. People can be obsessive without being neurotic; they can also have experiences that resemble obsessive-compulsive behavior and not really be afflicted by it. Everyone occasionally has a trace of these difficulties as, for example, when a favorite song runs recurrently through one's mind or a momentary urge to do something bizarre passes fleetingly through one's consciousness. An *obsession* is technically understood as a recurring thought that is unwanted and that cannot be excluded voluntarily from one's awareness. A *compulsion* is a recurring irresistible impulse to perform an act or a series of acts. It is, as some note, an obsession in action.

Obsessive rumination refers to a recurrent subject, a personal problem, or even some abstract idea that preoccupies an individual in a repetitive or stereotyped way. This is somewhat like obsessive doubting or indecision except that the individual ruminates about some choice without ever coming to a conclusion. These are not the same as normal recurring thoughts or preoccupations known to everyone; the big difference is that an obsessive thought is unwelcome and that the person cannot get rid of it.

An inhibiting obsession is a thought about doing something the individual doesn't want to do. Frequently this takes the form of hurting somebody close or jumping off a high building or out of an automobile. The idea horrifies the person and it is not carried into action. The compulsion may focus on a single act the person feels he must repeat over and over again in exactly the same way, such as hitting all the pickets in a fence. It can also refer to a series of acts such as those involved in arranging one's room or one's desk in a precise way before beginning work. This may manifest itself in compulsive rituals that cannot be interrupted or deferred; this behavior frequently surfaces in a religious context.

A person afflicted with compulsiveness may manifest it by doing things over and over or by constantly rechecking them. Obsessives never seem able to let things be; they rewrite something, for example, until all its life or spirit is destroyed. They are forever interrupting their journeys to go home to check the locks or the furnace and, although they may begin some jobs, they are constantly breaking them off because their efforts, as in essay writing, never satisfy them. Compulsive persons do not choose to act; they *must* act in order to save themselves from being overcome by anxiety. Such persons do not enjoy these problems; they cannot even enjoy the sympathy or the special concern they may get from associates who recognize their difficulty. They understand that there is something wrong, that what they are doing does not make sense and does not make for an integrated life, but they cannot do anything about it. The *obsessive-compulsive dynamism* has been described by Salzman as possessing three characteristics:

1. Behavior or thought that persists beyond the need for and/or in spite of voluntary action.
2. The presence of anxiety and somatic distress because of the ego-alien nature of such thoughts.
3. Insight into the illogical and unreasonable nature of the thought or action, which does not alter the behavior (Leon Salzman, M.D., *The Obsessive Personality*. New York: Science House, 1968, p. 10).

What Is Going on?

The use of these mechanisms in whatever form constitutes an external translation of some inner conflict and anxiety. Obsessives also use the ploys of displacement, condensation, and symbolization in this effort. The defenses of isolation, reaction-formation, and the mechanism of undoing are frequently observed in obsessives. They are, in other words, speaking a very special language, a dry and containing language that encases their emotions and enables them to live outside them. Researchers of the subject feel that these manifestations are frequently related to underlying conflicts about authority and external control, and that the threatening impulses the person strives to keep under check are frequently hostile or sadistic ones. It has been suggested that this conflict, which the person cannot consciously acknowledge, is between being *obedient* and being *defiant*, between wanting to please and wanting to act out against authority. It is not a pleasant life experience. The person is trying to get life down perfectly so that nothing can go wrong and no hurt can take place.

As Salzman has observed, the typical obsessive seems to have a need to "gain control over one's self and one's environment in order to avoid or overcome distressful feelings of helplessness. The concern about the possiblity of losing control by being incompetent, insufficiently informed, or unable to reduce the risks of living produces the greatest amounts of anxiety. The realization of one's humaneness—with its inherent limitations—is often the basis for considerable anxiety and obsessive attempts of greater control over one's living" (p. 16).

Many churchgoers are quite familiar with the behavior of obsessives, which is often generated in certain authoritarian ecclesiastical atmospheres that are able to achieve extensive control over a person's environment. They propose a perfectionistic scheme to persons to overcome the threat of damnation. Whole life-styles have been spun out on this psychological conflict, and many of the obsessive individuals who make their way into counselors' offices can trace their life-style to unfortunate experiences with organized religion.

Some of the patterns that have been described as characteristic of the obsessive-compulsive style include the following: *Cognitive rigidity,* an approach to living manifested in a fairly stiff, formal social attitude or in a severely dogmatic and opinionated thinking style; *preoccupation* with strain-laden, driven activity or work accompanied by a restless inability to relax and to enjoy leisure; *indecisiveness* that includes postponing decisions to avoid their turning out to be wrong; a regular *worrying* that the person cannot seem to do without; lastly, what David Shapiro terms a *loss of reality* manifested in an excessive concern about possible, even though not very probable, events such as future ill-nesses or accidents (E. B. McNeil, *Neurosis and Personality Disorders.* Englewood Cliffs, N.J.: Prentice-Hall, Inc., 1970, pp. 39ff).

Salzman also cites the person's seeming need for omniscience, not-ing that "the obsessional can be comfortable only when he feels he knows everything or is engaged in the process of trying to know everything." He uses such experiences as doubting, putting things off, or not deciding in order to prop up the illusion of perfection because they allow him to avoid situations that would reveal deficiencies or shortcomings. Obsessives sometimes show rather exaggerated ideas about their own self-importance. This is not based on reality but is related to the high standards and impossible demands such persons make of themselves. The ritualization of behavior becomes important because it provides a focus for the person's attention, "thereby," ac-cording to Salzman, "distracting interest away from other matters."

Unhappy People

It is clear that persons afflicted with obsessive-compulsive problems do not experience much joy in life. They tend to be conforming because they really do not experience or enjoy freedom very much. It is too scary for them at some level of their awareness, and they prefer to be dependent on someone who will tell them how they should live their lives. They really prefer security to satisfaction. That makes it very difficult for them to enjoy things even when they have the money and leisure to do so. Frequently they turn hobbies that are suggested to them by well-intentioned friends into new forms of compulsive work. They simply cannot let go of their style of dealing with things and there is no way to argue them out of the difficulty.

Obsessives cannot help but reveal their inner problems through their outer activity. Sensible counselors learn to read their style and do not fall into the trap of trying to manipulate their environment as a solution. Down deep such people resent the controls on their life, but they cannot express this directly with any great ease. Rather it emerges in symbolic form, and those who wish to understand and work con-structively with obsessive individuals need to interpret their behavior carefully to avoid misunderstanding or misjudging it.

It is not enough, of course, just to know about obsessives. The important learning for the counselor who may already be under considerable stress is how to relate to and work with these people when they come for assistance. An understanding of their dynamics and the highly symbolic way in which they express themselves is, therefore, indispensable for even a common sense kind of counseling with them. Anybody who has ever worked with obsessives realizes how easily one can be absorbed into their defensive system. It is like the protective inky fluid shot out by the squid to obscure its movements when it is in danger. So compulsives blur out perception, making it more difficult for us to see them, in order to keep at a safe distance from us. The first thing counselors can do to help themselves, then, is to reflect on this style, which is built on so much hidden and misunderstood anger, which seeks to confuse and keep counselors off balance, which avoids their getting at significant emotions, and can so easily engulf them in massive intellectualizations that characterize the syndrome.

Working with obsessives provides a different experience from working with most other troubled people. Once they get into the session, obsessive individuals give very little of themselves away. They are like old pros at a press conference who know how to fend off the reporters and say nothing in several different ways. They are not open and eager to talk about their emotional problems; they display, in fact, their overall difficulty by their strenuous efforts to hide them. Counseling sessions with these persons can seem to be long, difficult, dry stretches. Why is this so? Precisely because obsessives are trying to avoid emotional contact; they want to keep the insulation on the wires and, even though this is an unconscious evasive maneuver, it serves their purpose of keeping the interview under their own control.

Reflective counselors who have learned to be participant-observers in their work will be aware of the undulations within each counseling session. If the counselor manages to get inside, the obsessive ducks away to control the fear and anger that the counselor's getting close causes him to experience. Counselors will feel repeatedly that as soon as they get close to meaningful material the door will be slammed tightly shut in their faces.

Counselors need to distance themselves from this interaction in order to be able to discern the pattern that clearly emerges. As helpers grasp the way in which these obsessives avoid emotional material, they begin to understand better the whole style and approach that obsessives typically employ. The pattern itself can be effectively used in furthering the counseling as long as counselors are able to grasp this and not be rendered frustrated and irritated by it.

Good Beginnings, Good Endings

Some students of the treatment of obsessive-compulsives have noted that, because of their passion for categorization, these individuals detach the body of a counseling session from its beginning or conclusion. What happens before a session actually starts or after it is concluded is ruled out as being of no importance. That is why the beginnings and the endings of appointments with obsessives can be instructive for counselors. Obsessives may let more things out at these times than they do in the course of the counseling interview.

Perceptive counselors are alert to this and realize that everything the compulsive does is meaningful; nothing is neutral. Striving truly to understand these people, sensitive counselors observe everything about their style, from their clothes and their seemingly innocuous introductory remarks to the kind of statements they may surprisingly make at the conclusion of a counseling interview. This is rich ore to be mined carefully by the counselor for clues about the possible nature of the underlying conflicts. They also provide relevant subject matter the counselor can direct attention to during the session. The first or last statements may be the closest to emotional expressions the client makes.

A client may mention a key subject at the very close of a session. He or she may do it by saying, "I'm surprised you didn't ask me about my job today," or some similar statement. This is a signal to the counselor about the key element in the conflicts that underly the client's symptomatic difficulties.

Obsessives classically use offense as the proverbial best defense. Counselors, especially those without very much experience, may not understand what is occurring and may find themselves bewildered by the way in which these clients can set about seizing control of the counseling itself. For example, obsessives like to throw counselors off guard, to get them to explain something they have said or to defend some other aspect of their professional activity. When this occurs counselors are vulnerable to getting angry and then to responding to their own irritation rather than to the psychological reality that lies beneath this defensive maneuver. It is very difficult for these people to seek help even though they need it. They fend off the threat that such help symbolizes to them and, if counselors can appreciate this, they will be able to look beneath the strategies with less stress on themselves.

Since one of the principal objectives of counseling is to establish some genuine human contact with the other, and since this is precisely what the obsessive is trying to avoid, what can the counselor do? It is helpful, first of all, to check one's own reactions and to read in these some truth about the nature and development of the counseling activity itself. For example, if counselors inspect themselves and find that they are bored, they can be fairly sure that they have not established any kind of contact with the client. If, on the other hand, they find that they are irritated, counselors realize that they have come in contact with their clients but that they are engaged with their defensive systems rather than with their inner personalities. If counselors find themselves interested and humanly responsive, this is a clue that they have gotten much farther into their clients' personalities. This is a reasonably reliable guide to follow. It resembles checking one's own psychological thermostat and it can be helpful in guiding the counselor through the sometimes tortuous course of counseling sessions with these persons.

Communication as the Defense

It is the particular genius of the obsessive style to use the means of communication to destroy the goal of communication. It is characteristic of many obsessives to be present physically but to be absent psychologically during the counseling. They may look away from the counselor, avoid making eye contact, speak so that they are almost inaudible, and, as a final touch, refuse to listen very carefully to the helper—even when they look as if they are listening. They are good at not being there, and it is not surprising that counselors can experience great frustration in dealing with them.

Sometimes obsessives become tutorial, delivering little lectures or suggestions to the counselor about the way the counseling is proceeding or about some technical point of psychotherapy about which they may have consulted the authors themselves. The problem here for counselors is to resist what is clearly a frontal assault on their professional capability. The temptation is to hit back, to see this behavior in the context of the client's overall maneuvers. Such persons are trying to save themselves much more than they are trying to hurt the counselor. Counselors who can view this with some good-natured compassion do not allow their pride to be hurt because they see its meaning and can respond with acceptance as well as some recognition of what the person is trying to do. It is sometimes wise to point out to the person how we perceive this kind of maneuver. "You feel more comfortable when you can keep me under control, don't you?" is only one way of making a realistic response that is not punishing but appropriate to what is taking place.

MacKinnon and Michels (p. 99) offer a number of practical strategies for this situation. They suggest, for example, that when the counselor senses that the obsessive client is not paying attention and is not, therefore, hearing what the counselor says, it would be better to stop and draw some attention to what is taking place. This offers an opportunity to tap into what the client is really thinking but not communicating when the counselor is speaking to him. It provides, in other words, a way into the interior landscape of the person. When this can be done gently, for example, by asking what the person is musing about and then pursuing its theme, the situation is far more realistic than pretending that counseling is going on when it really isn't.

The theme behind these reflections, of course, is that counselors must not focus so much on the incidental elements of the counseling that they miss the overall maneuvers that constitute their clients' basic style. There are many clues to this in the resistance that the client manifests, and the counselor who wants to understand will not hesitate to follow these leads in a concrete but undefensive manner. These are the flags, tiny though they be, that indicate where the individual's concerns really are. It is easy to miss them or to shrug them off; they remain, however, as symbolic signals that convey important information when interpreted correctly.

28

More on the Complex Languages of the Obsessive Style

The obsessive person may come into the counselor's office with notes or lists of things to talk about, or things he wants to read to the counselor. It is obvious that the use of such devices enables the client to keep control of the situation very neatly. What will get talked about is only what he or she outlined on paper. Counselors who go along with this play right into the hands of their clients; the use of such techniques is almost always defensive and counselors cannot afford to let themselves be taken in by them.

When we do not permit people to use notes they may get upset. Counselors must learn to live with these upsets because they represent contact with the reality of the other's personality. Such clients will be anxious, but that only means that their real feelings have become involved.

It must be remembered that obsessive persons hate surprises; spontaneity is just what worries them. They want to be well-prepared to prevent the occurrence of surprises that may upset them emotionally. That is why obsessives come prepared or sound so well-rehearsed at times. The defense reveals something about the person, and a sensitive and understanding counselor can propose a question like this: "Why was it so important for you to be so well-prepared today?" That can open up a significant area. It is also clear that the counselor should avoid similar techniques—using notes or an outline—in dealing with such clients. They are poor solutions to stress and only complicate counseling problems.

Wherever they stand on the long continuum of the obsessive-compulsive problematic, these people can wear down their helpers with the systematic impersonality of a grindstone. They produce, for example, masses of irrelevant detail. You may, at one time or other, have read a book written by an obsessive-compulsive. They cannot leave anything out. They know how to waste our time and make it difficult for us to discern the shape of their lives by adding detail upon detail and keeping us effectively on the outside of their personal history. At the same time, they are sensitive to any criticism the therapist might offer about this defensive technique. That is why they are so taxing on the skills of helpers and the source of so much stress for them.

The key aspect of the challenge to helpers centers on their capacity to hear, accept tolerantly, and understand keenly just what the obsessive-compulsive person is attempting to do to them. Counselors cannot, in the long run, sit there and let it happen. Good counseling never means allowing oneself to be manipulated in the name of being understanding. That is a distortion of any authentic notion of psychological understanding. The art of therapy with obsessives rests on grasping the appropriate moment to intervene gently but clearly in order to stay the torrent of defensive words, and also to approach more closely the dynamic inner reality that motivates this bewildering style. Counselors cannot allow themselves to be trapped or they will lose their best opportunity to reach the emotional core of the client's behavior.

Being Quiet Is the Best Revenge

Although they may at times overproduce verbally, obsessives also have an instinctive feeling for the advantages of being silent. They can withdraw inside themselves in the presence of the counselor and, in the judgment of some clinicians, may tolerate this better than many other people who come for assistance. Sometimes they are able to tolerate silence better than counselors can. Helpers sometimes get edgy, especially if they have not learned to deal constructively with their own strong urges to do good or to do well. Obsessive-compulsives can throw silence at counselors quite skillfully. They may ask, "Don't you have something to say to me?" and if counselors are not careful, they may find themselves trying to explain. Here again the counselor's sensitivity is to what is going on beneath the silence. Sometimes very gentle questions such as, "What are you thinking about when you are quiet?" can lead into more emotional and meaningful material.

Questions are, however, another face of the defenses that are evident in this stressful counseling situation. Obsessives ask questions but they are not really looking for answers. That is why counselors who attempt to answer them merely contribute to their own dilemma. These clients place questions in order to get the interview under their own control; they are not really trying to foil counselors as much as they are trying to control themselves by controlling their relationship with their helpers. An awareness of the complexity of their psychological devices enables counselors to be more patient and to wait for the right moment to tap into the need that lies beneath all the questions. "It seems very important for you to get me to answer questions," is a far better response than any attempt to give the obsessive-compulsive direct answers.

The Heart of the Matter

Basically, obsessive defenses are, as has been mentioned, intellectual in nature. Obsessive-compulsives strain to find the right word; they may shift the words they use to indicate their dissatisfaction with the one they have just chosen. They jump from one place to another like children playing a game in the street and it becomes difficult and exhausting to follow them. They also may read up on psychology and psychotherapy and integrate scientific terminology into their statements. This not only supplies a whole new vocabulary for the defenses they use but it gives them some leverage against counselors who may not have kept up on things quite as well as they have.

They frequently use vague or neutral-sounding terms to describe genuine emotional events in their lives. They may, for example, say that they had a misunderstanding when they actually had a knockdown, drag-out fight with a member of their family. The counselor's task is not to let these bland words from which emotions have been distilled slip by. Counselors must catch the euphemism and baptize it with a more down-to-earth name almost as soon as it is uttered. Counselors must serve as translators as the client goes along or they may soon be lost altogether.

A very practical move in this regard is to remain concrete in our own terminology in order to avoid using the kind of intellectualized or jargonized language at which the client is adept. We thereby keep the field clear for improved communication. If, however, we succumb to employing their style, we may give obsessives just what they want; we provide the ammunition that they will quickly use against us.

Counselors must keep their sensors alert to where feeling may exist beneath the surface of so much dry intellectualizing. Part of the difficulties of these persons is that they live with the lid on their emotions. They exist by rote, carrying out what they think they have been told by someone else. They sometimes seem to live in abstract, almost third-person terms, saying things like, "A good husband wouldn't do that," or "It wouldn't be right to do this," without ever saying anything like "I don't feel it would be right to do this or that." Strangely, many people live out of touch with themselves in this way.

This is typical of the obsessive-compulsive who must isolate his intellectual interpretation of things from his authentic emotional reaction. Indeed, this is the motivation beneath the defenses they raise before our very eyes. It helps to sense the massive effort that is expended and to appreciate something of the fear and anger that are commingled inside obsessives. For people who have lived very rigidly, for example, the answer is not some sudden liberation of all their impulses. The last state of such people can be worse than the first.

How the Truth Comes Out

These clients are also good at using *denial*, that essential ingredient of all defense mechanisms. Counselors should not be surprised to encounter this in the classic defense of reaction-formulation. It is helpful, in trying to grasp the meaning of the denial that these persons employ, to remember some basic principles. Counselors who remember that *there is no negative in the unconscious* will be much better able to translate the statements or even the symbolic gestures made by these clients. When they deny something more than once this may be a clue that there is a pesky, emotion-laden truth that they are trying to obscure. Compulsives sometimes get tangled up in these defenses, such as going on to reverse the statement made earlier in the interview. When this happens it may be very helpful to reflect on it with the client. It is one of the signs of and avenues to the emotions they hide so diligently and so effectively. Other related clues center on any instance in which they make too much of telling the truth. This stands as a fairly good rule in life itself, of course, but it has special application with obsessives, with whom we must be very sensitive to catch the slightest flares that indicate the presence of emotion. Beware of phrases like, "To tell you the honest truth now," or "Well, to be perfectly frank . . ." They are always distant early warnings that what we are about to hear will neither be frank nor truthful. It also helps to watch for inappropriate laughter or self-conscious grinning that is not connected with anything really funny. Anger frequently lives just beneath a grin of this kind and counselors must be ready to read its paradoxical presence.

Counselors must always be prepared to have clients try to do something to them in the course of the helping experience. This happens in every genuine therapeutic relationship. Counselors can read their own experience with the client as a sample of the general way in which this person relates to others.

What are some of the things that may happen to us in the course of working with these clients? They may present themselves as dependent, helpless persons, which is obviously related to their desire for external control, for some mechanism that will keep them secure. They may, in pursuit of this, treat counselors as authority figures whose advice they are anxious to receive and follow. They confer omniscience on counselors, something that can be flattering but psychodynamically entrapping at the same time. This problem can manifest itself in religious behavior. One may recall the well-intentioned but hopelessly bad advice that was once given to pastors and other counselors working with such individuals. They were told, in effect, to take control of the afflicted person's life, to insist on absolute obedience to their dictates as a cure for what was popularly referred to as *religious scrupulosity.* It is clear that this approach reinforced their difficulty and hardened the defenses of the person seeking help. It also placed the guide into the very vulnerable position of taking responsibility for another's activity.

Obsessive-compulsives can keep at an emotional distance from even the most insightful kind of comment or response on the part of the counselor. They have prepared in advance for such things, and counselors should not be surprised or unnecessarily dismayed at the fact that their insights do not seem to be effective. This is one of the characteristics of these clients, because they are able to maintain the separation between intellectual interpretation and emotional reality.

Counselors need to be very careful not to fall into some kind of formula in dealing with these clients. Formulas are grist for their defensive mills. If we find that we are saying something to one client that we also said in almost exactly the same way to another, then we may be dulling our own vitality and removing ourselves further from the possibility of being truly effective.

Things to Remember

As we pick up the signs of the emotions beneath the systematic defenses of clients, we will look for early opportunities to point this out in our responses. We try, as always, to keep our responses as close to the client's experiences as possible, but we also remember that not far beneath the surface clients are angry and that any response that gets close to the truth may make them overtly angry. Counselors must learn to live with this if they hope to be effective. Obsessives can put on quite a show of being hurt or irritated but that is more a sign of progress than it is evidence of a serious mistake having been made.

Don't try to patch things up with them. This is a natural inclination for most helpers when their clients seem to be offended by something that takes place in the counseling. This is particularly true for people whose counseling is part of another professional identification. It is much better to let clients be angry, to let them experience what they have been hiding from and through this perhaps to find a way, for the first time, of dealing less defensively with this affect.

Don't strike back at them when they get angry. That is a response to our own needs rather than to the real meaning of this occurrence in the obsessive-compulsive relationship.

Don't let them patch up the situation. That may sound cruel, but once emotions are expressed in a relationship, it is not therapeutically sound to try to hide them or pretend that they did not occur.

Don't argue with the client. That is really a doomed activity as far as working with obsessive-compulsives goes. There is nothing they like better than an argument that simultaneously enables them to rebuild their intellectual defenses, waste time, and frustrate the helper. Obsessive-compulsives are good at getting into unreasonable arguments with you; the important thing is to remember that they *are* unreasonable and that logical responses are clearly doomed from the start.

The counselor's best effort is to relate the anger to its causes even when this must be done inch by inch by pursuing this emotion into the interior of the person, to find something of the truth that lies beneath the client's symptomatic behavior and his whole style of relating. After we do this the counseling actually can begin. Clearly this requires counselors who are tuned in correctly to the client, who have their own feelings under control, and who know what they are doing.

Behavior Modification

Although the reflections of these chapters have followed traditional dynamic lines, the techniques of behavior modification have also been applied to the treatment of obsessive-compulsives. There has been extensive research done in this field, and counselors should be acquainted with it. It is also important to realize that therapists who use behavior modification are not insensitive, robot-like individuals. The qualities we have been discussing about appreciating the style of the obsessive-compulsives are important for the behavior modifier as well as for the more dynamically oriented counselor. In fact, these attitudes are chiefly marked by respect for and understanding of the client, and are necessary in the context of any attempts to modify the behavior of other persons. It is only with sensitivity that these approaches can be effective.

Behavior modification emphasizes the learned aspect of behavior, suggesting that obsessive-compulsive symptoms are held onto because they have been acquired the same way we learn anything else—from the mistake in our golf swing to a preferred way of tying our shoes. Behavior modifiers feel that the symptoms reflect overlearning of specific thoughts and behaviors and that they are maintained because carrying out these symptoms brings an immediate reward through relieving anxiety. Although obsessive-compulsive symptoms such as hand-washing and ritualistic behavior may bring special disapproval, that only comes later on. The immediate reward—and the reason that the behavior is maintained—is sufficient in itself to help the person tolerate other more remote consequences.

Behavior therapists attempt, as Millon puts it, "to identify what behaviors are maladaptive and what behaviors should be reinforced to supplant them. . . . Then a program of reinforcement to shape the new behavior is devised" (Theodore Millon, *Modern Psychopathology.* Philadelphia: W. B. Saunders Co., 1969, p. 405. See also R. J. Yates, *Behavior Therapy.* New York: John Wiley & Sons, Inc., 1970).

Although there has been some success in this regard, there has been regular criticism that exchanging one pattern for another without dynamic insight is not productive in the long run. Most behavior therapists are, as has been noted, humane and understanding in their efforts to free people from the chains of learned behavior that punish them and keep them from enjoying a freer life.

Don't Be Discouraged

D. E. Cameron, noting that compulsives are very difficult to treat, states that they are "among the most refractory of all psychoneurotics. Indeed many psychotherapists avoid attempting their treatment at all" (D. E. Cameron, *Psychotherapy in Action.* New York: Grune and Stratton, 1968, p. 206). No one should be naïve about the problems associated with obsessive-compulsive persons. Not every one of them will be suffering from a full-blown neurosis, but the same style will be evident, emphasized here one way and there another, in the obsessive-compulsives who come for help. Sometimes professionals who are not counselors—clergymen, lawyers, and physicians—will deal with such people and will not realize exactly what is happening to them. They will try to be logical and they will find themselves in the web of the obsessive-compulsive's defenses. They will mark these people off as frustrating eccentrics, but a little understanding can improve their way of relating to them and their effectiveness in dealing with them.

Counselors of all kinds need patience in dealing with clients who have so much masked anger. It is wise not to push too hard, argue too much, or try to prove to them that we are good counselors. We may, in fact, only be able to free them a little. We may end up referring them to somebody else. A little help, however, is a great deal of progress for these people. Any better balance between their needs for security and their satisfactions can change their lives very positively. Understanding the people beneath the symptoms is the essential ingredient in achieving this.

29

The Histrionic Personality

The histrionic personality, formerly termed hysterical, is a common, complex, and yet fascinating challenge to everyone who engages in counseling. In common with all personality disorders, the hysterical difficulty represents a lifelong pattern of maladaptive behavior rather than a distinguishable set of symptoms. In other words, personality disorders do not manifest themselves in the clusters of defensive measures that are employed in specific configurations in order to check the anxiety that spurts from some inner conflict. People suffering from personality disorders have *problems in living* that are reflected in the overall way in which they establish relationships in their lives. A personality disorder is more like a life-style than an episode of illness with distinctive symptoms. The hysterical personality, then, does not exhibit the conversion symptoms that are common with the neurotic problem often termed hysterics.

The hysterical personality does resemble the hysterical neurotic in the use of dissociation and repression. Hysterics may, for example, behave as though their problem did not exist, thus acting out a fundamental denial of their difficulties. Persons of this type may, for example, find themselves in situations that call upon them to make some preparations for the future. This can occur, for example, if they are members of the faculty of a school that is closing at the end of the year, and yet they do nothing about it, going along as though this major change were not really about to take place. People may shake their heads and judge them as unrealistic without suspecting how this acted-out denial fits into their hysterical pattern of adjustment. Many people may judge them as foolish or improvident and not understand or even suspect the presence of a personality disorder.

Interesting People

Beginning counselors, as MacKinnon and Michels (p. 129) note, find "the hysterical patient one of the easiest to interview; the experienced psychiatrist finds him one of the most difficult." This is true because, on the surface, people with histrionic personalities seem extremely attractive and interesting. A new counselor, meeting one for the first time, may be impressed with their vivacious qualities, their attractive looks and way of speaking, their seeming warmth, and their apparently serious intentions about pursuing therapy.

Older therapists have worked with these people long enough to realize that things are not what they seem and that the superficial qualities mask an emotional impoverishment and uncertainty that make histrionic personalities difficult work indeed. Novice therapists may also find themselves flattered by the kind of attention they seem to get from these people who, as we will observe later, use seductive maneuvers as a matter of course. The younger therapist, in other words, often feels good about meeting an attractive patient. It is true that counselors never get bored working with these self-dramatizing persons, but they also find that they are walking across terrain that is shaped by subterranean forces that are complex and intertwined. They are not as easy to work with as they seem. Counselors can spare themselves much stress by carefully studying their own reactions when they are suddenly enthusiastic about a patient of this type. They should wait to hear what is going on beneath the surface and save themselves from the disappointment of discovering that these persons are not nearly so emotionally rich or able as they had supposed.

Other Characteristics

Histrionic personalities seem unaware of the impact of their behavior on others. They may also seem a rather mixed configuration, somewhat prudish in one moment and then quite the opposite in the next. That is why there can be some difficulty in being sure that one's understanding of them as "hysterical" persons is accurate.

One thing that comes across, however, is the energy these persons put into looking attractive. This is something that sensitive counselors can feel and trust as an initial indication of the kind of person with whom they are working. These people want attention, and self-dramatization is a chief feature of their self-presentation. This is but one of the features that make them interesting and place them in such sharp contrast with other persons who experience so many difficulties just in beginning to speak about themselves. And every counselor has met many withdrawn and uninteresting clients.

Histrionic persons entertain the counselor in speech, appearance, and the general way in which they conduct themselves. They emphasize, much to the delight of therapists, feelings and their inner experiences. They do not, like the phobic patient, talk concretely only about their external behavior. They can, in fact, exaggerate their experiences in a highly colorful way. To no other group can the old saying be better applied: it's not what they say but the way they say it that reveals the truth about them. They do not, of course, hide themselves consciously. They present themselves in the only way they have learned throughout the course of their whole lives. Counselors get a clear sample of what these people are always like with others. The problem is that the presentation contains elements that can prove seductive to the counselor in many ways.

These people demand a great deal of attention and they may employ their attractiveness, especially if the therapist is a member of the opposite sex—classically a woman patient with a man therapist—to season the counseling with an erotic flavor. This offers a sample of how they relate to everybody else; counselors must learn early that this is not some special response to their own attractiveness. Some counselors who have never experienced seductive behavior from an attractive client at close quarters may find the experience both exciting and flattering. If they get too mixed up in it by accepting the invitations of the seductive person, they set themselves up for the classic completion of the maneuver. These histrionic persons may seem to promise a lot, as the old saying goes, but they are not at all ready to deliver. If a counselor evinces any sexual interest in response to what seems like an open invitation, the histrionic personality will pull back, indicating that that is certainly not what was in mind. They seem genuinely unaware of the effect of their demeanor, and when they close the trap they leave others feeling frustrated, defeated, and puzzled. This, in fact, is one of the ways in which histrionic persons make their way through life. They flirt, lead people on, and hardly realize the way these maneuvers affect those around them. For them, this is a major problem in living because it does not deliver any satisfying relationship to them and it tends to leave them more alienated and lonely as people recognize and protect themselves against this behavior.

The histrionic person has been depicted often in the movies and on the stage. They can be observed in certain professions where their flamboyance and style is accepted and where their lack of follow-through in relationships is not considered such a surprise. They have a way of speaking like Bette Davis playing an edgy fashion editor or a movie queen, using gestures and delivering superlatives such as "fabulous" and "sensational" about even the most ordinary events. There is also some popular folklore about women who can seem so seductive and yet who remain so cold. The notion is that if the right man could get hold of them—usually the man who thinks he is the right man says this—and show them how to enjoy sex, they would be "cured." This is the kind of opinion that merely perpetuates masculine illusions about the therapeutic effects of their own potency. It is just another daydream resonating to a life already marked with daydreams; it is a dangerous prescription, not only because of its adolescent flavor but because counselors must remember the true significance of the seductive behavior of these persons. Their way of presenting themselves to others is not a matter of choice; it is the only style they know.

The histrionic personality is the outgrowth of complicated early experiences, especially, insofar as we can understand them, those related to what these persons have learned through their relationships with their parents. Counselors can save themselves much frustration by maintaining the perspective that allows their enlightened understanding to put the exaggerated and histrionic behavior into perspective. Unfortunately, other persons are frequently drawn close to these people because of their attractiveness; they never quite understand why they are always on the outside of their personalities, why their relationships fall apart, and why it is so difficult to do anything about it.

Where's the Love?

Basically, histrionic personalities have enormous difficulty with love and intimacy, with the substance of what it means to share life deeply with another person. They only *seem* to relate warmly, and the sensitive counselor will catch the fact that this is a superficial presentation of themselves. Helpers will note that the intimacy they seem to offer so generously in the beginning of counseling never goes anywhere. It is a flat and echoing vestibule to their personality. The doors never open to anything roomier. There is no place to go if one is not content to remain on the surface according to the terms allowed by these persons.

Just as the obsessive personality will work strenuously to avoid emotional contact in counseling, so histrionic personalities will seem to work very hard in order to achieve it. Indeed, much of their effort goes into trying to get some gratifying response from the counselor; this is not the response the counselor thinks he is asking for, however. When these people do not get the specific response they want—and it is more the response of a parent than a lover—they feel that they have failed and become quite upset and angry. This reveals the low level of tolerance for frustration that also characterizes their behavior. These things become more evident when counselors do not succumb to what the clients wish them to be. Experienced therapists, sensing the difficulties that lie behind their effusive beginnings in therapy, are not as enthusiastic as beginners about working with them.

The general seductiveness of the histrionic is a principle way in which they present themselves in counseling. They seem to use their bodies intuitively, trying to signal a concern for love and tenderness. They are not looking for this, however, but they do seek more shallow words of approval, applause, and protection. They do not really want to be close to another person; they would not know what to do with real intimacy, so physical proximity becomes a substitute for genuine emotional closeness. Anyone with much life experience realizes how unsatisfactory such an effort at relationship can be. They are always looking for love, using their seductiveness to achieve what they understand to be love, only to find that their approach cannot build or sustain any mature relationship. Most of these remarks concern the way hysterical persons relate to therapists of the opposite sex. With members of their own sex they are far more antagonistic and competitive, seeming to deal with them as though they were threats to the possibility of their achieving the adulation or attention they seem to crave so ardently.

One of the chief features of the histrionic woman is her presentation of herself as basically helpless and dependent. They do not present themselves as mature partners in a relationship that can develop into something. Rather, they place themselves in the role of someone who needs care and attention from a strong and fatherly figure. This follows closely the model of the parent-child relationship, with the counselor explicitly becoming the substitute parent. Parental concern is the reward the histrionic person attempts to wrest from the counselor through what appears to be erotic and seductive maneuvers. They do not want lovers; they want good fathers. This is why they seem so shocked and surprised if, in response to their seductiveness, a man might make some advances to them. Such intimacy is not at all what they are emotionally prepared for. They want a "parent" who will take responsibility for them, worry about them, and protect them. What they offer in return is their superficial charm and the kind of entertainment for the therapist that comes out of this.

This presentation of the self as a child needing protection is at the core of the histrionic person's style. It is beneath what inexperienced therapists may take as an invitation to a sexual or somewhat intimate relationship. This is not what is happening and, as the client begins to act in a possessive way in this regard, counselors may begin to realize and face the psychological facts. Only as counselors appreciate the unconscious determinants of their behavior can they begin to see hysterical persons in true perspective.

The Problems Here

It is clear that serious countertransference problems are possible with these clients. They are inviting, indeed promoting, countertransference through their seductive attention seeking. Counselors who do not recognize this may find their own position compromised, their own feelings confused, and their own ability to be helpful seriously impaired. It takes a sensitive and insightful counselor to keep these things in balance. Needless to say, histrionic persons can be a source of enormous stress. That is why it is so important for counselors to reflect periodically on their feelings as honestly as possible. They also come to appreciate the seasoned therapist's measured approach to such clients.

Male histrionics will not present themselves in exactly the same way as females. They may, in fact, present more of a facade of self-confidence, a studied capacity to run their own lives with serenity and self-assuredness. They may seem very "macho" but this kind of behavior is almost always a sign of the weakness that they feel inside themselves. They experience fear and anger, which they cover up with a more superficial kind of behavior. The man who feels that dressing the right way, having the right cigarette lighter, and wearing the correct fashions, as well as possessing an extensive knowledge of what wine to order, may make up for the lack of confidence he experiences within. Histrionics can seem to be very promising as candidates for counseling. That is why they need such careful and sensitive understanding.

Histrionic persons can sometimes seem to live outside of time with a great lack of concern for order, punctuality, or even for knowing what is going on in the world at any given moment. They are very different from the obsessive, who is so overconcerned about such things, and they are very poor at keeping records or organizing things. They respond much better in any assignment if they are guaranteed to get a good deal of attention in the process of carrying it out. This is one of the clues to understanding and relating with some effectiveness to them.

They are basically self-indulgent. Counselors can feel the self-concern the histrionic person generates in much the same way that ordinary, healthy people can feel the psychic emanations that come from self-centered persons. The vanity and narcissistic qualities of these people are quite obvious. They need attention and they want it now. This is one of the reasons they seem to be independent of the time frame that is significant in the lives of most other people. They cannot put things off, nor plan very well for tomorrow. It has been suggested by some observers that, for clear psychological reasons, histrionics sometimes are attracted to obsessives; they marry and supply each other for their own lacks. The obsessive keeps things in order; the histrionic provides a kind of vivacity and sense of freedom the obsessive cannot manage. That, of course, does not necessarily make a good match.

30

More on the Histrionic Personality

Histrionic personalities, despite what may seem like an assured and knowing sexual self-understanding, almost always present problems connected with their sexual functioning. These are related to their marriage, radiating out from their basic difficulty in establishing reciprocal relationships with anyone. There is a great variation in the forms that these difficulties take. This is a very complex scenario, with mainly unconscious cues that go back a long way in their lives. To approach these people with oversimplified solutions may merely ensnare counselors in a web of motivations that are not easy to untangle and may make the counselor ineffective. It is said that, at times, gamelike approaches to counseling are applied on a superficial level that does not take proper cognizance of what is really happening dynamically in histrionics. Such people cannot merely be given new roles to play and be expected to heal themselves through this process. Neither will these people be helped very much by some crusade for sexual liberation, an experience of "swinging," or urging them to read some new book that is supposed to add zest and novelty to their sexual lives.

Histrionics are classic examples of individuals whose problem is not that of technique. It is that of being able to meet another in an equal kind of relationship and to experience the deeper meanings of intimacy. Their basic psychological problem is that they do not want to give of themselves because they so definitely need someone to take care of them in a parental and protective manner. Despite the superficial sexiness that these people can exhibit, and which can be so beguiling to naïve observers, they are simply not capable of great or satisfying sexual adventures. They find themselves very upset because this is an area with which they cannot deal effectively. They can go through a lot of motions, but the basic problem is not one of helping them to perform sexually; it is the far deeper one of helping them to live more humanly. When people learn this, sex, as always, has a way of taking care of itself.

These remarks are made and emphasized because sexual clinics are proliferating throughout the United States. Many of the counselors who run these clinics are well-trained and sensitive, but others have a strong orientation toward treating what they perceive to be symptoms of sexual dysfunction; they either ignore or are unable to deal with the complex of interpersonal dynamics that lie beneath the marriage or sexual problems which histrionic or "hysterical" persons may bring to them. Sensitive counselors always look beyond the problem to the persons who experience it in order to grasp its dynamic meaning in the setting of their lives. This is essential in understanding and dealing with the presenting problems of histrionic persons. Not even curing the symptom will insure success because the roots of the problem are far different.

Female histrionics may complain of some kind of frigidity. This is generally a reaction to their fear of their own sexuality. This can be seen in their relationships with other women. They are hostile and competitive with them as they move toward gaining power over men through the use of seductive techniques. These maneuvers, needless to say, do not deliver peace or contentment very readily. They are never satisfied for very long with their apparent victories.

Histrionic women, as we have noted, tend to idealize the man they are after. They do not see him in his individuality but rather as the all-good and providing father who will really not make any demands on them. The process is very complicated because of their fear that they may lose their "good father." To guard against this, histrionic women sometimes select—unconsciously, of course—men they can hold onto because of the man's dependent needs. It is not uncommon for these hysterical women to marry men who do not seem at all suitable for them. They may, for example, marry those who are less well-educated, less talented, or they may marry older men in a clear signal of the kind of relationship they are seeking.

Male histrionic clients also experience disturbed sexual functioning. There may be problems of potency or concern about homosexuality; nor is it uncommon to find male histrionics who engage in Don Juan-like behavior. Dynamically speaking, it can be seen that neither the female nor the male have worked through the basic relationships in their own lives. These center on the parent of the opposite sex and the shadows of these unresolved problems lie across the rest of their lives.

The Complicated Part

Because of these powerful inner dynamics their range of freedom in choosing a marriage partner may be highly restricted. It is a fair question to ask whether they can consciously choose and join themselves in marriage to another person on anything like the equal footing that is required in a genuine marriage. They are moved to meet needs that they neither recognize nor understand. That is why it is not surprising to find a histrionic woman marrying an obsessive male who also has passive-dependent needs. Neither party in the marriage recognizes what is going on. They do, however, continue to act out the script written in their unconscious.

It is not surprising if the histrionic woman views her obsessive male as a self-centered and controlling individual who restricts her freedom. He, on the other hand, keeps guard over her because she seems like an idealized mother who can answer both his sexual and dependent needs without disturbing his passivity too much. These people can only struggle, hurting each other and slowing killing themselves, unaware of their authentic motivation, and hardly in touch with each other in any genuinely intimate way. Both husband and wife want to be cared for and this has never been a solid basis for a marriage. Those who engage in marriage counseling may profit from reflecting on this not unusual situation.

Some observers have seen this kind of marriage typified in the relationship of George and Martha, the leading characters of Edward Albee's play, *Who's Afraid of Virginia Woolf?* The problem with such persons, as is clear in the play, is that they do not often go for treatment. Instead, they center their lives somehow on their own destroyed relationships, maintaining themselves through conflict. This is filled with fantasy, and in the play Martha and George maintain both Martha's imaginary pregnancy and their mythical child. They are examples of what Cuber and Haroff described as partners in a "conflict-habituated" marriage:

> At best, the couple is discreet and polite, genteel about it in the company of others—but after a few drinks at a cocktail party the verbal barbs begin to fly. The intermittent conflict is rarely concealed from the children, though we are often assured otherwise. "Oh, they're at it again—but they always are," says the high-school son. There is private acknowledgement by the husband and wife as a rule that incompatibility is pervasive, that conflict is ever-potential, and that an atmosphere of tension permeates togetherness. (J. R. Cuber and P. B. Haroff, *The Significant American.* New York: Appleton-Century-Crofts, 1965, p. 44)

What keeps such couples together is what keeps them apart. They are only one example of the complicated kinds of marriages into which people quite often get themselves. They are worth studying in somewhat greater detail here because of our need to realize the true nature of their governing dynamics, as well as the restraint with which counselors should generally approach and attempt to assist them in their sexual or marital difficulties.

Somatization Disorder

Somatization disorder, first known as hysteria, has been observed for a long period, although the actual cause of the disorder is unknown. It is characteristic especially of women with a long history of medical complaints. This may go back to their adolescent years and continue throughout their lives. They can talk about these medical problems very dramatically and their physical difficulties can be as complex as a medical textbook. It is not unusual for them to get themselves regularly hospitalized. They may, in fact, have a great deal of surgery, especially for gynecological reasons. The presence of this kind of medical history does not necessarily mean that one is dealing with a hysterical person. It does, however, provide evidence that alerts a counselor to this possibility. Counselors must restrain themselves from expressing the anger that this medical history sometimes generates in them—this contorted language of pain is one of the languages that some of them speak. It is not fakery and it describes psychological pain; it is ordinarily a way of looking for help.

These patients achieve a great deal of secondary gain, because they so regularly make themselves the center of attention in so many different ways. They have a special problem, however, in the fact that other persons gradually begin to see through their means of presenting themselves. There is a cost-benefit ratio involved because, although they get the attention they crave, they never get anything like a mature and satisfying relationship. They experience loneliness and depression because they cannot involve themselves deeply with others. It is, in reality, a very touching situation.

Repression is a characteristic mechanism employed by these persons. The purpose of the repression is to defend against any reawakening of sexuality. This repression shows up in their lack of sexual feeling, their loss of memory about certain events, most of which have to do with their central and unresolved relationship with their parents. Counselors should be alert for the clinical signs of repression in these episodes of forgetfulness and reported lack of feeling. This is the way the repression expresses itself.

What the Counselor Can Expect

Counselors can expect things to start well. They seem to get in touch with these patients almost immediately and they are delighted, especially if they have other clients who are more drab and seemingly—but only seemingly—more demanding on them. Things go along fine because a mood of seeming rapport may come to life right away. Histrionics may, for example, seem very enthusiastic about the counselor, saying that they have found him or her just at the right time and that they seem to have just the ideal qualifications for helping them. This is all part of their typical self-presentation in life and it can have a very warming and gratifying effect, especially on counselors who are overworked and seldom hear kind words from anybody.

Counselors can confidently expect to experience the dramatic and seductive behavior that has been described earlier. Histrionic persons will also be very entertaining. They are ready to talk and they know how to do it. They sound like wonderful clients—bright-eyed, attractive, and vaguely romantic in their style. Sensitive counselors can pick up the essence quickly. One of the problems counselors have is to refrain from being defensive as soon as they recognize what is happening. Much of the art of therapy resides in being able to understand such behavior without reacting self-protectively. To maintain an understanding and self-possessed attitude is very helpful for counselors working with flashy and interesting persons.

Counselors can be ready for body language. Counselors will remain more understanding and less defensive or neurotically involved the more they are aware of how histrionic persons speak to them through using their bodies. Helpers who have a fairly mature understanding of human nature will appreciate that they are working with another human being rather than an exotic temptress; they will understand that this behavior is not aimed specifically at their personalities but is characteristic of the level of interpersonal functioning of the histrionic person.

There may come a time in the counseling in which the self-dramatizing techniques of the histrionic person will have to be remarked about and discussed. This cannot be done too hurriedly or the client may experience it as rejection. A premature discussion of the histrionic style will only occur if counselors are too anxious to handle the seductive maneuvering in order to avoid getting involved in it. Counselors must remember that histrionics will always deny the seductiveness that seems obvious to others. Counseling is no place to argue with them about this or to react excessively to the dramatic statements they characteristically make. Histrionics may, seemingly offhandedly, divulge something about themselves—that they have committed a crime—that can have a powerful impact on the counselor. These are examples of their techniques of self-dramatization. What they ordinarily dramatize is their perceived plight of being helpless, put upon, or rejected by others. That is the message behind their behavior just as it is behind the distortions and exaggerations that may mark their narrative. If counselors get hooked into this, they must get unhooked and move back from the situation in order to get things back into perspective.

Histrionic persons can seem so interesting that counselors can get absorbed in the details of their story and miss getting some of the fundamental information that is important for a true understanding of these persons. It is always a good idea to get some kind of life history, to take nothing for granted, and to be wary of being distracted by the intrinsically interesting character of what they have to say. Any individuals who exhibit histrionic personality traits as well as physical complaints should have follow-through visits with a qualified physician in order to rule out the possibility of organic illness.

It is also helpful for counselors to note the feelings about themselves that lie beneath the histrionic's self-presentation. These are often quite self-devaluative. It is to these deeper feelings that a response can be made. One theme can usually be identified as common to their example and self-dramatization. Alert counselors will listen carefully for this special tone and respond to that rather than to the illustrative material. Histrionics provide counselors with many opportunities to get beneath their surface behavior and dramatics; counselors merely need to be listening to the right things on the right level.

Counselors who can work toward this deeper level of reactivity begin to relate slowly but surely to the frightened and immature person beneath the showy exterior. They will not stop at the symptoms nor just treat the marriage or sexual problems. Because they can sense the overall meaning of hysterical maneuvers, counselors will not be distracted or unnecessarily involved in the seductive behavior exhibited by these persons. These individuals test the sensitivity and understanding of counselors but they also provide an extraordinary challenge to professional behavior. Well-informed and self-knowledgeable counselors learn to avoid the easy mistakes and to work with the hard truths of the counseling experience.

31

The Deceptive Language of the Antisocial Personality

This chapter is an extended study that centers on the *antisocial personality,* one of the most difficult of the personality disorders. It is discussed in depth because, first, it is not an unusual challenge for counselors in a wide variety of settings; second, it offers an excellent opportunity for helpers to examine themselves and to learn more about their own pattern of psychological reactions.

The antisocial personality has a long history in our consciousness and in psychiatry. Those suffering from this personality disorder constitute one of the groups that is most difficult for counselors to recognize and work with effectively. As in all personality disorders, those described as antisocial have suffered from a lifelong difficulty that reveals itself in disordered behavior rather than in symptom formation. Even now personality disorders are not well understood dynamically.

The history of describing these persons in psychiatric terms is instructive in this regard. In 1835 James C. Prichard used the term *moral imbecility* or *moral insanity* to describe them, writing that "the moral or active principles of the mind are strangely perverted or depraved; the power of self-government is lost or greatly impaired and the individual is found to be incapable of talking or reasoning upon any subject proposed to him and of conducting himself with decency or propriety in the business of life." These are century-old words describing what we now call the antisocial personality.

Descriptive terms always shift with varying theoretical emphases in the field of psychiatry. At the end of the last century, in which genetic explanations were favored, these patients were described as "constitutional psychopathic inferiors." Later they came to be terms "psychopathic personalities," "sociopathic personalities," and in the second version of the *Diagnostic and Statistical Manual* they were termed "antisocial."

What are these antisocial persons like? These individuals seem, in major ways, to be unsocialized. They live to meet their instinctual needs without apparent concern for conscience or the standards of the community in which they live. They persistently violate the laws, codes, and common sense of interpersonal behavior, and they keep on doing so even when they are severely punished after they are caught. Aversive conditioning has no effect on them; for this reason heavier penalties do not cause them to put aside their antisocial behavior.

In the *DSM-III-R,* the criteria for the diagnosis of the antisocial personality include, in those over 18, a history of behavioral disorders that began before they were 15, including at least three of this array: truancy, running away from home, cruelty to human beings and animals, forcing others into fights or sexual activity, covert or overt stealing, and the use of a weapon. After the age of 15, the imprint of irresponsibility is observed in an irregular job history when work is available, including failure to show up, giving up jobs unrealistically, or equivalent actions in a school setting. It is also evidenced in deviant social behavior that, whether taken into custody or not, would normally be grounds for arrest.

Antisocial persons may cause harm to others, including abuse of spouse and children, and defaulting on bills and other financial obligations. Driven by impulse, they may travel without clear plans or any fixed address for lengthy periods. Although they are superficially engaging and often charming, antisocial persons indulge in behavior that is dangerous for themselves and for others, are not good at sustaining monogamous relationships, and, seemingly unconcerned for the truth, frequently use a con man's tactics to wheedle things out of others with no concern for what their effect on others may be. Often romanticized in popular culture, their attractive qualities are no more than skin deep and they leave a wake of pain and unhappiness behind them.

Outlaws by Conscience

Our century has witnessed a rise in the number of people who have defied the laws of the state in the name of the convictions of their conscience. These people are not to be understood as antisocial personalities even though they may, in fact, place themselves in the same position of opposition to law that characterizes the antisocial person. To act from conscience is the very opposite of acting as though one did not have a conscience at all. The wide variety of those who have protested war, or what they have perceived to be unjust conditions in racial discrimination or labor relations, deliberately choose to make a public statement by violating the law. They are also ready, in general, to pay the legal penalty as a symbol of the sensitivity with which they respond to their consciences. And they are generally motivated by some feeling for human concerns.

The antisocial personality is very different; he or she has no such noble motives and frequently does not seem to secure any advantage through taking the risks of breaking the laws of the community. Antisocial personalities are strikingly different; that is the first thing to remember about them. It may be true that the antisocial personality and the conscientious protester intermingle at the edges of certain groups in society, but they are quite distinct types. Indeed, the deviant life-style and manner of reacting of the antisocial personality are two clear aspects of their maladjustment.

Antisocial personalities are difficult to identify, especially for inexperienced counselors. This is so because they exhibit a patina of charm and goodwill, and they know how to flatter those who may be able to help them. That's part of the way they get through life. Eager helpers are vulnerable to their manipulative style. Antisocial personalities constitute a clear and present danger for those who lack training or who are unaware of the dynamic configuration of this personality disorder.

There is at present a renewed interest throughout America in the rehabilitation of convicts that has brought many volunteers, including members of the clergy, into this field of work. Religious persons are ordinarily marked by a strong motivation to help other people. Their very desire to succeed in doing this, especially with a population that needs a considerable amount of attention and help, sometimes leads them into naïve and entrapping relationships with antisocial personalities. Unsophisticated but eager helpers may have bad experiences as, in wanting to do good, they find that they have been used and that their efforts to help have been considered neither significant nor important by the antisocial personalities involved.

One should not be cynical in reflecting on these realities. The failure to appreciate the nature of the antisocial personality leads clergymen—as well as lawyers, judges, and countless other members of society—into bad judgments about people who are ready to go on swindling, robbing, dealing in drugs, and even murdering their fellow citizens without any observable qualms about it.

In New York City in August 1974 a young man on parole was arrested on charges that he had committed a sex-related murder that was a carbon copy of one for which he had been indicted eight years before. In the original case his defense attorney had plea-bargained him into a prison sentence that made it possible for him to return to society through parole. His good behavior and seeming rehabilitation in prison even advanced the date of his eligibility for parole.

The postparole behavior of this person puzzled all those who were in any way connected with him during this sequence of events. The superintendent of the correctional facility in which the accused murderer served for three years reflected: "We thought that Yukl was a classic version of the rehabilitation system working at its best. He didn't get a harsh sentence, he became a model inmate who seemed to have learned his lesson. But I guess underneath it all he was a con man. He certainly fooled me and it's giving me a lot of sleepless nights." These are the words, one must remember, of an individual with long experience with prisoners. And the psychiatrist who worked with him said in retrospect: "We release so many people when they make their required minimum that I didn't have any concern about him. We were sure he was rehabilitated and one of the best, brightest, most articulate prisoners I have ever seen. I can't blame the system, there was no way of doing it differently" (*The New York Times*, September 3, 1974, pp. 1, 57).

Similar stories—many of them far less dramatic—can be read or heard about almost every day. It is not a call for a hardening of the heart against the antisocial personality to suggest that we need, for our own sake and for that of society, to be more aware of and sensitive to recognizing and properly interpreting the meaning of his or her behavior. Only this can lead to more informed ways of helping them. Counselors, whether it is the main focus of their work or not, need to sharpen their appreciation of the qualities and challenges connected with these persons.

All counselors would learn a good deal about the antisocial personality by reading such books as Norman Mailer's nonfiction novel *The Executioner's Song* (Warner Books, 1980). It is the story of the murderer Gary Gilmore, who became an international celebrity in the early seventies while his lawyers fought an extended battle to win commutation of his death sentence. So skillfully does the artist capture the flavor of Gilmore's pathology that the reader will feel something very close to the emotions generated by antisocial individuals in person. It is a classic evocation of this syndrome and its manipulative and disruptive role in American culture.

Many antisocial personalities are getting by without being detected or properly understood. Readers of Harvey Cleckley's *The Mask of Sanity* (Masbey, 1964) will be familiar with this. Counselors can reflect for themselves on the fact that an emphasis on impulse gratification—do what you like when you feel like it—is widespread, and only gradually disillusioning for those who believe in it. Many other actions are made to seem reasonable on the grounds that *no one else will know what happened;* another variation is that *everybody is doing it.* There is a tinge of the antisocial attitude in many of these cultural phenomena. Only counselors who have some understanding of their environment can see this problem in full perspective.

Where Do They Come From?

The fact that there seems to be something lacking—something almost literally missing—in the character of antisocial persons has led current theorists to associate this personality with experiences in their early home life. Some hypothesize that, especially in shattered families, there is a lack of opportunity for proper gender identification. Parental inconsistency in dealing with children and unreasonable standards and expectations have also been associated with the growth of psychopaths. Others mention some early experience of parental or community rejection.

As Widiger and Frances summarize (Talbott, 1989, p. 634, 635) about antisocial personalities, "The failure to develop adequate attachment to one's parents, their inconsistent discipline, and the availability of an appropriate peer group are important (Wilson and Herrnstein 1985). The principal biogenetic variables are unclear. Currently popular are low clinical arousal and reduced level of inhibitory anxiety (Fowles 1984; Gorenstein and Newman 1980), which may contribute to an impulsive, sensation-seeking lifestyle and a failure to be responsive to aversive consequences. Antisocial personality disorder also appears to be associated with alcohol abuse, with a mutually interactive effect. Alcohol may result from and contribute to the development of an antisocial lifestyle."

Lack of inner controls accounts for much of the apparently pointless nature of what they do. They may steal a car on impulse even though they may, without great inconvenience, legitimately get the use of a car. They may steal something from a store merely because they have no money with them. They cannot deal successfully with the delay that would be involved in doing a thing legally. They are also unable to tolerate frustration and, although they may be punished for what they do, they do not change their behavior as a result. They are simply not put off by punishment. It seems as though their inability to postpone pleasure prevents them from estimating the inevitable cost of their lawbreaking.

Antisocial persons also lack close interpersonal relationships. Friendship requires what the antisocial personality simply cannot give. No one can be a friend for very long without having to give up something of his or her own concerns or without postponing some gratification. Friends have to be considerate, just what the antisocial personality seems constitutionally incapable of being. They can take but cannot give, and this is almost always reflected in their stormy and disrupted marital histories. Their inability to form relationships that are close and meaningful also makes it difficult for them to profit from counseling and psychotherapy.

Major Signs

Characteristic of antisocial persons is their apparent lack of anxiety, guilt feelings, or any other subjective discomfort as a result of their behavior. Those who suffer from them usually display free-floating anxiety only when they are under external stress. It is not something that comes from inside. Antisocial personalities may sound sincere in expressing regret but this may be discounted; it is a feeling of which they are incapable. Their problem is also manifested clearly in their defective sense of judgment. This is apparent in the way they respond to psychological testing by giving socially inappropriate answers to simple questions. Sensitive psychologists recognize the test behavior of these persons who, even when they strive to make a good impression through answering the questions the way most people would, frequently "spoil" the response by laughter or a condescending attitude.

These people generally have a poor school and occupational history. They are indeed con men who have depended on their superficial charm to get them through the obligations that other people have to face more straightforwardly. They are bound to reveal themselves somewhere along the line, at least to the subtle observer. They end up not doing well in the military, although they may be found in the ranks of soldiers of fortune, mercenaries, and guerrilla warriors.

Coleman, in his *Abnormal Psychology and Modern Life* (Glenview, Illinois: Scott Foresman, 1964), also mentions the way in which antisocial personalities characteristically reject all constituted authority and discipline wherever they are. They also possess a quick ability to rationalize and to project the blame for their socially disapproved behavior onto others. Another important characteristic pointed out by Coleman, and one that is of significance for counselors, is the fact that, in the long run, these people are irritating, disappointing, and distressing to others. That is, they end up doing harm to other people, despite what might seem to be the charm or attractiveness of their initial self-presentation. Coleman (p. 364) cites Ferdinand Demara, Jr., "The Great Imposter," as an example of the antisocial personality. This man, who became something of an American legend, continually falsified physician's credentials, claimed to have carried out surgical operations, and engaged himself in a wide variety of assumed professions. His actions differ greatly from those of murderers or major lawbreakers, but the essential dynamics of his behavior remain the same. We may find these persons entertaining and so fail to appreciate how, in real life, they do end up hurting and disappointing other persons. The counselor should expect that the antisocial personality will do to them what they do to everyone else.

It is at times very difficult to diagnose antisocial personalities. This is complicated by the fact that in our culture the term "psychopathic" is used without much precision. Diagnosis is also made more complex by the fact that the behavior of certain other persons can, in some respects, closely resemble that of the antisocial person.

Antisocial persons, however, do differ from obsessive-compulsives who may involve themselves in certain disordered behaviors. These latter personalities generally commit only one type of offense, and they will give evidence of struggling with the impulse they experience as forcing them to carry out this offense. There is, in other words, a big difference between the antisocial personality and the person who acts out of a neurotic conflict in getting into deviant behavior. Those suffering from symptom disorders do not exhibit the other signs that are present in the antisocial personality. The former individuals, for example, feel a sense of guilt about their behavior. That is classically absent in the antisocial person.

Our culture has also become wise about the persons who seem to have a need for punishment that is related to masochism or guilt rather than to the constituents of the antisocial character. These people seem to leave clues and seek out detection and punishment; they are also quite different from the antisocial personality. Some care must be taken in making judgments about these matters.

This is also underscored by the fact that in certain brain syndromes behavior resembling that of the antisocial personality may be present. All these things should be checked out carefully by appropriate referral in order to provide sensitive and considerate understanding of the persons with whom we work.

Counselors should also be aware of the fact that retarded persons sometimes are persuaded into certain kinds of behavior that may make them seem like antisocial personalities. Again, this requires an appreciation of the total complex of the features of the antisocial personality in order to avoid making erroneous judgments. Needless to say, sharpening our clinical "feel" for others lessens pressures that generate stress for counselors.

Working with Antisocial Persons

For many of the reasons already cited it is clear that a counselor has a real challenge both to identify and to establish a helping relationship with persons suffering from this personality disorder. What is at the heart of their difficulty is also what makes it hard for these persons to be interested in or to involve themselves in anything like counseling. Counselors, who may naturally be an optimistic and helpful group, need a mature outlook in order to see these persons in perspective and to employ their own sensitivity and talents with maximum effectiveness.

It is helpful to realize that the antisocial personality is not "just like everybody else, only different." Antisocial personalities are quite different in the way they look at themselves, others, and the tasks of life. As MacKinnon and Michels note (p. 299): "[The antisocial person] sees other people only as potential sources of danger or gratification, having little concern about their security, comfort, or pleasure. Inner drives are experienced as urgent and overwhelming—delay or substitution does not seem possible . . . feeling that results from gratifying his drives is a quality of tension, relief, or satiation, rather than the more complex happiness with tender feelings toward objects and with increased self-esteem that characterizes the neurotic."

What Do They Feel?

While many observers state that antisocial persons do not experience anxiety, others say that an appreciation of their handling of their anxiety is central to understanding them. They exhibit little if any anxiety, but this is a result, according to some, of their low tolerance for anxiety. Many of the dynamic mechanisms employed by the antisocial personality react very early to fend off, defend against, or snuff out the slightest bit of anxiety. They seem to have an early warning system and will go to great lengths to keep anxiety from coming into their awareness. *Denial* may be a major feature of this defense, and their outer coolness gives the idea that antisocial persons do not experience anxiety at all. What seems like an indifferent exterior may be the outer evidence of a massive psychological effort to hold anxiety at bay.

It is also true that they show very little evidence of guilt or, again, have a low tolerance of a psychological phenomenon they keep at a great distance from their consciousness. They do experience some of the relatively undeveloped foreshadowings of guilt in such things as *shame* or in *fear of public disapproval*. They do not want to get into the discomfort of tight spots but that does not indicate that they have any true guilt about the behavior that may get them there.

In other words, antisocial persons do not feel much at all; their emotions seem to be shallow. Not much seems to be going on in antisocial persons, and counselors, aware that they are not making contact with these clients, may blame themselves. This is only one area of counselor feelings that is instructive in working with these persons. Counselors should not blame themselves too quickly, but they may profitably examine this lack of emotional contact for its dynamic information. It may be the first clue they get to the fact that they are working with the antisocial personality.

As a consequence of this superficial emotional life, antisocial persons seem to strive for external stimulation in order to cover up what they lack within. Any experience seems to them better than the tense, isolated feeling of aloneness that leaves them to seek excitement in order to escape aloneness. They make noise so they won't have to put up with the uneasy quiet.

It is not surprising to find them *impatient* and *oriented to immediate pleasure*. This does not mean that they enjoy things the way other persons do. They cannot have the same kind of deep appreciation of things, and it would be dangerous to read our own capacity for feeling into their reactions. There is, as MacKinnon and Michels note, "a primitive and oral quality" (p. 302) to the pleasures they seek. These are more related to psychological needs than to the rewards of genuine interpersonal relationships. They may look the same but they are not the same.

For this reason antisocial persons, through their impulsiveness, may be led to outbursts of aggression in response to frustration. And, because they do not feel the way others do, it is very difficult for them to experience empathy; that is why their actions can be marked by what we observe as cruelty or sadism. Another feature of their emotional reactivity is the *episodic quality of their outbursts*. They seem to come like sudden and violent storms that leave little aftermath. The ordinary person has a difficult time calming down after getting upset. This is not true of the antisocial personality, who may wonder at the unsettled reactions that other people have to their outbursts. They may seem genuinely surprised that what they have done has generated waves of concern around them. This is another important clue to identifying antisocial personalities—through the effects they have on others.

Relating with Others

The charm antisocial persons display is there merely to use people who pass by in transient roles. Others can come and go in their lives and they have little feeling one way or the other. Their whole style is to see other people in relationship only to what they can do to further their own purposes. It is sometimes difficult for counselors to appreciate how much antisocial persons are at the center stage of their own lives, how little feeling they have for others. This is one of the reasons it is difficult for counselors to develop empathy for these persons. In fact, it may cause some counselors to become morally indifferent about them.

There is a *sadomasochistic* character to their relationships with the persons in their lives, whether these are their parents, their spouses, or their children. The other people around them are always disappointed and hurt, which causes them to act out their disappointment—psychologically just what the antisocial person seems to want—and so to complete the cycle of reciprocal misery.

The antisocial person brings the same style to counseling sessions, and an awareness of this possibility is important right from the start. These persons have a diminished sense of themselves. They are striving for effects, for getting the combination that will enable them to use others as soon as possible. Interviewers should also be prepared for the fact that the characteristics that are sometimes judged to be assets in antisocial personalities—their apparent coolness under pressure—are precisely the skills they attempt to use in order to control the person who tries to help them. They intend to do unto counselors what they do to everybody else. They try to get the upper hand without much feeling for what happens to others in this pursuit. Again, counselors can read their own reactions for clues about this.

They also *transfer their anxiety* to those around them. This is something they attempt to do to the counselor. We have discussed the fact that persons suffering from phobias may even do this to their companions. This is done in a different way here, however, because antisocial personalities seem to enjoy generating an intense reaction in those around them.

Although phobic persons will become disturbed by the anxiety they cause in others and will move away from them, this is not so with antisocial personalities. It is not surprising to find them at the center of tense situations, like sieges in prisons and banks, or crises in schools and other institutions. These are perfect psychological environments for them. They make everyone else tense but maintain themselves through this process. An understanding of this dynamic is very helpful in making sense out of the kind of hopeless dilemmas into which they can get themselves.

Sometimes antisocial persons, in an effort to keep up their self-esteem, go through the motions of living like law-abiding citizens. They attend church and even participate in its activities. This, again, does not come from any internal conviction but rather from a desire to get the benefits of the effect achieved. It is also true that the lives of antisocial persons sometimes have severe secondary complications. They may organize their activities—and very carefully at times—around a hidden life based on taking drugs or any number of socially unacceptable behaviors. The person whose efforts are devoted to obtaining a needed drug, without caring how or what is involved in getting it, may be a good example of the antisocial personality in action in certain segments of society today.

Why Do They Come?

Antisocial personalities seldom come for help on their own. They are sent by others who have had to deal with their disordered behavior either at work, in school, or in some other setting. They come but, as is so characteristic of them, they may not even admit that they have been sent by authorities.

It is important to deal clearly with their reason for coming. This cannot be kept a secret, nor made to seem other than it is in reality. Deception is so much a part of everything they do that these persons are sensitized to any kind of behavior like that on the part of the counselor. Counselors must be open and honest, especially if they already have information from another source about why the person has been referred.

It is important to realize that *antisocial persons do not trust counselors.* Helpers should expect this and should look to their own feelings as vital sources of information in this relationship. Indeed, the emotional reactions of the counselor are powerfully helpful both in understanding antisocial personalities and in working out the challenges of helping them.

Antisocial personalities unconsciously *attempt to get counselors into the kind of sadomasochistic relationship* that will lead to disappointment for them. The counselor, in a way, is a "mark" for the con man side of the antisocial personality. He or she is being sized up beneath all the patter and the ingratiating efforts that may characterize the sociopath at the beginning of therapy.

What is important is that *counselors will feel this inside themselves*—they will feel that they are being watched and they will experience a certain defensiveness, a being on guard within themselves. This is an important clue to the dynamics of how antisocial personalities move swiftly to construct relationships in counseling similar to those they set up with other persons.

At this stage *inexperienced counselors,* unaware of or ignoring their own inner feelings, *may take the tempting bait* quite readily. They just add themselves to the long list of others who have been charmed by these persons and they take themselves out of the running as far as helping them goes.

A signal of this, especially in counselors just beginning their work, is *over-eagerness to help,* the sureness that, although this person may have had bad breaks before, he or she is on the road to rehabilitation now. Wanting too much to do good, these counselors end up in the classic sadomasochistic relationship. After they commit themselves wholeheartedly to this antisocial person, the counselor's hopes for helping him or her will soar. At some level sociopaths understand this and, as counselors get more warmly enthusiastic, the sociopath prepares to hurt or disappoint them.

This is a characteristic bind into which overeager and undersensitive counselors can get themselves. It is very hurting and disillusioning to them and they can withdraw after such an experience, much to the damage of their own counseling efforts. Some awareness of this possibility right from the start protects them from being conned and deepens their capacity to be effective in this and in other situations. Sensitive counselors can do much to avoid the worst stresses of their work, the ones they get themselves into.

It is said that all society has some liking for the outlaw. There is some truth in this. We can find ourselves rooting for the criminal even though we may not wish to admit this publicly. This kind of feeling can be present in therapy as well. Counselors may experience a certain envy for the seemingly carefree life-style of the antisocial personality. This is particularly true if counselors feel a great psychological burden in their own personal and professional commitments. This kind of subtle admiration may lead them to relate in a non-therapeutic way. They allow the antisocial person to be their surrogate at the edges of society and this can lead to many compromises in the counseling process itself. Enjoying the deviousness of the antisocial personality may lead counselors into deep waters.

Counselors should also be aware when they are excessively negative in their responses to these persons. Whenever they hear themselves being too negative toward certain counselees they may begin to wonder why this is so. It is frequently because they are unconsciously handling their own similar unacceptable impulses through this maneuver. They should not be afraid of discovering such truths because such awareness gives them valuable information about the unconscious factors that affect their style in relating to those they help. Sensitive counselors are always ready to learn; one of the things they listen to carefully is their own defensive system.

32

The Most Difficult
Language of All:
That of the Seriously Disturbed

Most counselors understand their need to reflect on the problems connected with helping persons suffering from major psychological difficulties. Even though helpers may be aware that they have insufficient training to deal with these clients, they inevitably meet them at least in the role of referring them on to other sources of assistance. It is essential that counselors know both how to recognize serious psychological illness and what, within their limitations, they can constructively do when they are confronted with it. The amount of stress associated with such helping work can be reduced noticeably through anticipating some of the specific problems of working with the seriously disturbed.

The greatest stress for the average counselor arises from the fact that it is extremely difficult to form a relationship with individuals suffering from psychoses. Helpers may not even be able to generate much empathy for the experiences of the severely disturbed; they may not feel comfortable being with them. Counselors are struck by the fact that these people are so different; they seem to represent not just an extension or exaggeration of neurotic conflict but a separate and more impenetrable psychological mystery. Counselors find themselves reacting differently to psychotic persons; they feel more distant from them and they may be intimidated by what is perceived as the strangeness or "craziness" of psychotic individuals. It is very difficult to find the human message in their confused communication—thus the search for the person behind the symptom can be intense and fearful. Counselors may sometimes feel "infected" by the feelings of the seriously disturbed and they end up being frustrated and angry because they cannot seem to break through to the other's personality. This may affect the self-confidence of counselors and challenge their sense of being helping and considerate persons—not the least of reasons for careful reflection upon the complexities of working with psychotic individuals.

Defeated From The Start

Some counselors feel totally inadequate even with the idea of relating to persons suffering from major psychological problems. All too often such individuals transform their uneasiness into a self-fulfilling prophecy and so they do not even attempt to do any of the many sensible and helpful things that are within the powers of most healthy and perceptive individuals. The fact is that all counselors, whether full- or part-time, will have to deal with seriously disturbed persons at one time or another. They may, in fact, need to assume a responsibility for decisions connected with helping these persons in specific situations, such as in a school or a parish where in a personal crisis the counselor is looked to for immediate assistance. Even if counselors anticipate referring these persons for more intensive professional help, there is a great deal they can do until the doctor comes.

Shifts in Attitude

For many years, but especially after the development of anti-psychotic drugs, it has been widely held that the sooner patients could be freed from mental hospitals and returned to their communities the better things would be for all concerned. It was felt that many patients stayed far too long in hospitals and that they sometimes remained there because society was uncomfortable with them—because, in other words, they had no other place to go. People have been relatively unsophisticated in their perception of seriously disturbed persons; they have also been afraid of them. A growing body of research came to suggest that deeply disturbed persons were not as dangerous as was thought and that a return to more normal living circumstances would be positively helpful for almost all of them.

American Practices

The task of depopulating state hospitals began in 1955 but it was twenty years later before governmental and professional organizations started a serious study of the process and its characteristics. Limited data were available about the demographics or the diagnoses of patients released from hospitals. The chronically mentally ill population, most of whose members would have been hospitalized a good portion of their lives encompasses, as noted in Talbott, (p. 17) "those who suffer severe and persistent mental and emotional disorders that interfere with their functional capacities in relation to such primary aspects of daily life as self-care, interpersonal relationships, and work or schooling, and that often necessitate prolonged hospital care."

These persons may be understood under the following headings: (1) the estimated three million people who suffer a diagnosable severe mental disorder; (2) 2.4 million of these who experience moderate and severe disability; (3) those with prolonged and severe disability who number 1.7 million of the original number. Counselors are most likely to encounter the 1.3 million individuals who do not suffer from prolonged, severe disability and who, although they are seriously ill, are still able to function in a limited way in society.

Counselors should appreciate the need to secure accurate diagnoses of mentally ill persons. Although most of these patients are psychotic and suffer from some form of schizophrenia, a significant number of them experience chronic depression, a severe personality disorder, bipolar (manic-depressive) illness, or some form of organic problem such as Alzheimer's Disease. Important advances have occurred over the last twenty years in the field of diagnosis and treatment of severe mental illness. Many patients with such problems as manic-depressive illness as well as some organic mental disorders are therefore treated effectively and are spared the ordeal of long-term hospitalization. Many of the latter are able to function at a relatively high level in society.

This massive effort to depopulate mental hospitals has not been an unqualified success in the United States. The process has given rise to new problems including those connected with young adults with severe mental problems, the phenomenon of homelessness, as well as those challenges specific to the expanding population of elderly citizens.

There is, for example, a new population of mentally ill young adults that is the result not of *de*institutionalization but of *un*institutionalization. Pepper and Ryglewicz (in Talbott) outline the forces that contribute to a totally new problem in society. They observe that, as a result of the new policy about the institutionalization of patients, many persons now live in society emitting behaviors that, in the past, would have triggered their hospitalization. In addition, with the growing brevity of hospital stays, many persons are discharged into the community before they are ready. The legal climate relating to mental illness has also had a profound impact on this situation. There are constraints governing hospitalization, even when the latter is medically indicated, and there are no constraints on patients to accept aftercare arrangements or to take their prescribed medication.

As a result there now exists a large population of young adults who may exhibit major psychiatric symptoms but who have never received treatment of any kind. As a matter of fact, their symptoms may well have been masked by their participation in the drug culture because the latter universe easily tolerates such a range of aberrant behaviors. Having mingled with the general population all their lives, they do not view themselves as "psychiatric patients." As a result, as their healthy peers begin to meet the normal life expectations, such as entering a career or getting married and raising a family, these disturbed persons suffer repeated failures in attempting to behave in the same way. They may well have their first contact with a counselor in connection with job failure, marital stress, or problems with being parents.

As greater numbers of Americans live for longer periods, counselors will find themselves in situations in which well-functioning adults—often in their own retirement—must manage their own aging parents who can no longer care for themselves. The disability of the latter group is often caused by another severe form of mental illness, dementia. It is estimated that approximately five percent of the general elderly population (defined as those 65 years of age and older) living in the community suffer a chronic primary or secondary dementia. Another 2.5 percent of this population with a similar diagnosis live in long-term care institutions.

The counselor should know that dementia may have many faces. Primary dementia, such as Alzheimer's Disease, has no known cause. Secondary dementias occur in relation to some known or highly suspected etiology, such as neurological illness, AIDS, or a variety of metabolic and/or chemical agents. A dementia should be suspected whenever persons who formerly functioned well become forgetful, lax about taking care of themselves or their daily activities, or give evidence of some change in personality. A medical referral is imperative in order to establish a clear diagnosis so that such secondary dementias that can profit from treatment may receive it promptly.

It is highly likely that counselors will be called upon to work with the families of persons suffering from Alzheimer's Disease rather than with the patients themselves. They should, therefore, acquaint themselves with the community resources, such as social service agencies or support groups that can be of great assistance to family members.

British, Canadian, and American studies of the effects of deinstitutionalization have found that, accompanying the phenomenon, are growing numbers of psychiatrically disabled homeless people. Up to fifty percent of the homeless have been found to be suffering from chronic, serious mental disorders. The problem of homelessness, especially in large cities, is extremely complex and has yet to be addressed in a thoroughly satisfactory way. In 1981, in New York City, for example, the Mental Health Department initiated a five-year plan that insisted that "the basic needs of 'street people'—food, shelter, bath, clothing, medical care—are the responsibility of the social welfare system." (See Baxter and Hopper, "Troubled in The Streets," Talbott, p. 53.) Near the end of the same decade, the *New York Times* reported (May 22, 1989) that "substance abuse is one of the major issues causing people to be homeless and keeping them homeless." The provision of shelters to these people, "only makes the drug problem worse." These disturbed homeless use the fruits of provided housing and jobs to maintain their drug habit, thus isolating them more from rather than integrating them into society.

In the same edition of the *New York Times,* Senator Daniel Patrick Moynihan acknowledges the decline of the institutionalized mental patients in New York from a peak 93,314 in 1954 to 18,699 in 1988. The failure in the program, however, can be traced, Moynihan contends, to the failure to provide adequate funds and planning for the other side of the program, the construction and staffing of community mental health centers. For example, although 2,000 such centers were to be established by 1980, only 768 existed almost ten years after that target date. A vital link in the system was never forged into place and, as a result, the patients end up out of the hospital but untreated, homeless, or inadequately monitored.

What Does It Mean for Counselors?

Every counselor must be aware of these contemporary problems and attitudes that may complicate efforts to help the seriously disturbed. Such well-publicized problems also deepen the public fear about mental illness, make them mistrust professionals even more, and cause them to question sound theory because of poor execution in practice. But many people seem to want to give sympathy at a distance and they do not want what they consider to be dangerous and annoying people turned out of hospitals and back into their community. One of the functions of contemporary counselors is to help people see these problems in perspective, assist in educating them about the true facts, and try to prevent panicky and harmful reactions to what is already a very complex problem.

These facts have been discussed in some detail because counselors will be caught up in them, sooner or later, in almost every part of the country. They will have to work with families, employers, and others who are strongly affected by cultural attitudes toward the seriously ill. Not only does every counselor need to understand the situation in general, but all counselors must also examine and sort out what they themselves understand and feel about the challenge of working with the severely disturbed. It is not a task that can be avoided or handed on to someone else.

Classifying Serious Illness

We have previously discussed some of the principles relevant to serious mood disturbances. The *DSM-III-R* also considers forms of schizophrenia and paranoia as major psychotic difficulties. The immediate concern of counselors, however, centers on understanding the special language of the major psychological difficulties and using themselves effectively in their particular role in responding to these persons.

The term "schizophrenia" was first used by Eugen Bleuler in 1911. This problem ordinarily emerges by the end of adolescence or in early adult life. Almost three-quarters of those identified as schizophrenic are between the ages of fifteen and forty-four. It is a major problem that interferes markedly with the capacity of persons to have anything like a normal life. The principal characteristics of this illness include the presence of typical psychotic symptoms such as delusions and hallucinations, and a deterioration in social and occupational functioning. Such patients should always be referred for psychiatric evaluation.

The characteristic symptoms of schizophrenia are those that the popular consciousness frequently associates with "craziness." These include delusions, or false beliefs, that frequently possess a symbolic communicative quality to which counselors must be alert. There is a metaphorical quality to schizophrenic delusions at times. A related manifestation is found in hallucinations, or false perceptions, which are very common in schizophrenic patients. Such persons also experience *ideas of reference,* through which they take almost anything that is said and refer it to themselves. They may coin new words, many examples of which can be seen in the well-known novel *I Never*

Promised You a Rose Garden by Hannah Green (Holt, Rinehart & Winston, 1964). This book, perhaps better than many scientific treatises, gives the counselor a feeling for the flavor of "schizophrenese," the special language of the seriously disturbed.

Their Inner Experience

Schizophrenics experience great difficulty in relating to others. They have few friends and they seem to distrust other people. Sometimes they strike up a relationship—more like an association—with someone else who also lives on the edges of social approval. They may end up being excluded from ordinary society as they function in a marginal relationship with each other. These relationships are fragile and difficult at best.

The counselor's fundamental challenge is to understand what it is like to look out at the world and be afraid of the experiences that most healthy persons prize and seek out for themselves. Schizophrenic patients fear closeness. They are ambivalent about the reactions of others toward them. At the same time they may develop a dependency on others to guide and direct their lives.

For a long time it was thought that such seriously disturbed persons were not capable of forming "relationships," and that they could not, therefore, have a transference experience with a therapist. The work of people like Federn, Sullivan, and others has indicated that this is not so, and beneath all the strange surface behavior and withdrawal there exists a person capable of relationships.

Indeed, these persons who seem so different are not quite as different as we sometimes suppose. Their problems generally come from the same kind of situations that confront all persons. Deep within them we find the capacity to react to the warmth, acceptance, and understanding that is little different from our own. Counselors who remember this feel more comfortable with them and can better hear and understand their apparently strange language because they are less anxious about their work with them. It is vitally important that counselors present themselves as willing and interested human beings rather than as slightly intimidated or uneasy evaluators in their work with the seriously disturbed. A little bit of humanity goes a long way in working with these individuals; there are real persons beneath the disfiguring symptoms.

Indeed, it sometimes happens that the transference response of the deeply disturbed person is quick and intense. However, their own sudden experience of intense feelings toward their counselors may frighten them. They may move back into their lonely psychological exile. The problems associated with developing what is called a "therapeutic alliance" between the counselor and the client are very trying. It is difficult for counselors to work at close range and keep their balance with these persons who seem to need and demand so much. Their sometimes violent and confusing reactions can bewilder even seasoned counselors.

It is helpful for counselors to remember that these persons will present to them the same patterns that they have used to defend themselves in other settings. They will, for example, produce in therapy the same behavior they have used in their families. One of the techniques at which they are quite adept consists in making those around them feel guilty. They can manage this very subtly. The evocation of guilt in others represents a very controlling maneuver. For a seriously disturbed person to tell a counselor that he or she is only making their problem worse may not be a statement of fact; it may be the kind of psychological maneuver that characterizes the disturbed persons' way of controlling the responses of others. They get the counselor to feel guilty and gradually to feel irritated, thus confirming the ineffectiveness of which they have been accused. Such maneuvers can tie counselors up in knots if they get tangled in the literal content of these statements. At every stage the counselor must ask the familiar question about what is really taking place within the other person to cause them to act in this particular way. What is the other's inner experience that results in this surface behavior? To watch the patterns—the style of the individual—is very helpful because this provides the context that gives meaning to many of their otherwise confusing individual statements and actions. Counselors who stay at the literal level—trying to explain themselves, for example—miss what's really going on.

Translating the Language Correctly

The symptoms, which have been previously described, are to be understood as dynamic statements, part of this special language that counselors are charged with translating. Even if we can only get a small fraction of the message they are attempting to convey, we make a significant step in working with them. These are their efforts to get in contact, and we should not hurriedly dismiss them as mere delusions or hallucinations that are random and without meaning. Counselors may wisely step back to try to see or hear them in context. A hallucination, for example, may be a good example of a disturbed person's trying to adapt to their psychological deficit. Through a hallucination, after all, persons may externalize their inner conflicts. Hallucinations can also deliver a sense of self-importance and significance. These are primitive efforts to get back in contact with reality, but they should not be dismissed as merely unmeaningful examples of disordered behavior. There is a message locked into them, and it is the counselor's task to catch at least the flavor of it.

The problem for counselors is to discipline their tendency to react negatively to such behavior. They may, like so many people, be unaccustomed to interpreting these symptoms as metaphors. It is easy to ignore them or to write them off as "craziness." Behind them, however, deeply disturbed persons are revealing themselves in the only language they are able to speak.

The steady effort to hear and understand despite all the static and confusion is a major plus for all counselors, both for their own self-confidence and the positive assistance of others. It is slow work and it tests the patience of the helper sorely. People suffering major psychological problems are, however, not totally beyond our capacity to reach them. We may not change them dramatically but even to receive some of the messages they send—to establish even minimal contact—is a solid therapeutic achievement.

Elements of Understanding

Counselors are often helped by realizing that they are caught up in their clients' ambivalence about wanting to join themselves with other people and their terrible fear that this may actually happen. This fear may be expressed in bizarre fashion, but it is an understandable reaction when we can relate it to their shifting and uncrystallized sense of themselves. Such people cannot "pull themselves together," despite the urgings some may make on them to do just that. Their feelings about themselves resonate with a basic fear of being lost or absorbed in the people around them. They are torn painfully where their feelings intersect. Counselors can understand why such persons may draw back if the helper pushes toward them too closely. At the same time, if the counselor is too removed or neutral, too afraid to express any real concern, these persons may feel neglected or abandoned altogether. The balance of a healthy presence is one of the most important gifts counselors can bring to these individuals; that is, an unselfconscious presentation of the self that neither overwhelms nor undercuts the client.

Seriously disturbed persons may also exhibit feelings of dependency because of their emotional conviction that they are unable to care for themselves or to cope with life. This feeling of helplessness is one of the reasons that these clients sometimes regress to what seems to be a very primitive and dependent mode of adapting to the world; they sometimes seem ready to settle for almost total care of their needs by others. It is painful for these individuals to express dependency because such self-revelation further attacks their sense of self-esteem. The passivity—the willingness to be shaped and sheltered by others—that marks this presentation of themselves in life is also very threatening. Healthy people realize that they are not totally independent and that letting themselves be dependent is an important part of living. Nobody can be close to others, or love them, without at times sharing a mutual dependence. However, this very notion is appalling to the seriously disturbed. Again, realizing their reaction tempers the enthusiasm of counselors for pushing too far too fast into the intimate areas of their lives.

Strong Feelings

Counselors can also expect hostility to exist even beneath what seems to be a bland exterior. Persons with major problems are often very anxious lest their strong hostile feelings do come out. Some analysts feel that their suppression of hostility and rage explains the apathy that so often characterizes schizophrenics. Counselors should be ready to find these strong feelings bubbling just beneath the surface of such patients' behavior. Indeed, these rumblings represent something else that counselors must hear and understand very carefully. The presence of these feelings also explains why disturbed persons may seek to control the counselor in the interview. This is their way of making up for their own feelings of inadequacy. Counselors who resent this behavior may miss its meaning; counselors who interpret it personally as a direct attack quickly get lost. When the effort to control can be seen as part of these persons' struggle to pull themselves together, it can be accepted and responded to with more mature understanding. Counselors who can retain perspective can catch the sweep and pattern of the dynamics of the deeply disturbed and, by responding more effectively, they reduce the stress of the entire experience.

Things to Remember

Counselors should not be surprised at the difficulties they experience in establishing emotional contact with schizophrenics. This is not, as has been noted, because these patients are incapable of it but because they are so sensitive to human interactions that they draw back into their own private world of isolation to protect themselves. Gestures or statements of counselors that can be handled without concern by other clients will loom as threatening and punishing in an extreme way to these schizophrenic persons. Counselors who are aware of this will manage their own responses with a greater respect for the vulnerability of the schizophrenic. They may find that they must be more active in their therapy, more reassuring in what seems an almost naïve way in dealing with these persons. Seriously disturbed individuals need these sincere, concrete signs that counselors recognize their needs and are trying to respond to them.

Counselors may find it necessary to express their own feelings in trying to reach into the isolation and withdrawal of these patients. Establishing some relationshp with them is not an occasion to be too analytic, too intellectual, or too neutral and detached. This latter stance, which can sometimes be a defensive posture for counselors who are uneasy working with very disturbed persons, can easily be interpreted as a rejection. And they may be right; they catch the counselors' moving back from even the effort to make contact. Counselors who can expect little emotional feedback, and can live comfortably with it, will do well with these patients.

The Chaotic World

One of the greatest challenges in working with these persons is the chaotic picture they present of themselves and their world. It has been suggested by some observers that this schizophrenic disorganization is their way of defending themselves against the threats of the world and other persons. This mechanism is at once both unconscious and effective. Such disorganization represents a test for counselors while keeping them at a safe distance at the same time. These people may be very difficult to follow but, if we can sense this disorganization as part of their defensive sparring, we may be able to catch the lonely and frightened persons beneath these maneuvers. It is to the persons rather than to their surface strategies that we must respond.

In these situations it is fatal to pretend to understand when we do not. Seriously disturbed persons are astute at picking up any hypocrisy, inconsistency, or failure to attend to them and what they are trying to say. Counselors must constantly return to an old question: "What is this person trying to tell me through the way he is treating me?" This will enable them to keep the whole therapeutic situation in clearer perspective, to manage their own stress better, and to be more effective as counselors.

Some Basics

There are certain basic kinds of information which counselors may need to get, especially if they are responsible even for a brief time for taking care of these disturbed persons. It is important to find out as concretely as possible why these individuals have come for help and whether they have had assistance before. Some inquiries about previous episodes may be very helpful in understanding the nature and prognosis of the present difficulty. Some gentle inquiry into their history, even into the kinds of symptoms they have experienced before, may provide equally helpful knowledge. Counselors may be called up in an initial interview to help the severely disturbed person define the problem that has brought them for assistance. They may be able to do this only in a very primitive and symbolic way. This is better than nothing, however, and if counselors are alert to teasing out the stress that precipitated the search for help they may go a long way in a few moments in assisting these individuals. The patients may have arrived at the counselor's office as a response to the feeling of being overwhelmed, or having faced the final humiliation, or some other "last straw" experience. A readiness to to identify the occasion of the need for help may be an important key that allows the person to communicate his or her special vision of the world.

Counselors who are sensitive to the fact that there is meaning in the jumble of communications will try to identify themes and topics even when the conversation is very rambling or full of intellectualizations and circumstantial details. It may be helpful for them to realize that accuracy in making counseling responses is not the only quality that is important in working with severely disturbed persons. Catching the whole pattern or mood of the other at the right moment is the most important role of the counselor. It is vital to communicate their commitment to understand rather than to judge. Counselors should never underestimate the importance of this effort to understand, even when final and complete meanings are not grasped. Understanding helps even when it is not perfect.

It is improtant to respect the privacy that these deeply disturbed persons need. They are afraid of the world and they need secrecy. This is related to their shaky feelings about their own identity. Again, sensitivity to these persons allows us to accept them and not to push them too hard to behave in a fashion of which they are incapable.

Counselors should avoid giving the idea that they can read the minds of these people. They can do this by overeager responses or interpretations, by any maneuver that puts them too far ahead of their patients in displaying insight about the situation. Proving one's skill does not necessarily help others.

In the long run, counselors who can rid themselves of their prejudices, intimidations, or fears about severely disturbed persons will be able to perceive them more clearly as individuals, and they will be able to make themselves present to them in a more genuine and helpful way. There should be no great tricks—any manipulations would be destructive—employed by counselors in working with these persons. Their own humanity, sensitively shared, remains the strongest asset counselors have in this and every other type of therapeutic work.

A Summary:
What Counselors Should Know about the Seriously Disturbed

Because counselors will often be called upon to work with the families of such patients, they should understand that it is generally thought that genetic factors play a role in some or all forms of schizophrenia but that environmental factors are also influential. Their precise roles and interaction is not well understood.

Much current research focuses on factors that contribute to relapses on the part of schizophrenic patients. Here, one of the major issues is the quality of the family environment. Those families characterized by frequent intense expression of emotion—especially those with the hallmarks of demandingness and criticism—are judged, not surprisingly, to contribute to the relapse of these patients. These families are described as "high expressed-emotion," or EE, and many current treatment efforts center on educating members of these families to new patterns of relationship to the schizophrenic patient.

All severely disturbed patients should be referred for psychiatric evaluation and treatment. Most of them can benefit from medication as well as from other modalities of treatment. Counselors should appreciate that even when treated individuals take their medication regularly, thirty to fifty percent will experience another psychotic episode. Without taking their medication properly, seventy percent will suffer relapse. If contacted by family members with the complaint that the individual is again developing symptoms, prompt referral to the treating physician is indicated. More often than not—although sadly at times at the advice of some well-meaning but harmful person—patients stop taking their medication on their own. The most seriously disturbed patients do best when they receive a combination of pharmacotherapy and some form of psycho-social treatment.

33

The Paranoid Personality Disorder

Paranoia drifts like the acrid fumes of ammonia in America's air. W. H. Auden's age of anxiety has yielded to one of paranoia, understood as a widespread sense of vulnerability to malign forces—to random violence, untrustworthy institutions ranging from church to state, to a loss of safe places and secure relationships, to the pressures of the paranoid distortions that overpower reality. Paranoia seems the seasoning of the age. Counselors cannot function, however, on vague understandings of this unsettling phenomenon. What does it mean and how are they likely to encounter it?

For our purposes, we emphasize the paranoid personality disorder. This differs from the psychotic state labeled as paranoid, which is marked by at least one systematized delusion with frequent auditory hallucinations centered on a common theme. That major problem is real but is not the incarnation of the paranoid with whom most nonprofessional counselors will deal. The paranoid as a type of personality disorder—that is, as an example of the lifelong pattern of behavior in which subjective discomfort and self-observation are minimized—often enters the life of a busy counselor.

Such individuals are identified by their long-term dispositions, in a variety of settings, to interpret the actions of other people as purposely threatening or demeaning. Their attitudes, according to *DSM-III-R*, are marked by at least four of a number of psychological features, including unwarranted expectation that they will be used or harmed by others; unjustifiable questioning of the loyalty of others; the attribution of veiled meanings into harmless statements or incidents; an unforgiving feeling about insults or slights and a single-minded bearing of grudges; a hesitation to trust others or confide in them because of fears that the information will be used against them; flaring counterattacks and anger in response to perceived slights; a suspicious questioning of a spouse's or lover's faithfulness. These manifestations occur outside the context of a psychotic disorder.

What Are They Like?

Few people suffering from major psychological problems are exactly the way ordinary people imagine that they will be. Madness may have one terrifying and bizarre stereotyped face for many people, but in reality serious problems have many faces. Parnoid persons may seem quite intact to many observers. They may appear a little distant but they can be quite impressive, especially on first being associated with them. This quickly wears thin, however, and, as MacKinnon and Michels note, "As people know him better, they like him less" (p. 270).

These persons have the power to make us uneasy. Our feelings, as in so many similar situations, are a fundamental source of information in developing an appreciation for the problems of those with whom we work. This particular uneasiness is generated by the hostility that lies just beneath the surface of the paranoid's self-presentation. They are people who can curdle the atmosphere in a room. They make other people argumentative and resentful; they sometimes seem totally preoccupied with fairness and its application to life. Although there is no one close to them, they can be acutely sensitive to the inner states of others. Paranoids generate a kind of suspiciousness that keeps other people on guard.

In a society in which people may not know very much about their next door neighbors, these persons can keep their delusions—that is, their false beliefs—to themselves without very many other people knowing about them. Because they are suspicious, they don't confide readily in others anyway. Their capacity to form delusions is what tells us that they have a major problem and is central in understanding the paranoid. The exact nature of their delusions, no matter how fascinating, is not as significant as the way they can manufacture and use delusions to manage their way through life.

If we view those experiencing paranoid states from the stance of how and what they communicate to others, we can develop a better feeling for them. Their capacity for delusions represents a confusion in their sense of identity between what is a part of their personality and what is separate from it. Through this capacity for delusions, they pull back from communicating except to themselves. That is one of the reasons that they sometimes have hypochondriacal complaints. This reflects their intense focus on their own person and their inability to reach out and invest themselves in others. Their communication has an odd flavor; they are fascinated with unusual means of communicating—or being communicated to—including such things as ESP, mysticism, and similar phenomena. These strange means of communication reflect their impoverished effort to make contact with others, to move away from self-concern and to reach other persons. Their whole distorted receiving and sending system is clearly involved in their paranoid difficulty. When, however, we can see that these signals represent the efforts of lonely, isolated, and frightened persons, we have a better understanding of them. This perspective also enables us to keep ourselves free of becoming tangled in the specifics of their delusions. It is not the specifics but the whole mechanism of constructing and using them that must be remembered.

Food for Delusions

Counselors may wisely recall that the content of the delusions reported by paranoid persons does change across the generations because they are so strongly determined by cultural events. Strangely enough, the persons who a generation ago focused on Communists as a source of persecution may at the present time shift 180 degrees and blame the FBI for their troubles. Recent years have seen the development of what we might informally term the parnoid distortion in public life. This describes an event that is fictional in nature, that is a construction based on some paranoid motivation—such, for example, as the celebrated Tawana Brawley case in New York in the late eighties. In that situation, a young girl, in order to avoid punishment by her stepfather, invented a tale of being abused and raped by white police officers. This distortion, supported by quickly assembled patrons and politicians, took on a life of its own as it was projected day after day in the media. The incident, finally refuted by a grand jury and the girl's own admission, took on the character of reality for long tortured months and was treated, with all its ramifications for racial strife and political gain, as if it were a real occurrence. This kind of paranoid distortion, while not classifiable in the literature, is the kind of phenomenon with which nonprofessional counselors may well have to deal. They must be prepared to take its measure, identify its dynamics, maintain their own balanced view of matters, and interpret its meaning and power to others.

Culture supplies the paranoid with different "pseudo-communities"—as psychiatrist Norman Cameron calls them—at different times. This partially explains the intense hatred and persecution of certain religious and racial groups at different periods in history. It also explains why we are never free of "conspiracy theories" about major historical events. There are many vague groups—the media as well as the mafia—to whom paranoids can turn their attention these days. The specific qualities of the paranoid delusion may also be affected by their family background as well as by other features of their own psychodynamics. It is not the story, colorful as that may be, that is the prime concern of the counselor. It is the reason for using such stories, the motivation for this style of communication that is important for the helper to grasp and understand.

The Delusions Themselves

The delusions are generally of persecution or grandeur. These are ordinarily touched off by some event that threatens their self-esteem or causes them to taste failure in one way or another. The loss of a job or a lover, or the anticipated or fantasied loss, all work the same way. Sometimes competitive experiences may occasion paranoid behavior. Confinement, as on a ship or in a jail for a long time, may precipitate it as well. It has been observed that the paranoid state is sometimes the result of these persons being forced to submit passively to an actual or an imagined attack on themselves. There is almost always some grain of truth to support the development of their delusion, something they can point to or cite to support their interpretation of events.

Persecution: Delusions of persecution lead these people to think that someone else is going to harm them. They can specify an "enemy" who is following them, listening to their conversations, or who is bent on ruining them or their career. Although this can be an individual it is more often a group. Paranoid persons may also develop strong jealousy and deep suspicions about their spouses, centering on some presumed betrayal of trust in the married state. That is one of the most fertile grounds for the growth of paranoid fear.

Grandeur: These delusions are represented by the persons' feeling that they have some great if unobserved talent and can manifest it in a variety of ways. Such persons may feel that they are wealthy, powerful, or important to a world that does not recognize them quite fully. They may have a new invention that they are convinced will solve the energy crisis, or they may have a new theory of salvation that they feel will change the course of history. The person who proclaims himself as the awaited messiah is a good example of the paranoid state in action.

Erotomania: It is not unusual for persons in a paranoid state to believe that someone of the opposite sex is in love with them or is making an effort to attract or seduce them. This condition has been given the technical name *erotomania*. The individual who is presumably doing the seducing is ordinarily a prominent or attractive individual who really knows nothing of the paranoid person and has no interest in him or her. While this delusion must be distinguished from the kind of crushes students can sometimes get on their teachers, it can be a serious problem. As a matter of fact, counselors may sometimes have to deal with the individuals who are the subjects of the delusional passion of paranoids rather than with the paranoids themselves.

Ready to Fight

These paranoids always seem ready for a fight or a court suit. This is further evidence of the hostility bubbling beneath their surfaces. They can be suspicious, feeling themselves to be loners, but they are good at collecting injustices and can be quite quarrelsome, always attributing bad will to those around them. Everybody is "out to get them."

That is why they are sometimes very preoccupied with law and order and the rules governing them. They may even take up some training in self-defense, or gather guns or other weapons for their protection. Paranoid mistrust leads them to insist on the letter that kills the spirit of every law. These individuals have to be this way; it is a sign of their psychological need and difficulty, but it does not represent a free choice. They cannot appreciate the spirit of a law because it is so difficult for them to appreciate the meaning of any other person's experiences. They just cannot make room in themselves for others. Laws serve the function of controlling their own inner emotions, of keeping them in check. They may project an impression of great capability, and that they can get along without the help of anyone.

Paranoids are very upset when sufficient attention is not paid to them. They may believe and act on the principle that the end justifies the means and so they invoke a missionary-like zeal in pursuit of their rigid and distorted opinions. It is not unusual to observe paranoid persons associating themselves with militant crusading groups. Their special pathology would make them great consumer advocates; it would give them free rein for distrust and accusation. As they associate themselves with an extremist group, however, they soon find themselves uncomfortable because they cannot trust the other members. If the group is composed of relatively sane persons, these healthy people will soon feel that there is something wrong with this new member. The dynamic is always the same; their pathology leads them back to isolation. Although they want to be close, they have a strong fear that they will be betrayed. That is one of the reasons that they are so suspicious. Some feel that the paranoid state is a defense against depression, a way of handling the challenge of melancholy. Paranoids are caught between wanting to be close and being afraid of what others might do to them. Sometimes they strike out to beat others to the punch, to get them before they can be gotten themselves.

Other Clues

Counselors may pick up a feeling for these people through noting the deadness in their sense of humor. They are not alive, spontaneous, or capable of reacting with the kind of easy laughter characteristic of healthy people. There is a lacing of sarcasm in paranoids' efforts of humor; they use it in the service of their psychodynamic needs but the humor is controlling and hurting. The jokes they make leave others feeling uncomfortable. Paranoids are not easy to win over by some innocent endearment. They cannot appreciate it, will read other meanings into it, and will be put off rather than be won over by such attempts at rapport on the part of counselors.

Working with the Targets

The targets for the paranoid's delusions, as mentioned before, sometimes are the ones who come to counselors for help. They may come for many reasons other than erotomania. It is not uncommon, for example, for paranoid persons to accuse others of crimes or shameful deeds, or to threaten to circulate the news of these to damage their reputation. Sometimes people shrug their shoulders and say that such persons are merely "crazies" who will do no harm. Others, however, see them as potentially dangerous and become quite disturbed by finding themselves the object of their suspicions.

It is true that most paranoid persons are harmless. They seldom attack their persecutors, although this is not entirely unknown. Counselors are well-advised to evaluate the history of the aggressive behavior of paranoid persons, whether they are dealing with them directly or with the persons suffering from their accusations. Their attacks generally come in the form of false accusations, although they may occasionally hurt others in what they fancy to be self-defense. A careful and prudent judgment about the paranoid's potential for real aggression is fundamental, and it is essential in evaluating such a situation.

What to do: If the person the counselor sees is the object of the letters or accusations, what can the counselor do? It is clear that such persons may need legal as well as psychological advice and that counselors should limit suggestions to areas about which they have some knowledge. They should refer them for other advice to a lawyer. In general, these people should be urged to be courteous but distant in their dealings with such bothersome individuals. There are a number of things, however, that it is wise for people *not* to do.

What not to do: These include *ignoring the situation.* This can be especially dangerous if the accusations continue and if there is really no hard information about the nature of the accuser and his potential aggression. When there are a number of unknowns, it is dangerous to counsel persons to "forget" such a problem.

Persons should not be urged to try to win paranoids over by being nice to them. This is sometimes the spontaneous reaction of accused people. The difficulty here is that being nice to persons who are made more defensive by friendly gestures generally makes things worse. Neither is it wise for a person to try to frighten the paranoid accuser or to try to fend him or her off by some show of force. This kind of involvement at close range almost always worsens the situation.

Occasionally, persons think they can solve the problems of paranoids by admitting that their accusations are true. They hope that this will put an end to the situation. It hardly ever does. It merely involves people in a new and complicated way with them. Avoiding doing the wrong thing is a way of doing the right thing in dealing with paranoid persons in such circumstances.

Cautions and Expectations

It is difficult to place these persons in perspective, but it is important to do so with as much sensitivity as possible. They are suffering a major disturbance rather than a mild aberration. It is not a question merely of handling or coping temporarily with them. The challenge is to grasp the twisted and hostile communication in order to be able to understand and respond to the person who is driven to make it.

One of the reasons that it is difficult to be sure of a paranoid diagnosis is that these people are generally referred from other sources and, because of the essential nature of their problem, they are uncooperative. It is also difficult at times to prove that they are experiencing false beliefs. This is because there is so often a kernel of truth that can be interpreted as suspicious even by fairminded persons. They can always hook their case into some facts. Healthy people may not pay much attention, but there are a number of times in every day when they are under electronic surveillance. This happens in banks, in stores, and in the lobbies of apartment houses and office buildings where television equipment monitors peoples' comings and goings. What the ordinary person can accept as routine, the paranoid persons can use as solid evidence that people are gaining information surreptitiously all the time about them.

Paranoid persons generally make a negative and uncooperative presentation of themselves. They say, in effect, "I do not need to be a patient." Theirs is a primitive form of denial and it can be observed in almost all paranoid patients. Reaction-formation and, of course, projection are other defenses also employed. They use these to protect themselves against their own consciousness of aggressive impulses, their need for dependency and any warm or affectionate feelings. They also protect themselves from being betrayed or put off by other persons. The use of denial also allows paranoid persons to blot out certain painful parts of the human situation.

Counselors, then, can expect paranoids not to be ready to accept their role as clients or patients, a stance that is intensified by the fact that they are generally referred for counseling by others. They have been forced into coming for help or they have been strongly advised that they must talk over certain difficulties with a counselor. Counselors sense the seething anger and hostility that is paranoids' inner reaction to having their lives thus arranged. They use projection to express this resentment and anger toward others.

Paranoids' passion for law and order—or for the control of rules and regulations—insulates them from their own fantasied acts of aggression toward others. Projection is used, as in cases of erotomania, because it enables the individual to feel loved by someone who is attractive. This can also protect them against the negative feelings they have within themselves. That is why the caricature of the spinster who imagines that men are breaking into her home or apartment is, as MacKinnon and Michels note (p. 266), a good example of these mechanisms in combination. A frightened woman projects her sexual difficulties and her own hostility out onto men by such a perception.

Counselors will sense clearly the anger in these people even when it is expressed silently. The air brims with the feeling and only the most insensitive person could fail to pick it up. When paranoid persons are referred for help against their own judgment, they frequently express their hostility by refusing to speak. This does not mean that they are withdrawn, in the manner of a catatonic schizophrenic, from awareness of the environment. They sense quite clearly everything that is going on and their silence is an overt hostile act. This silence both conceals and expresses their anger at the same time.

Counselors must be able to understand how the meaning of the paranoid is compressed into this display of the self. It is obviously not a time to try to win them over by actions—gestures at friendship or rapport making—that might easily border on insincerity. Paranoids are not easy to charm or to trick into talking. They are already saying something through their silence, and counselors should be able to hear it and to catch the nub of its challenge. There is much to hear in this hostile silence. As counselors do hear it they can make entrance into a world in which paranoids feel oppressed and offended by other persons. Contact is made, not on the surface level but with the lonely and frightened individuals who are behind this hostile behavior.

Sometimes paranoid patients fix their gaze intently at those who attempt to help them. This can make counselors very uneasy because they feel they are being thoroughly scrutinized. Despite this, they can maintain their calm and express their interest while also demonstrating that they will not be intimidated or be made to turn away by such glances. This is a way of meeting them, eyeball to eyeball, not to stare them down but in an effort to see behind this defensive style of presenting themselves.

Other Characteristics

It is also quite characteristic of paranoid persons to talk a good deal, especially at the beginning or ending of a counseling session. They do it at these points because beginnings and endings have special meaning as times of contact and separation, experiences that are especially difficult for them. It would surprise us if they did not have problems with these issues; this is precisely why they do talk so much. They have very diminished self-esteem beneath this flow of words and, although counselors may have to put up with a good deal of verbiage from these persons, they should not get lost in it.

Counselors who try to make sense out of every detail in the kind of story or statement that can be related by a paranoid will never find their way toward a therapeutic goal. Here, as in the question of feeling scrutinized, counselors must make their own presence felt. They cannot allow themselves to be dominated by the paranoid nor to yield total control of the conversation. This does not demand immediate and stark confrontation, but a far subtler game that depends on the counselor's genuine capacity to retain control of what he or she is doing without getting into an argument with the patient.

Not Being Trusted

Counselors should, of course, expect to experience mistrust. That is a prime characteristic of these individuals. The management of this mistrust and hostility constitute the crucial issue for counselors working with these persons. The perspective that allows counselors to see beneath the hostility and enables them to pick up the paranoid's deep longing for and fears of a close, trusting relationship is essential.

Paranoids can reach out and defeat the counselor in any of a large number of ways by rejecting them. As noted, they want to beat the counselor to it; they want to reject in order to defend themselves against rejection. Seeing this clearly helps counselors to maintain self-possession and keeps them from becoming overly defensive in explaining themselves or in trying to win the paranoid over. Counselors may have to be more restrained and slightly more distant than they would otherwise be in trying to express their interest and concern. This does not mean that counselors should be cold, but they are wise if they do not try to reach paranoids by overwhelming them with attention. One does not push too fast or too far into the intimate territory that is so uncomfortable for paranoid persons.

Counselors should expect paranoids to test them and their trustworthiness constantly. This can come out in a wide variety of ways. They may, for exmaple, accuse the counselor of arranging his or her desk in some way designed to get a reaction out of them. They may even verbalize this or accuse the counselor of trying to trick them in some way or another. Counselors who have been through these kinds of experiences realize how trying and stressful they can be. Paranoids sometimes behave like hurt animals; one naturally wishes to reach out to them, but as the helping hand gets closer, one is not surprised by an animal response of self-protective biting. It is a very painful situation in which they find themselves, desperately wanting someone close and yet fearful of allowing anybody to get close.

Action Now

Paranoids sometimes confront counselors with demands for immediate responses to their grandiose plans or delusions of persecution. Something must be done right now, they seem to say, and they can countenance no delay. They want to get counselors to commit themselves one way or the other right from the start. Helpers should not panic in the face of the startling kinds of announcements these people sometimes make—that they are picking up signals from Mars in their earlobes or that they are plotting to assassinate some local officer in order to save the country for democracy. Patience and understanding, as well as a careful effort to evaluate the full meaning of such statements, is more in order.

Their efforts to get the counselor to agree to certain conditions are different. For example, they may want the counselor to promise not to send them to a hospital. Those who do give immediate and complete promises in this regard may find themselves embarrassed later on when they feel they cannot or should not fulfill them. The outcome may be a broken promise, just what the paranoid needed as proof that the counselor was untrustworthy.

The Language of Delusion

Therapists who are anxious to confront patients sometimes move in very strongly on paranoid persons when they recount their false beliefs. At times, inexperienced counselors attempt to argue paranoid persons out of their delusions with some kind of logic. These may be dangerous rational responses to what is essentially a very different kind of language. These persons do not speak a logical tongue; they communicate in a paranoid metaphor, and those who try to respond with their own careful logic find themselves quickly confounded. A premature challenge of a person's delusional system may, in its ill-timing, work more harm than good. A good-natured effort, the kind often used by beginning counselors, to cajole paranoids out of believing that people are spying on them merely enmeshes the counselor further in their pathology.

In general, counselors should avoid agreeing or disagreeing with the points or statements made by paranoid persons. It is very easy, in the name of trying to make things run smoothly, to seem to go along with them. We think that faking them out a little will not hurt. It almost always does, however, because paranoid patients are intensely sensitive to any signs of untrustworthiness or inconsistency.

It does not pay to debate paranoid patients. This is not the meaning of counseling in the first place and, in the second place, it is a grievous therapeutic error. Some counselors, however, caught up in the surface of what they hear, involve themselves in this before they know it.

The counselor's task is not even to try to figure out how much of the individual's delusion is true and how much of it is false. The important things center on clients' preoccupation with the delusion and their unreasoning certainty that it exists in just the form that they describe. Also significant for counselors to understand is the way that paranoid persons use their delusions to cover or explain their failures or other life experiences. As in other forms of therapy, the counselor must steadily attempt to see what the meaning of this delusion is to the person who generates it; the question becomes: What function does it serve?

While avoiding overenthusiasm, the counselor may at times have to involve himself in stimulating paranoids' motivation to get help. Many counselors feel that they should refer them to a more skilled therapist who will be able to take them on as long-term patients. Counselors can anticipate difficulties in this attempt; just the idea of it may disturb paranoids greatly. They are very sensitive to any restrictions on their freedom or to any manipulation of them into a forced passivity. Openness and consistency are the hallmarks of the understanding counselor in working with paranoids. Their effort must be to reach what is healthy in these people.

Perhaps the most important thing to remember is that it is not the delusion that needs treatment but the troubled and anguished person who gives birth to it. This is difficult to do because these patients can be so hostile, and at times may even intrude into the private life of the counselor. Counselors must preserve limits, shielding their own lives and not allowing such persons to be physically destructive in their offices or other settings in which they may work with them.

What Does the Counselor Feel?

This is always a significant issue but it is especially important here because some counselors do experience a real dislike, occasionally even a fear, of paranoid persons. If this is their experience—and if they have not dealt with it in some way—they should not try to help such clients. They will only make things worse for themselves and their patients. It is wise to remember that paranoid persons will do to the counselor what they do to everybody else. All persons who try to make a relationship with them find their efforts frustrated. They may wonder why this is so, but it is clearly the result of the paranoid's reaction to the threat of growing intimacy. Paranoids disrupt relationships; that is one of their prime characteristics. They have been doing it all through their lives.

They are also good at making other people feel anxious. When they get them to experience anxiety, they then perceive this reaction in the other as some form of rejection of them. Paranoid persons are very good at accomplishing this, and they can trip up and ensnare inexperienced counselors very easily. They can humiliate them, for example, by trying to wheedle some bland reassurance from them, and they can make the good-intentioned helper feel foolish.

Counselors need self-possession and an ability to accept their own deficiencies so that they will not become defensive when these are challenged by paranoids. They also need a capacity to handle people who are suspicious and mistrustful. Such individuals are not easy to work with and they strain the helpers' enormously in their efforts to understand them. Counselors who cannot accept these conditions are better off not getting involved in the first place.

Counselors should also be ready, at a certain stage of counseling, to be overidealized by these persons. This unrealistic overestimation is not, in reality, any more helpful than their suspicions and distrust were. Counselors must be aware of the paranoids' sensitivity in all of these situations. One practical thing for helpers to remember is to prepare such persons very early for any absences or vacations that the counselor can anticipate with any accuracy. Otherwise these will become very disruptive for the whole process of counseling. The more counselors can plan ahead, the better they can keep the whole process of counseling in perspective. There is enough stress involved in working with paranoids without causing any that, with a little thought, can be avoided.

34

Borderline and Narcissistic Personality Disorders

If the metaphor of the seasons has been applied successfully to the lives of human beings, it may also serve well for the universe of psychological diagnosis. Of no two personality disorders is this more true than the borderline and the narcissistic. These classifications appeared relatively recently in the diagnostic literature and considerable discussion and debate has attended their entrance into our diagnostic consciousness since then. These diagnoses seem, indeed, to have been made as often as their theoretic nature has been argued in recent years. That they are in season may be rather a function of greater clinical acuity and sensitivity than of a sudden epidemic outbreak of these problems. In any case, nonprofessional counselors must be acquainted with these entities for at least two reasons.

First, helpers will want to understand the vocabulary of current diagnosis so that they can understand whatever background reading they are able to do to discuss such problem clients with professionals and the other community resources with whom they regularly interact. Even more important for nonprofessionals is the help that some in-depth knowledge will give them to take sensible measure of the specialized difficulties they may experience with persons suffering from these disorders. The almost unique pressure exerted by borderlines, for example, can seem as heavy and stifling as the weight of the sea. Narcissists require proper identification because of the severe complications they can introduce into, for example, the already challenging work of marriage counseling.

The Borderline

James Joyce's H. C. E., Here Comes Everybody, comes to mind in examining the borderline classification. The heterogeneity and overlapping nature of this diagnosis have been noted by many researchers.

295

Counselors should not, therefore, be surprised at the confusion they may experience in trying to understand this problem. Widiger and Frances (in Talbott, p. 636) describe the borderliine's behavior as a "pattern of intense and chaotic relationships, with affective instability, fluctuating and extreme attitudes regarding other people, impulsivity, directly and indirectly destructive behavior, and a lack of a clear or certain sense of identity, life plan, or values." Counselors, or those they involve in their problems, will feel at times that they are experiencing all of these at once. Observers speak of the "storm" of which such persons are the psychological energy source. The stress caused by close work with a borderline is difficult to exaggerate. This makes more urgent a good working understanding of their characteristic pathology. This can often be read in the impact that borderlines have on counselors.

Among the behaviors that the *DSM-III-R* associates with the borderline personality are some that will be intense and unmistakable. Perhaps the borderline's capacity to switch from overidealization to devaluation in interpersonal relationships is one of the signals that will help identify this condition for nonprofessionals. The latter will be the subjects of this usually mercurial, unpredictable, and, for the unprepared, highly bewildering emotional shift. The typical "splitting" of the borderline is one of the principal clinical indications of the presence of this complex disorder. The split may, as mentioned, occur with one person, such as the helper, or it may divide the staff or other groupings as part all good and part all bad. This splitting can wreak havoc in certain settings, such as in an office, and its disruptive effects may be traced back, like a trail of gunpowder, to the borderline personality holding the match.

Borderlines indulge in impulsive behavior in ways that may damage them, as, for example, in sexual activities, eating binges, shoplifting, or substance abuse. Such activities are distinguished from their not infrequent fashioning of suicidal threats or gestures and their engaging in self-mutilating behaviors. One feels the borderline pathology in their sudden shifts from what seems to be normal into depressive, anxious, or irritable moods. They often complain of feelings of emptiness or boredom and experience persistent uncertainties about who they are, how they want to be, and with whom they want to relate. They sometimes strive to ward off real or hypothesized abandonment. Their real impact on helpers, however, is through their anger, samples of which will predictably occur in the context of counseling. This anger is strong, poorly controlled, and intimidating.

Other Features to Note

Recent research has suggested that there may be a genetic antecedent for both the borderline and the narcissistic personality disorders. Counselors should not be surprised, therefore, to hear possibly confirming evidence of this diagnosis in the individual's family history. Indeed, family cohesiveness seems to play a role in the development of these problems; its lack may create the setting for a genetic disposition to manifest itself. Psychiatrist Samuel Perry, of the Cornell Medical Center in New York City, has identified these factors while also noting the evidence for the increased role of child abuse in the genesis of the borderline personality. The most important predictor of later suicide by borderlines may be the presence of physical abuse in childhood. A high incidence of suicide also occurs in those who have suffered a major loss, as of a parent, early in life. The diagnostic picture also often includes the coupling of borderline problems with some other disorder. Just as alcohol abuse is often associated with dependent personality, so borderline personality is linked with affective, or manic-depressive, disorder.

What Should the Nonprofessional Do?

Helpers will help themselves greatly by being able to free their observing self from the welter of borderline entanglements in order to view these persons with some clinical objectivity. One of the main problems caused by these suffering individuals emerges in the countertransference reactions that they generate in those who try to assist them. They are easy to dislike and therefore to reject or to punish, reactions that incorporate the helper into the long line of persons who have succumbed to their involving pathology. Perspective is therefore essential in maintaining the counselor's own sense of balance. Many experts suggest that consultants be used frequently by those working with borderlines in order to manage the countertransference issues effectively. Obviously, nonprofessionals can take some sensible steps on their own as, for example, not seeing such clients more than once a week, monitoring the intensity of the meetings, and not seeing them for extended periods of time before referring them, if this is in order, for professional treatment.

It is, at this point in our understanding of these persons, difficult to judge the efficacy of psychotherapy. Nor is it clear that any specific medication, except one aimed at a target symptom, will be of ultimate value. Some researchers have observed that certain borderline patients, especially those who also suffer from affective problems, seem to settle down as they enter middle age. Intermittent periods of treatment have been recommended by some therapists and others have come to identify the worth of supportive treatment and religion in assisting these persons. Pastoral counselors may, therefore, serve well in religiously oriented supportive help.

The main challenge, however, lies in the engulfing self-presentation of borderlines. Nonprofessionals will need their wits and their good sense, as well as the assistance of others, in identifying the heavy load of transferential material they will find piled on themselves. Sorting out the transference and noting their own countertransference reactions in a healthy way are essential for counselors who want to preserve themselves and be of even measured help to these very unhappy people.

The Narcissistic Personality Disorder

As a sign of their overall cultural struggles, Americans have been preoccupied about narcissism for over a generation. The widespread self-reference and self-absorption of the late twentieth century—being both engrossed with and imprisoned in the ego—have provided an attentive audience for psychiatry's debates about this personality disorder. Elements of narcissism are found in every personality, of course, and the maintenance of adequate self-esteem is not always easy even for the most psychologically robust among us. If we all understand the devastation that can follow from a blow to our self-image we are not, for that reason, all suffering from the kind of disorder that experts have in mind when they discuss this entity.

Widiger and Frances (Talbott, p. 633) describe pathological narcissism as "a behavior pattern characterized by expressions of grandiosity, entitlement, exploitation, shallowness, low empathy, and preoccupation with fame, wealth or grand achievements." Certain rock stars, politicians, and "celebrities" are sometimes cited as contemporary examples of this personality disorder. As Widiger and Frances further note, perhaps the most important feature that counselors will experience in authentic narcissists is their sensitivity "to evaluation by others, reacting with shame, rage, humiliation, or a gross indifferent denial. They are conceited and arrogant but also envious of others, including those who are satisfied with simple but meaningful lives."

What Counselors Must Understand

Here again, nonprofessionals will profit both as persons and as helpers from their careful appraisal of those who suffer from this problem. As with borderlines counselors will experience the pathology that flows from these clients in a firsthand and often confusing and upsetting manner. The need, therefore, to identify transference material, as well as to recognize countertransference reactions, is paramount if the counselor is to survive and be helpful. This is particularly so because the narcissist will exert intense pressures on any potential helper, viewing the counseling as a competition, for example, and seeing the helper in a disdainful way.

While experts still debate about the best method of treating narcissistic personality disorders, the first concern for nonprofessionals is to avoid being incorporated into their psychological maneuvering. Counselors should recognize the potential gravity of the narcissist's reactions to loss or the threat of loss. Their rage can be literally murderous in nature and effect and it may well be the pathology beneath the killing or other physical harming of spouses at the time of marital breakup.

Persons with narcissistic personality problems may, therefore, be disruptive to the already challenging nature of marriage counseling. Their sense of grandiosity and entitlement, coupled with their seeming inability to feel empathy for others, make them difficult to work with and, in certain circumstances, dangerous to others. Counselors should consult professionals if they have any questions about such clients and refer them promptly if they feel that their problems need evaluation and treatment by more highly trained therapists.

Recommended Reading:

Alfin, P. L. (1987). Agoraphobia: A Study of Family of Origin Characteristics and Relationship Patterns. *Smith College Studies in Social Work, 57:* 134–54.

Antonovsky, A. (1987). *Unraveling the Mystery of Health: How People Manage Stress and Stay Well.* San Francisco: Jossey-Bass.

Appley, M. H. and Trumbull, R. A., eds. (1986). *Dynamics of Stress: Physiological, Psychological, and Social Perspectives.* New York: Plenum Press.

Arieti, S. (ed.) (1974–75). *American Handbook of Psychiatry, second edition.* New York: Basic Books.

Barlow, D. H. (1988). *Anxiety and Its Disorders: The Nature and Treatment of Anxiety and Panic.* New York: Guilford Press.

Beck, A. T. (1972). *Depression: Causes and Treatment.* Philadelphia: University of Pennsylvania Press. (First published under title of *Depression: Clinical, Experimental, and Theoretical Aspects,* 1967.)

Beckfield, D. F. (1987). Importance of Altering Global Response Style in the Treatment of Agoraphobia. *Psychotherapy,* 24: 752–58.

Berglas, S. (1986). *The Success Syndrome: Hitting Bottom When You Reach The Top.* New York: Plenum Press.

Bernstein, G. A. and Garfinkel, B. D. (1986). School Phobia: The Overlap of Affective and Anxiety Disorders. *Journal of the American Academy of Child Psychiatry,* 25: 235–41.

Birnbaum, J. (1987). A Replacement Therapy for the Histrionic Personality Disorder. *Transactional Analysis Journal,* 17: 24–28.

Bleiberg, E. (1988). Developmental Pathogenesis of Narcissistic Disorders in Children. *Bulletin of the Menninger Clinic,* 52: 3–15.

Bruch, H. (1974). *Learning Psychotherapy.* Cambridge, MA: Harvard University Press.

Chance, S. (1988). Surviving Suicide: A Journey to Resolution. *Bulletin of the Menninger Clinic,* 52: 30–39.

Cohen, L. H. (1988). *Life Events and Psychological Functioning: Theoretical and Methodological Issues.* Newbury Park, CA: Sage Publications.

Colbach, E. M. (1987). Hysteria Again and Again and Again. *International Journal of Offender Therapy and Comparative Criminology,* 31: 41–48.

Coleman, J. C., Butcher, J. N., and Carson, R.C. (1980). *Abnormal Psychiatry and Modern Life, 6th Edition.* Glenview, IL: Scott, Foresman, and Co.

Coryell, W., Endicott, J., Andreasen, N. C., Keller, M. B., et al. (1988). Depression and Panic Attacks: The Significance of Overlap as Reflected in Follow-up and Family Study Data. *American Journal of Psychiatry,* 145: 293–300.

Craske, M. G., Sanderson, W. G., and Barlow, D.H. (1987). The Relationships among Panic, Fear, and Avoidance. *Journal of Anxiety Disorders,* 1: 153–60.

Dahlem Workshop on the Origins of Depression: Current Concepts and Approaches (1982). New York: Springer-Verlag.

Diagnostic and Statistical Manual of Mental Disorders: DSM-III-R (1987). Washington, DC: American Psychiatric Association.

Diamond, D. B. (1987). Psychotherapeutic Approaches to the Treatment of Panic Attacks, Hypochondriasis, and Agoraphobia. *British Journal of Medical Psychology,* 60: 79–84.

Drinka, T. J., Smith, J. C., and Drinka, P. J. (1987). Correlates of Depression and Burden for Informal Caregivers of Patients in a Geriatrics Referral Clinic. *Journal of the American Geriatrics Society,* 34: 522–25.

Evans, E. (1986). Facilitating the Reparative Process in Depression: Images for Healing. *Pratt Institute Creative Arts Therapy Review,* 7: 43–53.

Fand, B. T. (1986). Irritability and Resistance in Obsessional Neurosis. *Psychotherapy*, 19: 289–93.

Finkelstein, H. (1988). The Long-Term Effects of Early Parent Death: A Review. *Journal of Clinical Psychology*, 44: 3–9.

Fyer, A. J. (1987). Agoraphobia. *Modern Problems of Pharmacopsychiatry*, 22: 91–126.

Fyer, A. J. (1987). Simple Phobia. *Modern Problems in Pharmacopsychiatry*, 22: 174–92.

Ganellen, R. J., Matuzas, W., Uhlenhuth, E. H., Glass, R., et al. (1986). Panic Disorder, Agoraphobia, and Anxiety-Related Cognitive Style, *Journal of Affective Disorders*, 11: 219–25.

Garvey, M., Noyes, R., and Cook, B. (1987). Does Situational Panic Disorder Represent a Specific Panic Disorder Subtype? *Comprehensive Psychiatry*, 28: 329–33.

Gedo, J. E. (1988). *The Mind in Disorder: Psychoanalytic Models of Pathology*. Hillsdale, NJ: Analytic Press.

Geller, J. L. (1985). The Long-Term Outcome of Unresolved Grief: An Example. *Psychiatric Quarterly*, 57: 142–46.

Georgotas, A. and Cancro, R. (eds.) (1988). *Depression and Mania*. New York: Elsevier.

Goodwin, D. W. (1986). *Anxiety*. New York: Oxford University Press.

Gorman, J. M. (1987). Generalized Anxiety Disorders. *Modern Problems in Pharmacopsychiatry*, 22: 127–40.

Gorman, J. M. (1987). Panic Disorders. *Modern Problems in Pharmacopsychiatry*, 22: 36–90.

Greenberg, D., Witzum, E., and Pisante, J. (1987). Scupulosity: Religious Attitudes and Clinical Presentations. *British Journal of Medical Psychology*, 60: 29–37.

Hazelton, L. (1984). *The Right to Feel Bad: Coming to Terms with Normal Depression*. Garden City, NY: Doubleday.

Hirsch, I. (1986). Sexual Disorders: A Perspective. *American Journal of Psychoanalysis*, 46: 239–48.

Husaini, B. A. and von Frank, A. (1985). Life Events, Coping Resources, and Depression: A Longitudinal Study of Direct, Buffering, and Reciprocal Effects. *Research in Community and Mental Health*, 5: 111–36.

Jacobson, E. (1972). *Comparative Studies of Normal, Neurotic, and Psychotic Conditions*. New York: International Universities Press.

Jenike, M. A., Baer, L.,and Minichiello, W. E. (1987). Somatic Treatments for Obsessive-Compulsive Disorders. *Comprehensive Psychiatry*, 28: 250–63.

Judd, F. K., Burrows, G. D., and Norman, T. R. (1985). The Biological Basis of Anxiety: An Overview. *Journal of Affective Disorders*, 9: 271–84.

Kapur, R. (1987). Depression: An Integration of TA and Psychodynamic Concepts. *Transactional Analysis Journal*, 17: 29–34.

Katon, W. (1987). The Epidemiology of Depression in Medical Care. *International Journal of Psychiatry in Medicine*, 17: 93–112.

Klerman, G. L. (1986). Current Trends in Clinical Research on Panic Attacks,

Agoraphobia, and Related Anxiety Disorders. *Journal of Clinical Psychiatry,* 47: 37–39.

Lapierre, Y. D. (1987). Clinical and Biological Correlates of Panic States. *Progress in Neuro-Psychopharmacology and Biological Psychiatry,* 11: 91–96.

Lieberman, P. B. and Jacobs, S. C. (1987). Bereavement and Its Complications in Medical Patients: A Guide for Consultation-Liaison Psychiatrists. *International Journal of Psychiatry in Medicine,* 17: 23–39.

Liebovitz, M. R. (1987). Social Phobia. *Modern Problems of Pharmacopsychiatry,* 22: 141–73.

Lin, N., Dean, A., and Ensel, W. M., (eds.) (1986). *Social Support, Life Events, and Depression.* New York: Academic Press.

Long, B. C. and Haney, C. J. (1988). Coping Strategies for Working Women: Aerobic Exercise and Relaxation Interventions. *Behavior Therapy,* 19: 75–83.

Margraf, J., Ehlers, A., and Roth, W. T. (1986). Biological Models of Panic Disorder and Agoraphobia. A Review. *Behavior Research and Therapy,* 24: 553–67.

Marks, I. M. (1987). *Fears, Phobias, and Rituals: Panic, Anxiety, and Their Disorders.* New York: Oxford University Press.

McNamara, M. E., Southwick, S. M., and Fogel, B. S. (1987). Sleep Apnea and Hyperthyroidism Presenting as Depression in Two Patients. *Journal of Clinical Psychiatry,* 48: 164–65.

Meares, R., Hampshire, R., Gordon, E., and Kraiuhin, C. (1985). Whose Hysteria: Briquet's, Janet's, or Freud's? *Australian and New Zealand Journal of Psychiatry,* 19: 256–63.

Michaelson, L. and Ascher, L. M. (eds.) (1987). *Anxiety and Stress Disorders: Cognitive-Behavioral Assessment and Treatment.* New York: Guilford Press.

Millon, T. (1981). *Disorders of Personality: DSM-III, Axis II.* New York: Wiley.

Monat, A. and Lazarus, R. S. (eds.) (1985). *Stress and Coping: An Anthology.* New York: Columbia University Press.

Moos, R. H. (ed.) (1986). *Coping with Life Crisis: An Integrated Approach.* New York: Plenum Press.

Nespor, K. (1985). Stressful Life Events: A Preventative Approach. *International Journal of Psychosomatics,* 32: 28–32.

Nesse, R. M. (1987). An Evolutionary Perspective on Panic Disorder and Agoraphobia. *Ethology and Sociobiology,* 8: 73–83.

Pecknold, J. C. (1987). Behavioral and Combined Therapy in Panic States. *Progress in Neuro-psychopharmacology and Biological Psychiatry,* 11: 97–104.

Pollack, J. (1987). Relationship of Obsessive-Compulsive Personality to Obsessive-Compulsive Disorder: A Review of the Literature. *Journal of Psychology,* 121: 137–48.

Rachman, S. and Lopatka, C. (1986). Do Fears Summate? III. *Behavioral Research and Therapy,* 24: 653–60.

Rapaport, J. L. (1986). Childhood Obsessive Compulsive Disorder. *Journal of Child Psychology and Psychiatry and Allied Disciplines,* 27: 289–95.

Rice, P. L. (1987). *Stress and Health: Principles and Practice for Coping and Wellness.* Monterey, CA: Brooks/Cole.

Romanis, R. (1987). *Depression.* London: Faber.

Ross, C. A. and Gahan, P. (1988). Techniques in the Treatment of Multiple Personality Disorder. *American Journal of Psychotherapy,* 42: 40–52.

Roth, M., Noyes, Jr., R., and Burrows, G. (eds.) (1988). *Handbook of Anxiety.* New York: Elsevier Science Publishing Co.

Roy-Byrne, P. P., Geraci, M., and Uhde, T. W. (1986). Life Events and Course of Illness in Panic Disorder. *American Journal of Psychiatry,* 143: 1033–35.

Roy-Byrne, P. P. and Katon, W. (1987). An Update on Treatment of the Anxiety Disorders. *Hospital and Community Psychiatry,* 38: 835–43.

Ruple, S. W. (1985). Grief: The Hidden Crisis. *Emotional First Aid: A Journal of Crisis Intervention,* 2: 10–15.

Rutter, M. (1985). Resilience in the Face of Adversity: Protective Factors and Resistance to Psychiatric Disorder. *British Journal of Psychiatry,* 147: 598–611.

Rutter, M. (1987). Temperament, Personality, and Personality Disorder. *British Journal of Psychiatry,* 150: 443–58.

Seagrave, A. (1987). *Free from Fear: New Help for Anxiety, Panic, and Agoraphobia.* New York: Poseidon Press.

Secunda, S. K., Swann, A., Katz, M. M., Koslow, S. H., et al. (1987). Diagnosis and Treatment of Mixed Mania. *American Journal of Psychiatry,* 144: 96–98.

Selby, J. J. and Neimeyer, R. A. (1986). Overt and Covert Hostility in Depression. *Psychology: A Quarterly Journal of Human Behavior,* 23: 23–25.

Signer, S. F. (1986). Is There an Obsessive Psychosis? *Canadian Journal of Psychiatry,* 31: 178–79.

Silver, H. (1987). Physical Complaints Are Part of the Core Depressive Syndrome: Evidence from a Cross-Cultural Study in Israel. *Journal of Clinical Psychiatry,* 48: 140–42.

Slavney, P. R. (1987). The Hypochondriacal Patient and Murphy's "Law." *General Hospital Psychiatry,* 9: 302–3

Solyom, L. (1968). "Is There an Obsessive Psychosis?": Dr. Solyom Replies. *Canadian Journal of Psychiatry,* 31: 178–79.

Solyom, L., Ledwidge, B., and Solyom C. (1986). Obsessiveness and Adjustment. *Comprehensive Psychiatry,* 27: 234–40.

Steinhausen, H. C. and Radtke, B. (1986). Life Events and Child Psychiatric Disorders. *Journal of the American Academy of Child Psychiatry,* 25: 125–29.

Swallow, S. R. and Kuiper, N. A. (1988). Social Comparison and Negative Self-Evaluations: An Application to Depression. *Clinical Psychology Review,* 8: 55–76.

Thyer, B. A. (1987). *Treating Anxiety Disorders: A Guide for Human Service Professionals.* Newbury Park, CA: Sage Publications.

Torch, E. M. (1987). The Psychotherapeutic Treatment of Depersonalization Disorder. *Hillside Journal of Clinical Psychiatry,* 9: 133–43.

Tuma, A. H. and Maser, J., (eds.) (1985). *Anxiety and the Anxiety Disorders.* Hillsdale, NJ: L. Erlbaum Associates.

Vriend, J. and Dyer, W. (1973). Counseling the Reluctant Client. *Journal of Counseling Psychology,* 20: 240–46.

Wiener, R. L. and Merkel, W. J. (1987). Relation of Depression to Specific Medical Complaints in Psychiatric Inpatients. *Psychological Reports,* 60: 147–52.

Williams, S. L. (1987). On Anxiety and Phobia. *Journal of Anxiety Disorders,* 1: 161–80.

Wolf, A. W., Schubert, D. S., Patterson, M. B., Grande, T. P., et al. (1988). Associations among Major Psychiatric Diagnoses. *Journal of Consulting and Clinical Psychology,* 56: 292–94.

Zal, H. M. (1987). Panic Disorder: Is It Emotional or Physical? *Psychiatric Annals,* 17: 497–505.

PART
4

35

Marriage Counseling

There is enough stress connected with counseling only one person; it increases almost logarithmically as we add others because it puts greater demands on our skills and attention. A prime challenge is found in counseling husbands and wives together. It is a strange paradox that, although marriage counseling is one of the most sensitive and difficult of therapies, it is also the area in which many counselors, wisely or not, feel supremely self-confident about giving advice. It seems that everybody knows how to run everybody else's marriage. This may be a distraction from their own troubles in life, or because they feel that what they have learned the hard way is worth sharing. The effectiveness of our counseling married couples varies inversely with the degree of our uninformed self-confidence. Marriage counseling is stressful precisely because, like a land-mined buffer zone, it is filled with psychological traps and surprises. You enter humbly and cautiously, always more ready to learn than to teach.

There is perhaps no activity in which preconceptions, hunches, prejudices, or other attitudes of counselors can interfere so easily or disastrously with the process of counseling. Such hazards abound because of the ease with which transference and countertransference problems can arise and, like swiftly multiplying cells, can come to dominate and destroy the relationship. The intimacy that is intrinsic to the marriage relationship, the complications caused by conscious and unconscious attitudes and experiences of our own, as well as influences such as prevailing cultural expectations over which we have no control, combine to build pressure on all those who participate in this therapy.

In order to minimize the stress and its possible distorting effects on counseling, helpers should begin by increasing their sensitivity to their own inner experience. It helps a great deal if we are aware of the wide range of emotions we all have about marriage and friendship; we also have a store of personal hurts or triumphs in relationship to these. We will profit by examining any strong feeling we have in this area, not only to be able to sense its presence but also to monitor and control its influence on the counseling relationship. Marriage counselors who want to manage stress sensibly should model themselves after surgeons preparing for an operation. They must "scrub up" beforehand to cleanse themselves of the emotional infections that can interfere with counseling. These include an inventory of our past and current feelings about our own experiences in human relationships. We must permit ourselves to hear them in order to understand and deal with them.

One of the subtle feelings to which counselors must give their attention before involving themselves in marriage counseling centers on their potential readiness to choose sides with either the husband or the wife. Counselors may not set out to support one spouse against the other but, unless they are aware of how smoothly and swiftly they can be emotionally enlisted by one or the other, they are easy prey to this complicated difficulty. This is probably the major source of stress for many sincere counselors who, deciding that one spouse is right and the other wrong, invest their energies quite partially on the side they consider correct. They are no longer mediators of communication; they are more like seconds shouting advice to their "fighter" and providing refreshment and moral support between rounds.

If the counselor sees one of the spouses before the other and is therefore vulnerable to being persuaded by his or her view of the situation, choosing sides is likely to result. This is, of course, a particular danger for people who counsel only part-time in relationship to other professional activities. It is not unusual for the first spouse to be seen to get his or her viewpoint across with a maximum amount of illustration and conviction. For many counselors this is the story that permanently affects all their subsequent perceptions of the relationship. Unless helpers are able to sense their potential vulnerability, they may be trapped by it and the subsequent counseling may be permanently distorted in favor of the first person they see.

This is the kind of thing that can happen, for example, when a tearful and attractive woman speaks to an inexperienced counselor about the difficulties she is having with her husband. Such a counselor, not clearly aware of the conflicts of the transference that is taking place, may sympathize strongly with the woman even on an unconscious level; before he knows it, he is on her side. An examination of this counselor's feelings might reveal that he not only feels sympathy for the wife but that he is actually angry at the husband. Were he to examine himself he might be able to see why this happens. It may reflect his own experience or that of his parents or other members of his family. Such quick enlistments put a mortgage on understanding and counseling effectiveness.

Only balanced counselors can accept and deal with the fact that one of the partners may, even unconsciously, actively attempt to get their support from the first moment of contact. Counselors cannot ignore or react defensively to these preliminary issues without running the risk of crippling the counseling and markedly increasing their stress.

Alone or Together?

Closely related to this fundamental idea is the easily developed conviction that, viewed from the outside, a marriage in which one of the partners is receiving psychological help and the other is not, can be defined as "healthy one-sick one" relationship. It is an easy temptation in these circumstances to blame most of the difficulties on the partner who is receiving professional assistance. This does, after all, provide a handy explanation for what conflicts might be present. It is never so simple, however, and counselors must be wary of feeling that the only true perceptions are given to them by the spouse who is not in therapy.

Such spouses are in a relationship, and no relationship is a one-way street. Only if we try to remain open-minded can we appreciate the complexities of communication and experience that can bring a man and wife to the point of seeking help. Committing ourselves quickly to one spouse or the other, either out of sympathy or by concluding that the partner receiving psychological treatment is necessarily the one at fault, contributes twin dangers for all counselors but especially for those whose counseling is only one part of other responsibilities.

There are many theoretical arguments about the advisability of seeing married couples individually or together in counseling. This is the subject on which every counselor must reflect in order to be able to anticipate the counseling arrangements well in advance and to avoid having them arise haphazardly or by chance. Such a decision is based on the counselor's experience, the degree of comfort with which he or she can operate with more than one person, and the nature of the presenting difficulty. Although the arguments for seeing couples together are highly persuasive because this situation naturally recreates their ordinary interpersonal style, there may be good reasons for seeing couples separately, at least for a time at the beginning of counseling.

It may be important, for example, for the counselor to carefully evaluate the factors that contribute to a full and sensitive understanding of these two married persons. Sometimes it is only as counselors get a full appreciation of each individual that they can make a prudent decision about how the man and woman should be seen. A counselor may be able to conclude that in a particular case husband and wife must work together on some maladaptive pattern of behavior they have fashioned in their life together.

On the other hand, a helper may also judge that the partners have special and separate psychological problems that need individual treatment before the couple can come together to work on the specifics of their relationship with each other. This judgment is obviously important and can only be made if the counselor is acquainted with the relevant elements of psychological diagnosis. This is a significant issue that should be discussed jointly with the couple early in the counseling. If the man and woman have a voice in this basic decision, it strengthens the possibilities of continuing therapeutic progress. Such decisions are clearly sensitive and require a prudential judgment freed of emotional complications early in the counseling.

What are the goals the counselor has in mind and how clear are they before the therapy begins? This is a relevant question for those professionals whose main involvement is in fields other than psychology and counseling. They may be committed by their profession or by their particular work within their profession to viewing marriage in a certain way. For example, clergymen may want to save the marriage at all costs for reasons of religious belief and family integrity. Lawyers wish to evaluate the relationship in terms of a divorce settlement in light of other strictly legal approaches with which they are most familiar and concerned.

Physicians may handle only the medical aspects of a couple's difficulties, giving general advice about marriage strictly from the viewpoint of this specialty. In a number of states, couples seeking a divorce must first see a counselor for a prescribed number of visits. Such counselors may find that they are motivated in one way or another either to maintain the relationship or bring it to an end. Certain religious jurisdictions require premarital counseling, especially for very young people, sometimes with a view toward delaying their decision to marry. Counseling that is done under such pressures and with such goals in mind—even when these are not consciously verbalized—introduce elements that may well rob the counseling of its location on neutral ground. A heavy investment one way or the other on the part of counselors before their work with husband and wife begins can obviously predetermine the outcome.

There are many areas that need examination in relationship to goals. Some counselors have very strong feelings about the moral, ethical, or legal issues connected with marriage and divorce. Everybody has certain convictions about these emotionally laden questions. The challenge is not to sacrifice their convictions but to be able to take them into account so that they do not interfere markedly with the counseling. There are enough difficulties involved in marriage counseling without complicating them with factors that we can identify and isolate beforehand. In some situations, helpers may have to exclude themselves from cases in which their feelings are too involved.

This does not mean that counselors are persons lacking values. Currently, the notion of the therapist as a scientist operating from a value-free position is being questioned and put aside. Counselors, as mature adults, must have commitments to values, but in the particular work of marriage counseling, a prime value lies in concern about the integrity of the therapeutic process itself. In other words, a directing value of counselors is to discharge their obligations to their clients in a moral and responsible way. This calls upon counselors to be sensitive to the values possessed by their clients. They must, for example, recognize the place of values in life and in marriage and not rule these out as unimportant or irrelevant to therapy. People care about their values and counselors must recognize these and allow married couples to explore and express them in the counseling relationship.

It is also quite dangerous to force our own values on others, especially if these are foreign to their tradition and belief. That is not the role of the counselor. In the long run we must allow people to make decisions according to their own personal values. We best acknowledge the role of values and reveal our own when we respect those that are operative in the lives of persons with whom we work; counselors are not preachers or proselytizers, and they are false to the profound values that are the foundation of counseling if they assume these roles.

Kinds of Problems

What kinds of problems do married people have? The list reflects the human condition and the familiar staples of life; such as money, in-laws, abrasive personal habits, sexual problems. These are indeed the sore points, the intersections where people collide quite regularly. There are, in fact, many manuals packed with recommendations on how to handle these problem areas more constructively in marriage.

A marriage therapist in Chicago was recently quoted as saying that "marriage counseling is strictly arbitration, similar to that between Egypt and Israel," and that to accomplish it, he uses "Twelve Rules for Happiness" which include: *Live a Simple Life, Spend Less Than You Earn, Cultivate a Yielding Disposition,* and *Rule Your Moods.*" Where these obvious suggestions are applied they can, in fact, do great good. It is sometimes surprising to discover how poorly acquainted some people are with the simple steps—such as the use of a budget—that can reduce friction in their married lives.

While all these suggestions may in fact be helpful, they can easily lead us to become enamored of the *fallacy of the reasonable solution.* It is tempting to use practical solutions because they are aimed at specific problems and they offer positive activities or attitudes that often prove to be very helpful. The difficulty, however, is that reasonable solutions often fail even in the lives of fairly reasonable people. They don't work *because the problem is not a reasonable one;* it is an emotional one and it defies the laws of logic or rational analysis. Most people who are having difficulties with each other do recognize what would be a reasonable thing to do; their chief difficulty lies in trying to implement such notions. They are not reasonable precisely because of the emotional factors that block their capacity for rational solutions and tempered dialogue. There would be no need for any counseling if reasonable solutions could be easily applied. Sometimes it is very stressful for counselors to see reasonable solutions spurned. It seems unreasonable, impractical, and frustrating. But the essence of counseling lies in helping people to reintegrate reason into personality through exploring the emotions that cloud and inhibit it. Counselors should expect people to be unreasonable; that is why they come for counseling.

In order to respond to the married couple, counselors must listen to them rather than just to the problems they describe. Most of the problems are given only as illustrations of something they find difficult to define about their life together. They are trying to sort out their feelings and get to the bottom of themselves. It is a great relief for counselors when they realize that they do not have to have rational solutions to all the concrete problems presented in the course of marriage counseling. For that matter, they don't have to have solutions at all.

Now is the time to recall the basics of counseling, which require that we understand and respond to the persons having problems rather than to the problems themselves. We need not know how to solve the problem, but we must be able both to understand and to express our understanding of the individuals involved. The more counselors drift away from responding to the persons with whom they are working, the more they move toward quagmires and dead ends. They get trapped into these when they have read many lists of marital problems as well as too many rational "how-to-do-it" solutions to them. It all seems so reasonable that they are surprised to discover and rediscover that these "solutions" do not automatically work.

Counselors reduce their own stress when they get back just to understanding the persons involved in the counseling; as understanding helps husband and wife to appreciate their emotional entanglements, they become reasonable on their own.

36

More on Marriage Counseling

Nowhere is the role of mediator of communication more important than in marriage counseling. Counselors are called upon to hear the deep and sometimes confused messages being conveyed by couples who cannot hear each other, and to translate these so that husband and wife can again begin to communicate directly. This requires extreme sensitivity and a practiced and disciplined skill, for which textbooks, "reasonableness," or quick solutions are no substitute. Communication is dead center, the bull's-eye we cannot afford to miss, in marriage counseling. This is where our skills are put to the test. Unless we hone them carefully they quickly grow dull. For example, if we allow ourselves to become stale and distracted, either through overwork or not enough balance in our lives, we may diminish our effectiveness in this payoff area.

This is the reason that marriage counseling places so much stress on those who engage in it. It requires constant attention to the emotional nuances of the strained communication between husband and wife and the ability, without being enlisted by either side, to convey what they are saying to each other. This is the only thing that can reopen a long shut-down relationship. If we miss in the process of communication, we miss in everything.

This is a fairly fundamental thought, and the important question becomes: "How can we miss doing the thing we realize to be one of the most important aspects of counseling?" We fail as agents of communication when we stop hearing, when, in other words, we suffer from the same difficulty that plagues so many worried people. Counselors slip into this for similar reasons: routine, familiarity with similar cases, preoccupation with our own problems, a dullness brought on by overextending ourselves.

Counselors need to be in shape for their work; this constitutes the first ground rule of marriage counseling. The image of the counselor as a harried, overburdened practitioner who has already seen and heard everything has no place in the demanding work of marriage counseling. Being in shape insures our readiness to hear accurately and humanely. It means getting enough rest, working with a reasonable counseling load, and keeping in touch with our own inner lives. Oddly enough, these basic rules are the ones most frequently violated, especially by professionals who let themselves get so busy that they lose perspective on their work.

Be Ready to be Surprised

No counseling has more unexpected turns in it than that involving married people. It illustrates the amazing and unexpected variety of life as one of the most charming aspects of human nature. People frequently do not do what we think they are going to do, especially when they are married to each other. Such peculiar discoveries teach us not to be overconfident in our own judgment about what other people should or might do. Some married people are willing to settle for less, or for only a bit more than we think they should get or deserve from life.

People define happiness in many different ways. In this regard, counselors must even let couples decide that they are going to move away from each other. Counselors may interpret such a decision as a failure on their part but, in many instances, a difficult choice may represent success. Couples who have never really been in touch with themselves or with each other may discover this through counseling and finally realize, for the first time in their lives, who they are and what their relationship really means. While no one may wish for this kind of outcome, and while it may challenge the religious and philosophical ideals of many, it is nonetheless the homely truth about life for which counselors should be prepared. Happy endings are not always the order of the day, and to be disappointed or to feel one has failed because of an unfortunate outcome is not always appropriate. Hard and good decisions are not necessarily happy ones.

Be prepared to not fully understand what is going on. The distinctive manner in which people satisfy each other's unconscious needs shapes their relationship and the course of counseling. This causes a great deal of behavior that is unpredictable precisely because we cannot accurately trace it to its unconscious source. Counselors must remain alert to these subtle shiftings that change the whole balance of the relationship and thus give it a new face. But they may not always be able to interpret or appreciate them fully. They only sense the shifts and see their effects.

Be prepared for the partners to grow at different rates. For example, if one begins to respond and improves in self-understanding and in behavior, this may have strong repercussions on the other partner. He or she is accustomed to relating to an individual who has remained fairly static for a long period of time. When a change comes about, the previous reactions no longer work very well. Something has happened but it is difficult to chart it accurately. Yet we can see the partner shifting in what is bewildering for them and for us. This kind of dynamic occurs in many combinations, and the husband and wife, long accustomed to their former ways of behaving, may be thrown for a loss. The counselor may be confused as well.

Another example may clarify this. A woman who had exhibited psychosomatic symptoms for years began, in the course of marriage counseling, to improve. She has fewer physical complaints but as she became less demanding her husband began to emerge from the passive and quiet role into which he had formerly moved to avoid upsetting her. Now he became more active. This reciprocal change happened too quickly for the wife, even though her initial improvement triggered it. Because she was not prepared for a change in her husband as a result of the change in herself, she could only revert to her former style and get psychosomatically ill again. Sequences of behavior like this can occur very easily in marriage counseling. They can be hard to follow. We need a measure of patience and an adequate perspective to be able to grasp what is going on.

Currents in the Air

Another influence on the course of marriage counseling arises from the philosophy and opinions about marriage that receive widespread publicity through the media and are favorite conversational topics in the social circles of the married couple. These include concepts about open marriage, companionate marriage, or living together with no marriage at all. While there is little that is historically new in any of these developments, they may represent startling and novel ideas about marriage for a great many persons. There are contemporary pressures on marriage, arising from complex ongoing sociological and psychological transformations. Counselors must be aware of these influences; they must hear not only the couple but the world that is the context of the marriage. Such discussions cause pressures because they reveal stresses and strains in the relationship that may have been better defended under previously unquestioned outlooks on man, woman, and marriage. People can say, "Yes, that's us," or "That's how I feel too," to a wide variety of contemporary descriptions of married experience.

This is a difficult area because so many shifts in these popular discussions take place, and also because these discussions can be used as a shield against other interpersonal problems. There is always a danger to human relationships when highly emotional issues can be compressed into a slogan that can seem to renew the familiar battle of the sexes. These slogans are powerful because they provide a forceful symbol for many hitherto unexpressed feelings. This is the advantage of the slogan or the cause; each draws out a wide range of psychological infections.

It is clearly common sense for the counselor to remain neutral about these issues and to be sensitive to the fact that arguments about issues and causes may mask other unnamed internal difficulties. It is also common sense to avoid the role of a crusader on any of these questions. The most that counselors can do is to assist people to understand and take greater responsibility for themselves and their relationships with each other. The high-voltage quality of many current discussions makes it all the more important for counselors to be aware of the many levels of significance that are present. Counselors also increase their own stress if they allow marital or any other kind of counseling to become a forum for the intellectual discussion of such issues. This takes counseling far afield and allows people an escape from their fundamental counseling task of exploring themselves.

When counselors hear too much discussion of contemporary issues going on, they can be fairly certain that this is a defense mechanism in operation. The key is that the dialogue may go round and round but it fails to move the counseling forward.

A further signal is the amount of vehemence attached to certain of these discussions. It is as if the complaining partner had suddenly discovered a way to express deep and frustrated feelings, some of them antedating the experience of marriage itself. For example, a twenty-five-year-old woman recently expressed almost violent feelings of anger at finding herself a wife and the mother of three children. It was not that she did not love her husband and her children; rather, it was the long pent-up emotion of having been cheated out of a better chance at life by her overdemanding father. She had always had these feelings but had only recently become aware of them because of the public discussions about other women who felt "trapped" in their lives.

This woman had carried these unresolved conflicts with her into her marriage. They had probably caused friction of one kind or another before, although their true nature had not been recognized. They lay, as it were, sleeping in her psyche until a contemporary discussion provided the symbols through which she could become aware of them. The resolution of these conflicting feelings—rather than an intellectual discussion of women's liberation—became the first order of the day. Until she could understand these long-repressed emotions she could not discuss her relationship with her husband.

It is clear from this example that although her discontent manifested itself in her married life, it could be traced back to a much earlier period. Working through the long-denied emotions of being robbed of her best chance at life enabled her to separate her own experience from that symbolized in general by the women's movement. It would not have helped to argue with her or to encourage her to be "reasonable." She was, in fact, far more realistic once she was able to express her frustration. Such situations are not uncommon.

Keeping Up and Keeping Open

While it may be difficult for counselors to keep abreast of everything that is going on in their culture, they should make some systematic effort to be informed about the major issues connected with areas of human development, marriage, and the family. An acquaintance with the contemporary world is essential for counselors who wish to understand their clients fully.

Most people who do counseling are familiar with professional publications that offer dependable information and perspectives. They should also try to take advantage of seminars and workshops for updating on the background material relative to their marriage counseling work.

Less often cited but nonetheless important are the other ways in which our culture speaks to us. We have to listen to films, popular magazines, and other shapers of our impressions about married life and related values. The popularity of certain magazines and books indicate that people identify or are intrigued with the life-views or life-styles represented. If we are going to be good listeners, we must also hear what is being said—and what lies beneath what is said—in these publications.

Sexual Dysfunctions

Human beings have suffered greatly from society's difficulty in articulating and dealing clearly with the sexual component of personality. The sexual problems associated with marriage can be very complex. They do not admit of any facile solution and, despite the flood tide of informational literature on sexual subjects at the present time, people do not seem to profit merely from theoretical or intellectual discussion. Currently, a number of sexual therapists of varying backgrounds are establishing themselves in various cities throughout the country. They purport to offer treatments for impotency, frigidity, and other problems that have been associated with the sexual life of married couples. People are still uneasy about their sexuality, and it takes mature and sensitive therapists to assist them in integrating it more successfully in marriage.

A temptation here is to focus excessively on the problem. This is a mistake according to pioneer sexual therapists William Masters and Virginia Johnson. They have consistently emphasized the need to deal with the persons who have sexual problems rather than just with the problems themselves. Sexual difficulties are to be seen in the context of the couple's relationship. Those who counsel, even those with medical competence, should hesitate to suggest or outline new sexual therapies as the total answer to people's difficulties.

Responsible counselors should be well acquainted with the current literature on human sexuality and should be reasonably aware of and comfortable with their own sexual feelings. They cannot rule these out of all therapy because they may well be involved in reacting to certain clients or couples. There is nothing surprising in this. Counselors who are uncomfortable with their sexual feelings—or who need to deny them in order to carry on—increase their own stress until they are willing to come to terms with their own reactions. This does not require psychoanalysis but a certain measure of openness to their own experience and a readiness to explore and integrate their sexual reactivity if and when it is related to their counseling work. In other words, the counselor must practice good mental hygiene; he or she treats sexual feelings as they would any other feelings. They are to be accepted and understood rather than repressed or acted out impulsively. The capacity to handle feelings this way is the hallmark of the ways in which counselors can most successfully manage stress in their work.

Counselors must be aware of their limitations and should not feel, as some contemporary authors and lecturers do, that they must solve all sexual problems or describe a new sexual ideal for their patients. It may be important at times for counselors to refer the married couple for more specialized help with their sexual difficulties, but, in the first instance, understanding persons who have sexual problems is the most important response that they can give. It remains the most significant and indispensable contribution counselors can make because sexuality is an area in which men and women are still easily intimidated. It is difficult for them to talk about their feelings or conflicts. We can assist them to clarify these instead of moving too swiftly toward a referral to sexual therapy. The reason for this is clear: Sexual difficulties are often symptoms of other relational difficulties. As counselors help people get their total selves into better perspective, the root causes of sexual difficulties are often seen much more clearly.

Even with no direct effort to treat their sexual problems, persons find them more manageable when they have a deeper understanding of themselves. Counselors must understand that a sexual problem in a personal relationship is almost always a sign of something deeper. This common sense approach will avoid excessive concentration on the symptom and will also put questions of referral to more specialized help in better perspective.

Referrals

Counselors should look into—but not necessarily use as a first recourse—the professionals in their area who are experienced sexual therapists. They should become acquainted with their professional qualifications, their ethics, and their sense of integrity in dealing with patients. These are generally safeguarded if the persons have the appropriate credentials and licensing but, in the area of fads, it may be that some persons would try to capitalize on the sexual difficulties of others through unprofessional exploitation. Every counselor has an obligation to safeguard men and women from such practitioners. Checking with local medical or other professional societies is the best way to verify the qualifications of such therapists.

We should not be ready to make sexuality and its conflicts the core of every marriage counseling experience. The persons involved in counseling will, if we let them, place it in perspective and allow us to see their relationship through their own eyes. There is nothing more basic to counseling, yet it deserves to be repeated—and perhaps inscribed and hung on every counselor's wall—when it comes to the sensitive business of marriage counseling.

What Counselors Should Know about Sexual Disorders

Counselors who recognize the histrionic use of sexuality should also remember that sexual dysfunctions may be symptomatic of biological problems, intrapsychic or interpersonal conflicts, or some combination of these factors. Sexual function can be adversely affected by stress of any kind, by emotional disorders, or by ignorance of functioning and physiology.

It is very helpful, even for nonprofessionals, to keep some basic principles in mind when they deal with persons who have sexual complaints. For example, it is sensible and helpful to get as complete a case history as possible. In connection with this, counselors should ascertain the client's age, general physical health and current life stresses in order to clarify their possible relationship to the onset of the complaint.

Counselors may already understand that ongoing physical illness as well as a wide variety of prescribed medications may have, as one of their side effects, some measure of sexual dysfunction in both men and women. Often, the average person's being able to talk about this sensitive area of experience brings great relief, a different, healthy side effect of simply offering human understanding to persons. Naturally, counselors should be alert to sexual dysfunction that seems chronic, long-standing, and resistant to psychological intervention. That is a signal for referral for professional evaluation and treatment.

37

Death in Our Culture

Working with dying persons is well recognized as a significant source of stress for counselors who do this only occasionally or as a regular part of their work. It involves being a helper with a patient, his family, physicians, and a wide range of friends and others who, like lawyers and funeral directors, are involved in some way or other in the dying person's life. In the background an increased interest in the subject of death has been noted and commented on extensively by social observers in the United States. This is not an interest shared only by those who are immediately contemplating their own death; many young persons have displayed concern with this subject and have enrolled in various courses and seminars in order to deepen their appreciation of death. There is, one might say, a clear and continuing fascination with death in our culture. Death and violence as a steady diet in our entertainment also focus on mysteries and conflicts in the depths of the human personality that we have hardly begun to investigate.

Americans also try to solve with characteristically pragmatic verve many of the problems associated with death that have been described in the growing body of literature about the subject. It is the same way that Americans have approached sex—with a determined effort to understand it and offer solutions through improved technique, therapies, and assorted other cures.

Death, for example, has been considered by some of its students as a problem of management, something that causes difficulties on a social as well as a personal level and is therefore amendable to improved methods of dealing with it. I recently read an essay describing the "trajectory of death," which can be plotted on a graph and marked, like a business curve, at its most significant or crucial points. But death, much like sex, eludes those experts who think that measurement and organization are effective or even efficient ways to deal with it.

There is a mystery—and a complex one—connected with both death and sex, which suggests that there is more than just a pragmatic challenge involved with both of them. The person is at the center of both death and sex and neither experience can be understood unless the person is kept in very close focus. The more death or sex is treated as something that can be abstracted from human personality, the more estranging is the effect of such investigations. Death and sex, if they are anything, are profound personal experiences and they cannot be understood, much less managed, aside from the context of the individuals who experience them.

The first relevant counseling principle, therefore, is based on the most fundamental perceptions of effective counseling: Just as we respond and relate to sexual persons and not to sexual problems, so we also relate to dying persons and not to the problems associated with dying.

Death and sex are interwoven subjects worthy of meditation more than measurement. We are just beginning to deal with both of them, and there is far more we do not know than what we do know about them. There is, for example, a strong erotic component associated with death. Although it is seldom discussed, it is nonetheless part of our cultural pull toward death; it is a psychological vector with which counselors should have some acquaintance. They should also realize that sex and death have been around a long time, longer even than taxes. Indeed, the recent interest in death is not in itself anything new. It is a revival of an interest that was very strong centuries ago; persons were quite concerned about dying, and many books and reflections were published on the subject of how to die well. The famous *Ars Morendi*, or *Art of Dying*, was first circulated in ancient Rome. The realization that not everything about either sex or death is absolutely new helps counselors to steady their own perspective and to trust the wisdom of their best human instincts in dealing with both subjects. Human sensitivity and common sense are still the counselor's best equipment in dealing with these subjects.

The Too Easy Management of Death

The counselor who wants to be effective needs a seasoned perspective from which to evaluate all the talk and suggestions about death that can be heard at the present time. It is possible to treat the subject of death superficially when the difficulties and challenges connected with it are handled in the way that sex education sometimes is, that is, by people who depend totally on the writings or observations of others because they have never thought deeply for themselves about the subject or the values associated with it.

Good things can always be done badly and it is common sense to recognize that not everybody has the sensitivity or depth that is required in dealing with the human issues connected with dying. It is difficult to imagine that these are fully achieved by some of the teachers who have attracted publicity by having their students plan the teachers' funerals—the teacher as substitute deceased, that is. What a splendid exercise in narcissism this can be for the teacher who, in the name of education, makes himself or herself the center of so much attention. Such examples make us ask: Whose needs are being served in these circumstances? When it turns out that they are those of the teacher, then we can be almost sure that the serious subject of death is being treated superficially.

Death as a fad—that is, working with the dying as a fad—is also possible. It would not be the first time that good has been corrupted by persons who need a cause far more than the cause needs them. Death, alas, has become this for some persons. They get "into it," the way they get into natural foods or Far Eastern mysticism. Working with the dying suddenly offers them a worthy occupational identity and they join themselves to it more for their own sake than for the sake of the dying. This has also happened to many otherwise dignified activities, such as prayer and prison reform. One must be alert for the self-centered people who deal with death as an "in" subject; they add to the stress for everybody else who is seriously concerned. No one has put the matter better than did the distinguished critic Benjamin DeMott several years ago. (*The Atlantic Monthly,* June, 1974, p. 99):

> The most dismal trend is death mongering. Elisabeth Kübler-Ross's *On Death and Dying* was an exceptional work but bad apples are strewn among its offspring. Writers who use—quite seriously—phrases like "low level grief" . . . books that nag the reader ceaselessly with the question, "Have you done your death work?" . . . chapters describing hospital conversations between a dying man and a base form of life called "Death Researcher." Friend, "the death researcher" seems ever on the point of saying, friend, are you aware you're dying? Lady, don't you see you're through?

Sensitive counselors reduce some of this stress by keeping such people as far away from patients, family, and staff as possible. No area demands unadorned humility more than that of working with the dying. Such work can be very stressful but it is also very deepening. The anxiety of uneasiness associated with working with dying patients is not all that there is to the experience.

Through entering into a person's efforts to come to terms with death, we can purchase life ourselves. We are changed for the better by such experiences rather than just depressed by them. That is why fundamental counseling attitudes, stripped of pretense or a need to impress, are essential. Only what is real works, and what is unreal always makes the stress surrounding death more intense.

A Fundamental Question

Helpers, as has just been mentioned, need to draw on all their insights and skills in order to respond to the symbolic and displaced expressions of feeling that are common during the process of bereavement. Some practical questions must also be considered because they have significant implications for the healthy resolution of the grieving process itself. They are issues in which the counselor finds himself involved.

Should the dying person be told of the situation? This has been argued for years but most evidence suggests that there are good reasons to be truthful with dying patients. They have a remarkable capacity for sensing their own condition and they also demonstrate a great willingness to talk about their illness and the prospect of death with those who listen to them without giving them bland reassurances of one kind or another. Human persons possess remarkable potential for facing difficult situations; the greatest tragedies may be those that occur because we leave this reservoir of strength untapped.

It is important to work this through in relationship to the sick person's husband or wife. This is, after all, a part of their life experience, an aspect of their relationship a couple should be able to deal with together. Several years ago, playwright Robert Anderson wrote of his own sadness that he had not told his wife of her imminent death. Looking back he felt that he missed sharing something with her that was very important. He felt that he had not been truthful with her and, in his quest to save her from pain, he now realized that he had ruled out something richer and more important—facing together the challenge of death.

If this can be done—and the counselor may oftentimes be the key figure in this area—people may be able to anticipate some of the problems of grief and even deal constructively with some of the practical questions that will arise at the time of death. One cannot force people to discuss these things, but if one is understanding and acceptant, he may be able to journey with people into feelings they need to explore about themselves and each other in view of the prospect of death. Obviously, one needs to avoid being morbid or dragging in such subjects unnecessarily. The key to this lies in listening, in that sensitive readiness to hear what the others are ready to talk about, and then helping them to put this into words. This is at the heart of all counseling; when it is done correctly it diminishes everybody's stress, including the counselor's.

Even nonprofessional counselors quickly learn that in working with children they often hear the unfiltered unconscious speaking directly. This is true in children suffering life-threatening illnesses who may ask or speak very directly about death. From the age of ten, as Cassem observes (p. 740), "the concerns of children can be strikingly adult." They understand its universality and irreversibility and often ask questions that go right to the heart of their concerns. These are questions, in a sense, for all of us and it is frequently best to allow the child to give his or her own answer. We are better as witnesses than as guides to their remarkable capacity to identify their own fears and wonders and to deal with them. Helping them give a name to their chief fear is a service of enormous benefit. Sometimes, as Cassem notes, giving them simple information, such as the reason in some treatments for hair loss, enables the children to deal effectively with this otherwise extremely upsetting development.

Doing the human thing spontaneously—as with hugging and touching—is what is called for in these circumstances. Perhaps our best support is given to the parents whose best instincts should be encouraged. It is sensible, for the sake of other siblings, to keep family life as normal as possible. It is better for the child to have days that are lived in an average healthy way, neither ignoring nor spoiling them.

In the same way, counselors, although not often the ones to make such decisions, should realize that most persons want to find out the truth about their own condition. Many of them sense it on a less than conscious level anyway. We should not conspire to disguise or dissemble when sensitive honesty, which differs greatly from blunt and crude bad-news breaking, can be helpful to the gravely ill individual.

Nonprofessional counselors should have some acquaintance with and knowledge of the Hospice Movement in their region. Founded by Dame Cicely Saunders in 1967, the programs of this widely expanded movement aim at allowing people, in special environments, "to live to the limit of his or her potential in physical strength, mental and emotional capacity and social relationships. . . . It is the alternative to the negative and socially dangerous suggestion that a patient with an incurable disease likely to cause suffering should have the legal option of actively hastened death, i.e., euthanasia" (quoted in Cassem, p. 753). This may be more important than ever in a culture in which publicity about the easy termination of death has mounted in recent years. Perhaps we are dangerously ignoring the fact that for many sick people life remains desirable and that they should be given every assistance to live it fully to the end.

Some Fundamental Attitudes

Among the familiar principles that counselors who work with the dying may recall are these:

Dying people want to talk rather than be talked to. We are not experts on what dying people should hear. However, in struggling to share with us those things they want to express while the light still lasts, they are experts on revealing to us what is important to them. And dying people will tell us what is significant to them if we give them a chance. We must restrain ourselves, then, especially from using the clichés with which we sometimes fill the uneasy space of a death room. Before dealing with dying persons, we must come to terms with whether we actually trust that common people do have some sense of what is important for them to deal with as they approach life's end. To sum up—let them tell us.

Presence plus the vulnerability that goes with it are essential. There is no way of antiseptically inserting ourselves into a relationship with a dying person. We have to be in the relationship, not on the side of it nor at the kind of safe psychological distance we can be so skilled at introducing. The best thing we have is who we are; who we are may not be the perfect instrument but it is eminently suitable for such work. It is, in fact, our flawed humanity that enables us to be counselors at all. Who we are needs to be revealed rather than hidden, exposed rather than protected, in the presence of dying persons.

Dying persons speak symbolically. We must hone our sensitivity in order to catch their meanings as completely as possible. The symbols may be in gestures, in stories, or they may be tied up in the kinds of memories or reflections they choose to share with us. If we are aware that dying persons are not merely passing time but trying to spend it in getting across important messages, we will be more skilled at reading their communication. There is always a message; it only remains to be translated. This is a principal function of a counselor with the dying— to give words to what they can only outline in symbols.

Dying persons are subjects not objects. It is very easy to begin to treat dying persons as objects, as persons who have almost lost their right to speak about themselves. Often other people—with the best of intentions—begin to make decisions about what is best for the dying patient. These people may not be aware of how this taking over of responsibility diminishes the sense of personhood that remains so important for the dying patient. People sometimes forget how much seriously ill people can hear and understand. Objects can be managed, but subjects must be listened to and allowed a voice in the matters connected with their treatment, their visitors, and other such subjects.

The counselor deals with more than the dying person. Frequently the one who bears the burden of the counseling responsibility relates not only to the sick person but also to physicians, hospital staff, members of the family, and other friends. This is taxing but significant and important work because these parties also experience tangled emotions and they can function much better if someone can respond to their often overlooked needs. Sensitivity that radiates out to all those connected with the dying person puts a strain on the counselor, which he can reduce by anticipating and planning his time in order to be able to deal with these issues.

What We Know

The research of recent years, as in the work of Dr. Elisabeth Kübler-Ross, has taught us things about the experiences of dying patients that help enormously in preparing counselors to do their best work more humanely and more effectively. An acquaintanceship with the literature on death and bereavement provides counselors with a base of reinforcing knowledge that reduces the stress they will otherwise experience. Some of the things we have learned about dying include the following:

People want to live until they die. One of the functions of counseling is to help dying persons to do precisely this, to invest as much of themselves as possible in experiencing life fully even in their last weeks or days of it. They do not want to be treated as "dying." The problem for many people who work closely with terminally ill patients is the degree to which they begin to perceive the patient as different from healthy persons. It resembles the way we occasionally talk louder to foreigners than we do to each other. If we find ourselves treating patients more as dying than as living, we should investigate to find out why this should be so. It may be our way of denying the relevance of death to ourselves.

Dying persons pass through stages that have been repeatedly observed. They cannot skip any of the stages of coming to terms with death, and the counselor who understands these stages notably increases his or her sensitivity to the real experience of the dying person. A helper can keep in tune with dying persons far more easily through observing the psychological map that charts the phases of a dying person's experience. It also aids in interpreting the numerous symbolic gestures and other communications during these phases. Dr. Elisabeth Kübler-Ross has pointed out these stages and commented on them extensively in her books and tapes. Many readers will already be familiar with them.

Dr. Ross first mentions *denial* with some effort to carry on as usual. The patient may go from physician to physician trying to disprove the diagnosis and he may avoid telling his family, just as he avoids telling himself, the truth about the situation.

The next stage is that of *anger* that the dying person should be the one chosen—the "why me?" phase. This is obviously a time for counselors not to take the client's anger personally.

Then follows what Dr. Ross describes as *bargaining*—the individual tries to gain some stay of execution from God with promises of better behavior and other reforms. There are real efforts made at striking this kind of bargain before the person can accept the fact that death is really coming.

The succeeding stage includes *depression,* in which dying persons mourn past losses and then begin to withdraw their interest from the world around them. The circle of those in whom interest is shown becomes smaller; the dying person is experiencing preparatory grief.

The final stage is one of *acceptance,* in which the person is able to meet death peacefully. Counselors will find in Dr. Ross's book extensive descriptions and examples of these phases of the dying process. (*On Death and Dying,* New York: Macmillan Co., 1969.) Others, such as Avery Weisman, have observed that the stages vary considerably in number from individual to individual. There is no point in trying to make dying people go through the stages as we conceive them. They must be allowed to go in their own way, at their own rate. We can only accompany them.

The Family

The family members also pass through these same stages once they realize that someone is seriously ill. They do not pass through them at the same time as the dying person, and a counselor must allow them to proceed at their own rate. Counselors cannot hurry them or make them skip stages, nor should they artificially contrive to have family members and the patient pass through the same stages at the same time. It just does not work that way.

The counselor's awareness of the fact that these stages are inevitable enables a better informed response to the grieving family as well as to the dying person. It allows us to omit the platitudes that hardly touch people when they are trying to work through the difficult realization of the death of someone close to them. It is a time for availability and presence rather than for words from the outside, no matter how supportive these may sound.

The Counselor

There are several things counselors may do to enlarge their capacity to respond to dying persons. First of all, they can acquaint themselves with the growing sensible literature on the subject of dying. They can also attend seminars or take advantage of other updating educational experiences that will help them to perceive the issues associated with dying in a clearer and more humane fashion. There is no substitute for the active acquisition of a greater understanding of the human experience of death.

Counselors can deal seriously with their own self-knowledge. They need some reverence for themselves, for their strong and weak points, and a genuine acceptance of their limitations. This is one of the reasons that those who work with the dying are notably assisted if they can be part of a reflective team of persons who, as in a hospital for example, work with dying patients. Working in a team allows counselors to handle their own emotions more clearly and to sort out the countertransference feelings with less ravaging of their own hearts. A group setting also allows discussion of the serious questions that arise in relationship to any particular individual or family. It provides a human setting of support for the difficult work of counseling the dying. No counselor should try to carry on alone in this kind of work.

For this reason nobody should have a steady diet of working alone with the dying. Counselors must respect their own needs and provide themselves with the kind of recreation or change in routine that enables them to keep fresh and so permits them to enter more deeply and effectively into the lives of dying persons. Overworked and overwrought counselors don't see things clearly. Counselors totally absorbed in death multiply stress and reduce their effectiveness. Working with the dying does not demand killing ourselves.

This work demands the simplest human responses we can give. These are the best. They are, in fact, all that we ever have to give. They are all that people seem really to be looking for: Somebody to be there, somebody who can accept and understand their experience and sense their meaning. Dying people want other persons there who will accompany them on this last uncertain pilgrimage. The greatest asset counselors can possess is the ability to make this journey without being lost on it, to be able to stay with the dying person even when they do not quite understand everything the person is trying to say, to look steadily into the face of death rather than to turn away.

38

Suicide Risks: Who Are They?

Sixty to seventy times a day some American succeeds in committing suicide. It is the ninth leading cause of death in our country and, although it is sometimes imaginatively associated with older people, it is the third leading cause of death among adolescents, ages 15 to 21. It is an occurrence any professional person who works closely with others must appreciate and understand. Although suicide has already been treated briefly, it needs a deeper analysis and more reflection if counselors are to be prepared to respond to this complex and stressful challenge.

Despite the fact of approximately 28,000 completed suicides in the United States every year, some observers feel that many genuine suicides are "lost" in the reporting process. The underreporting of suicidal death is, for example, considerable, with estimates that as many as 100,000 of these occur every year (Grinspoon, 1986). Some suicides are covered up by families who feel a sense of shame at its occurrence; others go unrecognized because the attendant evidence, such as a farewell note, is not present. These include automobile accidents, an estimated fifteen percent of which are truly suicides. Self-punishment and ritual suicide recur at different periods of history and in different cultures. A certain romantic illusion sometimes attaches itself to suicide; such tendencies all reflect shifting cultural attitudes and emphases.

According to Stevenson (Talbott, p. 1029), the rate of adolescent suicide has risen steadily for the past several decades, with some estimating that between 1960 and 1980 it grew by 237 percent. For those under 19, it has stabilized at about 6,000 completed suicides per year. These young people constitute the population that is the second most at risk for the completion of suicide. Stevenson notes, in one of the grimmest footnotes to our overall cultural problems, that twenty-five percent of all adolescent suicides are related to substance abuse, and that there is a fifty percent incidence of parental alcoholism in the victims of teenage suicide.

The crucial role of family life and early experience is underscored painfully by such findings. When there are major ruptures in the home life of the growing person, later illnesses and functional liabilities grow, at first imperceptibly but later undeniably, as weeds do in hairline sidewalk fissures. While the situation is complex, some studies have suggested that early loss and separation experiences as well as failures of healthy nurturance may so compromise the young person's capacities for adaptation in adolescence that they may be more prone to suicide. Stevenson notes that "additional causative factors in adolescent suicide center in the home environment, with disruption, separation, and a high degree of acrimony recognized as particularly stressful" (p. 1030). The sequellae of death, divorce, failures (such as in school or relationships), and frequent family moves also seem strongly negative. Nonprofessional counselors are often in the middle of such turmoil and may well reflect on what they can do, not only to identify the adolescent at risk, but to address these urgent, if somewhat remote, problems.

Stevenson provides a table of "frequent precipitants and events preceding adolescent suicidal behavior," which ranks them as follows:

1. Arguments between parents
2. Arguments with parents
3. Loss of parent
4. Divorce of parents
5. Breakup of close relationship
6. Failing grades
7. Loss of interest in usual activities
8. Complaints of boredom (op. cit., p. 1031)

A recent phenomenon in American culture is the contagion of adolescent suicide that seems to spread after a well publicized incident of teenage life taking. Some refer to this as a "cluster" of suicide. As Stevenson notes, recent research "positively correlates a rise in teen suicide of approximately two weeks' duration following such events. . . . [and] these subsequent suicides should be regarded as imitations of the events reported or viewed on television" (loc. cit.). Not only does such information help counselors interpret and perhaps even prevent such occurrences, but it also reminds them of the interest they should show, especially in their primary roles as clergy, physicians, and teachers, for example, in influencing opinion on the broader contextual issues. The need for restraint without censorship in reporting such provocative events may be a cause in which they could constructively participate. This sensible counseling to the culture at large may be one of their most significant contributions to the mental health of the nation.

Distinctions

There is a distinction between an *attempted* suicide and a *completed* suicide. Women attempt suicide four times more than men, but men complete suicide four times more than women (F. B. Davis, "Sex Differences in Suicide and Attemped Suicide," *Diseases of the Nervous System,* 29: 1968, pp. 193–194). It is also known that suicides peak in the springtime and at the Christmas holidays, periods during which many people experience the depression that is closely associated with self-destruction. Sixteen percent of suicides have previously committed murder, a finding that has held up in cross-cultural studies as well. It is estimated that over two million Americans have made suicide attempts.

The composite picture of the individual most likely to commit suicide is that of the depressed man over sixty years of age, single, divorced, or without close friends in his life; persons who live alone; alcoholics, of whom fifteen percent die by their own hand; persons who have recently suffered a great loss; or older people who are physically ill.

It is clear that suicide is a national problem and that all helpers need to sharpen their sensitivity to its signs, some of which may be very subtle but all of which need the kind of understanding that is characteristic of good counseling responses. To understand suicide is, after all, one aspect of trying to understand the complexity of human behavior.

Suicide is far from a simple problem; it cannot be mastered so that a counselor can keep all the possibilities under control. At some point almost every helper will be involved to some degree or other in a potential suicide situation. A compassionate but informed approach lessens counselors' experience of stress and enables them to respond more confidently and constructively.

Hard Truths

Suicide is not a subject people enjoy discussing. Neither are some of the facts that research has revealed about the circumstances of suicide. These must, nonetheless, be understood without embarrassment by those working in this sensitive area. They include, for example, an understanding that some suicides are committed quite accidentally by persons, often young, who are not seeking to end their own life but seem rather to be driven by the desire for the erotic kind of excitement that for them is associated with mock suicide. Even though counselors may not deal directly with these events, they may at times be involved with family or friends who will need special understanding in order to deal with this interpretation of the behavior of some member of their family.

Moreover, it is important to understand the possibilities of accidental suicide in some young person who might approach a counselor to discuss this kind of difficulty. It is ordinarily very hard for them to speak about suicide as an experience with erotic dimensions; it also may be hard for some counselors to listen. When the situation is this complex, the counselor's ability to grasp the meaning that the other is trying to convey takes on an added significance. Counselors not only need to understand but they may also be called upon to help bewildered and distraught survivors to understand.

People are becoming acquainted with some of the false notions that have been held over the years about suicide. Counselors can further the education of those with whom they have contact by helping them, for example, to understand that people who talk about suicide actually do commit it. Upwards of eighty percent of patients who have completed suicide have communicated their intent to others (Stevenson, citing Beskow's research, p. 1032). People are, as we have already noted, always trying to tell the truth about themselves although they often do this in disguised ways. Of no group is this more true than those who could be termed suicide risks. The problem is not that they do not tell us; it is usually that we do not hear what they are saying.

There is also some misunderstanding about unsuccessful suicides. Some believe this means that the persons were never serious in the first place. However, this interpretation betrays an inadequate understanding of the problem of suicide. As Stevenson observes, noting studies done by Hawton and Osborne in 1981, any efforts "to separate those individuals who attempt suicide from those who completed the act may have clinical disadvantages. Because at least ten percent of individuals who attempt suicide complete suicide at a later date, any attempts should alert the clinician that the patient deserves careful assessment and follow-up" (Talbott, p. 1032). People who attempt suicide mean business and they may stay at it until they are successful. The problem frequently arises because those close to them want them to get better, so they screen out the negative signals and reinforce in their own minds the favorable statements that those contemplating suicide may make.

Ambivalence is a main characteristic of potential suicide. This means, of course, that there are two sets of feelings. When only one of these can be heard, the potential suicide is misunderstood by those who want to be of the greatest help. That is why so many survivors say things like, "She didn't seem depressed. She seemed in good spirits last night." This is all they can see or hear because they are members of the same family or close friends. And their selective perception makes the role of other professionals, such as teachers, clergy, or counselors, all the more important. They may be the only ones who are able to catch the total communication of the suicide-prone individual.

The presence of *depression* has always been identified as the chief characteristic of the potential suicide. Not all depressed persons, of course, plan suicide, but very few who plan suicide are not depressed. The story of each suicide may be as complex as the story of each individual's life. This is why a willingness to let other persons take us into their experience in order to reveal it to us is more important than ready answers, inspiring sermons, or even untimely action to prevent suicide. Suicidal intent must, according to some observers, be perceived as a continuum ranging from some vague thought about self-destruction to the actual concrete initiation of such activity. The way people sound and act differs from one point to another along this line, but depression and hopelessness are common denominators that can be heard, faintly or loudly, all along the way.

Reading the Signs

Dr. Paul Pretzel (*Understanding and Counseling the Suicidal Person.* Nashville, Tenn.: Abingdon Press, 1972) lists two basic conditions associated with suicidal attempt. First of all there is *an increase in the stress* that is judged to be intolerable by the individual. Secondly, the person *experiences the lack of ability to cope* with this stress alone or even with the help of others. The suicidal person does not suddenly arrive at the point of contemplating self-destruction. There is a history connected with this, as has been mentioned, as well as repeated efforts to communicate the person's intent to others. Pretzel suggests that suicidal persons have a period of peak crisis during which suicide is highly probable for them. This, according to him, is the point at which counseling intervention can be most helpful. It can only be determined, of course, by a perceptive and sensitive observer.

James C. Coleman (*Abnormal Psychology in Modern Life.* Glenview,

Ill.: Scott Foresman & Co., 1972) describes three stress factors in the suicide-prone individual that are important for helpers to understand: *Interpersonal crises, failure in self-evaluation,* and *the loss of meaning and hope.* Edwin S. Shneidman has studied and written extensively on suicide. See, for example, his *On the Nature of Suicide* (San Francisco: Jossey-Bass, 1969). He has cited four constellations of symptoms that indicate clear suicidal intent. These are the messages being delivered fairly clearly by these persons; they only remain to be read accurately by those around them.

Shneidman first lists the common factor of *depression.* In this state suicidal persons shift away from being interested in others to a greater concentration on their own psychological life. They emphasize their own internal feelings rather than their feelings toward others. This depression is also manifested in an inability to sleep or to eat, and sometimes in withdrawal from ordinary social activities. These are important signals, according to Shneidman, which indicate that suicide-prone persons are losing hope and need the response of someone in the environment.

Secondly he cites organic mental disorders or psychosis, in which persons experience hallucinations (seeing something that is not there) or illusions (misperceiving something that is there). This may have organic causes or it may also be the product of a serious functional disorder.

Shneidman cites as the third syndrome *the defiant person* who, through suicide, is trying to reestablish control over the environment. Terminally ill patients sometimes give evidence of this by committing suicide in order to control the time of their own deaths.

Fourth, he lists *dependent-dissatisfied patients* who understand that they are dependent but are very unhappy with the condition. They are miserable in this deadly combination of activities.

These represent the classic psychological situations in which suicide potential exists; it remains for helpers to read and respond with understanding to these clear signals. Frequently an understanding response or even the capacity to tolerate what seem to be unreasonable demands on the part of depressed individuals in one or the other of these situations turns out to be very helpful.

More on Depression

Willard Gaylin ("The Meaning of Despair" in *Psychoanalytic Contributions to the Understanding of Depression.* New York: Science House, 1968) comments on the depressive features that are related to suicidal intent, indicating science's recent appreciation of the loss of self-esteem of such persons. He thinks this diminished self-esteem is better understood as the loss of self-confidence and that this takes place when the person is deprived of something on which he normally depends. There is, in general, a consensus about the gradual weakening of suicide-prone persons' capacity to deal with life and with the losses they have experienced in its course. They can, in the language of the day, no longer "get themselves together" in order to respond to life. George Engel (*Bulletin of the Menninger Clinic*, 32: 1968) refers to this as the "giving up-given up complex"; it must be watched carefully by those who would be aware of suicidal intent. The characteristics include:

1. Giving up feelings of helplessness or hopelessness.
2. A depreciated picture of oneself.
3. A loss of satisfaction from personal relationships or from one's role in life.
4. A break in one's sense of continuity between the past, present, and future.
5. A reactivation of memories of earlier periods of "giving up" on life.

Bernard Steinzor puts it another way (*The Healing Partnership*. New York: Harper and Row, 1967) saying that "he who takes his life has given up all hope of the possibility of affection. . . . I hear suicidal thoughts and the cries for help before the final spasm of despair takes over." The sucidal person does not hide this growing sense of hopelessness about life. It is the message that we can hear when we are realistic rather than naïvely optimistic or at such a distance from those with whom we work that we simply do not grasp what their experience means to them. It is important to achieve the internal view of suicidal patients. Without it we will be baffled by their actions because we will be looking at their lives from our own vantage point. The key to understanding suicidal persons is to see things—black as they are—from their viewpoint.

Counselors obviously need as much information as possible if they wish to be effective in dealing with potential suicides. They cannot, however, apply these facts without checking on their own attitudes toward self-destruction. Such an emotionally laden subject is bound to cause a variety of reactions at various levels of consciousness in each of us. We may have relatives or friends who have committed suicide; our religious or ethical convictions may influence us far more strongly than we suspect.

By understanding what is going on inside themselves counselors can, of course, take account of these influences and keep them from interfering—from blocking their capacity to hear the messages of the suicidal person, for example—in the heart of their counseling work. Listening first to ourselves is always the initial step in reducing stress and improving chances of hearing others.

39

Suicide: Weighing the Risk

Whether as a consultant or as a counselor working directly with suicidal patients, the question of making a judgment on the possibility of actual suicide is central in the helper's concerns. It is, indeed, one of the chief sources of stress for counselors working with such persons. Can this judgment be made in a more informed manner? If so, what are the factors that must be considered? It is already clear that suicidal persons are, in a real sense, cooperating with those persons who might be of assistance to them. They generally give clear signs of their distress and frequently clear signals of their suicidal intentions. Are there any guidelines available to assist helpers in making better judgments and, therefore, better therapeutic responses to those prone to suicide?

Dr. Paul Pretzel believes that determination to commit suicide is the clearest signal counselors can get. He also suggests that any suicide plan has three important facets: *specificity of the means, lethality of the means,* and *availability of the means.* When all of these are clear and strong, the likelihood of suicide must be judged to be very great.

The Los Angeles Suicide Prevention Center has developed a lethality scale to assess suicide potential as has the Center for the Study of Suicide Prevention of the US Public Health Service. Although counselors may not directly employ any of these techniques, they may use these categories to refine their own understanding of the suicide potential in those with whom they work. The lethality scale provides a checklist of factors that help to sharpen the perception and the prudential judgment of helpers; it recapitulates succinctly much of what is known about suicidal persons. It consists of the following information:

1. *Age and sex:* The potential is greater for men than women and for persons over sixty-five.
2. *Symptoms:* The potential is greater if the person is depressed, cannot sleep, feels hopeless, or is alcoholic.
3. *Stress:* The potential is greater if the person is under severe stress.
4. *Acute versus chronic aspects:* The potential is greater if there is a sudden onset of specific symptoms.

5. *Suicidal plan:* The potential is greater in proportion to the lethality, organization, and detail of the plan.

6. *Resources:* The potential is greater if the person has no family or friends.

7. *Prior suicidal behavior:* The potential is greater if the person has a past history of suicidal attempts.

8. *Medical status:* The potential is greater when there is chronic, debilitating illness.

9. *Communication aspects:* The potential is greater when the person has no outlet or has been rejected by others.

10. *Reaction of significant others:* The potential is greater if others punish or reject the person.

Stevenson offers the following table for the evaluation of suicide risk:

	LOW	HIGH
Sex	Female	Male
Age	Midyears	Adolescence; old age
Marital Status	Married	Single, divorced, living alone
Psychiatric conditions	Character disorders; situational disturbances	Depression; alcoholism; schizophrenia
Setting	Rural areas	Urban areas
Level of religious activity	Churchgoer	Nonchurchgoer
Geographic location		
United States	Mid-Atlantic region	Mountainous Western region
Other countries	Italy, Netherlands, Spain	Romania, Austria, Switzerland, Scandinavia, Japan, German-speaking countries

(Stevenson, in Talbott, p. 1023)

There is no substitute for prudence on the part of the helper deciding about the relative seriousness of a suicide attempt. He can assemble all the information and fail to integrate it properly because of some factor, perhaps within himself, that he has not weighed sufficiently. It is also possible that, on the basis of only some of this information, a counselor could make an inappropriate judgment about the danger of suicide and the way to handle it. Counselors cannot allow the dramatic aspects of suicide potential to hurry them or to make them misinterpret information that is obviously central to any effective response to suicidal persons. Making a recommendation in this area is intrinsically stressful; counselors who respect themselves will be patient with themselves in formulating this decision. Nonprofessionals should always work, however, toward having an evaluation made by a person with expert training and experience.

Things to Avoid

As counselors deal with the difficult and delicate question of potential suicides, their first enemy is *overreacting*. To be wary of this makes good sense in any emergency situation because part of the counselor's role is to be a stabilizing influence as well as a mediator during a time of confusion. Avoiding panic, counselors are freer to sort out the situation and to establish the priorities of things to be taken care of as calmly as possible.

In this age of idealizing "coolness" another danger is *underreaction*. This false ideal is not shared by many of the persons sensitive enough to engage in counseling activity. They may, however, observe it in some others who are dealing with suicidal persons, and the counselor's task may indeed be to help people develop a realistic sense of the danger rather than to repress it under a false mantle of calm. The difficulty is compounded because suicidal persons who are met with the reaction of overcontrol may feel that they have simply not gotten through and that their only resort is to take some more drastic measures. A sense of coolness, in other words, may push suicidal persons close to the brink of self-destruction precisely because it projects the kind of emotional unresponsiveness that is most painful to them.

It is also important for counselors or others working with potential suicides to avoid doing things that don't help. For some reason this is difficult to understand; doing exactly the wrong thing is precisely what some people—even when they know better—do in the face of a crisis. Whether they do these inapproprite things in order to avoid the challenge, or whether they simply do not understand the dimensions, the effects are the same. It does little good, for example, to try to cajole deeply depressed persons out of suicide. Neither is it sensible to try to distract them by talking about other things. It is a vain endeavor to try to get them interested in some other activity. The threat of suicide must be dealt with, the message must be taken seriously, and inappropriately trying to be "cheerful" can be very harmful.

Closely related to the overcheerful attitude is the approach that emphasizes the negative aspect of the suicidal person's characteristically ambivalent feelings. Arguing against suicide on the basis of its undesirable consequences ("This won't make things better," "Don't you know your church says that this is a serious sin?") may only reinforce the glum aspects of the person's outlook and convince him that nobody truly understands the situation. One of the easiest and most costly mistakes in all of counseling is to pick up and respond to only one part of a two-pronged statement.

Things to Do

Counselors obviously should be keyed to the total communication of suicide-prone persons and not hesitate to place the positive aspect of their statements in contrast with the negative: "You say you also have lots of things you like about life." "There are reasons for, as well as against, staying alive; can you tell me something more about these?" This gives suicidal persons an opportunity to investigate their positive resources at a time when these are vitally important to them.

Counselors need not be hesitant about verbalizing the possibility of suicide when they are dealing with depressed persons they judge to be suicide risks even before the individuals actually mention suicide. This does not put a new idea into their minds; it may, in fact, diminish the symbolic power of actual suicide by showing that the thought can be accepted and understood by others. Even if the person denies thoughts of suicide, the inquiry, if made sensitively, can be helpful in challenging them to see themselves in sharper focus. Fear of mentioning suicide only interferes with counseling effectiveness with those clients who otherwise manifest the qualities associated with this problem. It is what they want to talk about—except that many cannot find the right words without the counselor's help.

Because suicide can give rise to many difficult and uneasy feelings in counselors themselves, all share a need to explore their own attitudes in order to be able to deal with their feelings before they get involved in suicide work. It may be that some persons will judge that they simply have neither the temperament nor the patience to work closely with someone who is contemplating suicide. It is better for such counselors to recognize their limitations—they may have limitations with some other patients as well—and to refer these for assistance to others. Counselors can never hide what they are really feeling, and they should never carry on by using awkward mechanisms of repression or denial. A good therapeutic relationship can be the strongest bond that a depressed or hopeless person can have with life itself.

A counselor is challenged to relate to suicidal clients as persons and to balance concerns about their behavior with a genuine understanding and acceptance of them as individuals. This builds a relationship that can be strong enough to see the person through the more critical phases of contemplated suicide. In the long run it is always the kind of relationship that the counselor has with the client that will be the most important determinant. It is on the basis of such a relationship that counselors can make timely and sensible referrals to others more experienced and skilled in dealing with suicide risks. It is not a failure to refer but a mature decision to remain within the bounds of supportive helping. The suicide risk will profit from both the referral and the sense of strong support still available from an interested and trusted counselor.

The question of sensible referral arises regularly in the work of nonprofessionals. In no other situation is it more important for counselors to avoid panic while they expeditiously draw on the resources of their local communities to assist their troubled client. This necessarily presupposes the development by the counselor of good relationships with local physicians, psychiatrists, psychologists, social workers, and others who work every day with such emergencies. The preliminary counseling becomes that bridge of support over which the troubled person can confidently make passage to experienced professionals.

The Attempted Suicide

Sometimes the counselor only has contact with an individual after he or she has made a suicidal attempt. The general principles regarding sensitivity and understanding apply here, of course, but it may be helpful to review what could be expected in counseling after there has been an actual effort at self-destruction. Hamilton and Moss ("Psychotherapy for the Suicidal Patient," in *Clues to Suicide*, pp. 99–111) say that over ninety percent of the patients they have studied experience a reactivation of the suicidal drive after an unsuccessful attempt. Successful management of this recurrence of the urges to self-destruction becomes, then, the most crucial aspect of continuing counseling. Hamilton and Moss suggest, as a course of therapy, the following three phases: the *acute*, the *convalescent*, and the *recovery*.

During the *acute* phase counseling may be directed toward adequate protection for the individuals coupled with relief from their experience of anxiety and hopelessness, as well as some effort to improve their relationships with family and friends. Hospitalization is often necessary at this time because its environment lessens tension and the possibility of solitary isolation. Counselors must be aware of such an individual's feelings about having attempted suicide. It is not appropriate to probe for these but it is essential to listen, for they will come out. People will talk about what is important to them in the wake of what they have attempted to do to themselves; this is a crucial time to catch the pattern of their reflections even when they are seemingly disordered and disjointed. The heart of the matter will be there.

The *convalescent* phase for the attempted suicide begins when the person is ready to return to his or her former environment. During this and the *recovery* phase patients are, of course, vulnerable to the reactivation of the suicidal urge. This is because they are back in the situation that originally precipitated the difficulty. During this period counselors must be carefully attuned to the person who attempted suicide and, perhaps more importantly, to the members of the attempted suicide's family. It is not uncommon for the relatives of the person to need counseling as much as the one who attempted the suicide. This can be particularly helpful at the time of a return to old scenes and familiar circumstances. Successful counseling with the persons who live in closest contact with the patient may help to restructure attitudes in such a way as to relieve much of the stress that precipitated the original incident. It is also possible that this is the time for family members to make important decisions about shifts in lifestyle, jobs, and other circumstances that may need modification for the good of the suicidal person. Such discussions should be carried out in relationship to the one who attempted suicide rather than behind his or her back. The convalescent period is also a rich opportunity to acquaint family members with the kinds of psychological responses that are important as well as the types of resources that are available should an acute crisis arise again.

The convalescent phase provides the occasion to help family members read the messages that they may have missed before. For example, it has been found that an agitated person who finally makes a firm decision about suicide may then experience a period of tranquility and calm before committing suicide. This is frequently misinterpreted, however, as a sign of improvement on the part of the individual rather than as the consequence of a firm decision for self-destruction. During this calm before the final storm, family members may react with relief and look away with less concern; this, of course, only complicates the problems both for them and for the suicidal person. They are least prepared just at the moment that the person who intends suicide is most determined.

It is hard for counselors to realize that they are not God and that, although they approach their task with sensitivity and dedication, they neither prevent nor postpone suicide or any other unhappiness in life. It is a sad but true axiom for psychology that a person who wants to commit suicide will eventually be able to do so no matter how we may try to prevent it. Counselors need a sensible approach to their own mental health in these circumstances. They cannot make demands on themselves that they cannot possibly meet. They cannot take responsibility for all the things that their clients do. We say *yes* to life for our clients, but we must be prepared for the fact that some of them will still say *no*.

The capacity to be realistic in the dangerously unpredictable circumstances connected with suicide actually frees the counselor to be more sensitive and responsive to troubled individuals and their families. There are many good things counselors can do, but there are things they cannot achieve in the way of controlling the decisions of others. The counselors' ability to balance these considerations determines their success in managing their own stress.

40

Working with Grief and Mourning

It is time in these considerations to apply the principles of earlier chapters to a practical and common life situation. One of the most stressful and familiar of any helper's experiences is found in dealing with bereaved persons. When men and women suffer a loss such as the death of a spouse they undergo extreme stress; it is a disorganizing blow to their sense of themselves and its reverberations echo in the deepest levels of their personality. Grief is inevitable for all persons and, as such, constitutes an experience during which they need special understanding and support. Bereaved persons frequently turn to doctors and clergymen and other counselors for help at this time. To stand with and respond to those who mourn can be a major source of pressure for counselors. The more helpers can understand about reactions of the grieving—and about their own emotional responses in attempting to help them—the better they will manage themselves and the more effective they will be in dealing with others.

Helpers have complex feelings about grief, however, and they sometimes do not care to explore them. Grieving is a subject somewhat like religion has become and as sex once was; powerful societal taboos make the search of one's own self and the integration of counseling principles in a practical response to the problems of others very difficult.

Ultimately, even with the aid of research findings, counselors are entering deeply into the deepest of human territories. Here we experience, as Joyce put it, "all that is grave and constant" in our existence. In "The Person Confronting Death" (*the New Harvard Guide to Psychiatry*, ed. Nicholi, The Belknap Press of Harvard University Press, 1988, pp. 728–58) Ned H. Cassem quotes psychiatrist George Engel's observation that, because of its enormous impact on our functioning, grief should be considered a disease. But he also notes Rochlin's point that the "powerful dynamic produced by our losses is indispensable to emotional maturation. Mourning can lead to some of man's highest achievements as well as result in many pathological states when de-

347

layed or unresolved" (Cassem, p. 752). In short, we are, at this intersection of life and death, touching the essential mysteries of life.

That is why counselors who have an integrated philosophy or theology of their own—perhaps we should say, those who have preserved a sense of the tragic nature of life—bring that wisdom and spirituality to these telling encounters. Weisman ("Is Mourning Necessary?" in *Anticipatory Grief,* Columbia University Press, 1974) reminds us that love and grief reflect each other in their intensity, thereby enhancing each other. Counselors cannot, therefore, approach this profound subject with automatic or easy prescriptions. Nor can they attempt to eliminate the edge of suffering that is necessarily an aspect of something so thoroughly human. It is especially important for pastoral counselors to understand their role, not as deathbed proselytizers but as those capable of bearing witness through their presence and understanding to the human majesty of mourning and grief. It has been noted that persons with well-internalized religious beliefs—those for whom faith is an integrating force rather than a grudging external custom—are better able to handle the challenges of these solemn yet common experinces.

Grief as a major human experience provides a focus by which we can examine what we are like as counselors in action. In its harsh light we must face and come to terms with the interplay between our feelings and those of others. Grief also challenges us to read sensitively the symbolic expressions of those who mourn; these may seem irrational but they contain significant messages. Among studies that are helpful in this regard the classic work is recommended: *Bereavement: Studies of Grief in Adult Life,* by Murray Parkes, M.D., N.Y.: International University Press, Inc., 1972.

Grief as a Process

The counselor who appreciates something of the dynamics of human growth is equipped to understand grief as a complex process rather than as a fixed state or a huge obstacle that the bereaved person must somehow surmount. Grief considered as a process rather than as a state make it analogous to growth and permits us to see both its complex determinants as well as the helper's human role in assisting the person to work through it. Grief is, in fact, something that demands a special kind of growth because it confronts people with basic questions of their own identity and requires that they work them out in terms of human relationships and across a certain space of time.

Dr. Parkes has suggested four phases in the process of grief: *numbness, pining, depression,* and *recovery.* There is no way to collapse or shorten these phases any more than one can stunt anything else connected with human growth. The grieving process is precipitated by loss, of course, but the definition of exactly what is lost is not easy. The person's own perception of the loss can be very complex, and there are many secondary factors that may be related to the initial experience of loss. Moreover, there are related experiences that must also be appreciated by the sensitive helper. These include *stigma* and *deprivation.*

Although it may not be discussed very much, and although we may like to think we have advanced beyond it, there is still a stigma attached to the person who loses a spouse. This is especially true for widows; in many societies they are killed precisely because they no longer fit in. Western society prides itself on having moved away from such savagery, but its treatment of widows is still frequently quite harsh. Widows experience difficulty in finding a place socially; often they are pitied and isolated rather than respected and assisted in reincorporating themselves into the community. Many widows find that, although they have ample financial resources, they cannot get something as simple as a credit card. This is one small footnote of testimony to the stigma attached to those who mourn. Anthropologist Geoffrey Gorer has observed that in the western world "mourning is treated as though it were a weakness" rather than a functional and necessary human experience. The remarkable work of Phillip Aries in studying burial customs over the centuries reveals our change in consciousness and attitude. While a single death was once considered a loss that was suffered and mourned by an entire local community, it has now, especially in big cities, become something to be obscured, discreetly hidden from our common awareness, often to the detriment of those most intimately associated with it. The helper who does not appreciate this situation may badly misunderstand and perhaps, quite inadvertently, increase the widow's sense of being different and isolated from other people.

The problem for many women is intensified because social traditions have made them find so much of their identity as helpmate to a husband who was the possessor of the more significant identity role in society. If he is a teacher, a doctor, or a lawyer, these strong functional identities continue for him even if his wife dies. The woman who has, perhaps quite contentedly, surrendered the possibility of another identity in order to be a wife and mother finds herself extremely vulnerable when the children are grown and her husband dies. This is part of a general cultural concern for feminism, for making it possible for them to have an enduring identity in their own right that will not only offer them self-realization but a source of strength after the loss of their husbands through divorce or death.

Parkes distinguishes deprivation from loss by underscoring this as the result of the absence of the person who previously provided so many of life's necessities. The change in the social and financial status of a bereaved person gives them another dimension of vulnerability during a time that is already difficult. Widows, for example, are suddenly exposed to a world of tax returns, bill paying, and other decisions from which they have previously been protected. They are deprived not only of identity but of the strengthening effects of it. Those who understand and work effectively with the bereaved must appreciate the stress that is generated by this deprivation. This has only recently been identified as one of the reasons that widows feel so helpless and imperiled.

The loss that generates grief and mourning need not be that of death. A man or a woman can lose a person who is very important to them in other ways as well. The loss is just as real, and the experience of working out its consequences is similar in its dynamics, to that occasioned by death. An engaged person, for example, may suddenly lose the one he or she hoped to marry. This can occur through a change of heart, a new love interest, or a sudden and unexplained rejection of the relationship. Loss can also occur through divorce or unexpected and prolonged separation. In all these situations counselors will be helpful—and will feel more confident—if they assist the person *to identify the loss that has occurred*. Grieving cannot take place—it cannot even begin—unless the loss is identified.

The first stage in the process of grief is frequently marked by a seeming absence of feelings, a sudden freezing of the emotions so that they seem locked away tightly within the bereaved person. This follows from the stressful impact of loss through death even when the death is something that has been expected for a long time. Persons have a way of selectively perceiving even the worst of news, and of keeping their hopes up even when they have been told as explicitly as possible that the end is near. It is not unusual for persons to deny that a death has occurred. The news is just too much to absorb, and it must, for a while at least, be rejected while the person prepares really to hear and deal with it.

It is not surprising to see people act in a panicky way under the first impact of this major stress. They have, after all, lost something that has defined them in relationship to themselves and to the rest of the world. Now they are exposed to that world and the alarm that they feel is much like that which people experience in times of some great natural calamity or sudden disaster.

During this stage the bereaved individual suffers the most characteristic dimension of grief, which is not depression but rather the deep pangs of longing and anxiety that are associated with the loss that has been suffered. The bereaved person experiences an extremely painful wish for the restoration of the person who is gone.

It has been suggested that this painful pining is the way in which the bereaved person subjectively experiences something that is found during all periods of mourning—the search for the lost person. The grieving person knows that it is irrational to try to restore the dead person, but this urge is deep and frequently unconscious. This is why it is so painful and why it reveals itself in such indirect ways. Afflicted persons will be restless and almost obsessed with thoughts of the deceased person. They will be ready to see him or her on the street or in crowds, much as we are prepared to find a person we are expecting in an airport or bus terminal. Grieving persons lose interest in their appearance and in other things that were formerly quite important to them. They direct their attention to those places and occasions associated with the lost person.

It is important for the counselor to understand the symbolic nature of this aspect of mourning. *There is a search going on,* even though it is one that cannot be admitted into consciousness. This behavior is not aimless; it is clearly directed toward finding the lost person. Because neither the mourners nor those around them can accept the search as a valid quest, people judge that they are engaging in aimless activity. Any effort to classify it may frustrate one of the aspects of mourning that must be carried out. You cannot keep people from engaging symbolically in this search; the sensitive counselor can understand and allow this search to proceed, sensing in it an attempt to resolve the experience of loss.

In a more recent study, Parkes has identified three patterns of abnormal or blocked grieving (C. M. Parkes and R. S. Weiss, *Recovery from Bereavement,* New York, Basic Books, 1983). These are (1) unanticipated grief; (2) conflicted grief; (3) chronic grief. In the first, the loss is difficult to deal with because of its unexpected nature, while in the second the problem arises because of ambivalent feelings in the relationship to the deceased. In chronic grief, the overly dependent quality of the relationship with the dead person interferes with the resolution of grief through the mourning process. These obstacles, as Cassem notes (p. 750), work directly against "the three tasks of recovery: intellectual acceptance of the loss, emotional acceptance of the loss, and the new development of an independent identity."

The Work of Grief

The search for the lost person may be an aspect of what Sigmund Freud termed *grief work*. By this he suggests that mourning, far from being an inappropriate or mysterious reaction, is humanly appropriate and necessary if the bereaved person is to acknowledge, understand, and accept the losses he or she must face in life. There must be a mourning period if the person is to incorporate the loss and emerge once more into life with a successfully modified sense of identity. This is very difficult work, filled with pain; and those who stand with the grieving person may be so close that they cannot detect its meaningful and functional pattern. Counselors can facilitate it but they can also frustrate it by inappropriate interventions. Grief cannot be foreshortened; it must proceed at its own pace and in its own time.

The work of grief involves individuals in looking back at the relationship before it ended or was interrupted by death. They explore and examine what took place over the years. Mourners may review the last illness or the last day of that illness, and with pain-filled wonder, question whether they did everything within their power for the dead person. Were they attentive enough and did they give the medicine properly? They also try to understand the significance of the relationship, to place it into perspective, and to see it in the light of their philosophy or religious faith.

Although it is not easy, there is no substitute for permitting a person to face all of these difficulties directly. They deal with a drastic change in their identity; to exchange one's self-concept as a wife for one as a widow cannot be done in an instant. This demands major reorganization of the whole perceptual system; the person literally has to develop a new way of looking at the self. Again, this takes time and the freedom to be weak or depressed in the process. Grieving individuals may be preoccupied with the lost person and with the many memories of the past as they experience a deep loneliness. At the heart of all the range of feelings during grief, the bereaved are trying to come to terms with a major life experience. The concept of work—of needing slowly and thoroughly to process the many aspects of mourning—is appropriate for this struggle to come through on the other side of grief. Counselors will wisely recognize that it is inappropriate, ineffective, and often harmful to urge people, as if by an act of their will, to pass through the stages of mourning as they are described in some book. These stages may collapse on each other, assert their own sequence, or repeat themselves. The unconscious works as it will and counselors must respect it.

Recovery

This follows on a period that may be marked with more experience of depression, accompanied by occasional feelings of despair as the individual labors psychologically to overcome the loss and to develop a renewed identity. The pain lessens, according to researchers, as the person concludes the search that has marked the early stages of grief. The griever does this by finding the lost person again, not as a physical presence, but through sensing them or their spirit as somehow very near.

Grievers resolve their relationship in a symbolic way; it is common for this to be marked by statements about a new awareness of how the departed ones help or guide them in their lives and work. It is not surprising that the prolonged emotional search should end with a sense of discovery, making sense of the loss in a way that restores the other person in some degree. This is a time when religious support is important because it delivers a sense of meaning; it is also the point at which the individual, out of whatever beliefs and faith he or she has had, pieces together a sense of life again. They must be allowed to do this themselves; counselors must not intrude with ready-made answers or rational explanations that only obscure the symbolic nature of the process involved. Nor should one argue about the sense of restoration or psychological equilibrium that is achieved.

Things to Remember

We have sketched the process of grief as a living experience to provide a background of understanding across which counselors may formulate their responses to those who have suffered losses. These factors obviously condition their own emotional reactions. Grief offers an interplay of transference and countertransference feelings.

The work of grief may be delayed or complicated precisely because people who want to help do not understand the importance of letting people work through the various phases of their mourning. It is not helpful to try to modify or in any way to deter the individual from carrying out the work of grief that only they can perform. A counselor may inadvertently do this if he or she is unwilling to explore with the person the very feelings that must surface during this time of search and self-appraisal. The counselor cannot permit his or her inner stress reactions—whether they be of uneasiness, impatience, or revulsion—to dominate and possibly destroy the process of mourning.

The counselor who makes a habit of attacking other people's defenses will be unable to effectively assist grieving people. Mourners are in need of their defenses, especially at the earlier stages of grief, when they are emotionally unprepared to accept the death or to talk in utterly realistic terms about it. For people to be rational and undefended at a time of loss is unusual and cannot be forced on anyone. In mourning, we recognize the functional nature of defense mechanisms, especially in the way they permit individuals to buy time within which to readjust their perceptions of themselves and of the world in which they live. The helper must be ready to let the person deny or engage in other defensive behavior during the experience of grief.

In brief, the helper who faces and deals with grief regularly needs an understanding of its dynamic nature and purposeful course. This removes the sense of stress that arises when we feel we are dealing totally with the unknown or the unpredictable. It also enables us to see individual expressions of grief in a psychologically significant context, to hear in them their inner meaning and to see connections that would otherwise be obscure. The counselor who can see the grieving experience as a whole is better prepared to deal with his or her own reactions as well.

Through a deepened appreciation of the dynamic character and function of mourning, the helper is enabled to educate others to a better understanding of the experience of grief. The counselor can thereby assist other members of the family, parish, or community to respond constructively to the bereaved. A better grasp of the meaning of grief also frees counselors to enter into the sorrow of others with less fear that they will lose themselves. As a steadier presence, the helper can also give grieving persons increased freedom to mourn in their presence. By their very attitude, in other words, counselors can remove some of the stigma or sense of societal judgment that keeps people from the work of mourning they must inevitably carry out.

41

Aftermath of Grief

There is considerable uncalculated stress involved in working with the bereaved. Subjective pressure builds up not only because of the intrinsic nature of mourning but also because of the degree of concentration required to interpret and respond accurately to the extensive symbolic activity involved in the process. Good-heartedness, good will, and good instincts are helpful equipment for counselors, but some preparation for the various manifestations of the grief experience relieves the counselor's stress and permits freer engagement in the situation.

Anger

The helper must be able to tolerate expressions of anger, which are common during certain phases of the mourning process. The bereaved person wants to blame somebody for what has happened, for this calamity that has suddenly taken away their loved one and left them helpless in the face of a complex world. The widow, for example, can sometimes be angry at the husband who has, as she see it, abandoned her, or at the supposedly loving God who seems to have treated her unfairly. Both widows and widowers may blame the doctors who attended their loved one; this explains why some physicians find life so stressful. Everbody gets mad at them because they are convenient targets for displaced anger. The counselor's job is not to correct the anger the bereaved persons express but to allow them to get it out in the open. Once out, it dissipates more quickly and will be less directed toward inappropriate persons. The person's anger is real and it craves symbolization; it is, however, their own anger that bereaved people feel and it may only feed depression if it remains within. The counselor who understands the displaced nature of the anger will be able to avoid attempting to argue the bereaved person out of it and will instead be able to let it find its own route to the surface.

355

Persons who do not acknowledge their own anger—after all, it is hard to admit feelings of bitterness over supposed abandonment by the dead person—complicate their lives by making themselves more isolated from other persons. Until they can accept their own anger, the bereaved may direct it toward others—even toward old friends and neighbors. Psychologically speaking, in other words, they have to be mad at somebody; they have to blame somebody or something for what they have experienced.

The counselor can also understand that the person who has suffered a great loss finds it very threatening to have the enormity of that loss brought home too directly or too permanently. They must approach and absorb it on their own time schedule. The loss, as they perceive it, is still threatening and to force upon them a realization of what has occurred may subject them to a kind of psychological threat that worsens rather than improves their situation.

Guilt

Most people have ambivalent feelings toward each other at one time or another in life. When death occurs they may feel quite guilty about these feelings and may try, in some way or other, to make up for what they judge were personal failings with regard to the other while he or she was living. After the other's death, unresolved ambivalent feelings arise again as guilt. This is something that must be anticipated, not avoided or rationalized away as though it were of no consequence. Part of the work of grief is to deal with this mixture of feelings, even when they seem shamefully inadmissible. This is the way people look at themselves and at their world and they cannot be argued or cajoled out of it.

It is also helpful to be aware of the highly charged emotional atmosphere that surrounds many bereavements, especially when people begin to exchange blame for various things connected with the dead person's life or last illness. This sometimes is an occasion for a split in families—as between in-laws—that would not occur except under the stress of the circumstances. The counselor who is a sensitive intermediary may be able to help people to identify and express their feelings at this time without destroying their relationships with each other. The bereaved person needs the support of all the friends that he or she has had. Family quarreling, in generally vain attempts to prove who is right and who is wrong, only adds to the burdens of the bereaved. These fights do not help the counselor's composure either, especially if he is tempted to choose sides in them.

It is also helpful for the counselor to realize that bereaved persons are struggling to give birth to *revised identity*, to a newly fashioned concept of themselves through which they will be able to present themselves again in life. People dealing with this problem need all the understanding skills that the counselor can provide. It is a challenge many helpers do not realize because they do not understand the reality of the situation. They simply do not appreciate the nature of self-reorganization that is taking place.

The effort to let go of a former self-concept and to develop a fresh and appropriate one confronts the already stricken individual with a fundamental and tricky problem of self-identity. Bereaved persons may experience feelings from layers of the unconscious they had presumed to be closed off long ago. So too doubts or uncertainties that had been healed by a marriage relationship may, at least briefly, represent themselves. As mentioned previously, the widow whose main identity came from being someone's wife can experience this crisis in a sharp and intense fashion. The counselor is partner to an effort to rebuild a sense of the self; he does not merely soothe the pains of grief. Unless counselors are aware of the possibilities of identity problems in the wake of mourning, they may miss important cues, many of which may only be symbolic, during this period.

What Should the Bereaved Be Told?

It is helpful to understand that it is not always a kindness to shield people from the death of those they love. Experience and research tell us that human beings may fulfill an important human function by viewing the body, even if in poor condition, of the deceased. Widows of military personnel killed in Vietnam have reported that viewing their remains on their return years after their death was an important element in completing their work of mourning. It is often very helpful if they can do something for the deceased, as, for example, when parents are allowed to help prepare their child's body for the funeral.

Counselors may be very helpful, as Cassem suggests, by asking spouse or parents gently about the last days or hours of the dead person. They may also be able to supply useful information, such as the facts on the Sudden Infant Death Syndrome, or to refer persons to support groups for survivors of such a tragic event. Such special groupings have proved very helpful in assisting the bereaved to face and resolve the challenges of grief and mourning.

Should the bereaved be involved in making the funeral arrangements? Anybody connected with the arrangements that must be made after a person dies should not try to protect the spouse from participating in these significant preparations. This is an initial and important way for bereaved persons to deal with the work of grief. They should not be treated as though they were incapable of doing this nor, on the grounds of any other pretext, he denied the opportunity to plan the funeral. Grieved persons have a right and a need to do this. Sometimes we do not want to involve them, not because we want to spare them but because we want to spare ourselves from associating with them at a difficult time. We would rather that they stayed by themselves or took some sedative. It is far more difficult to be with them in these moments than it is to busy ourselves with what we consider important and useful things while they take the first steps toward isolating themselves from something they should experience. This can happen at any time in the process of mourning. It illustrates the interplay of the helper's reactions with those of the people he proposes to assist.

It is also important to allow the rituals of mourning to be carried out. Many observers feel that society has been impoverished by the lessening of appropriate ritual in many areas of life. Grieving persons need rituals the way they need light and air. It is psychologically important for persons to have a public and approved way in which to express their complex and deep feelings of grief. The rituals are, of course, for the living far more than they are for the dead, and they should not be oversimplified nor so blandly diluted that they fail to achieve their expressed purpose.

Bereaved persons need time and perspective in which to begin to absorb and deal with the impact of the loss. They need close friends, not to be doing everything for them but to be with them, or to be available during the weeks when they struggle to accept the varied feelings they have during the time of bereavement. It is not helpful to leave bereaved people alone, nor is it helpful to distract them with so many visitors and activities that they cannot get on with the grief that only they can and must experience. They do need other persons nearby, however, to listen to them and to stand with them as they search themselves at this difficult time. The counselor who is a member of the clergy, for example, should keep contact after the funeral. Brief but regular visits are helpful.

Should the counselor intervene in the work of grief? It is not helpful to probe or to reassure people in a shallow way during a period of mourning. One cannot keep them from accomplishing their "grief work" and, with a little familiarity with the experience, one can begin to appreciate the symbolic occurrences of this time.

It is actually far more stressful for persons, whether they are counselors or just friends, to enter into mourning without knowing what they are doing than to have some sense of its process and some of the possible feelings associated with it. When people don't know what to say—or when they back off from entering into the mourning—they make themselves and the grieving person uncomfortable. To substitute mannered concern for a genuine response to grief is to increase the burden for all parties concerned.

This is illustrated by the visits of Henry Adams to novelist Henry James after the death of a close friend of the latter. To a third person Adams wrote, "Even Henry James, with whom I lunch Sundays, is only a figure in the same old wall-paper, and really pretends to belong to a world which is as extinct as Queen Elizabeth. I enjoy it." Meanwhile, James wrote to a friend: "I like [Adams] but suffer from his monotonous, disappointed pessimism. . . . So what can I do for him? However, when the poor dear is in London, I don't fail to do what I can." To which biographer Leon Edel adds: "Each thus seems to have believed he was comforting the other. In reality they made each other uncomfortable" (Leon Edel, *Henry James, The Treacherous Years: 1895–1902*. Philadelphia: J. B. Lippincott Company, 1969. p. 57).

The helper must allow the feelings of the grieving individual to emerge. It is not important to insist that they come out in any prescribed way. The bereaved person will select the appropriate manner in which to express them. These emotions must, however, be heard and accepted by someone else; this is the key response at this time in helping the bereaved. When we can hear them in their grief they feel more understood, and this reduces their sense of isolation from the rest of the world.

Obviously this is not a time for pity or clichés, nor for the kind of stiff upper lip that prevents us from expressing our own feelings. Sometimes an expression our own feelings of affection or concern is extremely appropriate during the mourning process. Here again the helper must neither plan to do this nor to exaggerate it. It is done if it is the right thing in the context of the relationship that the counselor has with the bereaved person. Counselors need not, however, be neutral or totally unfeeling—a role that is sometimes rapidly urged on them.

The counselor's main work—to help other persons to say what the meaning of the loss really is and to express a new sense of their own identity—is indispensable in assisting bereaved individuals to work through their grief. The counselor's task, as Shakespeare once wrote, is to "give sorrow words." This not only facilitates the process of mourning but it enables grieving persons to emerge from it with a new and better sense of their own wholeness.

For too long counselors have been deprived of a sense of how importantly they may participate in the work of mourning. This is related to a general cultural uneasiness about the subject of death and loss and a well-established tendency to deny both. The person in the role of counselor not only responds to the bereaved directly but also to the culture's general need for sensitive and sensible reeducation in this regard. As counselors are better informed and more confident in their application of counseling attitudes and principles to the work of grief, they find that the experience is less stressful for themselves. They know what they are doing, they can read the symbols accurately, and what was once mostly a bewildering burden becomes a richer opportunity for assisting in the growth of others.

The Identity Problem

We have already discussed the fact that sudden widowhood may plunge a woman into a crisis about her own identity. She may not be able to verbalize it this way; indeed, for many, the notion that being a wife and mother may have kept them from recognizing and developing more of their own talents and interests is a forbidding one.

The issue, however, is closely related to the larger cultural concerns of women's changing role and may well become a more clearly defined problem in working with grieving persons during the next few years. Consciousness-raising on the subject may, in fact, make the question of a woman's identity a more critical issue for some women even before the death of their husbands.

What was once an unspeakable problem may become one that needs anticipation and discussion between couples before they even need to face the challenges of illness or death. Counselors, in this situation as in many others, need to acquaint themselves with the cultural forces that are already giving shape to this problem in our awareness. They will reduce their own stress if they become more sensitive to the psychological dimensions of an identity crisis in an older person, thereby enlarging their capacity to help those experiencing it to express it therapeutically.

The issues connected with a person's need to rediscover his or her roots and individual talents and abilities—many of which may have been put aside or sacrificed in view of other demands—are complex and real. There is no predicting how these should be handled; it is obvious that counselors, like surgeons or lawyers preparing professionally, need to review the literature on human developmental problems. This may also become more important as the emotional problems connected with retirement living—especially in "villages" designed for that purpose—cause older persons to search themselves for a better understanding of their identity than environments for "leisure living" can ever provide.

42

Emergencies: Being a Steady Presence

For many professionals, alarm bells ring regularly in the night. Whatever the actual severity of the situation, emergencies are perceived as serious by the person or persons directly involved in them. The one who is called—in many cases, you—is expected to *know what to do.*

Whatever their main professional identification, individuals called upon for counsel during emergencies have themselves as their first clients. They must be able to maintain control of their own reactions, to possess themselves, in other words, with sufficient poise to remain calm and in command. One of the therapeutic activities of the person consulted at a time of emergency is to be *a steady presence* in the situation. The counselor, whether physician, priest, or school principal, must be aware of two things: What he or she can do effectively and realistically and what the others involved in the situation can do as well.

The counselor must straighten out the roles of those enmeshed in the crisis situation and this can only be accomplished through calm and sensitive perception of what each participant is capable of doing. This is one of the first responses that is appropriate for a counselor to give. It immediately changes the nature of the emergency, lessening the tension associated with it and freeing the involved people to use their own strengths—their own capacities to adapt—in order to improve things. This is not just sending people out to boil water while a baby is being born. It is based, rather, on an understanding of how people can constructively interrelate in an emergency situation once it is organized by the counselor. This reduces the anxiety that, as in any stressful encounter, can so easily cripple or inhibit the effectiveness of the persons connected with it. We know that one calm person who keeps self-control in a disaster can save many lives. The whole notion of a triage officer, one designated to make crucial decisions in emergencies, is based on this. The counselor who remains assured in an

362

emergency is able to reduce the overall anxiety and thereby decrease the intensity of the emergency itself.

In order to do this effectively, counselors must be familiar with their own reactions at times of emergency. They cannot afford to be surprised by uncontrollable panic if they are leading lives in which they are frequently called upon for help in crisis situations. Counselors may wisely anticipate their reactions under stress. It is very sensible and not just romantic daydreaming to imagine how one would feel in a variety of demanding emergencies. Exploring the possibilities of our emotional behavior in an emergency gives us clues about our own stress-tolerance and allows us to manage ourselves— and therefore the situations in which we become involved—more securely. It is not an idle game for the person who may be called on for emergency help to prepare by framing various questions beginning with, "What would I do if ———?" Taking account of how we will react in certain circumstances is an extremely sensible stress reducer.

Experts classify most emergencies with which we will deal into: (1) *intrapersonal,* in which the individual is moved by internal depression, anxiety, and confusion; (2) *somatic complaints,* the complex of physical symptoms that are perceived by the individual as the cause of the emergency; (3) *interpersonal* problems, situations that ordinarily involve one person who is concerned or irritated by the behavior of another. It is frequently the complaining person who gets the individual to the counselor.

Kinds of Problems

The most common complaint in emergency situations is the experience of depression. This is usually related, as has been noted earlier, to some loss, real or imagined, in the individual's life. People may come for help with very similar subjective feelings of depression and yet be very different inside. For example, there is the individual who may be truly suicidal in his state of depression and who comes to the helper precisely because of this. Yet another person may be reacting to the death of a loved one; the depression is not suicidal but is an understandable part of the overall dynamic process of mourning. Acute subjective pain is present but it is part of a very different pattern of reactions. The work of mourning and the clues to understanding its dynamic and symbolic features have been discussed before.

The question of suicide risks has also been discussed but it is worth repeating some fundamental motives here. There is a distinction between *suicidal ideas* and *suicidal gestures*. A person with suicidal ideas takes the terminating of his or her life very seriously. They are planning it and taking the steps that will lead to killing themselves. People who make suicidal gestures are trying to do something to their social environment, to get attention, or to imtimidate it in some way in order to control the behavior of others. Both kinds of persons can appear at the counselor's door at times of emergency and it is helpful to be able to distinguish between them. Both need response, of course, but our ability to intervene constructively is helped if we can get a feeling for · the seriousness of the idea or the gesture. We can do this by putting the idea or gesture in the context of other factors in the person's life. There is, as Polatin (p. 284) notes, "no absolute indicator of suicidal risk," but the following may be associated with an increased risk of suicide:

1. In depressions, the greater the tension or agitation and the greater the expression of ideas of hopelessness and somatic delusions, the greater the risk.
2. A family history of suicide, or earlier attempts at suicide by the patient.
3. The patient who feels alone and angry.
4. Absence of any religious feeling or lack of faith in a higher power.
5. A history of preparation for suicide, without actual attempts, such as writing farewell letters, obtaining a weapon or drugs, visiting a chosen site, putting one's affairs in order.
6. Loss of a love one.
7. The patient's knowledge that he has an incurable disease.
8. Financial disasters, including loss of earning power, which seem irremediable.
9. Old age, with physical infirmities, financial stress, and symptoms like prolonged sleeplessness.
10. History of impulsive activity, aggressive acts, alcoholism, and drug addiction.

Perhaps the biggest indicator of the seriously depressed persons who have a clear intention of committing suicide is evidenced in the nonverbal signals they give. These telegraph to us the person's uncertain or conflicted feelings about living or dying. MacKinnon and Michels suggest that if the individual leaves doors unlocked, spends money that would otherwise have been used for the necessities of life, or calls a distant friend with whom he or she has not been in contact in a long time, the ambivalence is clear. The same holds true if the person is unconcerned about time and place, as though he or she were already detached in some way from present existence. The alert counselor may be able to pick up many clues that indicate the seriousness of the possibility of suicide in an individual case.

It is helpful for a counselor to prepare for such emergencies, both by anticipating them emotionally and by having alternative courses of action worked out in advance. Every counselor should have a contingency plan built on an awareness of what other help is available in the environment. Where, for example, can psychiatric or hospital assistance be obtained even at an awkward or difficult hour? It is frequently helpful for nonmedical persons to have some relationship already established with a competent medical colleague who will be able to be of assistance in these situations. It is clear that the stress the counselor experiences will be markedly reduced if he or she has practical options for sensible action available. It is not a time to improvise or to hunt frantically through the Yellow Pages for assistance. This is all the more important because such emergencies occur over weekends or at holiday times when, unless it has been planned for, it may be difficult to reach another professional colleague. When a counselor has a plan of action worked out, it is much easier to maintain the steady presence that is so important in alleviating such emergency situations.

The Cardinal Feature: Anxiety

Anxiety is almost always present in an emergency situation. It may even be the thing that the individual cites as a major symptom. When this occurs counselors must try to read the emergency in order to tease out the significant roots of anxiety in the individual. When persons complain of an acute increase in anxiety, it is usually a sign that their ordinary internal balance between drives and defenses has been dislodged in some way. When this occurs it may even give rise to their building new defenses in an effort to maintain their sense of themselves. Patients whose fundamental defenses have been disturbed may, for example, begin to use the defense of projection in an attempt to stabilize their internal difficulties.

Ordinarily we associate the expression of acute anxiety with one of the following factors: (1) Some current event stirs to life fears that have been sleeping in the person's unconscious life; (2) patients feel that they are losing control and may do something to act out their sexual or aggressive feelings. Their anxiety arises because they are terrified by the possible consequences of losing control. People in emergency situations are seldom aware of the specific fear that is affecting them. They cannot name it exactly. They present some overwhelming sense of panic and dread—a more diffuse experience. Counselors use their sensitivity to feel their way into and beneath these complaints. It is obvious that simple reassurance will not help when the roots of the problem are unconscious.

As we utilize this counselor's mode of perception to try to understand, we begin to appreciate something about the impulses or fantasies that cause such discomfort to these people. MacKinnon and Michels cite the common example of the adolescent boy who must share a room with another young man for the first time in college. "Homosexual feelings," they note, "become increasingly difficult to repress, and when he is under the influence of alcohol, his defenses are further weakened and he begins to panic" (p. 404). As mentioned previously, this kind of panic may lead the individual to build a new line of defenses. What we see on the surface are these new defenses. The use of projection, for example, leads him to express fears that his roommate is going to attack him. The real problem lies at a deeper level than this defensive accusation. This is a classic case of anxiety generated because of a sudden imbalance in a person's way of adjustment. It is precipitated by a new event—coming to college and the need to relate with another man on a level of intimacy that has never been experienced before. The counselor who can see this problem in the context of these events, who can sense the interrelationship of these dynamic events, has a much better capacity to respond positively and constructively.

The same need to understand the deeper dynamics occurs when the individual is brought in by another person. A wife, for example, may bring in a disturbed husband because she is afraid he is going to hurt himself, the home, or the children. She senses in him a breakdown of control that is more a source of anxiety for her and her family than it is for him. Again, the context of this situation provides the counselor with the understanding that it is essential for effective response in the emergency. Many persons respond to such emergencies by using reassurance or by trying to talk the person out of feeling the way he or she does. Nowhere is the fallacy of the "reasonable response" more obvious than in an emergency marked by quite irrational anxiety. In such instances, referral to a competent medical colleague or other professional resource is indicated.

Common Difficulties

Confusion is the symptom in individuals who seem mixed up and unable to locate themselves accurately in space and time. They are not easily able to manage their way through their environment and they involve themselves in emergency situations through inadvertence. There is frequently an organic basis for this difficulty; an underlying problem in the central nervous system that results in some handicap of memory, learning, or perception. Sensing their own confusion causes these people, who are sometimes elderly, to be bewildered and scared. Their actions are inappropriate and are noticed by others; frequently they are brought for assistance by a friend or relative. In these situations an accurate reading of the precipitating event in the context of the individual's life leads to the best management of the difficulty.

A major change in a person's life, for example, may burden a fragile personality with demands that it cannot meet. A person who moves to new surroundings after the death of a spouse, or any other major incident requiring great adjustment, may find that he or she is unable to make the transition easily or comfortably. Such persons get confused, forget where they are, or cannot manage the basic essentials of their lives. It is obviously important to gather practical information about whether such confused individuals can cope with life on their own or whether they need some kind of assistance. Several years ago an elderly couple from upstate New York were found dead in each other's arms. Their heat had been turned off because of their failure to pay their electric bills. There was money in the house and the local parish had, in fact, paid some of their bills for them. While people were angry at the utility company for its hardheartedness, it may be that friends and relatives had overestimated this elderly couple's capacity for managing their own environment. A sensible judgment, then, is obviously of the first order of importance in dealing with confused persons.

It is also important to include others in any emergency plan to deal with confused persons. They should be introduced to the situation and helped to understand its dimensions. They need to grasp the practical limits to which these confused people can be allowed to function on their own. Great complications can arise unless the feelings friends and relatives have about the situation are acknowledged and responded to. Unless the problems can be seen with insight and comprehension, friends and relatives may not provide the kind of help that counselors think advisable. Good plans often fall apart because the persons we depend on to carry them out have not been sufficiently integrated into the situation. These persons have needs both for information and for emotional reassurance, and the counselor functions as the coordinator who helps them fill the roles that are theirs in an emergency situation as effectively as possible.

Somatic Problems

There is a cultural tendency to dismiss some physical complaints as meaningless and imaginary because of our awareness that they often have psychological origins. Counselors responding to emergency situations in which the complaint is somatic cannot quickly or confidently make such judgments. The persons experiencing the emergency do not perceive their problems as psychological in origin. They are complaining of a physical symptom that may be symbolic but that is very real for them. Others around them may perceive their somatic complaints as psychological but they themselves do not. We must, then, treat them seriously as persons in the context of their total life and adjustment.

Quite often persons who have physical complaints deny their emotional problems and are unable to respond very well if we try to talk to them in psychological terms about something they insist is quite physical. It is common, for example, to find persons experiencing hyperventilation during a time of emergency. They are not satisfied by reassurances about the common and relatively nonserious nature of their difficulty. It doesn't help to say, "It's all in your head." Psychological sensitivity is appropriate in the emergency situation to enable us to understand why the persons have come to us and why they speak in a symbolic language of somatic illness. The physical symptom is their way of communicating to us. Any abrupt dismissal of the person may only complicate what for them is already an acute emergency problem.

Difficulties with Others

These ordinarily occur when one individual complains about the behavior of somebody else. Such an emergency situation has a courtroom air, as though you were being asked to hand down an indictment. One person is brought by another who wants you to do something about his or her behavior or the problems it is causing. The complexity of such interpersonal emergencies is obvious. A special vulnerability exists for professionals whose main identity is not with psychology or psychiatry. Parents, for example, may bring a son or a daughter whose behavior has generated great anxiety. They avoid bringing them to a psychiatrist or psychologist in the first instance because they do not want to interpret the child's problem as an emotional one. They want somebody else—the clergyman, the educator, or the physician—to "straighten out" the person's thinking, to get him or her on the right road again.

Counselors are well advised to avoid the Solomon role. They must not be judges, persuaders, or persons who can easily be enlisted to do the bidding of one or the other party in such situations. The best response is made to the emotional context of the event; this may have little relationship to the symptoms that are emphasized when the situation is first described and can only be pursued if we have an adequate perspective on the total relationship of the persons involved. It is not a time to respond only to one individual; the response is to the overall dynamic affecting the persons with whom we are dealing.

Counselors must approach emergencies well purged of their "rescue fantasies." They must realistically come to terms with the limitations that emergencies place on their capacity to solve the problems of others. They also need a grasp of their own potential countertransference feelings toward the persons who are caught in the crisis. Emergencies, by their very nature, occur when we do not expect them or when we find responding to them inconvenient and uncomfortable. If, as suggested before, we can anticipate our reactions to some of these situations, we can plan not only our mode of response but perhaps even our place of response as well. We should have some fairly comfortable office or room in which we can see people with minimal disturbance even in emergency situations. Jangling telephones, interruptions by secretaries or housekeepers—these interfere markedly with the kind of concentration that is needed for us to be effective in emergency situations. A counselor who has not gotten over the need to impress clients by having important sounding interruptions will not function very well at these times.

Counselors must also plan on spending their time freely when emergencies arise. There is no way to contain emergencies within a schedule, no way to tidy them up by a certain hour. The counselor who cannot live comfortably with this must either deal with his own feelings or avoid emergency situations. There is enough anxiety connected with a crisis already. If the counselor feels rushed, he is almost certain to compound the problem and add to the difficulty rather than relieve it. These are basic ground rules that are simply footnotes to the foundation of self-possession, which is the strong point of all effective emergency treatment.

Do We Include Others?

Whether to include others in handling the emergency is a practical difficulty of the first magnitude. The answer is, as in so many other important questions: *It depends.* Other persons frequently accompany the one who is experiencing the emergency, and the question becomes whether they should be included in the interview with the principal client or not. The counselor must follow professional instincts in this regard. Sometimes it is important to hold a joint interview with the client and with those who brought him, whether they are friends, roommates, or members of the family. Sometimes it is impossible for the client to communicate without the assistance of some friend or relative—as, for example, in the case of elderly and confused patients.

There are, however, some things to avoid. It is not good to talk privately to the person who brought the emergency patient before talking to the patient directly. All counselors need to do is imagine how they would feel if they were in such a situation. The client may think that, having seen the other person first, the counselor is now enlisted against them or clearly accepts the other's interpretation of his or her plight. Counselors should see the client first and only then bring in other members of the family or other friends.

In some situations, where the family is a problem in itself, it may be important to see all its members together to get some comprehension of their dynamic interactions. Counselors can, in fact, feel free to juggle the arrangements during the emergency situation when this seems called for. They can ask certain people to leave, or call in others, if they do this smoothly and with some willingness to explain their actions.

There are several practical questions that counselors can keep in mind as they move into the varied situations and sets of relationships that are found in emergencies. Perhaps the most important question is, Whose idea is this? A good answer to this will help counselors both in appreciating the overall dynamics of the crisis and in responding to the person who is most in need. It may be, for example, that persons who have been referred by members of their family or by their teachers may be quite reluctant to talk about any problems. Help cannot be forced upon these persons and, if they do not perceive the situation as an emergency, they cannot be motivated to do so merely on the authority of the counselor. Counselors prudently avoid being manipulated into this kind of role. They are not out to convince people that they are in trouble but to respond to them when they really are.

What of a Referral?

The matter of referral remains the center of our concern and the center of gravity for understanding the context in which the emergency has taken place. It leads us to explore the definition that the client gives to the problem, which may be presented in religious, legal, educational, or other terms. Not only a loss of religious faith but questions of academic performance may cause emergencies; in each case the roots may run in a different direction. Counselors in schools are familiar with these problems and realize that the academic emergency may signal some other emotional conflict which other members of the school faculty may not be able to appreciate.

The counselor's role is not to enforce the academic standards of the institution but to respond to the emotional needs of the persons referred for assistance. An associated question is, Why was I chosen as the person consulted in this emergency? Complex motivations may intersect in this regard, but if the counselor can get some appreciation of how he or she was perceived in order to be chosen, this may be a way of entering into the world of the persons with whom the counselor must deal. Why were my skills deemed appropriate and what role am I expected to play? It is very helpful for counselors to answer these questions before overcommitting themselves in an emergency situation.

What are the expectations? This central question offers us the opportunity to inquire with understanding about the recent past of the concerned parties. This is often very illuminating. The precipitating event may well be an anniversary, a move, or a holiday season. It may be a change of jobs, an imbalance in a marriage, or some frightening experience that the individual finds difficult to talk about.

Expectations are a part of every emergency situation. These exist both on the part of the individual and on the part of those people who refer or bring the person to our attention. Some people expect magic, some expect us to take responsibility for everything, while others may want only reassurance from us about the way they are handling things. Some may seek absolution or some kind of permission from us to act in a particular way. In certain emergencies, persons ask us, in effect, to control their behavior, while others may actively try to get us to intervene in some situation in school or at home. Still others may come to us because they want us to protect them from more serious psychiatric treatment.

It is sometimes necessary to urge treatment in a hospital, or to make a referral to some other colleague, even when we wish that this were not the case. It is also possible that we may have to do this when the client is unwilling to accept such a recommendation. This occurs when the person can no longer care for himself or when suicide is a serious risk and we are not able to manage helping him in any better way. These are difficult decisions and they can only be made after careful thought and evaluation of all the elements and alternatives related to the situation. In deliberating on these, however, counselors should never try to trick their clients by, for example, making hospitalization sound palatable under some other name. Counselors should be honest and straightforward and ready to explore the fears and unwillingness that people have about getting certain kinds of treatment. No one wants to hospitalize an unwilling patient, but a far greater risk exists if we attempt to please them by avoiding it. We may make what is already an emergency into a tragedy.

Pain by Telephone

The telephone is a mode of communication that has certain limitations, but it is frequently the only medium of communication at times of emergency. Brief, constructive contacts can be very helpful even over the telephone. Counselors are wise to remember that there is a person on the other end of the phone testing them in some way to see whether they are trustworthy or approachable. The phone can be a potent instrument for communicating our understanding and informed concern, and it should be used as skillfully as possible. It may be very helpful to try to personalize the conversation by finding something out about the individual so that he or she is not just a detached voice on the other end of the phone. It may also be practical to find out where they are, their age, and whether they have been getting help from anyone else.

All too often, the phone contact is the best that persons can manage when they are under severe pressure. It may be the last thing, as in the case of Marilyn Monroe, that certain people use in an effort to make contact with the world around them. We must make the most of it; sometimes we have to settle for at least another appointment on the phone if a face-to-face meeting cannot be arranged. Sometimes people announce their suicides to us by phone, telling us that they have just taken so many pills of this kind or that, and by such a gesture dramatically reach out for some kind of help. We should get the facts about the situation, including the name of the drug, as well as the address and telephone number of the person calling. It is useful to tell them that we are going to summon help and that they should leave their door open so that there will be no problem when help arrives. It is also wise to tell them that we will call back to confirm the imminent arrival of help. If there is time, it is advisable to get the name and phone number of a neighbor who may be able to be of assistance in the emergency.

43

Crises: Understanding and Intervention

Life itself may sometimes seem a crisis, especially for the busy pastoral worker, physician, or teacher. If the latter types encounter every day the kinds of emergencies described in the preceding chapter, they may also find themselves, from time to time, deep in what, for purpose of analysis from other viewpoints and traditions, we will term *crises*. In the exploration of these approaches, we will grasp better the appropriateness of the parameters of the nonprofessional's role that have been suggested frequently in this book. For it is during a critical incident that the counselor's ability to identify and support healthy defenses will often prove of crucial importance.

Background

The field of social work has long been deeply involved in crisis theory and technique. The impetus for this came from the pioneering efforts of Erich Lindemann, who worked closely with the survivors of Boston's Coconut Grove nightclub fire, a disaster that occurred in November 1942. Another pioneer, Gerald Caplan, developed, along with Lindemann, some of the basic principles about the nature and management of crises. Many others have since contributed to our understandng of the dynamics of critical incidents, including Lydia Rapaport, Howard Parad, David Caplan, Marvin Strickler, and Peter Sifneos.

Summarizing what they learned in life's own raw laboratory, crisis situations are, by their nature, episodic in the life span of individuals, families, groups, communities, and nations. Folklore has a saying, for example, that "every family can look back on one really bad year." These crises are usually initiated by some hazardous event, a blow from without, or an upset arising internally. There may be one catastrophic incident or a series of mishaps that have a cumulative effect on an individual or a group. We speak commonly today of the buildup of "stresses" to describe similar overload.

In these incidents, the basic human balance is upset and the person affected is rendered to some extent vulnerable. He or she then goes through a customary series of responses (things ordinarily done under pressure) in an attempt to regain balance. If these familiar responses do not work, anxiety grows and the person must find new ways to set himself or herself right again. If there is no resolution, however, and the tension builds to a peak, a *precipitating factor* can bring about the instant—the essential core—of crisis in which the person loses balance and suffers disorganization. This is termed the state of *active crisis*.

The events that take place may be interpreted by the person who experiences them under various names. They may be viewed as a threat to basic needs and independence; as a loss of self-identity or of some ability; or as a challenge to survival, development, or mastery. A response characteristic of the affected person will flow in accord with the nature of the perception. If, for example, the situation is regarded as threatening, anxiety will increase. A loss will prompt depression, deprivation, or mourning and, if it is experienced as a challenge, the moderate increase in anxiety will be mingled with incipient hope and expectation.

Counselors must appreciate that the crisis situation is not fundamentally a sickness or a pathological experience but rather a realistic struggle in which individuals are dealing with the actual circumstances of their lives. This is intensely human, therefore, and may touch off earlier life conflicts that, although previously covered up one way or another, have never been fully resolved. At this point, the counselor may well observe inappropriate or exaggerated responses. The counselor's task is, in view of all this, first of all, to help resolve the present difficulty. Secondly, the objective may be to rework the previous struggle, and, thirdly, to dissolve the linkage between the two.

These stages can be predicted and mapped, in a sense, so that such reactions may be anticipated and, when the person is blocked, counselors may, with a sensitive reading of the situation, understand the point of blockage. Counselors should also appreciate that each crisis state is limited in time. While this is true within variable limits, the actual state of intense disequilibrium is temporally finite. Most students of this phenomenon put the period at between four to six weeks.

During this phase, the afflicted person is ordinarily disposed to accept assistance from others. Defenses are down and previous techniques for coping are not working well. The person is, therefore, more available to a sensible intervention. The period of reintegrating can be one of profitably learning new and better modes of coping with stresses. It can also be true that, if such a person does not receive assistance, he or she may, during this time, learn maladaptive solutions that will not stand up well against future stresses.

Another Perspective

We have discussed the nature of emergencies as sometimes intrapersonal and, at others, interpersonal. The distinguished researcher Edwin Schneidman has offered a way of viewing them in relationship to life stages. Some crises may, according to his view, occur during a stage of development and be termed *intratemporal*. The crisis is appropriate, in this understanding, to some specific period, such as adolescence or old age. We may, however, also understand crises as *intertemporal*, that is, taking place at some juncture between life stages. As Schneidman has observed, some people may function well as adolescents but may have real problems in becoming adults.

It is also possible for crises to occur outside any time frame, in ways that seem—and may well be—mysterious. Often we are perplexed by an occurrence, a suicide, for example, that, from all that we can understand about the person's life, should not have occurred. Schneidman has done what he calls "psychological autopsies" in an attempt to grasp the reasons for such suicides. These questions have attracted the attention of novelists and other artists throughout history. John Gregory Dunne, for example, wrote *Dutch Shea, Jr.,* after being intrigued by a brief account of a lawyer's apparent suicide in Connecticut. In dealing with human beings, counselors must accept the reality of mystery, of things that will forever be beyond their full understanding. No framework, or approach, will therefore be completely satisfactory. They are vehicles to spur reflection and the organization of responses, however, that can be of enormous use in their work.

Responding to the Crisis

In addition to the already familiar notions of being a steady presence and of attempting to understand both the affected person, the life context of the crisis, and its existential arc or sequence, counselors should bear the following basic notions in mind:

In no situation is the inappropriateness of the approaches and attitudes of long-term therapy less applicable than in an emergency or crisis. This is not a time for withholding the self, giving vague or noncommital responses, or, in any other way, causing pressure to build up on unconscious defenses that are already under siege. Counselors want to stabilize the situation and one of their principal means of achieving that is through offering supportive responses, that is, the kind of counseling that controls unconscious rumblings by focusing on the present conscious field of the individual.

Counselors may, therefore, do things that would otherwise seem out of place. With a clear awareness of what they are engaged in, they may allow others to depend on them during the intense interval of crisis, they may let them "lean" on them, tell them what to do, take over the executive function of their lives. This is done in order to stabilize them psychologically and to prevent any unconscious conflicts from breaking through. Wise counselors will identify the person's strong points—what we term their healthiest defenses—and encourage their use in the struggle for equilibrium. A person's religious faith is an excellent example of a resource that, sensibly tapped, can be of enormous benefit to the troubled individual. So, too, may be some constructive skill or talent of theirs that, brought into play, may help them bridge the chasm of crisis safely.

Learning from Those Who Have Learned from Experience

Some institutions have lived a long time with human beings and, even without sophisticated psychological theory, have developed remarkably effective ways of dealing with a variety of human problems. One of these is the United States Armed Services, which has had a long and intimate experience with human beings under stress. It is worthwhile to note elements of their treatment plan as first articulated in 1929 by Salmon and Fenton (*Neuropsychiatry,* Vol. 10, The American Expeditionary Forces, Washington, DC, US Government Printing Office, 1929).

This approach, termed BICEPS after its principal elements of brevity, immediacy, centrality, expectance, proximity, and simplicity, is a distillation of wisdom hard-bought in the field of battle. There is an effort to identify the problem as quickly as possible and to limit the treatment period to a specified time, usually seventy-two hours. Delay, it was found, usually caused the symptoms to grow worse. In the central treatment facility, the soldier, sailor, marine, or airman, is not treated as a patient in order to keep individuals from assuming the "sick" role, the subtle side effects of which may retard improvement. Those working with the soldiers expect that they will be able to reintegrate themselves and return to their proper roles. The bonding of soldiers with their combat units is considered an invaluable source of support that stabilizes their identity as members of the military. The emphasis in treatment is on immediate, conscious experiences and current events, not on past or unconscious causes. When the latter are emphasized, progress is found to be delayed.

Nonprofessionals may not implement such an approach in exactly this way but the good sense of it—with its emphasis on supporting defenses and keeping the focus on current consciousness—is well worth their continuing reflection. Knowledge of its success will support them in their efforts to provide simple, straightforward human responses to persons in crisis.

44

Drugs: Use and Abuse

The expansion of the problem of drug use, among people of all ages, is well known to all those who participate in counseling, even in a nonprofessional or occasional way. The difficulty, swollen by its own publicity, has become a defining element for large parts of our culture, and, despite massive efforts at research and public education, it is a subject about which there still exists great confusion and uncertainty. Few educators or members of the clergy work in their primary professions very long without encountering the drug problem, either through those with whom they directly work or through the concerns brought to them by parents or other community leaders who wish to enlist their aid in dealing with a problem that affects America from the ghetto to the suburb.

It is true that there is nothing new about drug dependence. Even the problem of returning Vietnam war veterans who acquired an addiction to drugs is not a new situation. The hypodermic needle was invented shortly before the Civil War, thus making widespread use of morphine possible. The "soldiers' sickness" was the name given to the problems of Civil War veterans who had become addicted to morphine. And there is nothing new in the checkered and uncertain way in which we have dealt with the drug problem. While most people are familiar with the fact that modern-day use of methadone as a substitute for heroin led only to addiction to methadone rather than to abstinence, not so many realize that this same problem has happened many times before in the history of medicine. Thus heroin itself was once employed as a substitute for opium and morphine addiction and led only to a severe problem with its own self-created dependence.

Drugs and Youth

There are cultural problems, often ignored, which are related to drug addiction. Sometimes these situations are ignored because of our attitudes toward young people and their understanding of values and

379

goals in life. The personal upheaval that occurs when the family no longer constitutes the stable emotional surround that it presumably once was for growing persons is also of significant influence. There is a varied mix of social, psychological, and familial forces that shape the drug activity of young people.

It is important for all people who counsel to have a fundamental understanding of the nature of various drugs and the differences between them. Such knowledge is important in order for counselors to be able to communicate credibly wth younger people. Nothing betrays a counselor more than a lack of adequate information about an addictive substance. Quite frequently adults, for whom the drug culture is often an alien and forbidding territory, have only general notions, and they tend to lump all drug substances together in talking about them. This almost immediately invalidates them as trustworthy communicators in the eyes of younger people who regard basic accurate information as a basis for any kind of dialogue. The familiar challenge to older people—"Don't knock it if you haven't tried it"— builds on the kind of fundamental ignorance that is displayed by people who are unfamiliar with drugs and the distinctions between them.

It is obviously essential to have some grasp of the nature of the adolescent experience and the role that drug-taking plays both in that experience and in the American culture at this time. Most drug use in any form by adolescents is begun as experimentation. It is not very different than the kind of human experimentation that has been going on with other unknown or forbidden substances for years. Most adult counselors can probably recall this style of experimentation with alcohol in their own earlier years.

Such exploratory or frankly experimental use of these substances cannot be taken lightly, especially since society has witnessed such an enormous increase in the use of cocaine. The use of the term "recreational drugs" has offered a brutally deceptive rationalization for substances whose effects are far more destructive than recreative. The claims to heightened creativity under the influence of drugs, another justification for their use, has been given the lie in the shoddy, often almost incomprehensible products, such as some films that have been fashioned under their influence.

Recent survey data indicated that fully ninety percent of cocaine abusers used marijuana at the same age or an earlier age than cocaine (E. H. Adams, and J. C. Groerer, "Elevated risk of cocaine use in adults," *Psychiatric Annals*, September 1988). This is important information because of the once widely accepted notion that marijuana use by teenagers and young adults was no real predictor of drug abuse in adulthood. Now we know that quite the opposite may be the rule, particularly in relationship to cocaine.

Adolescence, as Erikson has pointed out, is the time when young people have the task of solidifying their identity, of coming to terms with the various aspects of their personalities and their newly developed sense of themselves as sexual, independent beings, so that they can move on to the stages of early adulthoo1 with a consolidated sense of their own personalities. Adolescence is difficult to define in a strictly chronological manner. There are late starters as well as those who develop prematurely. There are those who seem to achieve a sense of adult maturity without a great deal of struggle, and there are others well beyond the accepted age boundaries of late adolescence who are still struggling with the conflicts that should theoretically have been solved by that time.

Central to the adolescent's development of an adequate identity is the challenge of separation and individuation. Adolescents must separate themselves from their own family setting in order to develop an adequate sense of their own individuality. Their struggle is a familiar one but it is not one that is always carried out with great tension or difficulty. Obviously the presence of this struggle is normal. It is a difficult thing to move toward independence when one is not totally capable of independent financial or emotional self-support. Adolescence can be a time of bafflement and strained relations between parents—even the most loving and understanding parents—and their children, who can seem suddenly remote from them. It is a life problem, however, that most sensible people are able to manage without their family collapsing around them. Any notable lack of family stability complicates the problems of adolescents and makes this a time in which the person's vulnerability to involvement with drugs is increased.

Add to this the fact that adolescents in recent generations have received a great deal of attention—perhaps far more than generations at any previous time within memory—and one can better appreciate the difficulties they have in passing through the maturing crises of life successfully. One of the difficulties that today's adolescents face centers on learning to delay gratification. This experience, with which the members of previous generations are well acquainted and about which most of them had very little choice, is far different for younger people today. Contemporary young people have grown up with adults who wanted to give them everything they themselves were denied in their own youth, which was blighted by the depression or by World

War II and the later wars. They have been surrounded by the instruments of man's invention, which, like the thermostat and the television, respond immediately to their touch. Young people especially in the light of the Vietnam War experience, have been listened to far more carefully than any other group in the past. A certain wisdom has been attributed to them that may always have been present in youth but that, in the judgment of many, has been exalted far more than at previous periods and has become a source of political power as well as individual esteem. Young people have also been made a large and profitable independent commercial market for a wide range of products.

Add to this the enormous importance of peer pressure and counselors can understand how adolescents, even though they are difficult to define, can emerge as a separate cultural enclave in which drug use, which postpones dealing with reality while offering instant gratification, can be a serious problem. There is no simple solution to a situation that is so compounded by these complicated cultural difficulties. Adult counselors cannot merely point at younger people and challenge them to pull themselves together as they feel they did during that period in their own lives. Neither can adults make the opposite mistake of trying to enter into the adolescent culture and identifying with it in some futile quest for rapport. There is nothing more awkward or ineffective than a middle-aged counselor trying to take on the dress or attitudes of younger people in the hope of reaching them. Adolescents recognize these older people as being extremely needy in their own right, and they do not find in them the kind of models they need in order to pass through this complicated adolescent period successfully. Adult attitudes, correct information, and a capacity to participate in strengthening the community's values and institutions consitute the qualities that a nonprofessional needs in order to respond to the epidemic problem of drugs in our culture.

One may begin with a survey of the symptoms of drug abuse. What happens when young people are on drugs? The general symptoms of difficulty in this area include changes in school attendance, in homework quality, in discipline, or in grades. This list also includes changes in physical appearance followed by a sudden or unusual emotional outbreaks or flare-ups. Further indications of drug abuse may be found in the furtive behavior of younger people about drugs or the possession of drugs. Adults should also note any sudden change of associations or social patterns in adolescents. A subtle but important indication is found when young persons begin borrowing money from fellow students to buy drugs or when they begin to wear sunglasses at inappropriate times in order to hide the pupils of their eyes. Such activities as stealing small items from school or home also suggest that a drug problem may exist. When students are found in odd places during the school day—for example, in closets or storage rooms—a legitimate suspicion of drug usage may arise. Obviously counselors must not overinterpret the signs. They should, however, be familiar with them if they are to give their best informed judgment on any problematic situation that comes to their attention.

What can counselors do? Belkin, in *Practical Counseling in The Schools* (Dubuque, Iowa: M. C. Brown Co., Publishers, 1975), suggests that there are three areas with which those who function in counseling roles must be active. The first is *preventive.* This requires counselors to understand the drug problem and its manifestations as thoroughly as possible. It also requires counselors to participate in the development of drug education programs through which they can make adequate and up-to-date information available to younger people. Secondly, counselors may work *in a therapeutic way* with younger people. They may be the first ones to see those who have a serious problem with drugs, and they may need to refer them to other sources of ongoing help. It may be the role of the nonprofessional counselor to maintain lines of communication between all the interested parties while arrangements for further help are being made.

Generally, nonprofessional counselors will not try to interact therapeutically on a long-range basis with persons suffering from major drug problems. Their skills, however, are well used if they can keep the avenues of communication open between younger people, their parents, and other responsible persons such as educational administrators. Thirdly, counselors may be involved on the *administrative or legal* level. Here they will be involved with larger community efforts to respond to drug problems. This may engage them in specific activities or more general educational activities with special groups such as fellow teachers, members of the clergy, or parents. This may also require their developing a relationship with law enforcement authorities, not as informers but as agents of communication and understanding.

Drugs and Adults

Drug abusers are common, are often not recognized or even suspected, and are found in every walk of life and at every social level. They are not well understood. The drugs they use excessively are often from that grouping termed *psychoactive substances.* These include any substances taken into the body that can alter a person's consciousness or state of mind. A great variety of drugs—sometimes in their natural form, sometimes prescribed, sometimes illegally manufactured and obtained—can produce the changes described as psychoactive. Among these are sedatives, hypnotics, anxiolytics, opioids, cocaine, amphetamines, phencyclidine, hallucinogens, and cannabis.

Although these drugs can produce an almost panoramic range of disturbances, ranging from mild euphoria to delirium, counselors can profit by understanding the common kinds of behaviors and symptoms that suggest drug use as their cause. Some basic concepts allow us to grasp better the nature of drug use as well as to appreciate an individual client's relationship to his or her drug use.

Abuse should be suspected when an individual evidences a pattern of pathological substance use. For example, persons who claim that they can stop whenever they want, that they are in control, but yet are unable to reduce or stop their utilization of a drug, are projecting clearly the behavior and attitudes of an abuser. If such individuals manifest evidence of impairment in physical, social, or occupational functioning as a result of their drug use, abuse should certainly be suspected.

Important associated characteristics of excessive drug use must also be understood if counselors are to comprehend the problems and challenges that overflow from these patterns of drug use. These include:

1. *Tolerance*—characterized by the need for markedly increased amounts of the substance in order to achieve the desired effects.

2. *Dependence*—which may be either physical or psychological. *Psychological dependence* is also called *habituation* and is characterized by a continuous or intermittent craving for the substance in order to avoid the onset of disturbing emotions, especially depressive feelings. *Physical dependence* is manifested in the employment of the substance to ward off unpleasant physical symptoms that may follow after or during withdrawal from the drug. These symptoms may surface as the person abstains from or decreases the amount of the drug. Ingestion of the drug diminishes the symptoms and restores physical equilibrium. Counselors should understand that when these features emerge in the context of drug use, treatment of any kind becomes much more difficult.

Cocaine is the snowy Everest that dominates the landscape of the drug culture today. That it is the drug most seriously abused is supported by the fact that the number of people who tried cocaine at least once increased from 5.4 million in 1974 to 22.2 million in 1985. The estimated number of current users increased from 1.6 million in 1977 to 5.8 million in 1985 (Adams and Gfroerer, p. 523). What is particularly serious about the current cocaine craze is that in some forms it is highly addictive and its use puts the individual at high risk for medical complications.

These latter may include numerous complications due to arterial constriction and can lead to myocardial infarction, stroke, hypertensive episodes, and anoxia secondary to seizures; all of these can result in death.

When working with clients suspected of using or abusing cocaine, counselors should have some idea of the different forms in which the drug is used and their relative potential for producing dependence and toxicity (see K. Vereby and M. S. Gold, "From coca leaves to Crack," *Psychiatric Annals,* September 1988). These include the following:

Coca leaf chewing, an ancient method that is common in South America involves toasting the leaves and chewing them or their ash along with an alkaline material. There is a somewhat slow absorption so that effects may not occur for five to ten minutes but may last up to hours.

Oral use, in which cocaine is mixed with an elixir or some beverage, is absorbed slowly with the peak level of the drug reached in about one hour. The possibility of becoming addicted to drug use is less when the substance is taken in this manner than when it is taken intranasally.

Intranasal administration, better known as "snorting," is perhaps one of the best known ways of using cocaine. It results in a relatively rapid onset of the "high." The latter comes on within two or three minutes and begins to fade in about forty-five minutes. Cocaine is often snorted at fifteen- or twenty-minutes intervals to maintain the "high." Use by this method is complicated because of its potential for causing serious dependence as well as serious physical problems, such as nasal septum necrosis and perforation.

Intravenous cocaine use leads to a "rush" within thirty or forty seconds and its effect may last ten to twenty minutes. Because of its rapid onset and its short stimulation life, its potential for developing dependence is greater than the previous listed methods. A fearful complication of this method is found in the risk of becoming infected with the AIDS virus through the use of unclean needles. A further problem is caused by the inconsistent quality and character of street purchases for this intravenous usage. The user, therefore, cannot determine the effect of the drug so taken because the strength and purity of the dose cannot be determined accurately.

In smoking cocaine, coca paste is extracted from coca leaves with the aid of gasoline, kerosene, and sulfuric acid and is then mixed with tobacco and smoked in cigarette form or in a pipe. This results in a very rapid absorption of the drug (eight to ten seconds) with effects lasting five to ten minutes. Because the drug used this way acts so quickly—a "hit" as it is called—it is a most highly addictive method. It also presents particular risks for developing lung complications. Free-base and "crack" are essentially coca paste prepared in specific manners to produce products that generate a more rapid "high." According to Vereby and Gold (p. 517), "the financial success of crack is attributed strictly to a marketing and packaging gimmick which made small amounts of high quality cocaine available at low prices, especially to people of low economic classes and adolescents."

Counselors need to know that the use of cocaine is extraordinarily risky. "Cocaine," according to Vereby and Gold, "may cause sudden death, regardless of dose, blood levels of cocaine, or route of administration" (loc. cit.). Because of its rapid action and its highly pleasurable and addictive qualities, interrupting or breaking the use of this drug is very difficult. As a result, the habit becomes the focus of the client's life, often resulting in loss of job, deterioration or destruction of interpersonal relationships, and may even lead to alienation from society, to that state of homelessness that is the final result of the addict's need to spend every available dollar to support the habit. Almost invariably, successful treatment involves a structured program in an inpatient setting and long-term aftercare to aid in maintaining abstinence.

Another form of drug abuse involves opioids such as morphine, methadone, codeine and heroin, all of which are abused by persons who obtain them illegally on the street. They are often used by the young, especially from the lower socioeconomic population. The search for money to obtain these drugs accounts, in some communitites, for the majority of their serious crimes. The most common symptoms of such drug abuse may be observed in scarred veins, the "tracks" that indicate intravenous drug use. Users also display frequent drowsiness, "nodding off," apathy, and difficulty in concentration. As a result, the use of these drugs contributes to a vicious if familiar circle—its effects deprive the user of generating any motivation to change things. Once again, treatment, to be successful, usually begins with inpatient hospitalization.

Sedative hypnotics such as valium, librium, and barbituates involve drug abuse whose most appealing aspect lies in the capacity, similar to that of alcohol, to deaden the pain and/or discomfort that many people experience in ordinary living. As a result, such clients are often housewives or other relatively well-functioning members of society who are able to maintain some semblance of a normal life. They may, on occasion, be obtaining these drugs by prescription from well-meaning physicians who may not realize how much these patients have come to depend on these medications. To help these patients, counselors must suspect and inquire about their use, while recognizing that many of these people, like alcoholics, deny that they are using them too often or in such high doses. Careful evaluation, the development of an understanding relationship, and timely and strategic use of referral resources can help these clients.

45

Persons with Drinking Problems

Most people have some understanding of the enormous national problem—personal, social, and economic—that is created by alcohol and its misuse. One thing is clear: everybody who functions as a counselor in any capacity will sooner or later become involved in the problem of alcoholics, even if this is only indirectly, through dealing with affected members of their family or colleagues at work. There is also enormous stress associated with alcoholic problems. Difficulties with drinking involve many persons besides the drinker himself and so multiply sources of stress. Alcoholism radiates out to affect a cluster of people, each with a different intensity of emotion. Many counselors may never meet an alcoholic face-to-face, and yet almost every day they can feel the effects of an alcoholic problem in the person seeking help from them. This may be a spouse or an adult still pressed by memories of growing up in the shadow of an alcoholic parent. The mark and stress of the problem drinker is almost everywhere in American culture.

In recent years, the problem of alcohol use and abuse has become more amenable to study. Against a background of increased cultural concern and a better sense of the problem's dimensions and sequellae, research instruments have been fashioned to measure agreed-upon criteria for the diagnosis of various levels of severity of what are now termed "psychoactive substance abuse disorders." As a result, remarkable strides have been made in assessing the international public health parameters of alcohol use.

An important distinction, found in the *DSM III-R*, is that between substance abuse and substance dependence. *Substance abuse* signifies a pattern of pathological use of at least one month's duration that leads to impairment in social or occupational functioning. *Substance dependence*, on the other hand, describes a physical condition associated with alcohol abuse. It is characterized by tolerance—increasing amounts of alcohol are needed to achieve the same effect—and by withdrawal symptoms. Generally speaking, dependence suggests a more severe condition that may contribute to major illness and death.

As cited by Frances and Franklin (Talbott, p. 316), "Warheit (1985) found that approximately 30 percent of the general population are described as abstainers, 10 percent as heavy drinkers, and 5 to 10 percent as problem drinkers." They further note (p. 317) that in "the U.S. Department of Health and Human Services's fifth special report to the U.S. Congress on Alcohol (1984), it was estimated that 200,000 deaths per year are alcohol related."

An American Paradox

For counselors, countertransference problems with alcoholic clients frequently occur in response to the patient's transference reactions marked by rebelliousness, dishonesty, or aggression. Other sources of this difficulty may arise from the counselor's lack of knowledge about alcoholism and its treatment, or his or her experiences with alcohol, as a problem for themselves or in their close relationships with others.

Many people operating in the helping professions do so on a minimum of general impressions about alcoholism. Either they have not read much or they tend to respond out of instinct when confronted with the problem. This may be easy to understand because of the difficulties in getting a comprehensive and useful clinical picture of the alcoholic. Nonetheless, counselors have a professional obligation to read or to attend continuing education programs in order to fill out their knowledge about human problems.

Counselors can profit from examining their own feelings about alcohol and alcoholics. They may, for example, have strong feelings because of personal or family experiences with an alcoholic problem. Thus, some counselors may find it very difficult to be sympathetic to or interested in persons with drinking problems. They find that they do not like to work with them because they find them morally objectionable. No counselor can be of much assistance to an individual with a drinking problem if there are serious blocks to the basic acceptance of that individual as a person.

Another aspect of their feelings that is important for counselors to examine is their possible ambivalence about drinking. This seems to constitute the American paradox. According to research conducted in 1974 by the University of California (at Berkeley) Department of Public Health, in cooperation with the Mervin Field Public Opinion Research Corporation, Californians were prepared to denounce alcoholism but were strongly against anything that threatens to interfere with their individual drinking habits.

People do not like drinking drivers but until recently they were stubbornly opposed to any measure that might restrict the free use of alcoholic beverages. This reluctance to deal directly with the problem of drinking in our society has been transformed somewhat in recent years, largely due to the organization MADD (Mothers Against Drunk Drivers). Each year 25,000 persons die and 150,000 are permanently disabled because of alcohol-related accidents. The development of easily administered tests that measure Blood Alcohol Level (BAL) have furthered legal efforts to control drinking by providing reliable indicators of intoxication levels. The use of such instrumentation have had dramatic effects on this problem and added to the change in public attitudes toward alcohol abusers caused by the consciousness-raising effects of organizations such as MADD. The consumption of alcohol declined across the decade of the eighties and many legislatures initiated new and tougher policies in order to control the alcohol abuse problem.

We have to return to a basic principle about all counseling help. It is important to keep the person, rather than just the person's problem, in focus, an effort that seems to be easier in some situations than others. In working with alcoholics many counselors find it almost impossible to perceive them as persons. The problem itself looms so large—and with such an unpleasant emotional aura—that little compassion can be generated, and the efforts to establish a helping relationship are minimized. It is easy to turn a person with drinking difficulties into a problem case even when we are willing to believe that alcoholism is a disease rather than a personal fault. The effort to see the drinker as a person beneath all his or her disruptive and abhorrent behavior is fundamental to any counseling success.

Newer Understandings of Alcoholism

1. There is strong evidence, especially in findings on men, that alcoholism is, in most cases, related to a genetic vulnerability. The mechanism of genetic transmission, however, remains unknown. Whether such hereditary factors are also present in women is unclear.

2. With more refined criteria developed for the various mental disorders, it has been noted that almost two-thirds of alcoholic patients also suffer from an additional diagnosable mental condition. Such persons are referred to as "dual diagnosis" patients. Whether the alcohol or some other psychological condition is primary is not always immediately clear. This new understanding of the relationship between alcohol and other psychological illnesses, such as depression

and anxiety disorders, should help counselors better to understand and more sensitively read the symptomatology of their alcoholic clients. It is particularly significant for them to understand that, as Frances and Franklin observe (Talbott, p. 325), "recognition and appropriate treatment of the depression is important" because of the increased suicide rate that is found among patients suffering from primary and secondary affective illnesses.

3. Alcoholism is as high a risk factor as depression is for suicide. This means that alcoholics are nine to twenty-two percent more likely to commit suicide than are individuals in the general population.

4. Counselors are likely to have the children of alcoholics (COA) as clients. These individuals, especially men, are vulnerable to developing alcoholism themselves. In addition, they often suffer the effects of growing up with a parent who was inconsistent and emotionally depriving. Some of these grown children of alcoholics watched as their nonalcoholic parent, often the mother, experienced physical and/or sexual abuse at the hands of the alcoholic parent. In cases of childhood sexual and physical abuse, it is often discovered that the author of such abuse was the alcoholic parent. A popular literature on the problems of the children of alcoholics has developed and self-help groups have been a source of support for them as well.

5. In recent years, increasing evidence has been developed that a specific fetal abnormality results from alcohol abuse during pregnancy. Various studies have reported the incidence of women who are heavy drinkers during pregnancy as ranging from 2.5 percent to forty percent (see Talbot, p. 317). Fetal Alcohol Syndrome (FAL), which can result in children of such mothers, includes features of growth retardation, abnormalities of facial and cranial structure, smaller head size and mental retardation. There is some question whether the moderate use of alcohol affects birth weight or causes spontaneous abortions, but the National Institute for Alcohol Abuse recommends that women abstain from any alcohol use during pregnancy (see Talbott, p. 319).

6. Since nonprofessional counselors may be the first helpers in touch with alcoholics, it is important for them to recognize the clinical features of this problem. The timely recognition and treatment of alcohol abuse and dependency are frustrated and made more complicated by the use of denial not only by the individual but by the family and the general culture. Often, alcohol abusers are reluctant to see doctors and avoid them because of feelings of embarrassment or their own conflicts with authority figures. As suggested by Frances and Franklin (Talbott, p. 318), those working with these patients "should

be alert to the subtle signs and symptoms of early alcohol problems, including loss of communication in a marriage, frequent temper flare-ups, belligerent demands, and a loss of interest in the marital relationship." The early warning signals may also include a failure to complete projects on schedule, chronic lateness, or not showing up at all.

7. Counselors should work toward the evaluation and treatment of the family of the alcoholic (see Talbott, p. 326). The family system, as Frances and Franklin put it, "that has been altered to accommodate the patient's drinking may also reinforce it." The person often comes for help as a result of a family crisis, establishing a certain clinical logic for involving them in the planning of the treatment, a factor that seems to improve the success of the treatment itself. An emphasis on "the group and self-help aspects of treatment aids in the patient's resocialization, and practicing of object relatedness, impulse control, and acceptance of an identity as a recovering alcoholic" (loc. cit.). Setting limits in a structured environment provides the support the patient needs until he or she can take control of his or her own independent life again.

8. In some cases, alcoholics who cannot accept Alcoholics Anonymous or other group-related treatment may need individual dynamic psychotherapy. A clear sign that outpatient treatment will not be successful is found in a person's reluctance to practice abstinence as a condition for getting help.

9. Nonprofessionals should have some relationship with local chapters of Alcoholics Anonymous and appreciate its spirit and structure. The meetings offer members' experiences of acceptance, understanding, forgiveness, and even confrontation. Central is the twelve-step program which new members enter by admitting their problem, surrendering a sense of personal control over the illness, carrying out a personal assessment, making amends, and helping others. There is a strong employment of spiritual resources in this successful program that aims at restoring sobriety largely through dealing with individuals in terms of their conscious perceptions of their problems. The emphasis, as in nonprofessional counseling, is on strengthening the person's defenses, the very function that nonprofessional counselors can handle very well.

A Core Difficulty

Despite advances in our recent understanding of alcoholism, many lay persons as well as professionals still look at the alcoholic as an individual who makes a decision to drink too much. They view the alcoholic, in other words, as a kind of sinner, one who chooses his own uncomfortable fate. Because many are sure that the alcoholic causes his own problem, they feel it is still his responsibility to decide to stop and to pull himself up out of the pit where he threw himself in the first place. So people generally say something like, "Nothing can be done until he decides to do something for himself."

The excessive drinker is thought to act with intent and choice even though, at another level, it is recognized that an essential characteristic of alcoholism is that the person can't control his actions, especially where drinking is concerned. One of the realizations most helpful for counselors is that the most successful alcoholism programs are those that reach out to alcoholics rather than those that wait for alcoholics to come to them. Persons with drinking problems can respond to treatment when it is offered to them. Helpers should not construct an attitude that traps them into a role of waiting for alcoholics to prove that they are ready to get better.

Some Things to be Ready For

Counselors should be prepared for complications in dealing with alcoholic problems. Frequently alcoholism is the symptom of a deeper kind of difficulty, and, as described in this chapter, often is accompanied by a serious mental disorder. There may be, in certain alcoholics, evidence of harm to the body and to the central nervous system. A patient and careful evaluation of all the factors involved in an individual problem is obviously necessary. Counselors should work in cooperation with other specialists, with physicians and psychologists who are capable of carrying out the necessary tests or getting the biographical information that may be essential to helping the person involved. Oversimplification of an alcoholic's condition is the most counterproductive of all the counselor's attitudes.

The effort to understand the person of the alcoholic is severely tested because of the defenses alcoholics may use in their relationship with the counselor. Counselors who are prepared for alcoholics to be defensive will not be surprised to find them using rationalization, denial, or dissociation in their presentation of themselves. It is interesting to note how easily our inquiries about drinking make the use of such defenses possible. Many forms ask whether we drink or not and then provide the classification "socially" for everyone to circle. Counselors must be aware of providing the same easy kind of rationalizations out of some ill-conceived pity or the wish not to embarrass the alcoholic or hurt his or her feelings. An overall concern for alcoholics as persons is our best guarantee against hurting them.

There will be difficulties in establishing a therapeutic relationship with a person with an alcoholic problem. One of the main reasons for this is the fact that alcoholics frequently suffer from low self-esteem. They need to be respected and they are very sensitive to any kind of judgmental or critical attitudes toward them. These only make them withdraw and become more defensive in the presence of the counselor.

Counselors must also be very gentle—but not softhearted—in their approach. It is very easy for counselors to be used by alcoholics who have been through similar situations before. They know just how to play on the sympathy of the person, to keep them at a safe distance, and to get them on their side. Sensitive counselors will, of course, be aware of this and will attempt to see beneath this behavior in order to respond at a deeper level.

Attentive counselors are careful not to probe too much because of the sensitivity of alcoholics. Neither should they press them into expressive forms of therapy for which they are psychologically ill-prepared. One cannot push these people too fast or too hard. They are like packages stamped "fragile" and they cannot be thrown around. They have an injured sense of themselves and reinjuring it in the name of helping them is a real danger for an overaggressive or moralizing counselor.

Counselors frequently function best if they are part of a treatment team. All the resources that are available should be employed in assisting persons with alcoholic difficulties. It is sensible for counselors in a certain area to set up a working relationship with colleagues who are physicians, mental health experts, or members of the clergy. They may also become acquainted with any programs in business or industry that attempt to identify and respond to alcoholic problems at an early stage.

Joining in efforts to reach out to the potential alcoholic may be one of the most promising functions that a counselor can fulfill. It goes against the instincts of many counselors, however, because they are traditionally in the role of those who wait for persons to come to them. Some participation in a team that recognizes the effectiveness of moving out toward the potential alcoholic at an important time should not be underestimated.

Counselors should also use other established resources such as Alcoholics Anonymous. They should, however, avoid automatically passing over to such an organization everybody who comes to them, which may represent a way of getting rid of the person with the problem instead of responding to him. Alcoholics Anonymous has proved to be very helpful to a great many individuals. Before referring someone to such an organization, however, counselors may wish to have a more careful diagnosis made, employing, for example, the resources of a team of which they may be members. It may lead to a judgment that Alcoholics Anonymous is not the appropriate organization at the present moment.

46

Counseling the AIDS Patient

Nonprofessional counselors, like almost all Americans, will inevitably find themselves involved with the illness acquired immunodeficiency syndrome, or AIDS. This may be directly with an individual suffering from it, or, even more likely, with someone affected indirectly by it. While nonprofessionals will wisely attempt to refer victims of this disease to experts, especially to the remarkable teams of professionals found in most large hospitals, they still need an understanding of this haunting killer that, like a tornado, slashes a wide path of physical and emotional devastation.

Those who wish to channel their compassion into effective assistance to AIDS victims or to the widening circle of family members, friends, and associates who will be affected by it, need an accurate understanding of the disease. AIDS is the most serious of a complex of illnesses termed the *human immunodeficiency virus* infection, or HIV. Studies that used the serological test for antibodies to HIV developed in 1985 for blood screening demonstrated that HIV can be observed in various guises ranging from the person who, without symptoms or complaints, is a carrier to the person whose symptoms meet the technical definition of the always fatal variant of AIDS itself.

The latter term is reserved for those persons with this gravest, deadly form of immune deficiency and the clinical manifestations of some opportunistic infector, such as pneumonia, or malignancy, such as Kaposi's sarcoma. Not everyone with HIV, therefore, suffers from AIDS in this manner. That distinction is important for helpers to appreciate, not only because of the different challenges of responding to persons in these categories, but because, as a serious social complication, cases meeting the above medical definition of AIDS must, in most jurisdictions, be reported to local or state health authorities. The technical diagnosis and the responsibility to report this illness belong to medical professionals; other counselors, such as members of the clergy, teachers, and concerned friends and colleagues, will, however, find themselves dealing with the emotional aura that throbs brightly and painfully around such decisions.

AIDS is not an illness, however, in which counselors can automatically employ the kind of responses that work in situations in which the basic problem is, for example, the identification and exploration of feelings. As Francisco Fernandez, MD, has written in a primer on the subject for the American Psychiatric Association, "in any case where HIV infection may be possible, any symptoms of a psychiatric nature must be considered organic until proven otherwise." The basic medical complications must, therefore, be understood as powerfully damaging to the central nervous system, resulting in dementia and other morbid states to which the nonprofessional cannot directly respond by fashioning responses directed solely to feeling states.

Nonetheless, the reactions to a diagnosis of HIV, much as with the diagnosis of any terminal condition, include human experiences of fear and anxiety with which understanding helpers can deal directly and effectively. The afflicted immediately understand that the path before them may lead to disfigurement through Kaposi's sarcoma as well as racking fevers, increasing fatigue, and the possibility of increasing rejection and isolation as they grow weaker. They are also faced with disclosing to their parents or loved ones the true nature of their illness, a stressful and uncertain prospect.

It is not unusual, therefore, for patients to express themselves in angry, desperate ways, as the massive weight of the sickness settles on them. The nonprofessional can support them in these trials by identifying and buttressing their healthiest defenses; they can also offer them education on the subject in the rumor-filled universe of their suffering and provide the commonsense psychological benefits of just being with them when there is not much else that can be done.

Back to Basics

Nonprofessional counselors must deal with countertransference feelings. A study of health care professionals dealing with AIDS patients done in the late eighties revealed patterns of unresolved reactions that nonprofessionals may be presumed to experience as well. Sixty-three percent of the professionals "were skeptical or did not believe assurances by experts that health care workers who observe safety guidelines are at minimal risk of contacting AIDS from patients. . . . Twenty-six percent of all respondents feared that they would become victims of AIDS if they continued their present work" (J. J. Wallack, "AIDS Anxiety Among Health Care Professionals," *Hospital and Community Psychiatry,* Vol. 40. No. 5, May, 1989, p. 507).

Yet the remarkably human correlate of these fears is that "97 percent expressed a firm commitment to caring for AIDS patients throughout their illness and the dying process." That nonprofessionals harbor the same misgivings along with their desire to help should not be surprising. These feelings cannot be ignored without their eventually affecting the counselor's work.

Most sensible persons, unexpectedly involved in a critical situation, do not attempt to usurp the roles of trained professionals. Untrained counselors recognize that individuals who intervene by changing the sick person's medication or by the introduction of some nontraditional form of therapy, such as a special diet, may, for all their good intentions, do more harm than good. While medicine is just beginning to understand the nature of the immune system, and while untested alternative therapies may have some merit, the commonsense rule is to stay within the limits of one's own background and training when dealing with HIV or any other major illness. That obvious restriction, however, leaves plenty of room for nonprofessionals to be of assistance by being themselves.

Desperately sick people do want to talk, when they have the energy to do so, and they need listeners. The surrounding cluster of family and friends often want to talk as well, especially during the long, uniquely enervating hours of waiting in hallways and parlors that go with hospital visiting. This is obviously one of the principal areas in which amateur counselors can work effectively. Even here, however, they must put their basic human capacity simply to understand the woes of others before any attempt to explore their origins or, in any sense, to "treat" them by psychological means.

Counselors, as we have strongly emphasized, should work with other persons on the *conscious* level of functioning. Nonprofessionals do not, then, attempt to explore unconscious material, nor do they engage in strategies that may, even without their advertence, break through the surface of the ill person's psyche. It is extremely important to be consistent about this approach in dealing with those stricken with any manifestation of HIV and with the surrounding company of their relatives or friends. Commonsense helpers are never called upon to do *uncovering* or *reconstructive* therapy. There is hardly time for the well-trained to do this in a terminal illness and, in any case, it would work against the reasonable goals of really helping individuals to manage their way through an illness that is already overwhelming.

On the conscious level, the main objective is, as has been noted, to champion those resources of personality, imagination, and spirituality that are found, to some degree, even in the most gravely ill of us. Even when these can only be evoked in a muted and minor key, they can be the decisive strengths by which human beings not only manage but transcend the ravages of mortal illness.

Wise nonprofessionals do not tamper with the defenses of the HIV patient. Whatever they are—even if they include elements of rationalization or distortion at times—they ordinarily represent the best the individual can do at the moment. Confronting techniques are, therefore, not to be employed by the nonprofessional in dealing with people who, battered by chronic disease, have enormous difficulty in just inhabiting their own personality in any vital or resonant manner. Supporting conscious defenses of the AIDS patient, even when these do not seem ideal to the helper, is enormously beneficial. Many nonprofessionals have a healthy sense of their own limitations; they thereby draw on their own health in responding to persons in distress. This healthy sense of using wisely one's best reserves—and not trying to do the work of the psychiatrist or clinical psychologist—is the hallmark of commonsense helpers at their best.

The intermingling of physical and emotional reaction and causation is highly complex and the nonprofessional must take cues from the specialists who have a more subtle and informed understanding of how these operate in each individual case. This is of particular importance in an illness in which, as noted, the infection of the central nervous system may give rise to symptoms that may seem totally emotional in nature.

Common Psychological Reactions to HIV

Aware of the above cautions, helpers will still recognize in HIV patients psychological reactions that are also observed in other patients with terminal illnesses. Perhaps the most common—and, it might be said the most human—is *denial*. When we are suddenly faced with a crushing piece of news, even the healthiest among us employs the mechanism of denial, if only to gain time and space in which to begin to regroup ourselves psychologically and admit the truth of the event. Just as we can expect and accept such a reaction in ourselves, so we should expect and accept it in patients who have been given a diagnosis of an HIV-related illness.

We cannot survive without denial, so the helpful counselor will allow patients this necessary and essential defense by which they can look away from the cold shadow of threat long enough to ward off panic. Denial also allows individuals to express an insurrectionary reaction, a rejection, often bitter, of the medical verdict that so suddenly deprives them of their independence and their future. The ability to differentiate this reaction from a dangerous variant of it is indispensable to the counselor. At times, some individuals employ denial not to reorganize interiorly and to adjust to the illness but to mask its reality to cover their hostile and destructive impulses. Such massive denial is always primitive and dangerous.

Such persons may, for example, recklessly engage in sexual activity with many partners without regard to the consequences for themselves, others, or, eventually, the public in general. They seem bent on revenge, on infecting the world that has deprived them of their own health and is soon to take their lives. Such patients reject any therapeutic assistance. Their rebuffs to those who wish to help them are not difficult to identify even by nonprofessionals. When such potentially destructive impacted embitteredness is encountered, the nonprofessional should not try to temper the anger or to cajole such patients into more rational behavior. Because of possible neurological as well as characterological complications, these patients need immediate and careful evaluation by professionals with the resources needed to manage them.

Perhaps one of the most difficult groups to work with is composed of individuals who have tested positively for HIV but who have not as yet contracted the illness. These persons are faced with a painful and anxiety-provoking reality. They carry the HIV, but in their minds they do not know when or if they will be stricken with AIDS itself. The disease has been tracked only since 1981 and, every year, more of these persons do come down with the illness. Still, the medical evidence, while seeming to suggest a certain inevitability about AIDS following HIV positive testing, has not proved this. It is clear, however, that the longer one has had a positive test, the more likely one is to develop the disease. Such persons live, therefore, under a shadow and need the kind of understanding support that nonprofessional counselors can provide successfully. It may be that such individuals will confide their anxiety about their condition first to a member of the clergy, a general practicioner, or a respected teacher or coach. These first-line counselors are in an excellent position to assist them psychologically and spiritually and to refer them for professional help when, in their judgment, the time has come for it.

In a 1989 address to the American College of Psychiatrists, Samuel Perry, MD, of Cornell University Medical College, noted that, in the research done so far, "there are fewer disastrous responses to learning the result of one's HIV test than had been expected earlier in the epidemic" (*Psychiatric News*, April 9, 1989, p. 5.). He identified the pretest interval as one in which counseling is essential, with "at least an hour (or even six or seven hours) . . . usually necessary to discuss all the ramifications of being tested." These latter include the meaning of the tests, with the chance that false positives or negatives may be reported, a realistic yet hopeful presentation of the prognosis and treatments, if the results are, in fact, positive. Counselors must deal with questions of confidentiality, their own policies on notifying others of positive results, and the person's own feelings, often of guilt if they have close friends or loved ones who are infected. Their need to modify their sexual behavior must be on the counseling agenda as well. Follow-up meetings should be suggested, as Perry observes, "to deal with the rebound effects of an individual's telling others about his test results."

Additional Reactions

Counselors working with AIDS patients may be the first ones to notice the small signals of profound neurological changes under way. For example, when patients describe periods of forgetfulness, report or evidence difficulties in concentrating, or a loss of interest, these are often regarded as understandable incidental psychological reactions to the massive burden of the illness. These mild symptoms should alert nonprofessionals to the possibility that these reactions foreshadow deeper central nervous system disorders such as the *AIDS dementia complex,* that group of irreversible organic disorders that destroy brain function. Delirium, with features such as insomnia and restlessness, is frequently encountered in hospitalized HIV patients. At times this is misread as a depression or some other purely psychological problem. Nonprofessionals who pick up signs of these problems should again refer the patient for a thorough medical examination.

While nonprofessionals remain alert to these possibilities, they may more often encounter the truly psychological complications of this illness group. These include *demoralization* and *despondency,* desolating feelings that lay waste to the psyche. In turn, the damaged spirit of the patient, evidenced by a negative self-image, affects the entire world of the afflicted individual, straining social and work relationships until they are no longer manageable. This further isolates the individual, compounding the already severely compromised level of his or her psychological functioning.

Following the tradition of Elisabeth Kübler-Ross, some have described the reactions of the HIV patient as one of adjustment that can be charted out in rough stages. These include the initial crisis, with the reactions of denial, anxiety, anger, and sadness, and is marked by efforts to strike some bargain in regard to health and sickness. The second stage sees denial yielding to a mixture of other emotions, including guilt, anger, and self-pity. This period, marked by a sharp decrease in self-worth, may find the patient estranged from his family and friends. A return to drug use and dangerous sex practices may occur at this time.

In stage three, according to this schema, the patient begins to accept himself or herself as a person compromised by the nature of the illness. He may begin to appreciate the unique character and quality of each passing day. In the next stage the person actively prepares for death. This may be marked by a fear of complete dependency on friends or strangers. It is not uncommon for patients, during the darkest moments of this death sentence illness, to contemplate suicide. Nonetheless, those who work with the dying also see evidence of the life force continuing to assert itself in the individual's efforts to hold on to life.

People who have worked with gravely stricken individuals understand that these stages seldom occur in pure form. They may be scrambled, combined with other undescribed intervals, or they may be reversed or, like a new river, cut an unexpected and unpredicted path through the landscape. Sensible counselors understand that they cannot force persons to go through these steps in some orderly fashion. The person who would be of real assistance to the patient must respect the patient's unique journey and understand that they will die, not as the textbook or the expert suggests, but as best they can. This pilgrimage through a final illness is made, like the rest of life, humanly, imperfectly, and not without nobility.

The chronically afflicted HIV patient experiences an illness that, bad enough in itself, also carries the seeds of social disapproval and ostracism at the same time. Nonprofessionals can respond in this very area, for what they can bring, in place of medical expertise, is the gift of compassionate understanding. Nothing deepens the isolation of the chronically ill more than the pressure, sometimes generated even by well-meaning friends and relatives, for them to be "normal" again. This distinctive void can be entered, if not filled, by nonprofessionals who can sensitively grasp at least some of the feelings of such demoralized patients.

47

Taking Counsel with Ourselves

What benefit can counselors derive from a reflective experience on the way they interact with other persons in trying to assist them? It is not just a matter of learning how to minimize the negative effects of excessive stress in our daily helping activities. Lessening our stress is a by-product of knowing how to use ourselves in a mature professional manner. We seldom rid ourselves of stress by a direct, frontal attack. Stress is decreased, however, when we learn to enter more fully and more confidently into our work with other persons. How can we use ourselves even more sensitively so that our talents will be used fully and our effectiveness with others increased? This is the perennial question for thoughtful counselors; answering it sincerely, in and through their work, they discover that stress is much less of a problem for them.

Winging It

We live in the age of improvisation. "Winging it" has become in many occupations almost the accustomed way of performing. There are many rationalizations for doing things without adequate preparation. We may speak, for example, of freshness and spontaneity, of "playing it by ear," but we may, in fact, be explaining away carelessness instead of describing creativity. There is a strange myth abroad that creative persons are undisciplined. Nothing is further from the truth. There is an intense inner discipline, according to all observations and studies, that involves creative persons profoundly in their work. Only pseudocreative people lack discipline and, although they may call themselves poets or artists, their shoddiness is revealed clearly in what they produce.

Counselors run the same risks in an age that has also exalted improvisation in interpersonal relationships. Unfortunately, winging it in the helping professions may not only harm other persons but may also induce a great deal of stress in counselors. Tension is connected with any self-discipline, but it is not the grinding and destruc-

403

tive agency that stress becomes in an unplanned and uncertain situation.

Whether counselors work at helping others full- or part-time, their most important objective is to develop a professional attitude toward themselves and their work. This is not only the best protection against stress but it also helps define the counselor clearly—in terms of work situations, goals to be achieved, and people to work with—and describes well the limits and organization of therapeutic work. It also enables cooperation with other professional helpers in an intelligent and productive manner. Counselors with a professional attitude do not float around like protoplasm, snagging now on one thing and now on another, moving with the latest stream of fashionable activity because they lack an internal sense of direction.

A professional attitude generates an increase in self-confidence and self-esteem. These are the strengths that enable counselors to face difficult situations—even those in which they are not quite sure what to do—and work through them in a constructive manner. Counseling is an activity in which being an amateur is really not good enough. Unfortunately, in counseling, as in other responsible professions, we can know just enough to do a lot of harm both to ourselves and to others. To organize our sense of self around a professional definition does not necessarily make us impersonal or somehow part of the "establishment" or "institution." True professionalism gives us a healthy sense of independence because it enables us to understand the ground on which we stand. Operating on good will, or merely the desire to be helpful, is not really sufficient.

Elements of Professionalism

Some of the important features of continuing to develop a professional sense include the following:

We need to take time for regular study. Surprisingly enough, many people who engage in counseling activity almost every day hardly ever consult the literature or even their own textbooks. They feel, perhaps because they went through an educational system that made learning seem this way, that they have completed their formal study because they have passed certain courses. But all professionals go on learning throughout their lives. And, no matter how much experience we may have, it is always helpful to study again the particular psychological dynamics that may be involved in a current counseling responsibility.

Most counselors recognize that ongoing education is the natural state of things for all professionals at the present time. The heart of this is the desire to continue educating ourselves, to continue learning more about ourselves and the subject matter of our counseling work.

For example, as one detects that a client is an obsessive-compulsive, one can turn back to some book that deals with this subject. It will read differently after clinical experience because counselors will have seen new facets of the obsessive style that they have previously not noticed. They will have a personal feel for it. A thorough reading of at least one treatment of the obsessive-compulsive character, for example, will bring out added dimensions in the current counseling experience. Such reading takes time and must be done carefully. It is helpful to make notes and, at the conclusion, to try to draw up a brief résumé of the important insights gained from this research and study. Add to this, time for reflection in terms of the actual client with whom we are working, especially if we can examine how our interaction has gone up to this point, and we will be much better prepared to assist our client at the next meeting.

Such study does not merely produce information; it leads to a more informed sense of ourselves as counselors. We do not just learn about a certain subject; we penetrate it so that we have knowledge, not merely to answer questions, but to possess operational professional knowledge that affects our whole way of relating to others. We are different because we continue to study. We grow professionally in this way and there is no substitute for it.

Professionals try to read professional journals and reviews. These enable counselors to understand the important developments in the field and offer them an opportunity to appreciate changes in training and psychological techniques. These can also be provided, of course, by attendance at professional meetings or other continuing education seminars. Counselors can do a great deal on their own, however, especially with the variety of materials available in print and on cassette.

Personality Theory

One of the things, for example, some counselors may not see as directly related to psychotherapeutic technique is personality theory. Without it, however, we lack a context for our work or a framework for thinking about it. To deepen as much as possible our appreciation of at least one personality theory, whether it is that of Freud, Rogers, or Eric Berne, we should constantly refine our appreciation of its meaning. In a sense, it does not make any difference what personality theory one follows, as long as one follows it consistently. A professional increases self-confidence by operating in reference to a well-understood set of principles about personality development. When one grasps a particular theory in depth it is much easier to appreciate the work of others.

It has been noted that professionals with very different orientations are able to communicate without too much difficulty even though their personality theories may be different. What enables them to communicate is their thorough grasp of the underlying notions that guide their work. Real professionals can talk across differing schools of thought because they can make the translations necessary for understanding others when they are familiar with their own first principles.

We should run to cover when we hear a counselor describe his orientation as "eclectic." There are ways of understanding this notion properly, of course, but often enough it suggests a hodgepodge of notions about psychological functioning with no clear or consistent theory to hold it all together. A firm grasp of personality theory enables us to integrate our experience in a systematic fashion. It gives us a way of reflecting on what takes place between ourselves and others in counseling. This becomes a base for us to stand on and a source of therapeutic communication. Being eclectic may sound charming but it may mean that a person knows a little of some things and not a great deal of any one thing. "Eclectic" sounds impartial and vaguely wise, but it can represent an outlook that has never been thought through seriously. Counselors who wish to serve sensitively and professionally begin with mastering a guiding theoretical framework.

Always Something New

Counselors who continue to read and to work at understanding personality theory have an unusual but healthy experience all the time. They feel that they are always just beginning really to understand human personality and they are always discovering something they did not know before. Such discoveries might alarm amateurs, but professionals who are always moving deeper in counseling work experience them on many occasions. This sense of discovery comes regularly to people who keep themselves open to learning at every stage in their lives. Their work can never become boring because their attitude toward it disposes them to seeing it and the world of people always in a fresh manner. It is as simple as that. Counselors who don't think they know everything are in the refreshing position of still being able to learn. Such an attitude not only lessens stress but makes life and work more deeply enjoyable.

A sign of professionalism in helpers is their readiness to seek out continuing supervision. They are willing to pay for it in order to get it on a regular basis. This experience is probably more important than any other in assisting counselors to see themselves and their work always in a fresh perspective. Supervision is in itself a process of continuing education. Sometimes counselors feel that they cannot afford to pay for supervision but, in certain instances, counselors may be able to group together to get supervisory assistance in a seminar style. It may sometimes happen that supervision cannot be obtained. Some approximation of this, even if it is just talking one's case over with a colleague, is of great value. This enables counselors to express their own feelings, to explore them, and to perceive themselves and their clients from new angles. Self-examination—and that takes effort and time—is a professional necessity.

Time

What everybody needs, of course, is time. Its pressure on us is a chief cause of stress. Time, in fact, dominates many aspects of counseling activity. Despite its pressure, counselors must learn to take some time for themselves. Many do not do this because they feel guilty if they are not out helping people all the time. When counselors feel that they cannot take sufficient time, for example, to study about a certain problem with which they may be dealing, this is a signal that they are overcommitted or poorly organized. Something has gotten out of balance.

Counselors who feel guilty if they do not put in X number of hours every day seeing people directly have a problem with their self-image that also needs investigation. As they allow themselves some time for reflection and reading, they can use themselves fully and well in their counseling work. A great deal of unnecessary stress is traceable to unacknowledged feelings—like the driving power of their own guilt—in the counselors themselves.

Only those who take time to listen to themselves can appreciate the emergence of countertransference feelings, for example, in the course of therapy. Some counselors are afraid of the discovery of such feelings. They think they are not supposed to have them. They are upset if they occur because they seem inconsistent with their idea of themselves as counselors. Experience of countertransference feelings is not, of course, a bad thing. It is a sign that something is going on in the counseling work. Such feelings need to be heard and understood properly. Counselors who give themselves no leeway in their schedule—and the number of these is legion—can only be trapped, and sometimes badly hurt, by their failure to understand their own psychological processes. Time for themselves is of the essence here.

The Economy of the Helper

This phrase has been used by certain psychologists to describe the counselors' own resources in relationship to the demands made upon them. No one has an infinitely expandable economy. Counselors who wish to continue effective work can only do so if they respect the limitations, both human and professional, under which they operate. Understanding our psychological economy does not mean drawing up a balance sheet about it. It means rather that we appreciate the rhythm of our lives and have a sensible appreciation of what, as ordinary human beings, we can and cannot do. A healthy psychological economy includes an understanding that we always make mistakes.

One of the remarkable things about counseling is that it works even when the helper is imperfect. It is more like friendship or love than golf. Doing some of the right things in counseling makes up for doing a lot of the wrong things. If we get the main sense of things—and that centers on a true understanding of other persons and their dynamics—then there is a large margin for error. We need not worry about the fact that errors will always be with us.

Counselors can also say *no*. There may be times when we cannot help people, or must turn them away or refer them to somebody else. Sometimes we may need to say no in order to preserve enough time for our continued professional development. This may be one of the hardest lessons for some counselors to learn.

Counselors do not have to feel guilty and they should be particularly sensitive to clients who try to give rise to these feelings in them. These are the people who want to be dependent on counselors, who want to be treated only according to their own whim, and who may have mastered the manipulative arts of making others feel sorry for them. These clients, and a wide variety of others, tax the counselor's adjustment severely. When counselors feel free to let people be mad at them or disappointed in them, they are free indeed.

If, after all our best efforts, we feel that we do not function well as counselors—and there are people like this—we should at least try to avoid some of our bigger mistakes. And we should not represent ourselves as possessing psychological skills if we find that our personalities keep us from mastering the discipline that is required in good therapists. We can call ourselves advice-givers, philosophers, or whatever, but we must not delude ourselves into claiming that we are counselors if we are not. Such a decision is much better for ourselves and for those with whom we work. There is no shame in this; we may be involved in education, religious teaching, or pastoral work without apologies.

For most persons who can learn to listen to others and can employ psychological techniques successfully, the task of being a professional is not an achievement but a never-ending process.

Recommended Reading:

Aguilera, D. C. (1986). *Crisis Intervention, Theory, and Methodology.* St. Louis: Mosby.

AIDS Primer (1987). AIDS Education Project. Washington DC: American Psychiatric Association.

Aiken, L. R. (1985). *Dying, Death, and Bereavement.* Boston: Allyn and Bacon.

Alexander, B. K. (1987). The Disease and Adaptive Models of Addiction: A Framework Evaluation. *Journal of Drug Issues,* 17: 47–66.

Andrews, T. (1980). *A Bibliography of Drug Abuse.* Littleton, CO: Libraries Unlimited.

Angst, J. and Clayton, P. (1986). Premorbid Personality of Depressive, Bipolar, and Schizophrenic Patients with Special Reference to Suicidal Issues. *Comprehensive Psychiatry,* 17: 511–32.

Austin, G. A. and Prendergast, M. E. (1984). *Drug Use and Abuse: A Guide to Research Findings.* Santa Barbara, CA: ABC-Clio Information Services.

Bachrach, L. L. (1986). Dimensions of Disability in the Chronic Mentally Ill. *Hospital and Community Psychiatry,* 37: 981–82.

Balon, R. (1987). Suicide: Can We Predict It? *Comprehensive Psychiatry,* 28: 236–41.

Bane, J. D., et al. (eds.) (1975). *Death and Ministry: Pastoral Care of the Dying and the Bereaved.* New York: Seabury Press.

Barstow, C., (1986). Tending Body and Spirit: Counseling with Elders. *Hakomi Forum,* 4: 42–51.

Beck, R. L. (1987). Redirecting Blaming in Marital Psychotherapy. *Clinical Social Work Journal,* 15: 148–58.

Becker, A. H. (1986). Pastoral Theological Implications of the Aging Process. *Journal of Religion and Aging,* 2: 13–30.

Berkowitz, A. D. and Perkins, H. W. (1986). Problem Drinking among College Students: A Review of Recent Research. *Journal of American College Health*, 35: 21–28.

Bethune, H. (1985). *Off the Hook: Coping with Addiction*. London: Methuen.

Blane, H. T. and Leonard, K. E., (eds.) (1987). *Psychological Theories of Drinking and Alcoholism*. New York: Guilford Press.

Boldt, M. (1987). Defining Suicide: Implications for Suicide Behavior and for Suicide Prevention. *Crisis*, 8: 3–13.

Bonner, R. L. and Rich, A. R. (1987). Toward a Predictive Model of Suicidal Ideation and Behavior: Some Preliminary Data on College Students. *Suicide and Life-Threatening Behavior*, 17: 50–63.

Borison, R. L. (1986). Schizophrenia and Depression. *Carrier Foundation Letter*, 117: 1–3.

Bowling, A. (1987). Mortality after Bereavement: A Review of the Literature on Survival Periods and Factors Affecting Survival. *Social Science and Medicine*, 24: 117–24.

Brown, K. (ed.) (1981). *Family Counseling: An Annotated Bibliography*. Cambridge, MA: Oelgeschlager, Gunn and Hain.

Burks, V. K., Lund, D. A., Gregg, C. H., and Bluhm, H. P. (1988). Bereavement and Remarriage for Older Adults. *Death Studies*, 12: 51–60.

Burrows, G. D., Norman, T. R., and Rubenstein, G. (eds.) (1986). *Handbook of Studies on Schizophrenia*. New York: Elsevier.

Cassem, N.H. (1988). The Person Confronting Death In *The Harvard Guide to Psychiatry*, Nicholi, A.M. (ed). Cambridge: Harvard University Press.

Civin, G. and Lachmann, A. (1987). On Denying and Facing Cancer. *Dynamic Psychotherapy*, 5: 77–82.

Clum, G. A. (1987). "The Case against Suicide Prevention": Comment. *American Psychologist*, 42: 883–85.

Cohen, S. (ed.) (1986). *The Diagnosis and Treatment of Drug and Alcohol Abuse*. New York: Haworth Press.

Cole, C. L. (1985). Relationship Quality in Long-Term Marriages: A Comparison of High-Quality and Low-Quality Marriages. *Lifestyles*, 7: 248–57.

Cole, D. (1987). It Might Have Been: Mourning the Unborn. *Psychology Today*, 21: 64–65.

Coumos, F. (1986–87). Suffering in Chronic Mental Illness. *Loss, Grief, and Care*, 1: 53–56.

Cutting, J. and Dunne, F. (1986). The Nature of the Abnormal Perceptual Experiences at the Onset of Schizophrenia. *Psychopathology*, 19: 347–52.

Davis, S. (1987). Four Conceptualizations of Schizophrenia as Models for Treatment. *Health and Social Work*, 12: 91–100.

Denton, W. (ed.) (1986). *Marriage and Family Enrichment*. New York: Haworth Press.

DeSpelder, L. A. and Strickland, L. (1987) *The Last Dance: Encountering Death and Dying*. Palo Alto, CA: Mayfield Publishing Co.

Doka, K. J. (1986). Loss upon Loss: The Impact of Death after Divorce. *Death Studies*, 10: 441–49.

Dominian, J. (1985). *Make or Break: A Guide to Marriage Counselling*. Wilmington, DE: M. Glazier.

Evens, D. R., Heam, M. T., Uhlemann, M. R., and Ivey, A. E. (1979). *Essential Interviewing*. California: Wadsworth, Inc.

Everstine, D. S. and Everstine, L. (1983). *People in Crisis: Strategic Therapeutic Interventions*. New York: Brunner/Mazel.

Flynn, L. M. (1987). The Stigma of Mental Illness. *New Directions for Mental Health Services*, 34: 53–60.

Fulton, R. L. (ed.) (1976). *Death and Identity*. Bowie, MD: Charles Press.

Gallagher, B. J., Jones B. J., and Barakat, L. P. (1987). The Attitudes of Psychiatrists toward Etiological Theories of Schizophrenia: 1975–1985. *Journal of Clinical Psychology*, 43: 438–43.

Gallant, D. M. (1987). *Alcoholism: A Guide to Diagnosis, Intervention, and Treatment*. New York: Norton.

Geller, J. L. (1985). The Long-Term Outcome of Unresolved Grief: An Example. *Psychiatric Quarterly*, 57: 142–46.

Gemsbacher, L. M. (1985). *The Suicide Syndrome: Origins, Manifestations, and Alleviation of Human Self-Destructiveness*. New York: Human Sciences Press.

Gerstein, L. H., Bates, H. D., and Reindle, M. (1987). The Experience of Loneliness among Schizophrenic and Normal Persons. *Journal of Social Behavior and Personality*, 2: 239–48.

Ghafarri, K. (1987). Psychoanalytic Theories on Drug Dependence: A Critical Review. *Psychoanalytic Psychotherapy*, 3: 39–51.

Gitlow, S. E. and Peyser, H. S. (eds.) (1988). *Alcoholism: A Practical Treatment Guide*. Philadelphia: Grune and Stratton.

Glick, R. A., et al. (1976). *Psychiatric Emergencies*. New York: Grune and Stratton.

Goldberg, D. C., ed. (1985). *Contemporary Marriage: Special Issues in Couples Therapy*. Homewood, IL: Dorsey Press.

Goldberg, S. R. and Stolerman, I. P. (eds.) (1986) *Behavioral Analysis of Drug Dependence*. Orlando: Academic Press.

Goldney, R. D., Spence, N. D., and Moffit, P. F. (1987). The Aftermath of Suicide: Attitudes of Those Bereaved by Suicide, of Social Workers, and of a Community Sample. *Journal of Community Psychology*, 15: 141–48.

Goldstein, M. J., Hand, I., and Hahliveg, K. (eds.) (1986). *Treatment of Schizophrenia*. Berlin: Springer-Verlag.

Grant, B. W. (1986). *Reclaiming the Dream: Marriage Counseling in the Parish Context*. Nashville: Abingdon Press.

Grinker, R. R. and Harrow, M. (1987). *Clinical Research in Schizophrenia: A Multidimensional Approach*. Springfield, IL: Thomas.

Grollman, E. A. (1988). *Suicide: Prevention, Intervention, Postvention*. Boston: Beacon Press.

Haddox, V. G. (1986). What Power Does the Patient Possess? *Psychiatric Annals*, 16: 640–44.

Hafner, H., Gattaz, W. F., and Janzarik, W. (eds.) (1987). *Search for the Causes of Schizophrenia*. New York: Springer Verlag.

Harding, C. M., Zubin, J., and Strauss, J. S. (1987). Chronicity in Schizophrenia: Fact, Partial Fact, or Artifact? *Hospital and Community Psychiatry*, 38: 477–86.

Hatton, C. L. and Valente, S. M. (eds.) (1984). *Suicide: Assessment and Intervention*. Norwalk, CT: Appleton-Century-Crofts.

Hawkins, J. D., Lishner, D. M., Catalano, R. F., and Howard, M. O. (1985). Childhood Predictors of Adolescent Substance Abuse: Toward an Empirically Grounded Theory. *Journal of Children in Contemporary Society*, 18: 11–48.

Heilbrun, A. B., Diller, R. S., and Dodson, V. S. (1986). Defensive Projection and Paranoid Delusions. *Journal of Psychiatric Research*, 20: 161–73.

Hersen, M. and Turner, S. M. (eds.) (1985). *Diagnostic Interviewing*. New York: Plenum Press.

Hinton, J. (1975). *Dying*. Baltimore: Penguin Books.

Holland, J. C. B. and Tross, S. (1985). Psychological and Neuropsychiatric Sequelae of the Acquired Immune Deficiency Syndrome and Related Disorders. *Annals of Internal Medicine*, 103: 760–64.

Hyman, S. E. (ed.) (1988). *Manual of Psychiatric Emergencies*. Boston: Little, Brown.

Johnson, S. M. (1987). Marital Therapy: Issues and Directions. *International Journal of Family Psychiatry*, 8: 63–78.

Jung, J. (1986). How Significant Others Cope with Problem Drinkers. *International Journal of the Addictions*, 21: 813–17.

Kalish, R. A. (1985). *Death, Grief, and Caring Relationships*. Monterey, CA: Brooks/Cole.

Kamerman, J. B. (1988). *Death in the Midst of Life: Social and Cultural Influences on Death, Grief, and Mourning*. Englewood Cliffs, NJ: Prentice-Hall.

Kane, J. M. (1987). Treatment of Schizophrenia. *Schizophrenia Bulletin*, 13: 133–56.

Karon, B. P. (1987). Current Misconceptions about Psychotherapy with Schizophrenics. *Dynamic Psychotherapy*, 5: 3–15.

Kastenbaum, R. (1986). *Death, Society, and Human Experience*. Columbus: C. E. Merrill Publishing Co.

Kennedy, B., Kostantareas, M., and Homatidis, S. (1987). A Behavioral Profile of Polydrug Abusers. *Journal of Youth and Adolescence*, 16: 115–27.

Kennedy, E. (1981). *Crisis Counseling*. New York: Continuum.

Kilty, K. M., Leung, P., and Cheung, K. M. (1987). Drinking Styles and Drinking Problems. *International Journal of the Addictions*, 22: 389–412.

Knapp, R. J. (1987). When a Child Dies. *Psychology Today*, 21: 60–63, 66–67.

Kozel, N. J. and Adams, E. H. (1986). Epidemiology of Drug Abuse: An Overview. *Science*, 234: 970–74.

Kumpfer, K. L. and DeMarsh, J. (1985). Family Environmental and Genetic Influences on Children's Future Chemical Dependency. *Journal of Children in Contemporary Society*, 18: 49–91.

Kurtz, R. (1986). Cancer and Psychotherapy. *Hakomi Forum*, 4: 18–32.

Leon, R. L. (1982). *Psychiatric Interviewing: A Primer.* New York: Elsevier North Holland, Inc.

Lester, D. (1983). *Why People Kill Themselves: A 1980s Summary of Research Findings on Suicidal Behavior.* Springfield, IL: C. C. Thomas.

Lichtenthal, S. (1985). Working with a Terminally Ill Young Adult. *Pratt Institute Creative Arts Therapy Review,* 6: 11–21.

Logan, S. L., McRoy, R. G., and Freeman, E. M. (1987). Current Practice Approaches for Treating the Alcoholic Client. *Health and Social Work,* 12: 178–86.

Ludwig, A. M. (1988). *Understanding the Alcoholic's Mind: The Nature of Craving and How to Control It.* New York: Oxford University Press.

Maltsberger, J. T. (1986). *Suicide Risk: The Formulation of Clinical Judgement.* New York: New York University Press.

Mather, D. B. (1987). The Case against Preventing Suicide Prevention: Comments on Szasz. *American Psychologist,* 42: 882–83.

McDonald, P. (1987). Conflicting Messages. Marriage in the 1980s. *Australian Journal of Sex, Marriage, and Family,* 8: 73–78.

McIntosh, J. L. (1985). *Research on Suicide: A Bibliography.* Westport, CT: Greenwood Press.

McLeavy, B. C., Daly, R. J., Murray, C. M., O'Riordan, J., et al. (1987). Interpersonal Problem-Solving Deficits in Self-Poisoning Patients. *Self and Life-Threatening Behavior,* 17: 33–49.

Meissner, W. W. (1986). *Psychotherapy and the Paranoid Process.* Northvale, NJ: Jason Aronson.

Mello, N. K. and Mendelson, J. H. (1986). Cigarette Smoking: Interactions with Alcohol, Opiates, and Marijuana. *National Institute on Drug Abuse: Research Monograph Series,* 68: 154–80.

Metzger, L. (1987). *From Denial to Recovery: Counseling Problem Drinkers, Alcoholics, and Their Families.* San Francisco: Jossey-Bass.

Meyer, R. E. (1986). Old Wine, New Bottle: The Alcohol Dependence Syndrome. *Psychiatric Clinics of North America,* 9: 435–53.

Miller, F. and Chabrier, L. A. (1987). The Relation of Delusional Content in Psychotic Depression to Life-Threatening Behavior. *Suicide and Life-Threatening Behavior,* 17: 13–17.

Minn, S. M. and Weiss, R. D. (1986). Affective Illness in Substance Abusers. *Psychiatric Clinics of North America,* 9: 503–14.

Nace, E. P. (1987). *The Treatment of Alcoholism.* New York: Brunner/Mazel.

Nahas, G. G. and Frick II, H. C. (eds.) (1981). *Drug Abuse in the Modern World: A Perspective for the Eighties.* New York: Pergamon Press.

Oates, W. E. (1987). *Behind the Masks: Personality Disorders in Religious Behavior.* Philadelphia: Westminster Press.

Ostrow, D. G. (1988). *Models for Understanding the Psychiatric Consequences of AIDS in Psychological, Neuropsychiatric, and Substance Abuse Aspects of AIDS.* Bridge, T. P. (ed.). New York: Raven Press.

Overholser, J. C., Miller, I. W., and Norman, W. H. (1987). The Course of

Depressive Symptoms in Suicidal vs. Nonsuicidal Depressed Inpatients. *Journal of Nervous and Mental Disease,* 175: 450–56.

Parkes, C. M. (1987). *Bereavement: Studies in Grief in Adult Life.* Madison, CT: International Universities Press.

Peele, S., ed. (1988). *Visions of Addiction: Major Contemporary Perspective on Addiction and Alcoholism.* Lexington, MA: Lexington Books.

Phipps, W. E. (1987). *Death: Confronting the Reality.* Atlanta, GA: John Knox Press.

Poteet, G. H. (1978). *Death and Dying: A Bibliography, 1950–1974.* Troy, NY: Whitston Publishing Co.

Priebe, P. R. and Carman, R. S. (1987). Drinking Rates among College Students: An Update. *Psychologicl Reports,* 60: 78.

Pries, A. M. (1987). Marriage Burnout: A New Conceptual Framework for Working with Couples. *Psychotherapy in Private Practice,* 5: 31–44.

Rando, T. A. (1984). *Grief, Dying, and Death: Clinical Interventions for Caregivers.* Champaign, IL Research Press.

Rando, T. A. (ed.) (1986). *Loss and Anticipatory Grief.* Lexington, MA: Lexington Books.

Ray, O. S. (1978). *Drugs, Society, and Human Behavior.* St. Louis: Mosby.

Reid, R. F., Leggett, B., and Kabourakis, M. (1986). Counsellors' Beliefs about the Interviewing of Individuals in Marriage Counselling. *Australian Journal of Sex, Marriage and Family,* 7: 191–98.

Richman, J. (1986). *Family Therapy for Suicidal People.* New York: Springer Publishing Co.

Rosenbaum, C. P. and Beebe, J. E. (1975). *Psychiatric Treatment.* New York: McGraw-Hill.

Roy, A. (ed.) (1986). *Suicide.* Baltimore: Williams and Wilkins.

Roy, D. J. (1987). The "Spiritual" Need of the Dying. *Journal of Palliative Care,* 2: 3–4.

Sands, S. and Ratey, J. J. (1986). The Concept of Noise. *Psychiatry,* 49: 290–97.

Scheff, T. J. (1984). *Being Mentally Ill: A Sociological Theory.* New York: Aldine Publishing Co.

Schiff, H. S. (1986). *Living through Mourning: Finding Comfort and Hope When a Loved One Has Died.* New York: Viking.

Schucter, S. R. (1986). *Dimensions of Grief: Adjusting to the Death of a Spouse.* San Francisco: Jossey-Bass.

Semlitz, L. and Gold, M. S. (1986). Adolescent Drug Abuse: Diagnosis, Treatment, and Prevention. *Psychiatric Clinics of North America,* 9: 455–73.

Shapiro, S. A. (1981). *Contemporary Theories of Schizophrenia: Review and Synthesis.* New York: McGraw-Hill.

Shiffman, S. and Wills, T. A. (eds.) (1985). *Coping and Substance Use.* Orlando: Academic Press.

Shore, D. S., ed. (1987). *Special Report: Schizophrenia.* Rockville, MD: U.S. Department of Health and Human Services.

Simpson, M.A. (1987). *Dying, Death, and Grief: A Critical Bibliography.* Pittsburgh: University of Pittsburgh Press.

Soulen, R. N. ed. (1975). *Care for the Dying: Resources of Theology.* Atlanta, GA: John Knox Press.

Special Issue (1986): The Divorce Process: A Handbook for Clinicians. *Journal of Divorce,* 10: 169–87.

Stengel, E. (1969). *Suicide and Attempted Suicide.* Baltimore, MD: Penguin Books.

Stone, M. et al. (1983). *Treating Schizophrenic Patients: A Clinical-Analytical Approach.* New York: McGraw-Hill.

Stroebe, W. (1987). *Bereavement and Health: The Psychological and Physical Consequences of Partner Loss.* Cambridge: Cambridge University Press.

Switzer, D. K. (1986). *The Minister as Crisis Counselor.* Nashville: Abingdon Press.

Szasz, T. A. (1987). "The Case against Suicide Prevention": Reply. *American psychologist,* 42: 885–86.

Szmukler, G. I. (1987). The Place of Crisis Intervention in Psychiatry. *Australian and New Zealand Journal of Psychiatry,* 21: 24–34.

Torres, C. S. (1986–7). A Pastoral View of Widowhood. *Loss, Grief, and Care,* 1: 161–63.

Treece, C. and Khantzian, E. J. (1986). Psychodynamic Factors in the Development of Drug Dependence. *Psychiatric Clinics of North America,* 9: 399–412.

Van Praag, H. M. (1986). Affective Disorders and Aggression Disorders: Evidence for a Common Biological Mechanism. *Suicide and Life-Threatening Behavior,* 16: 103–32.

Vaughn, D. (1987). The Long Goodbye. *Psychology Today,* 21: 36–42.

Walsh, M. (1985). *Schizophrenia: Straight Talk for Families and Friends.* New York: Morrow.

Weisman, A. (1986). Terminality and Interminable Psychoanalysis: An Incomplete Report. *Psychotherapy and Psychosomatics,* 45: 23–32.

Westermeyer, J. (1986). *A Clinical Guide to Alcohol and Drug Problems.* New York: Praeger.

Wilcoxen, S. A. (1986). One-Spouse Marital Therapy: Is Informed Consent Necessary? *American Journal of Family Therapy,* 14: 265–70.

Wolk-Wasserman, D. (1987). Some Problems Connected with the Treatment of Suicide Attempt Patients: Transference and Countertransference Aspects. *Crisis,* 8: 69–82.

Woody, G. E., McLellan, A. T., Lubursky, L., and O'Brien, C. P. (1986). Psychotherapy for Substance Abusers. *Psychiatric Clinics of North America,* 9: 547–62.

World Health Organization (1986). *Drug Dependence and Alcohol-Related Problems: A Manual for Community Health Workers, with Guidelines for Trainers.* Geneva: WHO.

Wynne, E. A. and Hess, M. (1986). Long-Term Trends in Youth Conduct and the Revival of Traditional Value Patterns. *Educational Evaluation and Policy Analysis,* 8: 294–308.

Zigler, E. and Glick, M. (1988). Is Paranoid Schizophrenia Really Camouflaged Depression? *American Psychologist,* 43: 284–90.

About the authors

Dr. Eugene Kennedy, professor of psychology at Loyola University of Chicago, has written several best-selling books for those who help others, including *Crisis Counseling* and *Sexual Counseling*. Sara C. Charles, M.D., professor of clinical psychiatry at the University of Illinois Medical School, is coauthor of *Defendant*.